Mit unseren Begleitmaterialien zu English Network zu optimal

Unsere Lernercassetten bzw. -CDs enthalten alle mit **weißem** Cassettensymk
(mit Nachsprechpausen!) sowie Ausspracheübungen aus den jeweiligen Lektioı

Unsere Textcassetten bzw. -CDs enthalten Hörtexte, die für den Gruppenunterricht mit Kursleiter/in gedacht
sind; ein **schwarzes** Cassettensymbol weist auf solche Texte hin. Wenn Sie diese Texte zu Hause nacharbei-
ten möchten, dann empfiehlt sich die Anschaffung.

Unsere Nachschlagegrammatik unterstützt Ihren Lernweg sinnvoll durch alle Network-Bände. Vergessene
Grammatik kann so jederzeit nachgeschlagen werden. Das Workbook stellt zusätzlich Übungsmaterial bereit.

D1724334

Ich bestelle hiermit:

English Network Plus 1

○ **Lernercassette 1 (Units 1–4)**
(Best.-Nr. 3-526-57 573-8 / € 9,95 [D] / € 10,30 [A] / sFr. 18,40)

○ **Lernercassette 2 (Units 5–8)**
(Best.-Nr. 3-526-57 574-6 / € 9,95 [D] / € 10,30 [A] / sFr. 18,40)

○ **3 Lerner-CDs (Units 1–8)**
(Best.-Nr. 3-526-57 527-4 / € 20,50 [D] / € 21,30 [A] / sFr. 36,40)

○ **2 Textcassetten (Units 1–8) – Institutsversion –**
(Best.-Nr. 3-526-57 572-X / € 20,90 [D] / € 21,70 [A] / sFr. 37,10)

○ **2 Text-CDs (Units 1–8) – Institutsversion –**
(Best.-Nr. 3-526-57 523-1 / € 20,90 [D] / € 21,70 [A] / sFr. 37,10)

○ **Nachschlagegrammatik**
(begleitet alle Network-Bände)
(Best.-Nr. 3-526-50 412-1 / € 12,95 [D] / € 13,40 [A] / sFr. 22,70)

○ **Workbook 2 zur Nachschlagegrammatik**
(begleitet Network Plus 1 und Plus 2)
(Best.-Nr. 3-526-50 414-8 / € 5,95 [D] / € 6,20 [A] / sFr. 10,70)

Unterschrift/Datum   (Absender auf Vorderseite ---->)

Preisänderungen vorbehalten
- Zutreffendes ist angekreuzt -

Ich bestelle hiermit:

English Network Plus 1

○ **Lernercassette 1 (Units 1–4)**
(Best.-Nr. 3-526-57 573-8 / € 9,95 [D] / € 10,30 [A] / sFr. 18,40)

○ **Lernercassette 2 (Units 5–8)**
(Best.-Nr. 3-526-57 574-6 / € 9,95 [D] / € 10,30 [A] / sFr. 18,40)

○ **3 Lerner-CDs (Units 1–8)**
(Best.-Nr. 3-526-57 527-4 / € 20,50 [D] / € 21,30 [A] / sFr. 36,40)

○ **2 Textcassetten (Units 1–8) – Institutsversion –**
(Best.-Nr. 3-526-57 572-X / € 20,90 [D] / € 21,70 [A] / sFr. 37,10)

○ **2 Text-CDs (Units 1–8) – Institutsversion –**
(Best.-Nr. 3-526-57 523-1 / € 20,90 [D] / € 21,70 [A] / sFr. 37,10)

○ **Nachschlagegrammatik**
(begleitet alle Network-Bände)
(Best.-Nr. 3-526-50 412-1 / € 12,95 [D] / € 13,40 [A] / sFr. 22,70)

○ **Workbook 2 zur Nachschlagegrammatik**
(begleitet Network Plus 1 und Plus 2)
(Best.-Nr. 3-526-50 414-8 / € 5,95 [D] / € 6,20 [A] / sFr. 10,70)

Unterschrift/Datum   (Absender auf Vorderseite ---->)

Preisänderungen vorbehalten
- Zutreffendes ist angekreuzt -

Bitte geben Sie die Bestellkarte(n) an Ihre Buchhandlung oder senden Sie sie an unseren Verlag.

Absender:

_____

Name/Vorname

_____

Straße/Nr.

_____

PLZ/Ort

Bitte liefern Sie die angekreuzten Titel
über die Buchhandlung

_____

Name/Straße

_____

PLZ/Ort

(Sollte keine Buchhandlung genannt sein,
erfolgt die Lieferung über eine Buchhandlung
nach Wahl des Verlags.)

Antwort

**An den Verlag
Langenscheidt-Longman
Postfach 40 11 20**

80711 München

Absender:

_____

Name/Vorname

_____

Straße/Nr.

_____

PLZ/Ort

Bitte liefern Sie die angekreuzten Titel
über die Buchhandlung

_____

Name/Straße

_____

PLZ/Ort

(Sollte keine Buchhandlung genannt sein,
erfolgt die Lieferung über eine Buchhandlung
nach Wahl des Verlags.)

Antwort

**An den Verlag
Langenscheidt-Longman
Postfach 40 11 20**

80711 München

ENGLISH network PLUS 1

John Potts

Gaynor Ramsey

Langenscheidt-Longman
ENGLISH LANGUAGE TEACHING

English Network Plus 1

Autoren:
John Potts (Unitteil)
Gaynor Ramsey (Revision Plus, Homestudy)

sowie
Carolyn Kilday Wittmann (Language & Culture)
Dr. Dieter Kranz (Grammatikanhang)
Michael Rutman (Stories)

Beratende Mitwirkung:
Dr. Dieter Kranz, Dr. Donald Porsché, Silvia Stephan,
Gaynor Ramsey, Carolyn Kilday Wittmann

Projektteam:
Ingrid Boczkowski, EFL-Beraterin und Lehrbeauftragte, Saarbrücken
Michele Charlton, Kursleiterin, Genf
Carolyn Kilday Wittmann, Kursleiterin und Lehrbeauftragte, München
Dr. Dieter Kranz, Kursleiter und Akademischer Direktor, Münster
Dr. Donald Porsché, Programmbereichsleiter, Frankfurt
John Potts, Kursleiter und Lehrerfortbildner, Zürich
Gaynor Ramsey, Autorin, Kursleiterin und Lehrerfortbildnerin, Zürich
Michael Rutman, Lehrerfortbildner und Landesbeauftragter, Zürich
Silvia Stephan, Autorin, Kursleiterin und Lehrerfortbildnerin, Offenburg
Jutta Zopf-Klasek, Kurs- und Fachgruppenleiterin, Wien

Projektleitung:
John Stevens

Verlagsredaktion:
Doris Michels

Redaktionelle Mitarbeit:
Coralia Pastora

Illustrationen:
Shirley Bellwood

Graphik und Layout:
Jürgen Bartz
Frank Fischer

Umschlag: Zero Grafik & Design GmbH

Umschlagphoto: Opernhaus von Sydney, Australien

Lehrwerkskomponenten:	
Kursbuch	50 402
Textcassetten (2)	57 572
Text-CDs (2)	57 523
Lernercassette 1	57 573
Lernercassette 2	57 574
Lerner-CDs (3)	57 527
Lehrerhandreichungen	50 403
Einstufungstest	50 392
Lehrwerksbegleitend:	
Network Grammar	50 412
Grammar Workbook 2	50 414

Der Innenteil dieses Buches wurde auf chlorfrei gebleichtem Papier gedruckt.

1. Auflage 1993

© 1993 Langenscheidt-Longman GmbH, München

Druck: LANDESVERLAG Druckservice, Linz
ISBN 3-526-50402-4

11 12 13 13 14/06 05 04 03

Wegweiser

Hier geben wir Ihnen einen kurzen Überblick über das, was Sie von diesem Englischkurs erwarten dürfen. Mit Hilfe der folgenden Hinweise werden Sie sich bestimmt schnell im Buch zurechtfinden.

Für wen ist das Buch gedacht?

English Network Plus 1 ist die Fortführung von *English Network 1-3*, eignet sich aber auch als Einstiegsband für alle, die über entsprechende Vorkenntnisse auf dem Niveau des Grundbausteins verfügen.

Was lerne ich?

In diesem Band beschäftigen Sie sich mit einer breiten Vielfalt unterschiedlicher Themen: Auswandern nach Australien, unser Zusammenleben mit Tieren, Älterwerden, Werbung usw. Sie bauen Ihre Fertigkeiten im Lesen, Hören, Sprechen und Schreiben weiter aus und wiederholen und erweitern systematisch Ihre Wortschatz- und Grammatikkenntnisse. Sie lernen, wie man Ratschläge, Begründungen und Erklärungen formuliert, Meinungen äußert sowie Zustimmung und Widerspruch ausdrückt.

English Network Plus 1 baut auf dem Kenntnisstand von *English Network 1-3* auf und erweitert diesen. In *English Network Plus 1* setzen Sie sich mit längeren Hör- und Lesetexten auseinander und können sich in Gesprächen und Diskussionen zunehmend freier äußern. Außerdem lernen Sie, wie Sie sich effektiv mit einem zweisprachigen Wörterbuch helfen können.

Wie lerne ich?

Mit *English Network Plus 1* lernen Sie nicht allein, sondern in einer Gruppe mit anderen Kursteilnehmerinnen und -teilnehmern. Im Unterricht hören Sie die Textcassetten (= ▬), üben das Sprechen, lesen Dialoge und Texte und schreiben kurze Texte auf. Sie arbeiten mal alle zusammen, mal alleine, mal mit einem anderen Kursmitglied oder einer kleinen Gruppe von Kursmitgliedern zusammen. Ihre Kursleiterin / Ihr Kursleiter steht Ihnen mit Rat und Tat zur Seite. Mit Hilfe der Lernercassetten (= ▭) und dem *Homestudy*-Teil können Sie Ihre fremdsprachlichen Fertigkeiten auch alleine vertiefen. Außerdem finden Sie im *Homestudy*-Teil zu jeweils zwei Units eine Seite mit Lerntips und Hinweise zur Wörterbuchbenutzung. Anhand der *Test yourself*-Seiten können Sie in regelmäßigen Abständen Ihre Fortschritte und Ihren Lernerfolg selbst überprüfen.

Wie ist das Buch aufgebaut?

Das Buch besteht aus acht Units, die in vier Gruppen mit je einem übergreifenden Thema zusammengefaßt sind. Jede Unit ist in zwei Steps aufgeteilt. Im ersten Step steht das Lesen und das Sprechen im Vordergrund. Sie lernen, einen Text (Zeitschriftenartikel, Annonce, Buchauszug) in seiner Gesamtaussage sowie im Detail zu erfassen und diskutieren die angesprochene Thematik. Ferner lernen und üben Sie wichtige Redewendungen. Den Schwerpunkt des zweiten Steps bildet die Grammatik. Hier werden Ihnen systematisch die wesentlichen Grammatikstrukturen vermittelt, die Sie mit Hilfe verschiedener Aktivitäten einüben. Außerdem wird das Hörverständnis und das freie Sprechen systematisch geschult. Am Ende einer Gruppe von zwei Units bietet *Panorama Plus* interessante Informationen aus aller Welt zu den Themen der beiden vorangegangenen Units. Dieser Teil ist gegenüber *English Network 1-3* deutlich erweitert worden: das Lesen, Hören und freie Sprechen in größeren Zusammenhängen wird hier gezielt geschult.

Die Units bearbeiten Sie mit Ihrer Kursleiterin / Ihrem Kursleiter. Die *Homestudy*-Seiten (Sie erkennen sie an dem blauen Streifen am Rand) mit zusätzlichen Übungen sind für die Nacharbeit zu Hause gedacht. Wenn Sie Ihren Lernerfolg absichern möchten, sollten Sie versuchen, diese Seiten regelmäßig miteinzuplanen. Die *Learners' letters* geben Ihnen Hilfen, wie Sie Ihr Wissen und Lernen verbessern können. Die *Dictionary skills*-Seiten vermitteln Ihnen, wie Sie Ihr zweisprachiges Wörterbuch optimal nutzen können. Ausführliche Informationen zum *Homestudy*-Teil finden Sie auf Seite 63.

Im übrigen Anhang des Buches finden Sie Informationen, die Ihnen beim Lernen helfen. Unter der Rubrik *Language & Culture* erhalten Sie interessante Tips und Hintergrundinformationen über das Leben in englischsprachigen Ländern sowie nützliche sprachliche Hinweise. Eine Zusammenstellung der gesamten Grammatik, die in diesem Band auftritt, finden Sie in der Sektion *Grammar*. Auf diese Sektion wird in den Grammatikkästen in Step 2 jeder Unit verwiesen (☞ G ...). Dem Wortschatzlernen und -nachschlagen dienen *Vocabulary* und *Dictionary*, die den gesamten Wortschatz des Buches mit Beispielen und deutscher Übersetzung auflisten. Das *Dictionary* enthält darüber hinaus auch noch die wichtigen Wörter aus *English Network 1-3*.

Viel Spaß und viel Erfolg beim Lernen
wünschen Ihnen

Autorenteam und Verlag

Contents

New moves

Unit 1 **A fresh start**

Unit 2 **Country life**

Units 1&2

It's only natural

Unit 3 Sport for all

Unit 4 Animals and us

Units 3&4

Contents

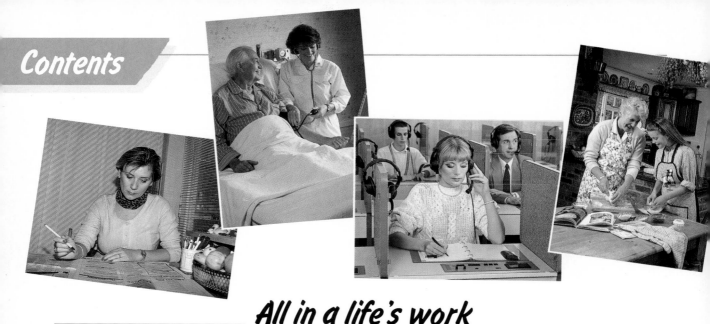

All in a life's work

Unit 5 Just the job

Unit 6 The third age

Units 5&6

Reading between the lines

Contents

Anhang Unitteil

Anhang Homestudy

Anhang Grammatik und Wortschatz

■■ Texte und Übungen mit diesem Symbol finden Sie auf den Textcassetten.
⌐⌐ Texte und Übungen mit diesem Symbol finden Sie auf den Lernercassetten.

Starter: Things we have in common

Work in groups of four. Try to find two countries you have all visited, two countries you would all like to visit, two things you all like, and two things you all dislike.

1 Reading: A new life in Australia

Before you read

Work with a partner. What do you think of when you hear the word *Australia*? How many things can you think of in three minutes?

Now read this article about two families who moved to Australia to start a new life there. Underline the things they liked about their new home.

A new life in Australia

Every year more than 30,000 people decide they want to leave crowded Europe and move to Australia.

Tony Simpson, from Leeds in the north of England, was one of them. "We went to Australia in 1988. I was really looking forward to it. I'd read a lot of books about the history of the country, and I'd found a job as an engineer in Brisbane, Queensland. But when we got there, it wasn't what we'd expected. People were very friendly, but we couldn't settle down. We missed our relatives, and spent a lot of money on long-distance telephone calls! We felt so homesick that we had to come back in 1990."

However, there are many success stories, too. Doreen and Dave Clark moved to Perth, Western Australia, in 1976. Doreen said: "At first we had a few problems, but I think that's natural. We love it here – the sunshine, the space, the freedom. There are so many interesting places to visit. We're going to fly to Alice Springs next year, and then drive through the National Parks to Ayers Rock – that's something I've always wanted to see. Our children are doing

very well at school and they'll probably go to university later. We're all very happy here."

How does Tony Simpson feel now that he's back in Leeds? "Well, it was a good experience in many ways, and we've got some lovely photographs to remind us of the two years we spent in Australia."

☞ *Language & Culture (page 58)*

1a Comprehension

Are these sentences true or false?

1 Tony Simpson wanted to go to Australia very much.
2 He stayed there for four years.
3 Doreen Clark found her new way of life difficult at first.

4 She wants to see Ayers Rock next year.
5 Her children are at university.
6 Tony is sorry he went to Australia.

1b Vocabulary

• Look at these new words from the article. Find their correct definition in the list below. Careful, there's one definition too many.

1	crowded	3	expect	5	relative
2	move	4	settle down	6	remind

- ☐ think that something will happen
- ☐ make somebody remember something
- ☐ somebody from the same family, e.g. an uncle
- ☐ go to live in a new house/town/country
- ☐ feel unhappy about the past
- ☐ full of people
- ☐ feel happy in a new place/job/home

• 📷 Look at this table. Can you fill in the missing words? Then listen to the words on the cassette.

north	
south	
	eastern
west	

• Match the four countries of the United Kingdom with the numbers on the map and the nationalities of the people who live there. They're all British but they're not all English. What are they?

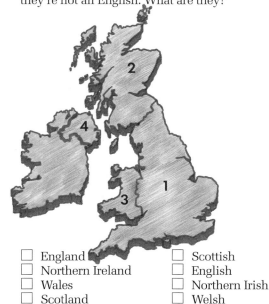

- ☐ England
- ☐ Northern Ireland
- ☐ Wales
- ☐ Scotland
- ☐ Scottish
- ☐ English
- ☐ Northern Irish
- ☐ Welsh

☞ *Language & Culture (page 58)*

1c A ten-minute conversation!

Work in groups of four. If you decided to live in another country, where would you go and why? What would you miss most if you left the country where you live now?

2 📷 How to say it: Giving advice

• The magazine article mentioned that Tony Simpson read a lot about the history of Australia before he moved there. Listen to the following radio interview with Annette Givens, an expert on the problems of emigrating to other countries. Which of these things does she advise people to do before they move?

- ☐ read a lot about the country
- ☐ find out about schools
- ☐ see a doctor
- ☐ buy new clothes
- ☐ think about how much the move will cost
- ☐ learn another language

• Now look at these expressions. Listen again, and number them in the order that you hear them. Careful, you'll hear only four of them. Which one isn't used in the conversation?

- ☐ **My advice is** to talk to people as much as possible.
- ☐ **If I were you, I'd** try to be very realistic about the move.
- ☐ **I think you should** read about the country.
- ☐ **It would be a good idea to** think about the cost, too.
- ☐ **You ought to** look at practical things before you decide.

2a And now you!

Work with a partner. Write three sentences giving advice to someone from another country who has just moved to your town or city. Use some of the expressions above.

▶ **Before you go on** ▬▬▬▬

Look at these examples.

infinitive	past simple	past participle	
want	wanted	wanted	(regular)
see	saw	seen	(irregular)

Now do the same with these verbs:

be	decide	drive	have	say	try
buy	do	eat	learn	stay	visit
call	drink	go	live	think	write

☍ page 62

Now do Exercise 1 in the Homestudy Section.

📷 Speaking practice. Listen and do the exercises on the cassette.

Starter: Find someone who ...

Find people in your class who can answer *yes* to these questions. The first question is: *Do you drink tea for breakfast?* If someone answers *Yes, I do,* then write his/her name on the line.

Find someone who ...

- drinks tea for breakfast.   ....
- reads a newspaper every day.   ....
- lives more than 2 km from school.   ....

- works in an office.   ....
- goes abroad every year.   ....

1 Grammar: Review of tenses

1	**Present simple**	**Do** you **miss** England?	I **miss** my friends.
2	**Present progressive**	**Are** you meet**ing** many new people?	I'**m** meet**ing** new people at work.
3	**Present perfect**	**Have** you settl**ed** down?	Well, I'**ve found** a job.
4	**Past simple**	What **did** you **do** last Saturday?	I **stayed** at home.
5	**Past progressive**	What **were** you do**ing** at ten o'clock?	I **was** work**ing**.
6	**Past perfect**	**Had** you **heard** about Ayers Rock before you read this article?	Yes, I'**d seen** pictures of it before.
7	**Future using *will***	Where **will** you **be** on Sunday?	I'**ll be** at home.
8	**Future using *going to***	What **are** you **going to** do next year?	We'**re going to** fly to Alice Springs.
9	**Future using *present progressive***	When **are** you leav**ing** for Australia?	We'**re** leav**ing** next month.

☞ G 1

1a Negative sentences

Look at the grammar box. The questions all have positive answers. Make a negative answer for each one, like this:

1 *I don't miss my neighbours.*
2 *I'm not making many new friends outside the office.*

1b What are your plans?

Work with a partner. Decide on a country or city you would both like to visit in the future. Make some plans for your trip, like this: *We're leaving on ... We're going to see/buy/visit ... We'll probably ...*

Now work with two more students. Ask and answer questions about the plans you've made. Here are some questions to help you:

When are you leaving?
What are you going to ...?
What do you think you'll ... there?

1c Have you ever been to New Zealand?

Work with a partner. Choose a country to talk about. Look at this example:

Have you ever been to New Zealand?

No, I haven't.

Have you ever been to Canada?

Yes, I have.

When did you go there?

I went in ...

What did you do there?

I visited/saw ... (etc.)

Did you like it? (etc.)

1d Memory test

The Adams family are emigrating to Canada next week. You went round to their house last Saturday to help them get ready. When you arrived, this is what you saw.

Look at the picture for one minute, then close your book and write down as many sentences as you can, like this:
A girl was holding the cat.

1e Penny's new life

Penny and Mary are in a pub. Penny is telling Mary about the changes in her life. Work with a partner. Complete the sentences with these verbs in the past simple or past perfect: *decide, enjoy, find, finish, get, give, go, have, hear, like, meet, move, take, work, write.*

1 Four years ago, she .... she didn't want to work in a library for the rest of her life.

2 So she .... a course in

computers, and she really .... it.

3 When she .... the course, she

.... a job with a small company in Scotland.

4 After she .... in Scotland for

about two years, she .... about a really exciting job in Germany.

5 So she .... to them, and

.... to Cologne for an interview.

6 They .... her and they

.... her the job.

7 She .... there two years ago,

and she .... to learn German.

8 Then she .... a lovely German guy from another computer firm and they

.... married about six months ago.

 Now listen and check your answers.

2 🎦 Living and working abroad

Listen to the rest of the conversation between Mary and Penny. Put a tick (✔) if you hear these things mentioned.

1 ☐ the USA   3 ☐ friends
☐ Australia   ☐ parents
☐ New Zealand   ☐ children

2 ☐ different weather
☐ different people
☐ different way of life

Now listen again. What did Penny say about the three things you've ticked? Take notes.

2a What do you think?

Work in groups of four. How would you feel about leaving your home and family and working abroad? And how would you feel about going to a country where you don't speak the language?

▶ 🖭 Before you go on to the next unit, do the speaking exercises on the cassette.

18-24 July

Radio Review

MAGAZINE OF THE YEAR

Starter: Word ping-pong

Work with a partner. One student says a word that belongs to the topic of towns and cities (e.g. *car*). The other student must then say a contrasting word that belongs to the topic of the countryside (e.g. *horse*). Take it in turns to start.

1 Reading: The changing face of Britain

Before you read

Work with a partner. You'll read about changes that are taking place in British villages. Which of the following words do you expect to find in the article?

bookshop	pub	school	cinema
television	railway	tree	town
supermarket	horse	factory	river
restaurant	farm		

The changing face of Britain

You can hear Margaret Templer's report on *The changing face of Britain* on Channel Seven next Thursday at 8pm.

For most of us, the typical British village has pretty cottages, little shops, a village school, an old church, and of course a friendly old pub full of friendly old farm workers. All around, there are farms and grassy fields. There might be a stream running through the village centre, or perhaps a river and a narrow bridge.

This is the image we see in so many advertisements, TV programmes and travel brochures. But what is life there really like? Channel Seven's Margaret Templer has been visiting small villages all over Britain to find out. "There are still some unspoilt villages, of course, but in many villages the school has disappeared, the small shops have closed, or sell antiques instead of milk and bread, the church is locked. Perhaps even the pub has closed, or has become an expensive restaurant or wine bar instead. The pretty cottages are still there, but they belong to rich people from London or other big cities. It's sad, but there's often nowhere in the village for the ordinary country people to live. The railway line closed years ago, and now even the bus services are disappearing. And some people have been feeling angry for a long time now ..."

☞ *Language & Culture (page 58)*

1a Comprehension

Read these statements about the text. Two statements are true and five aren't. Correct the statements that aren't true.

1 Most people think that a typical British village is very attractive.
2 There are now no unspoilt villages left at all.
3 It can be difficult to buy food in some villages.
4 All the pubs have now closed.
5 The cottages usually belong to rich local people.
6 The railway line closed last year.
7 The bus services in the countryside are getting better.

1b Vocabulary

- The words 1-8 are from the article. Match them with a word on the right which means the opposite.

1 little	5 expensive	☐ cheap	☐ spoilt
2 unspoilt	6 friendly	☐ happy	☐ open
3 locked	7 sad	☐ poor	☐ wide
4 narrow	8 rich	☐ big	☐ unfriendly

- Here are some ways of saying how nice something or someone is: *pretty, sweet, pleasant, beautiful, good-looking, attractive.*

Choose the best combination of words, like this:

a) a pretty — cottage ✔ / factory

d) a beautiful — man / woman

b) a sweet — job / smile

e) a good-looking — man / cat

c) a pleasant — person / animal

f) an attractive — face / baby

📼 Now listen to the words on the cassette.

1c A ten-minute conversation!

Work in groups of three. Would these changes be good or bad for the people living in a small village? Why?

- closing the small shops and opening a big supermarket
- building new houses
- making the pub into a restaurant or wine bar
- opening a small factory
- opening a fun park near the village

2 📼 How to say it: Giving reasons and causes

Rose – born in Boslem

Ben Wilson – runs an antique shop

- Margaret Templer went to the village of Boslem to interview both the villagers and people who had moved there. Listen to her radio report. Who mentioned these things, Rose (R) or Ben (B)?

...... the village Co-op shop

...... developing new business

...... feeling angry

...... tourists

...... friends moving away

...... the problem of finding a job

- Now look at these sentences from the radio programme you've just heard. Listen again and fill in the missing words.

1 It became an antique shop – **that's why** ....
....

2 Lots of my friends have moved away **because of**
....

3 Most of the ordinary shops have closed, and **as a result** ....
to Telford to do their shopping.

4 Not all the problems here are **due to** ....
...., you know.

5 **Another cause of** ....
.... is the problem of finding a job.

2a And now you!

Work with a partner. Write three sentences explaining why people move from a small town to a big city. Use some of the expressions above.

▶ **Before you go on**

How do you spell the *-ing* form of these verbs?

buy	live ....
do	see ....
drive	swim ....
feel	travel ....
go	work ....
have	

Now write out these sentences. Be careful about the tenses (they aren't all *-ing* forms!) and the word order.

1 Excuse me. I (*look*) for Bond Street. You (*know*) where it (*be*)?
2 We (*not play*) tennis at the moment because it (*rain*).
3 Hey, you! What you (*do*)? Those (*be*) my bags!
4 Please (*not make*) so much noise. The students next door (*have*) a test.

🔑 page 62

Now do Exercise 1 in the Homestudy Section.

🎧 Speaking practice. Listen and do the exercises on the cassette.

Starter: What's happening?

Work in pairs. Think of two situations (e.g. *buying something in a shop*) and practise miming the situation together. Then work with two other students. Mime one of your situations to them. They try to guess everything that's happening, like this: *I think she's opening the door. Now she's looking at ...*

1 Grammar: Present perfect with *for* and *since*

Do you know Susan? How long **have** you **known** her?	She's my best friend. **I've known** her **for over twenty years**. **I've known** her **since 1973**.

For is used with a period of time (*8 days, 12 months, 14 years* etc.). *Since* is used with a point of time (*Monday, May, Christmas, 1984* etc.).   ☞ G 8

1a *For* or *since*?

Do you use these words or expressions with *for* or *since*? Make two lists.

Saturday	nine weeks	1980
ten years	last summer	March
Easter	twenty minutes	two o'clock
six months	yesterday morning	three days

1b A questionnaire

Work with a partner. First look at the ideas below. Make them into questions, starting *How long have you ...?*. Then ask your partner. Partner: when you answer, sometimes use *for* and sometimes use *since*.

be   in your present job, at this school, married, etc.

have   your car, flat/house, bike, etc.

know   your teacher, best friend, neighbours, etc.

2 Grammar: Present perfect progressive

1 You look really tired. What **have** you **been** do**ing**? 2 How long **have** you **been** liv**ing** here?	**I've been** play**ing** tennis. **I've been** liv**ing** here for over twenty years. **I've been** liv**ing** here since 1972.
3 Do you know where Mike is?	No, **I've been** try**ing** to phone him all morning.

1 We use the present perfect progressive to talk about activities that finished very recently.
2 We also use this tense to talk about situations that started in the past and have continued up until now, for example with verbs like *live, work, learn*.
3 We can also use this tense to talk about events that took place several times between a point of time in the past and now.   ☞ G 6, G 9

2a Match the sentences.

Look at sentences 1-6. Then look at the sentences below them and find the best reply to each one. Complete the replies with one of these verbs: *come, feel, look, sleep, try, wait*.

1 Hi, Petra. Am I late?
2 Hello, Tony Clark speaking.
3 Goodness, Mary, you look tired!
4 Excuse me, is this your wallet?
5 Is this your first visit to England?
6 Are you all right, Peter?

☐ Oh thanks. I've been .... for it everywhere.

☐ I don't think so. I've been .... strange for the last few minutes.

☐ Yes, you are! I've been .... here for hours.

☐ No, I've been .... here every summer for the last six or seven years.

☐ Hello Dad! I've been .... to get through to you for the last two hours!

☐ Well, I've been .... very badly recently.

▪️ Now listen and check your answers.

2b It's been a long time!

David works for a TV station.

Liz and Eric sell antiques.

Barbara teaches English.

Marina writes books.

Tim and Sandra run a restaurant.

Ian and Peter live in Italy.

Jenny makes films.

Clare and Tony help immigrants.

Alan now lives in Canada.

Look at this old photo from your last day at school some years ago. A friend has sent it to you and has written some notes about all the people in the picture. Your teacher has extra information: ask him/her questions to find out more about your old school friends, like this: *How long has Alan been living in Canada?*

(Teacher: The information is on page 57.)

3 📼 Life in the country

Emma and Chris are talking about their new life in a very small village in Devon. Listen to the conversation and fill in the table below. Put in an E for the things Emma says, and a C for the things Chris says.

	quieter	cleaner	more friendly	transport	post office	cinemas	museums	shops	theatres
things they like									
problems									
things they miss									

Now compare your answers with a partner.

3a What do you think?

Work in groups of four. Emma and Chris mentioned some of the positive and negative things about living in the country. What advantages and disadvantages do you think there might be for:

- teenagers   • families with young children   • old people?

▶ 📼 Before you go on to Panorama Plus, do the speaking exercises on the cassette.

Starter

Work with a partner. You are both going to an information evening on Australia. What do you already know about the country? What would you like to hear about it?

Where do you think these words go in the text? Number them 1 to 16.

☐ doctors	☐ farms	☐ train	☐ longest	☐ 50
☐ teacher	☐ hospital	☐ motorbike	☐ hundreds	☐ 90
☐ kangaroos	☐ school	☐ largest	☐ million	☐ 478
☐ sheep				

Factfile on
Australia

Some animals and plants are found only in Australia – for example, **(1)**. They carry their young in a pouch or 'pocket'. These animals developed only in Australia. The grass tree is also found only in Australia. This strange tree can grow only after a fire!

Most Australians live in cities or their suburbs, but a few people live in the outback, miles from even the smallest town. They live and work on **(2)** stations – huge **(3)**, some as big as a quarter of a **(4)** hectares, where they raise sheep for their wool. Even the children need a **(5)** to get around.

Life in the outback can be difficult. The great distances mean that it's impossible for the children to go to **(6)**, and so they listen to the School of the Air. This is a system of two-way radios that allows the **(7)** and the children to talk to each other, even though they are three or four hundred kilometres apart. The Flying Doctor Service provides medical help. The **(8)** also use two-way radios to talk to their patients, and in an emergency, a plane can take someone to **(9)** in the nearest large town or city.

Transport in Australia is special. On the roads you might see a road train – a truck with several trailers, carrying **(10)** of sheep. On the railways, the

Flying Doctor Service

Trans-Australian **(11)** runs from Adelaide in the south to Perth on the west coast. It crosses the Nullarbor plain, which is an extremely dry, flat and hot area at the edge of the Australian desert. The maximum temperature can be almost **(12)** C°. Here you will find the **(13)** stretch of straight track in the world: **(14)** kilometres. The train driver has to press a special button every **(15)** seconds – if he doesn't, the train will stop.

The Australian desert is the second **(16)** desert in the world.

1 Which three facts about Australia did you find the most interesting?

2 What do you think people in Australia know about your country?

3 What questions might they ask you? Think of three questions.

4 Imagine you wanted to drive from Adelaide to Perth, across the Nullarbor plain and the desert. What should you take with you? What would you do if your car broke down in the desert?

☞ *Language & Culture (page 59)*

Did you know?

◆ Talking of deserts, the USA has some, too. The Sonoran Desert in Arizona is the eighth largest in the world. The Mojave Desert in California, which includes Death Valley, is one of the hottest places in the world, with a maximum temperature of almost 57 C°.

◆ The city with the longest name in the USA is El Pueblo de Nuestra Señora la Reina de los Angeles de la Porciuncula, or Los Angeles. Many people call it LA, which is the shortest name for a city in the USA. But LA itself isn't small – it has a population of over 3 million (and growing), over 100 suburbs which spread out 80 kilometres in each direction from the centre, and almost 100 km of coast.

◆ By the year 2000, half the world's population will live in cities.

◆ There will be twenty-five cities with over 10 million people.

◆ And there will be more than 30 million people in Mexico City.

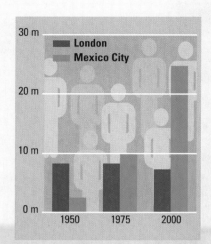

Australia and the USA

🖭 You will hear a professor talking to some American students about Australia and the USA. First, listen and number the words below 1 to 5 in the order you hear them.

Boston, USA

☐ population
☐ cities & suburbs
☐ size
☐ suburban life
☐ states

Listen again. This time make notes on what she says about each of these topics.

Sheep station in Renner Springs, Australia

Now compare your notes with a partner. Use your notes to write three sentences comparing Australia and the United States.

House in Maryborough, Australia
Family having a barbecue

You've won a month's holiday in either Australia or the USA. Which one will you choose?

1 Starter: Have you ...?

One student should give a piece of information like this:

for three years   or   since last Christmas

The others in the class should ask questions like this:

*Have you been living in
your flat for three years?*   No, I haven't.

*Have you had your car
for three years?*   No, I haven't.

Have you ...?

How many questions did you have to ask in order to get a positive answer (*Yes, I have.*)?

2 How much do you know?

Work with a partner. Read each starter sentence carefully. Then decide if the statements that follow the sentence are true (T) or false (F).

1 *They lived there for ten years.*

...... They live there now.

...... They used to live there.

...... They've been living there for the last ten years.

2 *They've been married since 1973.*

...... They are married now.

...... They've been married for more than nineteen years.

...... They were married but they aren't now.

...... They got married in 1981.

3 *He's been waiting there for twenty minutes.*

...... He arrived there half an hour ago.

...... He left there twenty minutes ago.

...... He's there now.

...... He started waiting there twenty minutes ago.

...... He waited there for twenty minutes, but then he gave up and left.

Now compare your answers with another student. Discuss any differences you've got, and try to decide which answer is correct.

3 Preposition practice

Where do these words go in the text? Write them in the gaps.

about   down   into   on   through
at (2x)   in   of (2x)   out   to (4x)

When Anna looked .... the house she didn't know if she wanted to buy it or not,

.... first. Then she talked .... the owner. The house belonged .... an old lady who reminded Anna .... her grandmother. Her grandmother had, ... many ways, been a mother to Anna when she was a child. As she walked .... the rooms, the house suddenly seemed friendly instead .... old and ordinary. So Anna bought it and soon moved .... the small town where the house was. Before she moved, she found .... a lot of things .... the town, and so she settled .... very quickly. She soon began to look forward .... her first summer there. She spent a lot of money .... plants for the garden – too much money, she thought.

But she made the garden .... a very pretty place, just like her grandmother's garden that they had both always loved!

What nostalgic memories have you got of a person you used to know?

4 Words, words, words: making nouns into adjectives

You can make some nouns into adjectives by adding the letter *y,* like this:

health —> healthy
sun —> sunny
wave —> wavy

Work with a partner and write down the adjectives that you can form from these nouns.

cloud ....

cream ....

dirt ....

dust ....

fog ....

fun ....

grass ....

luck ....

noise ....

rain ....

salt ....

sand ....

sleep ....

smell ....

smoke ....

wind ....

Now go back and add a word that can follow the adjectives above, like this:

a healthy person
a sunny day
wavy hair

If you don't know the meaning of a word, look it up in the *Vocabulary* section.

5 Write as much as you can!

Write about a place you have been to or used to live in, a place that you liked very much. Write about the place and say why you liked it so much. Write as much as you can in ten minutes, then exchange papers with another student and read what he/she has written.

Now write two questions to find out more things that you'd like to know about your partner's place. Exchange papers again and tell your partner the answers to his/her two questions.

6 With your partner!

Partner A, look at this page. B, please look at page 56. Partner A. You're going to ask B for some advice in the following situations. Before you ask B, write down the advice that you would give someone else in the same situations.

- You want to learn Spanish quickly.
- You aren't a very creative cook.
- You're overworked.
- Your neighbours are very noisy.

> My advice is to ...   I think you should ...

> If I were you, I'd ...   Why don't you ...?

Now tell B your problems and see if his/her advice is the same as the advice you would give (or is B's advice even better?).

7 Out and about!

Before the next lesson, try to buy or find an English or American newspaper (it doesn't matter which paper you choose). Look through the paper carefully. How many times does it mention Australia? And where? Is it mentioned in the sports section, the weather forecast or weather report, the business section or somewhere else?

13

In 1960 I started work for a London newspaper as a reporter. I was still quite young but I liked to think I was older. The work wasn't difficult but I had expected more exciting things. Reports on social events weren't so interesting after the fourth time. So just think of my reaction when my boss called me into the office one day and said, "Our man in Malaya is ill again. We've recently brought him back and he's now in hospital." At that time there was a war there and all the newspapers had their 'man in Malaya'. They now wanted to send me to Malaya immediately to report on the war. I returned to the small flat, where I lived with my mother, and packed. Forty-eight hours later I was at the hot, crowded airport in Singapore with one suitcase and a camera.

I quickly settled down. However, I soon found out that a reporter's life in Singapore wasn't more exciting than in London. I spent most of my time in government offices and also talked to local people, even taxi-drivers (people say that they're experts on everything). I spent my evenings in my hotel room, wrote my reports and tried to make everyday events more exciting than they really were.

I began to spend more time in the hotel bar, where you can find out quite a lot for the price of a drink or two. For example, I found out that my sick colleague, the one now in hospital in England, had spent nearly all his time in the bar and only left it to write his reports. I began to wonder what his problem was. One evening, I was sitting there as I usually did, when another hotel guest came into the bar. This was a man with a very red face, grey hair and a small moustache. I had seen him before at the hotel reception with an older, good-looking woman, who looked very rich. He was an

STRANGE MEETING

Englishman of about fifty and I wondered if they were married. His eyes looked everywhere, but never directly at you. I thought that he might have an interesting story for me, so I bought him a drink, and then another. He began telling me stories about his life. He said that he was just an ordinary man from the North of England. At that moment I knew that wasn't true. I'm from the West of England myself, and he had the same accent as me. He told me his name was Sharp and that he ran a business a short distance from Perth in Western Australia. "I'm spending a holiday here with my wife," he said and quickly looked over his shoulder, perhaps afraid that she was standing behind him.

I asked other people in the hotel about him. They told me a few stories about his life, some of them quite strange. "Which ones are true?" I wondered. Some people didn't even believe his name was Sharp or that the older woman was his wife. He didn't seem to know very much about Perth, either. When we met in the bar again, I bought more than one or two drinks for 'Mr Sharp' and after a time he told me a story that sounded true. When he was younger, he left England in a hurry – there was some story about a pretty girl who was expecting a child. "I liked the ladies a lot in those days," he said. "Things haven't changed much," I thought. "I didn't want to be a father," he said. "I wasn't ready for that." He looked sad. "So I decided to go abroad." At that moment 'Mrs Sharp' arrived. "I ought to go," he said and left with her.

I didn't see him very often after that. When he saw me in the hotel, he walked past me very quickly and didn't look at me.

A few months later I was at the airport on my way back to England. At the passport desk, I saw someone I knew in front of me. It was 'Mr Sharp' from the hotel. He was alone. He didn't see me. I followed him to the desk and managed to stand very near him. Then I looked over his shoulder at the name on his passport when he showed it. The name on the passport was 'Mr Harold Deacon'. Not 'Sharp' but 'Deacon'. 'Harold Deacon'. That was *my* name, too, and I knew I had the same name as my father. I'd never known my father. He'd disappeared, my mother always said …

It's only natural

UNITS 3 & 4

Starter: Finish the sentences.

Work in groups of four. Think about the topic of sport and then finish these sentences.
Playing sport is better than ...
You're never too old to ...
If you do some sport regularly, you might ...

1 Reading: Sport for all – your free guide to getting fitter

Before you read

Work with a partner. You are going to read about sports which are especially good for adults of all ages: exercise classes, swimming, tennis, and walking. Why does the brochure mention these four sports do you think?

Welcome to *Sport for all,* your guide to sports for adults. Sport is fun if you remember these three golden rules: first of all, start slowly; then, do it regularly; and finally, enjoy it!

EXERCISE CLASSES These have become very popular recently, and are great ways to meet people, have fun, and generally keep fit. Make sure the class is the right one for you – ask your teacher if you can try a class before you join. Most classes are quite cheap.

SWIMMING Swimming is an ideal sport for most people, and is great for general fitness. If you are overweight or suffer from a disability, it's especially good because the water supports your body. Going swimming shouldn't be expensive – ask about special prices and tickets at the pool. All you need is a towel and a costume! And if you can't swim, you can learn – it's never too late. Find out about lessons locally.

SPORT for all

TENNIS Tennis is good for improving your all-round fitness, and the rules are easy to learn. You can play at private clubs, but these can be expensive. Fortunately, public courts are much cheaper, but can obviously be crowded at times.

WALKING Walking is the most natural exercise you can have. It's also extremely good for helping with stress. Don't try to walk too far at first – just walk to work, or to the shops. You can increase the distance later – join a club and discover the local countryside. If you walk in the hills, you'll need strong, comfortable shoes and warm clothes. Buy good-quality shoes – your feet will appreciate the extra cost!

If you'd had the opportunity, would you have started any of these sports when you were younger? Yes? Then why not start one now – it's never too late!

☞ *Language & Culture (page 59)*

1a Comprehension

The table below also contains information about these sports. Which of the points with a tick (✔) did the brochure mention? Then check with a partner.

	exercise classes	swimming	tennis	walking
free				✔
can be quite expensive			✔	
good for disabled people		✔		
good way to meet people	✔			✔
good for general fitness	✔	✔	✔	
you need special shoes	✔		✔	✔

1b Vocabulary

• Complete these sentences with a word from the text.

1 Football is a very p............................... sport all over the world.

2 I didn't like jogging by myself, so I decided to

j............................... a club.

3 Riding your bike in the countryside is an

i............................... way to stay fit.

4 Most sports are good for i............................... your fitness.

5 Over the next few weeks, try to i............................... the distance that you walk.

6 Go swimming regularly and d............................... how good it feels to be really fit!

7 After finishing the Boston Marathon,

I a............................... an hour in a hot bath.

8 At school we didn't have the o............................... to do sports like tennis.

• ▰ Now match these sports with the pictures. Then listen to these words on the cassette.

☐ ice hockey   ☐ basketball   ☐ squash
☐ cycling   ☐ volleyball   ☐ motor racing
☐ sailing   ☐ handball

1
2
3
4
5
6
7
8

1c A ten-minute conversation!

Work in groups of four. Which sports do you play? Which sports did you use to play, but don't play now? Why did you give them up? Which sports do you like watching? Why?

2 ▰ How to say it: Explaining something

• Some students are playing a game in their English class. They have to explain a sport but not say what it is. Listen to two of the students and tick the two sports they talk about.

☐ tennis   ☐ skiing
☐ badminton   ☐ skating
☐ table tennis ☐ windsurfing

• Now look at these sentences that Chantal and Frank used. Listen again and complete them.

1 **You need a** ....

.... equipment.

2 **It's used for** hitting something ....

.... a ball.

3 **The point of the sport is to** hit this thing over ....

....

.... the room.

4 You try to hit it **so that** the player ....

.... hit it back.

5 You might wear special clothes **in order to** ....

....possible.

6 **First you** ....

stand up. **Then you** learn ....

.... slowly.

2a And now you!

Work with a partner. Think of a sport which you both know well. Describe this sport in the same way that Chantal and Frank did. Use some of the expressions above.

▶ **Before you go on** ▬

Put the words in each sentence into the right order.

1 you / do / you / would / wanted / to / if / fit / sport / which / get / ?
2 the / five / every / country / run / lived / if / would / I / day / km / in / I
3 you / would / if / jogging / go / couldn't / what / you / do / ?
4 bicycle / would / I / buy / think / instead / a / I

⊶ page 62

Now do Exercise 1 in the Homestudy Section.

▱ Speaking practice. Listen and do the exercises on the cassette.

Starter: What would you do if ...?

Work in groups of four, like this:

> What would you do
>
> if you met
>
> a famous sports star?
>
> I'd take her photo.

Here are some verbs to help you: *meet, see, win, have, lose, find*. Take it in turns to start.

1 Grammar: The third conditional

If I'**d trained** more, I **would have been** fitter.	= I didn't train enough so I wasn't fit.
If I'**d been** fitter, I **would have finished** the race.	= I wasn't fit so I didn't finish the race.
If I'**d finished** the race, I **wouldn't have felt** so disappointed.	= I didn't finish it so I felt disappointed.

> We use the third conditional to talk about the past. When the if-clause comes first
> in the sentence, we usually write a comma after it. Notice that *I'd* means *I had*;
> for example: *If I'd trained … = If I had trained …*   ☞ G 10

1a Make the sentences.

Work with a partner. Take turns to begin and complete these sentences.

1 If you hadn't shouted at the trainer,
2 If you'd been fitter,
3 If they'd played better,
4 If they'd won,
5 If you hadn't fallen,
6 If you hadn't taken so many risks,
7 If they'd practised more,
8 If they hadn't cheated,

☐ they would have won the Cup.
☐ they wouldn't have played so badly.
☐ you wouldn't have lost so many points.
☐ you wouldn't have lost your place in the team.
☐ they wouldn't have beaten us!
☐ they would have been national heroes.
☐ you would have finished the race.
☐ you wouldn't have fallen so often.

1b An ex-football star

Look at these notes about Mark, an ex-football star. Write sentences using the notes, like this:

1 *If he hadn't been lazy, he wouldn't have become unfit.*

1 was lazy – became unfit
2 went to discos – was always tired
3 was careless – made a lot of mistakes
4 hit the team captain – lost his place in the team
5 ate too much – put on weight
6 shouted at the crowd – became unpopular
7 took drugs – went to prison

1c What would you have done?

Work with a partner. Take turns to ask and answer these questions. Ask like this:*What would you have done/seen/said if ...?* Answer like this: *If I'd ..., I would have ...*

• if you'd won a million in the lottery at the age of eighteen?
• if your parents had taken you on holiday to America as a child?
• if you'd left school when you were fourteen?
• if your friends had given you ten flying lessons for your last birthday?
• if you'd …

2 Grammar: More adverbs

1 **First of all**, start slowly. **Secondly/Then**, do it regularly. **Finally**, enjoy it!

2 Private clubs can be expensive. **Fortunately**, public courts are much cheaper. **Obviously**, they can be crowded at times.

1 We use adverbs like *first of all, secondly/then* and *finally* to put a list of points in order.
2 We can use adverbs like *fortunately* and *obviously* to comment on what we've said or written.

☞ G 3

2a Scrambled sentences

Write the words in each sentence in the correct order.

1 is / swimming / all / people / suitable / of / for / ages
2 keeps / condition / first of all / your / it / good / body / in
3 can / secondly / your / improve / even / figure / it
4 cheap / is / free / or / fortunately / quite / even / swimming
5 can't / you / ask / to / someone / you / could / finally / swim / teach / you / if

2b Active holidays

David works at an activity holiday centre. He is speaking to a group of people who are interested in going there. How do you think he will combine these sentences?

1 First of all,
2 Obviously,
3 Fortunately,
4 In fact,
5 Naturally,
6 Finally,

☐ everything is included in the cost of your holiday.
☐ we've got the most modern private sports hall in Wales.
☐ we offer special low prices in May and October.
☐ I'd like to welcome you to this information evening.
☐ our centre is in one of the most beautiful parts of Wales.
☐ we can't offer all sports.

📼 Now listen and check your answers.

3 📼 A choice of sports

Listen to the rest of David's talk. While you listen, fill in the table with the information you hear.

canoeing   climbing

golf   riding

sport	page	booking number	adults	children
canoeing	9		£425	
climbing		CL84		£199
golf	16			—
hill walking			£380	
riding	26			£275

☞ *Language & Culture (page 59)*

3a What do you think?

Work in groups of four. Have you ever done any of the above sports? Which do you think is the most dangerous? What do you think could happen? What about other sports like skiing, cycling, or motor racing?

▶ 😐 Before you go on to the next unit, do the speaking exercises on the cassette.

Starter: Blackboard zoo

Work with a partner. In two minutes, write down the names of as many animals as you know. Can you guess any more? (Some, for example *elephant*, are like the German words!) Then collect your words on the board. How many words does the whole class know?

1 Reading: Your A-Z guide to pets

Before you read

Match the drawings and the names of these common pets. Then read the text and find out if it says anything about them.

☐ bird   ☐ cat   ☐ dog   ☐ guinea pig
☐ hamster   ☐ rabbit   ☐ fish

Your A-Z guide to PETS

CHAPTER I

Although a pet can be the perfect companion for young and old, it may be difficult to make the right choice. However, if you use your common sense, and follow this simple guide, you should be able to avoid making a mistake. Think before you make your decision. It's not a good idea to get a pet if you haven't considered it carefully first. Perhaps the worst thing to do is to give somebody a pet as a present if you don't know whether they can look after it or not.

The amount of time the owner has is important. Some pets need more attention than others – dogs, for example, often need a lot of care and daily exercise. They shouldn't be left inside the whole day, either. Cats, small birds and fish, on the other hand, are usually easy pets to look after and can be left alone during the day.

CHAPTER II

Now that you've chosen your pet, what's the best way of looking after it? A good person to ask is your vet, of course. He or she can give you plenty of helpful advice about how to care for it. Your pet should be examined by the vet, too. Obviously, it's important to feed your pet properly, to keep it clean and healthy, and to make sure it has all the exercise it needs. More information about these points can be found later in this chapter.

However, it's also important to remember that your pet lives in your home, and this can sometimes lead to problems.

☞ *Language & Culture (page 59)*

1a Comprehension

The information on page 20 is from two different chapters – Chapter 1 *Choosing your new pet*, and Chapter 2 *Looking after your pet*. Here is some more information about pets. Does it belong in Chapter 1 or in Chapter 2?

1 Every home has its dangers for pets. In the kitchen, all sharp knives and other dangerous objects should be kept in places where your pet can't reach them.
2 The size of your pet and the size of your home are also important. More space is needed by dogs, for example, so think carefully if you live in a small flat.
3 Think about the age of the owner, too. Can older people deal with a big dog that's got lots of energy?
4 Always remember to tidy up immediately after working around the home. In the garden, all tools should be put away so that your pet can't hurt itself.
5 And if you have very young children, be especially careful. Some dogs are made nervous very easily, and may then attack your child.
6 Smaller animals, such as hamsters, might be much more suitable for younger children.
7 Valuable furniture can be damaged by pets, especially by young cats and dogs, so be prepared for this. Even rabbits, guinea pigs and hamsters can cause a lot of damage!

1b Vocabulary

• These sentences contain words from the book about pets. Finish each sentence yourself.

1 I'll be away this weekend. Could you **look after** ...?
2 Some **common** pets are ...
3 Our teacher was very **helpful**. He/She ...
4 That knife's very **sharp**. Be careful, or you'll ...
5 Could you help me to **tidy up** – for example, could you put ...?
6 **Suitable** presents for young children are things like ...

• 📼 Here are some more words that are connected with animals. Work with a partner and match the words with the pictures. Then listen to the words on the cassette.

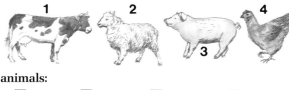

animals:
☐ pig   ☐ cow   ☐ chicken   ☐ sheep

meat:
☐ beef   ☐ lamb   ☐ pork   ☐ chicken

other products:
☐ wool   ☐ milk   ☐ leather   ☐ cheese
☐ bacon   ☐ butter   ☐ sausages   ☐ eggs

1c A ten-minute conversation!

Work in groups of four. Which pets have you got now? What about when you were children? What are the problems of keeping pets? Which pets might be suitable for the following people: an old lady, a ten-year-old boy, a young woman living alone? Why?

☞ *Language & Culture (page 60)*

2 📼 How to say it: Having a discussion

• You're going to hear a reporter interviewing the owner of a private zoo. Listen and note who mentions these things first, the reporter (R) or the zoo owner (Z).

☐ exciting animals
☐ the weather
☐ toys for the animals to play with
☐ learning about different animals
☐ small cages
☐ feeding the animals

• Now look at these expressions from the interview you've just heard, and number them as follows:

1 giving an opinion
2 agreeing with someone's opinion
3 politely disagreeing with someone
4 strongly disagreeing with someone

☐ I'm all for ...
☐ It's just the opposite.
☐ I doubt whether ...
☐ I accept what you say, but ...
☐ I can see your point, but ...
☐ It's important for us to ...
☐ Surely you don't really mean ...
☐ I support ...
☐ I completely agree with you.
☐ I don't really know whether ...

Listen again. Notice how the expressions were used.

2a And now you!

Write a sentence giving your opinion about keeping animals in zoos or as pets. Use one of the expressions you numbered 1 above. Then read it aloud to the rest of the class. The others should agree or disagree with your sentence. Use expressions numbered 2, 3 or 4.

▶ Before you go on

Here are some more regular and irregular verbs. What are their past simple and past participle forms? Make a table like the one you made in Unit 1.

answer, break, catch, enjoy, feel, find, get, give, keep, kill, leave, make, move, put, stop, test

⊶ page 62

Now do Exercise 1 in the Homestudy Section.

📼 Speaking practice. Listen and do the exercises on the cassette.

Starter: Chain sentences

Work in groups of three. Student 1: choose a word from the first box. Student 2: continue from the second box. Student 3: finish the sentence from the third box. For example: *Chianti is often drunk in Italian restaurants.* Take it in turns to start. How many sentences can you make in three minutes?

chianti	bread		is	often	drunk	sold		on picnics	for lunch
pizzas	champagne		are	usually	eaten	cooked		in Italian restaurants	at work
sandwiches	vegetables			sometimes	made	...		for breakfast	at home
coffee	...							at weddings	...

1 Grammar: The passive

1 Sometimes people **are attacked** by animals.
2 In the 1950s, dogs and monkeys **were sent** into space by the Russians.
3 The dog **has** already **been fed**, but it **hasn't been taken** for its walk yet.
4 Big dogs **shouldn't be kept** in very small flats.

We form the passive with the verb *to be* and the past participle. We can also show who did something, but only when this is important or interesting. See sentences 1 and 2: **by** *animals,* **by** *the Russians.*   ☞ G 13

1a History quiz

Work with a partner.
First make a question from boxes 1 and 2, like this:

Who made the first space flight?

Then use box 3 to give your answer, like this:
I think the first space flight was made by Yuri Gagarin.

discover	the Nobel Peace Prize in 1990
invent	the *Mona Lisa*
make	*Murder on the Orient Express*
paint	America
shoot	many Agatha Christie murders
solve	the ballpoint pen
win	the first space flight
write	President Kennedy

Lee Harvey Oswald	Leonardo da Vinci
Sherlock Holmes	Christopher Columbus
Mikhail Gorbachev	Hercule Poirot
Pablo Picasso	Agatha Christie
Marco Polo	Laszlo Biro
Yuri Gagarin	Mother Teresa

1b 📼 An office memo

You'll hear a message from a vet to one of her receptionists. First listen and note what she says about the following points, like this: *cancel all appointments.*

1 all her appointments
2 the bills
3 the cages
4 the new medicine
5 Mrs Redford's cat

Now write out the information as a memo for the receptionist's colleague. Use the passive with *should,* like this: *All her appointments should be cancelled immediately.*

1c A busy Saturday

Nicola and Andy have a lot to do. First, look at the list they wrote in the morning. The picture shows their house and garden at lunchtime. Now make sentences about what's been done and what hasn't been done yet.

Things to do
* do the shopping
* cut the grass
* water the plants
* wash the car
* paint the garage door
* repair the garden gate
* hang up the washing
* put the garden tools away

2 Grammar: Infinitives

1 Most children **want to have** a pet.
2 It may be **difficult to make** the right choice.
3 It's not **a good idea to get** a pet if you haven't considered it carefully.
4 Our vet told us **what to do**.

> Notice some of the different ways we can use infinitives: after some verbs (1), after some adjectives (2), after some nouns (3), after question words (4). ☞ G 14

2a The best way to learn German

Complete each gap below with one of these words:

☑ *decided* ☐ *happy* ☐ *places* ☐ *how*
☐ *difficult* ☐ *helped* ☐ *where* ☐ *what*

Two years ago Stephen **(1)** to go to a language school in Germany. He had the names of various schools, but it was **(2)** to choose the right one. So he asked his teacher **(3)** to do. She was **(4)** to help, and told him that smaller towns were good **(5)** to consider. She **(6)** him to write to a couple of schools, and showed him **(7)** to complete the forms they sent. Stephen didn't know **(8)** to stay either, and she suggested a family not a hotel.

Was each of the words you used a verb, an adjective, a noun or a question word?

2b The Glenmore Centre

You're going to hear part of an interview with a vet about how pets can be used to help old or ill people. Work with a partner. Read the sentences below and think of verbs that make sense for each of the gaps. More than one verb is usually possible.

1 The right person to .... is Dr Marion Stewart.

2 She invited me to .... her at the centre, to talk about her work.

3 Dogs are very often used, because they're usually easy animals to ....

4 Glenmore is a perfect place to .... the ways we can use animals as companions.

5 This gives us a very good opportunity to .... at how animals can help people.

6 It's a very good idea to .... small animals with old people.

📼 Now listen and fill in what you hear on the cassette.

3 📼 Pets and people

Listen to the rest of the interview. While you listen, decide if the following statements are true or false.

1 In France, 98% of old people's homes accepted pets.
2 Dogs were less popular than birds.
3 Dr Stewart has less information about Britain than about France.
4 In Britain, only 16% of the staff at old people's homes had used animals.
5 Dr Stewart says that animals help people to feel happier.
6 She says that animals aren't used in prisons in America.
7 She says that contact with animals can help prisoners.

3a What do you think?

Work in groups of four. If you lived alone and felt lonely, which animals would be a good companion for you? Are there any animals that you are afraid of? If you could come back to the world as an animal (or bird), which would you choose to be? Why? Ask your teacher too!

▶ 📼 Before you go on to Panorama Plus, do the speaking exercises on the cassette.

Starter

Work with a partner. How would your life be different if you were a top-class sportsman/woman? Would you enjoy such a life? Why?/Why not?

Too old at twenty?

♦ Boris Becker was only 17 when he won the Men's Singles title at Wimbledon for the first time. Jennifer Capriati won her first match there when she was 14. Aurelia Dobre from Romania won the women's world gymnastics title also at 14, and Fu Mingxia from China was the women's world diving champion at the age of 12.

♦ These recent examples of world-class sportsmen and women (or should that be sportsboys and girls?) have shown that success can come very early in the world of sport. But what happens to teenage sports stars when they get older? It's true that some continue to be successful – Becker, for example – but for others, their sporting life ends before they are 20.

♦ And what about the part played by their parents and trainers? There have been stories of parents who force their children to practise for hours and hours in the hope that they will become a champion – and rich. And of trainers who take complete control over the lives of their young starlets, and stop them from enjoying a normal childhood and perhaps even ruin their adult lives.

♦ However, young champions are nothing new. Lottie Dod won the Ladies' Singles title at Wimbledon when she was 15 – in 1887! Jay Foster was an international table tennis champion at the age of 8 in 1958, and a French boy (nobody even knows his name) took part in the Olympic Games in 1900 – at an unknown age, but perhaps as young as 7!

♦ What *is* new is the money – the few who become champions can earn millions of dollars. And, unfortunately, when some parents and trainers see that amount of money, they push their children harder and harder. No friends, no toys, no fun – just practice, practice and more practice. You can see it for yourself – baby-sized Beckers on the tennis courts, mini-Maradonas on the football fields. The sad fact is that hardly any of these kids will make it to the top – and even if they do, there is a terrible risk that some of them will be too old at 20. ▬

1 What are the positive and negative aspects of being a child sports star?

2 Imagine you're interviewing someone who used to be a child sports star. (You can decide which sport, and the other details.) What questions would you ask him/her about his/her life, both then and now? Work with a partner and write the questions down.

Now change partners. One student is the reporter, the other is the ex-star. Ask and answer the questions, as in an interview.

☞ *Language & Culture (page 60)*

Did you know?

◆ The oldest person to take part in an international competition was William Pattimore from Wales, at the 1970 Commonwealth Games, when he was 78.

◆ The fastest a human can run for 100 metres is just over 36 km per hour. The fastest animal is the cheetah, which has a maximum speed of around 100 km per hour over a short distance. The fastest bird is the swift, which can fly at around 170 km per hour.

◆ Some falcons can reach speeds of 350 km per hour when they dive down through the air, and in 1960 Joseph Kittinger reached a speed of 1,005 km per hour when he jumped from a balloon at 31,333 m!

A working relationship

🔲 You will hear several people talking about their relationship with an animal or bird. First, look at the photographs, and then number them 1 to 4 in the order you hear them.

☐ dolphin

☐ sniffer dog

☐ show jumper

☐ falcon

How do you feel about animals being used in sport? Number these sports 1 to 6, from the most acceptable to the least acceptable. What are your reasons?

☐ show jumping ☐ fishing
☐ bull fighting ☐ horse racing
☐ fox hunting ☐ dog racing

Listen again. This time, make notes on what each person says. Then compare your notes with a partner. Use your notes to write three sentences about the different ways that people and animals work together.

1 Starter: If he ...

Tom never liked school. In fact, he hated it every day. Continue this story about Tom. One person starts a sentence and the next person finishes it.

> If Tom hadn't hated school,

> he probably would have stayed there longer.

> If he had stayed there longer,

> he would have learnt French.

> If he had learnt French,

> perhaps he would have ...

2 How much do you know?

Work with a partner. Read each starter sentence carefully. Then decide if the statements that follow the sentence are true (T) or false (F) or not clear (?).

1 *If she had seen the accident, she would have phoned the police.*

..... There was an accident.

..... She saw the accident.

..... She didn't phone the police.

..... Nobody phoned the police.

2 *If they hadn't found that beautiful but expensive house, they wouldn't have moved to that town.*

..... They found a beautiful house.

..... The house was in the only town that they wanted to live in.

..... The house cost more than they had wanted to pay.

..... They moved to that town.

3 *Look, Susan's windows have been cleaned.*

..... Susan has cleaned her windows.

..... Someone else has cleaned Susan's windows.

..... Susan's windows are clean now.

..... Susan's windows need a good clean. Now!

4 *Mr Charlton's report has already been written.*

..... The report is finished.

..... Mr Charlton's secretary wrote the report.

..... The report was written yesterday.

..... Someone really must write Mr Charlton's report.

Now compare your answers with another student. Discuss any differences you've got, and try to decide which answer is correct.

3 With your partner!

Partner A, look at this page. B, please look at page 56. Partner A. You and your partner have got six questions together. First of all, put the words in the correct order to make the first half of questions 1-3 and the second half of questions 4-6. Then read the beginnings of 1-3 to your partner. He/She will tell you the second part so that you can complete them. Your partner will do the same with 4-6. In the end you should have six complete questions.

1 you / have / what / bought / would ....

What would you have bought

....

.... ?

2 have / what / cooked / you / would ....

What

....

.... ?

3 bought / have / which / magazine / you / would .....

Which

....

.... ?

4 ..... out / dinner / gone / for / if / you'd / yesterday ?

....

if you'd gone

.... ?

5 ....decided / if / weekend / you'd / go / to / away / last ?

....

if

.... ?

6 ......lesson / thirsty / been / you'd / the / if / before ?

....

if

.... ?

When you've got the six questions, tell each other your answers.

4 Write as much as you can!

Choose one of these pictures and write about how you feel about the situation in the picture. Write about your own personal experiences if you can. Write as much as you can in ten minutes.

Exchange papers with a partner. Read what he/she has written. Do you have the same feelings as your partner?

5 Words, words, words: adjectives ending in *-ful*

Some adjectives end in *-ful*, like *useful*, for example. Fill in the missing letters to make the adjectives in these sentences, and then complete the sentences. If you need help, you'll find the missing letters for each word in brackets at the end of the exercise (in the wrong order, of course!). Work in groups of three and try to do the exercise without looking at the help first.

1 A b _ _ _ _ _ ful woman is a woman who ...

2 A s _ _ _ _ _ _ _ ful student is a student who ...

3 A h _ _ _ ful person is a person who ...

4 A w_ _ _ _ _ ful city is a city which ...

5 A c _ _ _ ful driver is a driver who ...

6 A u _ _ ful birthday present is a present like ...

7 A p _ _ _ _ ful car is a car which ...

You can replace the *-ful* at the end of three of these adjectives by *-less* to make an adjective with the opposite meaning. Which three?

(Help: 1 utaei, 2 ecussc, 3 pel, 4 doren, 5 rae, 6 se, 7 ewro)

6 Preposition practice

Write prepositions on the lines and passive verbs in the boxes.

Prepositions: 1 *at, by, of, of, to*
                     2 *as, at, for, for, of*
                     3 *by, by, for, of, on*

Verbs: *damage, hit, kill, sell, tell*

1 He   to stay late .... work yesterday, due .... the amount .... work he had to finish .... the end .... the day.

2 Computers   .... things that are ideal and necessary .... nearly everybody, but .... times they cause a lot .... problems .... some people.

3 When the towns .... the coast .... the hurricane last night, people were not prepared .... it and, unfortunately, hundreds .... houses   .... it. Fortunately, nobody

7 Out and about!

Before the next lesson, look at the sports section of a newspaper that is written in your language. Find ten words in your language that you think are important to know in English. Write these words down and look them up in a dictionary. If you need any help with the pronunciation of the words, ask your teacher at the beginning of the next lesson.

A story

Emily Parsons lived alone in a small flat in a quiet road in the suburbs. When we say 'alone', we should also mention Emily's two cats, Smokey (the grey one) and Mr Britling (the black one with the green eyes). Emily had never married. She had very few friends, although she got on well with her neighbours and the people she met. Her cats were her true companions and she used to enjoy bringing home a special piece of fish or chicken for them when she went shopping.

Emily had taken the flat many years before when she used to give piano lessons. People didn't want piano lessons these days. Obviously, they spent their free time in other ways. She didn't pay a high rent for the flat and this part of the town was ideal for her. It was quiet and the air was good. Of course, the area had changed. There were more office buildings now and cars parked everywhere. The little shops had disappeared. Emily now had to walk to the big supermarket three streets away.

One morning in summer, she was making breakfast for Smokey and Mr Britling (today it was a meal of fish with some milk) when the post arrived. Emily Parsons didn't get much post, so she was always a little nervous when a letter arrived. This one came in a brown envelope and looked important. Letters like this were either bad news or bills. She opened the envelope. It *was* bad news. The owner of the building where she lived had died and Supernova, a large property company, had bought it. Supernova wanted a higher rent. Emily was not so worried about this because she had expected it. However, it was the second point in the letter that made her really very worried: "From January 1st next year animals will not be allowed in our flats."

Emily sat down quickly. Smokey and Mr Britling stopped eating and looked at her. "No animals." How could she live without Smokey and Mr Britling?

When she went shopping that day, she could think of nothing else. Her neighbour, Mrs Bruce, had to say 'hello' twice before Emily answered. "What's wrong, dear?" Mrs Bruce asked. Emily told her the whole story. Now, Mrs Bruce's son worked for the local newspaper. He wrote articles about local events. In the summer, however, there isn't so much news because most people are on holiday. When Mrs Bruce's son heard about Emily Parsons, her cats and the problem with the flat, he went to see her at once with a tape recorder and a camera. The next day Emily was front page news. Under a photo of Emily and her two cats, it said, "DON'T TAKE MY PETS AWAY" and the article began, "Miss Emily Parsons, 64, started crying last night when a property company told her that she had to give her cats

away." There was also a photo of a man from Supernova. Under his photo it said, "Has this man got a heart?" Soon the national newspapers had the story: "CATS MUST STAY" and "MY PETS ARE MY LIFE." There were more photos of Emily with her cats. Reporters wanted interviews and people from the radio phoned her nearly every hour for news. The next day there was a much bigger photo of Emily in the newspapers and the words: "DAY 3: EMILY: 'I WON'T GIVE UP'." That day the TV people wanted to talk to her. Emily soon became a media personality. She was interviewed on the radio and television about cats, gave advice and answered questions about food and health. Animal magazines wanted regular articles. Letters arrived every day from her many fans. Emily didn't mind. She enjoyed talking about her cats and liked answering questions. About this time Supernova wrote to her again. They said that she could stay in her flat and live rent-free if she wanted to. Obviously, they were worried about their image.

One day in late summer the phone stopped ringing. There weren't so many letters for her, either. It was the end of the holidays and there was more important and, probably, more urgent news. No one seemed interested in Emily and her cats now. Emily began to feel sad and alone. Then she suddenly had an idea. She opened the telephone book and started looking through the pages. "S... Superdrugs... Superkids... ah, Supernova!" And with the book on her knees and the receiver in her hand, she began to dial their number ...

All in a life's work

UNITS 5 & 6

Starter: Guess my job.

Your teacher will think of a job but not tell you what it is. Try to guess the job by asking questions. Your teacher can answer only *yes* or *no*.

Ask like this: *Do you work inside? Have you got a uniform?* etc.

(Teacher: There are some suggestions on page 57.)

1 Reading: Thinking of changing your career?

Before you read

Work with a partner. Imagine you want a better job. Look at these points and number them from 1 to 6, depending on how important each one is to you:

- ☐ longer holidays
- ☐ higher salary
- ☐ more/less travelling
- ☐ more responsibility
- ☐ shorter working week
- ☐ more interesting duties

Now read this advertisement from a job-finding service, and part of a letter from a woman who wants a better job. Does she mention any of the above points?

Jackie Woods, 21 Vicarage Lane, Bath

PDA

Professional Development Agency

Are you satisfied with your present job? Or are you ready for a change? Are you always applying for jobs, but without success? Do you get as far as an interview – and then fail?

Let PDA help you to find the perfect job – and get it! Write to me, Sue Conway, at the address below. Send me details of your qualifications and work experience, and the kind of job you're looking for. Come and find the job of your dreams!

'Applying for jobs was a waste of time – until PDA showed me how!'

LG, Bristol

Sue Conway, Professional Development Agency, 26 Maddox Street, Bath BA7 6ST

I am 29 years old, divorced, and have been working as a secretary for a lawyer for three years. Before that, I worked for the director of a small firm for five years. I can type and take shorthand, and I have a good knowledge of German. My present job is well-paid, but I find it dull and boring.

My positive qualities include a good sense of humour and a wide number of interests, and I consider myself quite practical and bright. Unfortunately, I get very nervous at interviews. I get embarrassed and then I'm not very good at expressing myself, though in ordinary conversations I am perfectly calm.

I would like an interesting job that gives me more responsibility. I would also welcome your advice on giving a better performance at interviews.

I am looking forward to hearing from you soon.

☞ *Language & Culture (page 60)*

1a Comprehension

Here is the personal information form that PDA uses.
Fill in the missing details.

Surname	*Woods*
First name(s)	*Jackie*
Age	
Status	
Experience	
Present job	
Strong points	
Weak points	
Aims	

1b Vocabulary

• Look at these groups of words. Which word
doesn't belong in each group?

1 secretary / firm / director / lawyer
2 boring / funny / interesting / pleasant
3 duties / salary / responsibilities / performance
4 happy / satisfied / angry / pleased
5 divorced / single / young / married
6 embarrassed / upset / angry / calm
7 experience / knowledge / holidays / qualifications
8 hobby / job / profession / career

• 📼 Now look at these words. Make pairs of
'opposites'. Then listen to the words on the cassette.

a) agree	☐ argue
b) ask	☐ boring
c) be calm	☐ clever
d) customer	☐ employee
e) employer	☐ female
f) exciting	☐ be nervous
g) fail	☐ pass (*verb*)
h) have a job	☐ reply (*verb*)
i) male	☐ salesman/woman
j) stupid	☐ be unemployed

1c A ten-minute conversation!

Work in groups of three. Ask the others what they
like and dislike most about the work they do every
day. Here are some ideas to help you: *travelling,
working hours, people, place, problems ...*

2 📼 How to say it: Developing a conversation

• Jackie goes for an interview with Sue at PDA.
Listen. Which of these points do they mention?

1 ☐ Jackie's colleagues   3 ☐ selling something
  ☐ Jackie's boss   ☐ organizing some-
                              thing
2 ☐ French   4 ☐ meeting people
  ☐ Italian   ☐ flying a lot

• Now look at these expressions. Listen again and
decide who says each expression. Write an S for Sue
(the interviewer) or a J for Jackie.

☐ Do you know what I mean?
☐ I mean, (I wish I could ...)
☐ Sorry to interrupt, but ...
☐ While we're on the subject of ...
☐ Talking of (tourism, have you ...)
☐ ... don't you think?
☐ Could you explain (what ...)
☐ You know, (sometimes I ...)
☐ What do you think?

2a And now you!

Work with a partner. Choose one of the topics below,
and discuss it together. While you're talking, try to
use some of the expressions above. Don't be afraid to
interrupt your partner.

• the ideal job
• the ideal employer – or employee

▶ Before you go on ▬▬▬▬▬

Make gerunds from these verbs (e.g. *buy – buying*).
Be careful with the spelling.

be, eat, fly, get up, lose, ride, run, stand up

Now choose the gerunds that fit each of the following
sentences.

1 Most people don't like ... early to go to work.
2 She hates ... when she plays tennis!
3 He keeps fit by ... in the woods and ... his bike.
4 We're looking forward to ... in New Zealand at
  Christmas.

⊶ page 62

Now do Exercise 1 in the Homestudy Section.

📖 Speaking practice. Listen and do the exercises on
the cassette.

Starter: I'd love collecting the tips!

Work in groups of four. What would you love doing, like doing, enjoy doing and hate doing if you were a waiter/waitress, a taxi driver, or a teacher?

1 Grammar: Gerunds

1 I **like meeting** people, and I really **enjoy travelling** in my job.
2 **Have** you ever **thought about changing** your job?
3 Are you **good at expressing** yourself?
4 What's **the point of going** to interviews if I always fail?
5 **Applying** for jobs was a waste of time until PDA showed me how.

> Notice some of the different ways we can use gerunds: after some verbs (1); after verbs + prepositions (2); after adjectives + prepositions (3); after nouns + prepositions (4); as the subject of a sentence (5). ☞ G 15

1a What's the answer?

Look at the sentences in the first box. For each one, find the best reply from the second box.

1 How is Mark doing at school now?
2 Would you like to change your job?
3 What's the biggest mistake you've ever made?
4 Why don't you ask your boss for more money?
5 Would you like to live abroad?
6 How do you keep so calm when your boss shouts at you like that?
7 What can I do about my cough?
8 Would you like me to lend you some money?

a ☐ I can't. I'm afraid of losing my job!
b ☐ Well, I think you should give up smoking.
c ☐ Yes, I often think about living in a different country.
d ☐ It's hard, but what's the use of getting angry with him?
e ☐ No thanks. I'd be worried about paying it back.
f ☐ Well, I really regret not travelling more when I was younger.
g ☐ No, I can't imagine doing anything different.
h ☐ OK, but he seems to have no interest in learning other languages.

🔊 Now listen and check your answers.

Then work with a partner. Look at the replies, and the grammar box above. Take it in turns to describe each sentence, like this:

In sentence a, the gerund comes after an adjective and preposition.

1b In my spare time

Work with a partner. One student chooses a picture and asks a question, like this:
Do you like listening to music?

When you answer, use one of the expressions below and start with a gerund, like this: *Yes, listening to music is one of my favourite pastimes.*

> … one of my favourite sports/pastimes.
> … my favourite way of spending the evening.
> … something I often/seldom/never do.
> … something I love/like/hate doing.

Take it in turns to start.

2 Grammar: *Always* + present/past progressive

Are you **always applying** for jobs, but without success?

He made me nervous – he **was always looking** at his watch.

> You can use *always* with the present or past progressive to show you're not happy about things. Here, *always* means *too often* or *(I) don't like it.* ☞ G 7

2a They're driving me mad!

Look at the picture below and imagine you are the lady in bed in the ground-floor flat. Complain about the situations, using *always* and the present progressive.
Here are some verbs to help you: *bark, come home, cook, dance, dig, have, leave, make, pick, play, practise.*

Now work with a partner. Tell him/her three things about your family, friends or neighbours that are driving you mad.

2b You should meet my new boss!

Kim and Bob are friends who work for different companies. They're in a pub, complaining about past and present bosses. Work with a partner. What could be the missing words in the sentences below?

1 She never listens to me – she's always ... with her pen or ... at her watch.
2 He was always ... me extra work at ten to five on Friday afternoon!
3 Another thing – she's always ... about all the important people she knows.
4 Mine did that too – and he was always ... me about all the clever things he'd done.
5 She's always ... away on business trips too, while I have to do all the work!
6 I know. And he was always ... golf and ... it was 'good for business'.
7 She's always ... three-hour lunch breaks.
8 Yeh. I wouldn't mind, but mine was always ... about how hard he worked!

📼 Now listen to Kim and Bob and compare your answers with what they say.

3 📼 Working at home

Before you listen to the rest of the conversation, read the sentences below. Then listen and decide whether answer a or b is correct.

1 Kim says that in future people
  a ☐ will have several different jobs.
  b ☐ won't travel to the office so much.

2 Bob says he
  a ☐ would miss seeing his boss.
  b ☐ would feel lonely working by himself.

3 Kim says that every day it takes her
  a ☐ an hour to get to work.
  b ☐ two hours to get home.

4 Bob says that working at home would probably
  a ☐ mean he could have more holidays.
  b ☐ give him less free time than he's got now.

5 At the end of the conversation, Kim
  a ☐ starts to agree with Bob.
  b ☐ still thinks working at home is a good idea.

3a What do you think?

Work in groups of four. If you could choose, would you prefer to go out to work or to work at home? What are the advantages and disadvantages of each? Do you have a lot of stress in your job? Choose the three most and three least stressful jobs from this list: teacher, waiter/waitress, farm worker, train driver, shop assistant, pilot, air hostess, typist, police officer.

▶ 📼 Before you go on to the next unit, do the speaking exercises on the cassette.

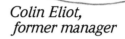

Starter: Now and then

Work in groups of four. Compare your daily life now with what it was like ten years ago. What do you think it will be like ten years from now?

1 Reading: After work

Before you read

Work with a partner. Think about a retired person that you know. What did he/she do before retirement? And now?

Now read these interviews with two retired people.

Colin Eliot,
former manager

When I was fifty-six, I decided to stop working and start enjoying myself. I've never regretted it. The children had both married and left home, so my wife and I moved into a smaller house in Vancouver and I retired. Suddenly we had time for each other, and for all the things we wanted to do – gardening, reading, sport, theater and, above all, traveling. Now we've been all over the world and seen all the sights – sunrises in the Sahara, sunsets over the ocean in Portugal, museums in most of the capitals of Europe. I've taken thousands of photographs, and kept a diary as a record of all the places we've visited. Perhaps I'll write a book one day! It's all a dream come true – I should have retired when I was fifty!

Mary Bishop, former office worker

I retired when I was sixty-two, and at first I rather enjoyed it. But after a while I became tired of having nothing to do. I h̲a̲d̲ ̲t̲h̲e̲ ̲f̲e̲e̲l̲i̲n̲g̲ ̲t̲i̲m̲e – I suppose I felt guilty about having nothing t̲o̲ ̲o̲c̲c̲u̲ group that organizes courses and activiti̲e̲s̲ ̲f̲o̲r̲ old people, immigrants, ex-prisoners, an̲d̲ ̲n̲o̲w̲ ̲I̲ ̲h̲e̲l̲p̲ ̲t̲o̲ ̲t̲e̲a̲c̲h̲ and write. The work is part-time, and u̲ I̲ ̲m̲e̲e̲t̲ ̲t̲w̲i̲c̲e̲ weekly, and it's really satisfying to see t̲ colleagues also work for the group – it's c̲ ̲a̲n̲d̲ ̲t̲h̲e̲y̲ enjoy it as much as I do. I think we all f̲o̲u̲ and we're trying to prove that we're no̲

☞ *Language & Culture (page 60)*

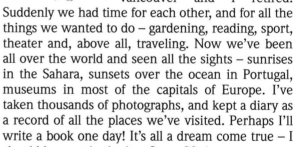

1a Comprehension

Can you find two words in Colin's text that are spelt differently in British English?
Now choose the best answer (a, b, c or d) for each question, and then compare with a partner.

1 At the age of fifty-six, Colin
  a ☐ found a new job.
  b ☐ gave up his job.
  c ☐ bought a bigger house.
  d ☐ got married.

2 Colin thinks he
  a ☐ retired at exactly the right time.
  b ☐ was happier before he retired.
  c ☐ should have stayed at work.
  d ☐ stayed at work too long.

3 When she retired, Mary
  a ☐ felt unhappy immediately.
  b ☐ felt tired all the time.
  c ☐ was quite happy for a while.
  d ☐ wasted all her money.

4 In her new "job" she
  a ☐ earns more than she did before.
  b ☐ works mainly with children.
  c ☐ works longer hours than before.
  d ☐ sees each class twice a week.

1b Vocabulary

• Match these words from the interviews with the correct meaning.

1 come true   5 contact
2 waste   6 organize
3 suppose   7 make progress
4 feel guilty   8 prove

☐ get better at doing something
☐ write to, phone, or go to see somebody
☐ show that something is true
☐ really happen
☐ feel that you have done something wrong
☐ not use something in a useful way
☐ think that something may be true
☐ make plans for something

• 📼 Look at the words in the boxes below and listen to them on the cassette. Then match a word from the first box with one from the second, and then make a short sentence, like this: *Europe is a continent.*

The Mediterranean	Everest	Portugal
The Sahara	Europe	The Rhine
The Atlantic	Corsica	Loch Ness

continent	country	desert
mountain	lake	island
ocean	river	sea

1c A ten-minute conversation!

Work in groups of four. Who was your favourite old person when you were a child? What was so special about that person? What did you learn about his/her earlier life?

2 📼 How to say it: Meeting people you know

• Mary Bishop is having a visit from James and Cathy and their daughter Emily. Listen and note down the three special occasions they are celebrating.

• Now look at these expressions. Listen to the conversation again, and tick the ones you hear.

1 ☐ Happy birthday!   4 ☐ Take care.
  ☐ Many happy   ☐ Look after yourself.
    returns of the day.
2 ☐ How are things?   5 ☐ Cheerio.
  ☐ How are you   ☐ See you.
    keeping?
3 ☐ Here's to you!   6 ☐ Give my regards to ...
  ☐ Cheers!   ☐ Give my love to ...

2a And now you!

Here are six possible reactions to expressions 1-6 in Exercise 2. Match the reactions with the expressions.

☐ Bye! Keep in touch, won't you?   ☐ You, too.
☐ Yes, of course I will.   ☐ Cheers!
☐ Fine, thanks.   ☐ Thank you.

Now work with a partner and use suitable expressions and reactions in these situations. Take it in turns to start.

• You meet your partner in the street (you haven't seen him/her for some time).
• Your partner is a good friend – you say goodbye.
• You buy your partner a drink.
• It's your partner's birthday.

▶ Before you go on ▬▬▬▬▬

One of the verbs in *italics* is not correct in these sentences. Cross it out.

1 If you feel so ill, you *might/should/must* see a doctor.
2 *Could/Will/May* you help me with my suitcase, please?
3 In the UK, you *have to /must/might* drive on the left.
4 You *needn't/can't/mustn't* park here – it's not allowed.

⊶ page 62

Now do Exercise 1 in the Homestudy Section.

📼 Speaking practice. Listen and do the exercises on the cassette.

Starter: Help!

Work in groups of three. For each of the situations numbered 1 to 4 below, give some helpful advice.
Use a different modal verb for each piece of advice, like this:

> I think my English is terrible!

> You could go to the UK for a month.

> You should buy an English paper every week.

1 I'm putting on so much weight!   3 I don't like my job!
2 I feel very lonely!   4 I'm really unfit!

1 Grammar: *Could have done* and *should have done*

Why did you drive so fast? You **could have had** an accident! (But luckily you didn't.)

Colin **should have retired** when he was fifty. (But he didn't.)

He **shouldn't have worked** until he was fifty-six. (But he did.)

> We always make sentences like these with a modal verb + *have* + past participle.
> Notice the word order! ☞ G 16

1a You could have had an accident!

These risky situations all took place yesterday.
Luckily, nothing bad happened. For each one, make a
sentence about what *could have happened*, like this:

1 She could have caught a cold.

1b Dangerous mistakes

Read this newspaper story about four climbers who
did everything wrong and almost died. Work with a
partner and make eight sentences about what they
should or shouldn't have done, like this: *They should
have told somebody their plans.*

Four Saved on Matterhorn

Zermatt. Local guides today saved four
climbers from certain death on the world-
famous Matterhorn. The four got into trouble
at over 10,000 feet (3,000 metres). 'They made
every mistake in the book,' said Alex Weiss,
one of the guides. 'They didn't tell anybody
their plans, they chose a difficult route, didn't
ask for advice and didn't take a local guide
with them.' Alex and his colleagues couldn't
believe their eyes when they finally reached
the four. 'They weren't wearing proper
clothes, they didn't have any emergency food
with them, they started in poor weather instead
of waiting for it to improve, and they even
tried to climb when it was dark.' The four 'are
very lucky to be alive,' he said.

2 Grammar: Comparisons and contrasts

1 She works much harder than **me** / than I **do**. (= than I work)

2 They enjoy the work as much as **me** / as much as I **do**. (= as much as I enjoy it)

3 She retired later than **him** / than he **did**. (= than he retired)

4 I can speak French, but my husband **can't**. (= my husband can't speak French)

5 We all found retiring more difficult than **expected**. (= than we expected)

In sentences 1-4, notice how we don't repeat the verb we used in the first half of the sentence.
In sentence 5, notice how we can use a different verb without repeating the subject.   ☞ G 2

2a Partner interview

Work with a partner. Find out which of you:

- is taller.
- goes to the cinema more frequently.
- got up earlier this morning.
- drank more coffee yesterday.
- can swim further.
- has been abroad more often.

Then tell the rest of the class what you found out.
Say it in two different ways, like this:
Karin is taller than me. She's taller than I am.

2b A visit from Tim's parents

Ann is interviewing Tim, her English teacher, about his parents. They're spending a holiday with him in Switzerland. Here are some of the things he says about them. What could be the missing words in the sentences below?

1 They're much older than .... of course, so we have to plan things carefully.

2 They can't walk as far as I ...., so we go for short, easy walks.

3 The last time they were here, they always got up

earlier than we ....!

4 My Mom knows a lot more about art and history

than I ....

5 He's done a lot more things than I ...., so he has a lot of stories to tell the kids.

6 They're easier to please than I ....!

7 Last year my Mom wanted to go to a concert but

Dad ....

8 My father eats meat but my mother ....
She's a health food fan!

▣ Now listen to Tim and compare your answers with what he says.

☞ *Language & Culture (page 61)*

3 ▣ Retirement plans

Listen to the rest of Ann and Tim's conversation.
Decide if the statements below are true (T) or false (F).

1 Tim's parents live in Chicago.

2 They are definitely moving to Florida.

3 They'd like to have their own apartment.

4 Ann's parents want to move to Italy.

5 Tim has decided to go back to America when he retires.

6 Tim and Laura have already bought a cottage for their retirement.

7 His wife wouldn't be happy if they lived in a city.

8 Tim and Laura are looking forward to a quiet life when they are older.

3a What do you think?

Work in groups of four. Suppose a retired person came to stay with you for two weeks. Plan a programme of things for him or her to do – some alone, and some together with you.

▶ ▢ Before you go on to Panorama Plus, do the speaking exercises on the cassette.

Starter

Work with a partner. Imagine that for the next ten days you met only people who were the same age group as you, or older. How would you feel about this? What would you miss if you never met any younger people?

Sun City, Arizona

◆ From the air, it looks strangely beautiful, like something in a dream or from a science-fiction film. A huge area of white curves and circles, spread out across the hot and silent surface of the earth. Nearer the ground, you can begin to recognize buildings and roads. But if you look carefully at the people driving around, or playing golf, you won't see many young ones. This is Sun City, where 80,000 people live – nearly all of them over 50.

◆ You can't live in Sun City if you're young. If you *are* under 50, then your husband or wife must be at least 50. Such couples are very much the exception. There aren't any schools in Sun City, because there aren't any children. They aren't allowed to live here – if a couple had a baby, they would have to leave.

◆ Everyone here is retired. So what does the average citizen do all day? Well, there's golf, and swimming, and tennis, a library, and classes in every kind of activity you can imagine. Enjoying yourself is the main aim. The people here feel safe, and free from the stress of living in our modern, youth-oriented society. They all share the same problems and interests. They understand each other here.

◆ Some people spend only six months a year in Sun City, usually over the winter, when it's cooler. Others prefer to remain inside the safety of this special environment the whole year round. Is this what the future holds for us, too?

1 Imagine you are seventy and someone is trying to persuade you to live in a place like Sun City. Think of arguments against going to live there.

2 What difficulties do old people face in their daily life in your country? How could we make life a bit easier for them?

Did you know?

◆ Augusta Bunge, from Wisconsin, USA, became a great-great-great-great-great-grandmother in 1989.

◆ Charlotte Hughes, from the UK, flew to New York by Concorde on her 110th birthday. She is one of the oldest people to fly.

◆ The longest anyone has ever lived is 120 years and 237 days. Shigechiyo Izumi, from Japan, was born in 1865 and died in 1986. Other 'records' can't be proved.

◆ The record for the longest working life also belongs to Izumi – he started work in 1872 and retired 98 years later, at the age of 105.

Number of hours worked per week in industry:

Egypt	58.0
South Korea	54.0
Singapore	49.2
Peru	47.4
Japan	46.3
Switzerland	42.4
UK	42.2
US	41.0
Germany	40.1
Finland	32.2

◆ Dr Paul Ashton, a British hospital doctor, had a working week of 142 hours in June 1980. He had an average of 3 hours 42 minutes sleep each day.

◆ One of the lowest unemployment figures ever recorded was in Switzerland in December 1973. From a population of 6.6 million people, only 81 were out of work.

◆ In Denmark 75% of the women of working age actually work. The figure for the UK is 62%, Germany 52%, and Switzerland 38%.

◆ British women earn 32% less than men. Swiss women earn 30% less, and German women 28% less.

Losing your job – it might be a good move!

Match these pictures with the jobs below.

☐ manager
☐ teacher
☐ engineer
☐ stewardess
☐ computer specialist
☐ travel agent

📟 You will hear three of these people talking about what they did when they lost their job. Listen and decide which three you hear.

Now listen again. This time, make notes on what the speakers say about their experiences.

Then compare your notes in groups of three. Use your notes to write three sentences about what one of the people did.

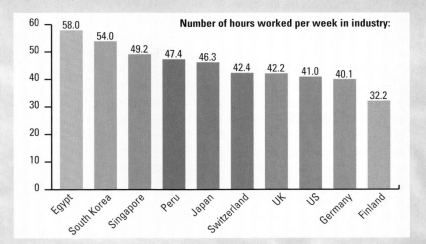

What do you think are the problems and new opportunities for a 30-/45-/60-year-old person who has suddenly lost his/her job?

1 Starter: Past lives!

Use your imagination! You all had a life before this life, or maybe more than one! What can you say about your past lives? Use the words given here:

a doctor	an elephant	like	be good at
a dog	a pilot	hate	be bad at
a teacher	…	enjoy	

In my past life I was a dog …

So was I, and I used to enjoy barking at the postman!

2 With your partner!

Partner A, look at this page. B, please look at page 57. Partner A. You are a travel agent and you want someone to work with you in your agency. Interview B for the job. Decide the following things first:

How old would you like the person to be?

☐ 20-30   ☐ 30-40   ☐ 40+

Which <u>two</u> of these languages would be most useful?

☐ English   ☐ Italian
☐ French   ☐ Spanish

Would you prefer a person who can drive a car?

☐ yes   ☐ no

Choose the <u>two</u> most important things here.

He/She should

☐ enjoy travelling.
☐ be good at using a computer.
☐ be willing to work at weekends.
☐ be good at speaking to large groups of people.

Which of these special wishes have you got?
Choose <u>two.</u>

He/She must

☐ be a non-smoker.
☐ live less than a kilometre from the nearest station.
☐ like big dogs (you've got one and you bring it to the office every day).
☐ have at least five years office experience.

Now interview B to find out if he/she is a suitable person for the job. When you've finished your interview, make a group of four with two other students and explain to them why you gave or didn't give the job to B.

3 How much do you know?

Work with a partner. Read each starter sentence carefully. Then decide if the statements that follow the sentence are true (T), false (F) or not clear (?).

1 *Tom's always parking his car there.*

...... He always parks there and nowhere else.

...... The speaker doesn't mind when Tom parks his car there.

...... The speaker doesn't like it when Tom parks his car there.

...... There = the speaker's parking place.

2 *She really regrets leaving school at sixteen instead of eighteen.*

...... She was eighteen when she left school.

...... She's happy now that she left school at sixteen.

...... She's doing an evening course now.

...... She now thinks that it was a mistake to leave school at sixteen.

...... She now thinks she should have stayed at school longer.

3 *He shouldn't have driven home yesterday in that bad weather, he could have had an accident.*

...... Other people tried to stop him from driving home.

...... He decided not to drive home.

...... He drove home in the bad weather.

...... He had an accident.

...... It was bad weather for driving yesterday.

4 *Martin found the test more difficult than Anna did. In fact he found it much more difficult than expected – but she didn't.*

...... Anna found the test easier than Martin did.

...... Martin expected the test to be more difficult than it was.

...... The test was easier than Martin expected.

...... Anna found the test more difficult than expected.

...... They both expected the test to be difficult.

Now compare your answers with another student. Discuss any differences you've got, and try to decide which answer is correct.

4 Preposition practice

Work with a partner. Make ten expressions that were in Units 5&6 using words from the left and words from the right with *of* in the middle.

1	what kind		☐	humour
2	a good knowledge		☐	fifty-six
3	a good sense		☐	interests
4	a wide number		☑	job
5	on the subject	of	☐	German
6	afraid		☐	photographs
7	most		☐	having nothing to do
8	thousands		☐	the capitals of Europe
9	tired		☐	languages
10	at the age		☐	losing my job

5 Words, words, words: making nouns (that end in *-tion*) from verbs

Make nouns ending in *-tion* from all these verbs:

apply   expect   interrupt   qualify
complete   imagine   organize   satisfy
correct   inform

Write the nouns here:

1 change the *'y'* to *'i'* and add *'cation'*

   application.................................. ....

2 add *'ion'* ....

3 drop the *'e'* and add *'ation'*

   ....

4 add *'ation'* ....

5 drop the *'e'* and add *'ion'* ....

6 drop the *'y'* and add *'action'* ....

Use five of these nouns in the gaps:

a) They were disappointed because their

   .... were too high.

b) The phone rang ten times during the meeting. We would have finished an hour earlier if we hadn't

   had so many ....

c) A writer of children's books usually has a good

   ....

d) They started building the house in May 1992, and

   April 1993 was the date of ....

e) As a nurse, she doesn't earn much, but when her patients get better, she gets a lot of job

   ....

6 Write as much as you can!

Choose one of the pictures and write about the job the person is doing there. Perhaps you could write about

- what the person has to do.
- what they had to learn.
- what you think about the job.
- whether you'd like to have the job.

Write as much as you can in ten minutes.

Exchange papers with a partner. Read what he/she has written about one of the jobs. Then find out how your partner's everyday life is different from the life of a person who does that job.

7 Out and about!

Before the next lesson, try to find a person who sometimes has to speak or read English in his/her job.

Find out

- when and where he/she learnt English.
- who he/she speaks English to.
- if he/she uses English in other situations, too.
- if there are any special English words he/she often uses.

If you can, ask your questions in English.

41

A story

Graham worked for The Happy Love marriage bureau. Their adverts said, "Are you lonely, are you blue? Happy Love has a partner for you." Graham was very good at finding partners for the people who wrote to Happy Love. He read their letters very carefully and then wrote suitable ads for the newspapers. Graham was popular with the other people at the office. He was friendly and helpful and his colleagues enjoyed his great sense of humour. However, there was one cloud in Graham's life and none of the people at the office knew about it. That was the fact that he felt very lonely. Although he had many positive qualities, Graham did not make friends easily. And strangely, although he worked for a marriage bureau, he found it difficult to meet girls. There were some pretty girls in Graham's office, but he never invited them to a cinema or a restaurant. When he wanted to say, "Would you like to go dancing tomorrow?" or "Are you interested in going to see a film?" he got very nervous and embarrassed. Finally, he talked about something else. After work Graham used to return to his empty flat and think about his lonely life.

MADE FOR EACH OTHER

One day a letter arrived at the office. It was from a girl called Susan. "I'm looking for my dream man," she wrote. There was something interesting about the letter. This one was special, Graham felt. Susan was 25, attractive, and – like him – she had a great sense of humour. She liked dancing, going to the cinema and having long talks. He did, too! Graham read the letter again. He went to the mirror on the wall and looked at himself. He did not look like anyone's 'dream man,' he thought. Graham wasn't very handsome. He wasn't exactly fat, but he wasn't slim, either. He was just, well, ordinary. Graham stopped looking at himself. It made him sad. He wanted to write to Susan himself, but there was the problem of photos. You had to send a photo. What could he do?

At that moment Alan came in. Alan wasn't one of Graham's friends at the office. Actually, Graham didn't exactly like Alan too much. Alan was the office playboy. He was tall, slim and handsome and looked like a fashion model. Alan wanted to give him a photo for the office files, which Graham looked after. When Alan left, Graham looked at the photo of Alan's handsome face and he began to think.

◆

Susan read the letter again. It was a beautiful letter, which told her a lot about the writer. He seemed interesting and kind. He wanted to meet her and he suggested a time and a place – a café in the centre of the town. Susan looked at the photo. He was certainly handsome, but the eyes looked cool, she thought. No, she didn't like the eyes very much. But the letter was different. It was special. She tried to imagine the man who had written it. "Please send me a photo of yourself," he said in the letter. "Then I'll know who you are when we meet." She looked at a photo of herself. "I look terrible," she thought. "What will he think of me?" No, she couldn't send this one. In her letter she had written 'attractive'. That had been Angela's idea, Angela was her best friend. But best friends can make mistakes sometimes. Susan phoned her. "Angela," she said, "have you got a photo?"

◆

The café wasn't full. Graham quickly found a seat and waited. He tried to read a magazine, but couldn't. He was too nervous. He looked at Susan's photo again. She looked very attractive. What would she say when she saw him? He was beginning to regret sending her Alan's photo. He shouldn't have done that. He tried to think what to say. A girl sat down at the next table. She seemed very nervous. She was obviously waiting for somebody because she looked at her watch again and again. "She's waiting for her boyfriend," Graham thought. He looked at her. She had nice hair, long and very attractive. Suddenly, she looked up and saw Graham. She smiled. "She *is* attractive," Graham thought. Her boyfriend's very lucky. "Are you waiting for someone, too?" she asked. "Yes," said Graham, "but I don't think she's coming. I've been here for half an hour." "I don't think my friend's coming, either," the girl said. "Would you like another coffee?" Graham asked. He found it very easy to talk to her. He wasn't nervous at all. Soon they were talking like old friends. Half an hour later they left the café together. When the waitress came to the table, she found two photos, one under each cup.

Reading between the lines
UNITS 7 & 8

HIGH QUALITY COPIES COPO

Starter: It's the greatest.

Work in groups of four. Think of as many super-
latives as you can that you could use to describe a
car, like this: *It's the fastest, it's the most expensive ...*
etc. Then do the same for a camera. After four
minutes, tell your ideas to the rest of the class.

1 Reading: Advertising – who needs it?

Before you read

Work with a partner. Think of as many different
places where you find advertisements as you can
(e.g. on the radio, on ball pens, on sports shirts).
After three minutes, compare your list with another
pair.

Now read these four points of view about advertising.

Advertising – who needs it?

Sally Churchill, teacher: "I know that advertisements are necessary, and that newspapers and
magazines would be much more expensive if they
didn't have them. And some of the adverts are
good, especially on TV. But others are silly, and a
few are even quite nasty, or use too much sex. They
often show women in a way that makes me angry.
And of course some of the things they say are nonsense. There was one that said I would speak
French fluently after only three weeks with their
cassettes! I don't pay much attention to most
adverts. But I really do think that ads for tobacco
products and alcohol shouldn't be allowed."

David Macmillan, head of an advertising agency:
"Our clients spend millions of dollars a year on
advertising, mainly on TV and in the press, and our
job is to make the best adverts we can for them. It
makes no difference whether they're for frozen peas
or electric shavers. I think good ads can show the

product in an original and interesting way. The
main purpose, however, is to sell. But don't forget,
adverts provide an important public service because
they help us to decide what to buy and give us
information about new products. Anyway, I think
they bring some colour into our lives."

Liliane Goodman, psychologist: "A lot of ads try to
make us think we will be happier, more successful,
better-looking, or more popular – especially with
the opposite sex – if we buy their products. As a
result, people *do* buy things they don't need, or
can't afford. Very often, ads work on our subconscious feelings. In other words, we don't realise the
influence they have on us. Children in particular
are at risk, I think."

Simon, aged 9: "All my friends have got a mountain
bike like the one they show on TV and I want one,
too. I asked my mum if I could have one but she
said I had to wait until Christmas. That's not fair!"

☞ *Language & Culture (page 61)*

1a Comprehension

Decide whether the following statements are true (T) or false (F). If the text doesn't tell you, write a question mark (?).

1 Sally Churchill speaks French fluently.
2 She's against advertisements for cigarettes.
3 David Macmillan's clients advertise a lot in
  newspapers and magazines.
4 He thinks that the main point of advertising is to
  give information about new products.

5 Liliane Goodman thinks TV adverts are more
  successful than adverts in the press.
6 She says that people sometimes buy unnecessary
  things because of advertising.
7 She says that children understand the influence of
  adverts better than adults.

1b Vocabulary

• These sentences contain words from the text you've just read. Finish each sentence yourself.

1 The weather was really **nasty** yesterday – it ...
2 Supermarkets sell a lot of milk **products**, for example ...
3 There's no **difference** between these two cassettes. In other words, they're ...
4 The main **purpose** of dictionaries is ...
5 I can't **afford** to go abroad for a holiday this year, and so I ...
6 My mother was a very good **influence** on me – she ...
7 His company sells foreign cars, and **in particular** cars from ...

• 📼 Now look at these words. Put them into five groups of three. Use each word only once. Then listen to the words on the cassette.

☐ alcohol	☐ frozen (peas)	☐ tinned
☐ cassette recorder	☐ fruit juice	☐ tobacco
☐ cigar	☐ pipe	☐ toothbrush
☐ comb	☐ shaver	☐ walkman
☐ fresh	☐ stereo	☐ water

1c A ten-minute conversation!

Work in groups of three. Look at the pictures of the tree, the apple, the sheep and the cheetah. How might they be used in advertisements? For which products? (Think of as many different products as you can.) What would these pictures say about these products?

2 📼 How to say it: Expressing satisfaction and dissatisfaction

• You will hear a local radio programme. It's reporting the results of a questionnaire on what people think about advertisements in the press. Listen and note the three topics from the questionnaire that are mentioned.

1 .... in adverts

2 .... of adverts

3 things people ....

• Now look at these expressions from the radio programme. Then listen again and fill in the missing figures about the three topics.

1 (I'm)	very pleased with (it)	...........%
	quite satisfied with (it)	...........%
	not satisfied with (it)	...........%
2 (I'm)	quite happy with (it)	...........%
	not happy with (it)	...........%
3 (I'm) sick and tired of (it)		...........%
(I've) had enough of (it)		...........%
It's / They're boring.		...........%

Now compare your figures with a partner.

2a And now you!

Work in groups of four. What do you think about the TV advertisements that you see in your country? Use some of the expressions above.

▶ **Before you go on** ▬▬▬

Put the verbs in these sentences in the correct tense. Use the simple past, past progressive or past perfect.

1 Yesterday, when I ....……….......... (*drive*) to

   work, I suddenly ....……………........ (*remember*)

   that I ....……………........ (*not lock*) the front door.

2 When we ....……………........ (*arrive*) in

   Munich, it ....……………........ (*rain*) and we

   ....……………........ (*realize*) that we

   ....……………........ (*forget*) to bring our
   umbrellas.

⊙━ page 62

Now do Exercise 1 in the Homestudy Section.

📼 Speaking practice. Listen and do the exercises on the cassette.

Starter: Who is it?

Work in two groups. In each group, one of you is a famous person. If you can't think of a suitable person, ask your teacher for a suggestion. The other students must ask questions to find out more information about the person, like this: *Are you a man or a woman? What do you do?* etc.

Then each group reports the information to the rest of the class, like this: *She says she's a pop star. She says she's got blonde hair. She says she wasn't born in Europe.* etc. Can the class guess who the person is?

(Teacher! There are some suggestions on page 57.)

1 Grammar: Reported speech

"**I don't pay** much attention to most adverts," Sally said.	Sally said **she didn't pay** much attention to most adverts.
"**I am learning** English with *Network Plus*," Martin said.	Martin said **he was learning** English with *Network Plus*.
"**We have seen** the new adverts on TV," the customer said.	The customer said **they had seen** the new adverts on TV.
"**I bought** a bike because of the adverts," Simon's mother said.	Simon's mother said **she had bought** a bike because of the adverts.
"**You will speak** French fluently with our cassettes," the advert said.	The advert said **I would speak** French fluently with their cassettes.
"**I can understand** parents' fears about advertising," Liliane said.	Liliane said **she could understand** parents' fears about advertising.

Notice how the verb tenses and pronouns change in the example sentences.   ☞ G 12

1a An awful holiday

Read this text from a travel company brochure.

Sand, sea & sun – have a super time in Marvella!

The Palm Tree Hotel is right next to the beach in Marvella. It's in the centre of town, but it's very quiet. The hotel has got a wonderful restaurant, and you can dance all night after dinner. All the rooms have a view of the sea, and they've all got private bathrooms. Our local agent speaks perfect English, so you don't have to worry about a thing! And when you arrive, our private taxi will meet you at the airport. You can be sure you'll have a really good holiday!

You booked a holiday, but when you got there you found none of the things were true. Now you've gone back to the travel company to complain. Work with a partner and make at least eight sentences, like this: *You said the hotel was right next to the beach.*

1b ▄▄ What did they say?

Listen to Alan and Barbara. They are giving their points of view on advertising. After each sentence, your teacher will stop the tape. Write down what Alan and Barbara said, like this: *He/She said ....* Then check your sentences with another student.

1c Writing a report

Read these comments that people made about a new pocket computer that can translate languages.

language students	language teachers
I'm looking forward to getting one. (Mark)	I've already ordered one for myself, and another for my colleague. (David)
It'll help us with our vocabulary. (Ben & Silvia)	We saw it at the Frankfurt Book Fair, and we really liked it. (Ann & John)
It's very good, but I can't afford one. (Sue)	I hope all my students can get one. (Christine)

Work with a partner. Write a report; use reported speech. One of you should write what the students said, and the other should write what the teachers said. Then compare your sentences with another pair.

2 Grammar: Special uses of *do* and *did*

1 I really **do** think that adverts for tobacco products and alcohol shouldn't be allowed.
2 People don't mind most advertisements but they **do** complain about the nasty ones.
3 No, that's not true. Your adverts **did** say that I'd learn French in three weeks.

> We can use *do* and *did* with positive verbs when we want to stress the verb (1), express a contrast (2), or contradict what somebody said (3).   ☞ G 5

2a It's not my fault!

Work with a partner. Look at the drawing and make a sentence, like this: *Why didn't you close the window?* Your partner should contradict it, using *did*, like this: *But I did close it. I'm sure I did.*
Take it in turns to start.

Here are some words to help you:

put the phone back	close	lock
switch it/them off	tidy (it) up	type
wash (them) up	water	post

3 ▄▄ The rules of advertising

You will hear a radio interview with an expert on advertising. He's talking about the rules that advertisements have to follow. First read the statements below. What do you think the answers might be?

1 The book of rules has got about
  ☐ 100 pages. ☐ 200 pages. ☐ 800 pages.

2 The rules say adverts
  ☐ should not be too long.
  ☐ should not break the law.
  ☐ should tell the truth.
  ☐ should not be sexy.

3 There are special rules about
  ☐ children. ☐ alcohol. ☐ medicines.
  ☐ animals. ☐ soap. ☐ clothes.
  ☐ cigarettes. ☐ shampoo. ☐ diet foods.

4 The rules are followed by
  ☐ 19% ☐ 83% ☐ 93% ☐ 99%
of the adverts in the press.

5 Every year, about
  ☐ 800 ☐ 1,800 ☐ 8,000 ☐ 80,000
people complain about adverts.

Now listen and tick the information you hear.

3a What do you think?

Work in groups of four. How do you feel about all the direct mail advertising that you find in your letter box? What kind of things are advertised in this way? Do you get a free weekly paper in your area? What other kinds of information does it give?

▶ ☐ Before you go on to the next unit, do the speaking exercises on the cassette.

Unit 8 The world of words   STEP 1

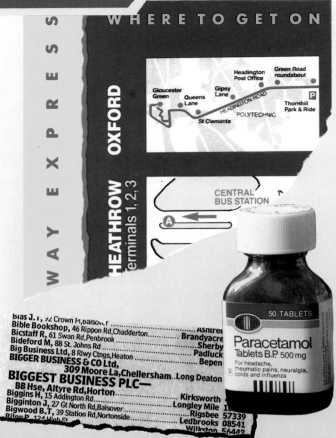

Starter: Partner interview

Work with a partner. Does he/she do any of these
things?

- read a weekend paper
- take a book on holiday
- read in the bath
- read the small print on bus/train tickets
- buy more than one magazine a week
- keep an English dictionary in his/her bag

Then tell the class some of the things you found out
about your partner.

1 Reading: Course #208

Before you read

Work with a partner. Imagine you're in a country
where you can't read the language at all (e.g. Japan,
Greece). Think of some situations where this could
cause you a problem.

Now read this article about people who have
difficulties reading in their own language. What
problems does it mention?

Course #208

Reading is a skill most of us learn
at school. By the age of eight or
nine, children can usually read
simple texts, and by fourteen or
fifteen they should be able to
read most things. As adults, they
will need this skill in almost
every area of life – further education, work, entertainment, travel,
shopping. But what happens
when pupils fail to learn to read
at the 'normal' age? And how
will they handle the problems of
daily life later on? Obviously,
children who can't read aren't
going to do very well at school,
they probably won't get a very
good job afterwards, and they
will face many other difficulties,
both practical and personal, all
their lives. It is thought that at

least 10% of adults in the UK
have quite serious problems with
both reading and writing, and in
the USA about 4% of adults cannot read or write at all.

However, if they are willing to
make the effort, adults can go
back to school – to learn how to
read. Rod Lewis went to City
College in Chicago. He attended
Course #208, which is Basic
Reading for Adults, for three
years. "It changed my life. For
years I was ashamed that I
couldn't read. I couldn't travel
much because I couldn't read the
signs, I didn't know what it said
on the packets of food at the
supermarket, I couldn't understand the instructions on my
walkman. I couldn't even look up
a number in the phone book. It
was hell – I felt threatened almost

every minute of the day, because I
might be asked to read something. I decided to go to college
when my daughter wrote me
from her new home in Germany.
She didn't know I couldn't read –
I'd kept it a secret because I was
afraid of what she'd think. Now
I've lost that fear. I keep a notebook with me, and write down
new words when I meet them.
I've got a shelf of books at home.
Now I can look anyone right in
the eye."

Beth DeLillo, who organizes classes at City College, is proud of
people like Rod. "It was a real
struggle but he refused to give
up. Now he works part-time at
the College at the information
desk, where he helps new students, some of whom are interested in Course #208."

☞ *Language & Culture (page 61)*

1a Comprehension

Here are the answers to some questions on the text you've just read. What were the questions? Write them down.

1 Most people learn it at school. *(When ...)*
2 Because it's needed in most areas of everyday life. *(Why ...)*
3 About 4% of the population. *(How many ...)*
4 Because somebody might ask him to read something. *(Why ...)*
5 Because he couldn't read his daughter's letters. *(Why ...)*
6 She organizes classes. *(What ...)*

Now compare your questions with a partner.

1b Vocabulary

• Work with a partner. Seven of these explanations of words from the text are wrong. Which one is correct? Correct the other seven.

1 A **simple** text is difficult to read.
2 A **pupil** is another word for a teacher.
3 When you make the **effort** to do something, you have to try more than usual.
4 If you feel **ashamed** about something, you want everyone to know about it.
5 When a person **threatens** you, you usually feel very happy.
6 You normally use a **shelf** to carry your books to school.
7 When something is a **struggle**, it's quite easy to do.
8 She **refused** to help me means that she wanted to help me but couldn't.

• ▄▄ Now look at these words: sentence, page, paragraph, word, chapter, phrase/expression.

Put them into the correct order in the lines below.

letter (of the alphabet) ....

....

....

.... **book**

Then listen to the words on the cassette.

1c A ten-minute conversation!

Work in groups of four. Find out as many answers as you can to these questions.

• What different kinds of things did you read last week?
• Where did you read them?
• Why did you read them?
• When did you read them?
• Which ones did you enjoy reading?

2 ▄▄ How to say it: Talking about likes, dislikes and preferences

• Listen to this English class talking about which book they would like to have as a class reader. First, look at this list of different kinds of books. Then listen and number the six that are mentioned in the order that you hear them.

☐ biography   ☐ play
☐ classic novel   ☐ romance
☐ detective story   ☐ science fiction
☐ easy reader   ☐ short stories
☐ non-fiction book   ☐ travel book

• Now look at these expressions from the discussion you've just heard, and put them into three groups. Label them a, b or c:

a = talking about likes
b = talking about dislikes
c = talking about preferences

☐ I'd really like to read ...   ☐ I dislike ...
☐ I'm keen on ...   ☐ I'd prefer to read a ...
☐ I'd love to read a ...   ☐ I'd rather we didn't read a ...
☐ I hate ...   ☐ I don't think much of ...
☐ I can't stand ...   ☐ I prefer ... to ...
☐ I'd rather read a ...   ☐ I'd prefer not to ...

Listen again and notice how the expressions are used.

2a And now you!

Work in groups of four. Try to choose the type of book you would all like to read. Use some of the expressions above.

▶ Before you go on ▬▬▬

Complete these sentences with *who, which, where* or *when*.

1 He couldn't read the instructions .... came with the walkman.

2 She's the teacher .... taught him how to read.

3 There was a time .... I used to read a lot.

4 We went to see the house .... Shakespeare was born.

⊶ page 62

Now do Exercise 1 in the Homestudy Section.

▭ Speaking practice. Listen and do the exercises on the cassette.

Starter: Definitions

Work in groups of three. Make sentences by choosing a word or phrase from each of the three boxes, like this:

An English teacher   is someone who   teaches English.

bookshop	fax machine	library
camera	journalist	photocopier
English teacher	kiosk	student

someone who
something which
a place where

borrow	learn	take
buy	sell	teach
copy	send	write

1 Grammar: More relative clauses

1 Beth DeLillo, **who** organizes classes at City College, is proud of Rod.

2 Rod attended Course #208, **which** is Basic Reading for Adults, for two years.

3 Rod Lewis, **whose** daughter lives abroad, can now read and write.

4 Most students in Course #208, **some of whom** were in their 40s, couldn't read at all.

5 These courses, **most of which** last for three years, are always full.

Notice the commas in these sentences. In sentence 3, *whose* means *Rod's*. We use it for people. After expressions like *some of / most of / all of*, we use *whom* for people, and *which* for things. (Sentences 4 & 5)   ☞ G 11

1a Correct the sentences.

Work with a partner. In each sentence in box 1, the relative clause is missing. First, choose a clause from box 2 to fit each sentence. Then fill in the missing word(s) in each clause.

1

1 Jane Fonda, ..., is very active in American politics.

2 Leonard Cohen, ..., is a famous Canadian singer.

3 Agatha Christie, ..., is the world's most successful fiction writer.

4 Cockney slang, ..., comes from the East End of London.

5 This old atlas, ..., is very valuable.

6 The students from Course #208, ..., read their stories aloud.

7 The word *set*, ..., has got the most meanings in English.

8 Our English teacher, ..., explained that commas are used differently in English and German.

2

☐ .... novels are available in translation

☐ .... is also an actress

☐ .... has also written books of poems

☐ some .... had beautiful voices

☐ some .... is hard to understand

☐ .... speaks very good German

☐ .... is a second-hand copy

☐ .... has got 464 meanings

1b Five sentences about me

Look at the grammar box again. Write a sentence like each of the five example sentences. Your sentence should say something true about you and your life,

like this: *1 My younger sister, who lives in Berlin now, is also my best friend.*

Then compare your sentences with a partner.

2 Grammar: *Some, any, both, either, neither*

1 Would you like **something** to drink / **some** wine? (= an offer)
Shall I ask **someone** to help you? (= a suggestion)

2 You can ask **any** teacher / **anyone** if you have a problem. (= it doesn't matter which teacher/person you ask)

3 You can have **both** books. (= the two books)
Both are very interesting. (= the two books)

4 You can choose **either** book. (= choose one or the other, both are OK)
Either will do. (= both are OK, it doesn't matter which one I have)

5 **Neither** book is the one I really want. (= both aren't right for me)
Neither of them is very interesting. (= both are boring)

Notice how we can use *some* in questions (sentence 1), and *any* in positive sentences (sentence 2). ☞ G 4

2a Offers and suggestions

Work with a partner. Choose one of the situations below, and make a short dialogue, like this:

I've got
a headache.

Shall I get you
some aspirins? /
Would you like
something to drink?

Oh yes, please.
That might help.

Take it in turns to start. The situations are: *headache, toothache, thirsty, hungry, lonely, worried, bored.*

2b *Both* and *neither*

For each of the pairs of words below, make a sentence with *both* and one with *neither*, like this:

1 Wales & Scotland
Both are in the UK. Neither is as big as England.

1 Wales & Scotland
2 coke & fruit juice
3 Munich & Hamburg
4 tiger & gorilla
5 salad & sandwich
6 swimming & jogging

Here are ideas to help you with some of the answers:
alcohol, ball, capital, drink, Germany, hot, sport, zoo.

2c ▣ In a bookshop

You will hear a customer and a shop assistant in a bookshop. Listen and complete the sentences below.

1 She likes ..... that's about different ..... .
2 Or ..... book on ..... .
3 Or ..... by Graham Greene. She loves those ..... writers.
4 She said I could get her ..... book of short ..... .
5 She said I could ask ..... in the bookstore.
6 She said I could go ..... downtown and I'd find a ..... that could help.

Now compare your answers with a partner.
Bookstore and *downtown* are what American people say. What would British people say?

3 ▣ Popular books

Now listen to the shop assistant talking about when and why different types of books are popular. Match the months/seasons with the different types of books.

1 Christmas   4 September   6 February
2 spring   5 May   7 June
3 summer

☐ art book   ☐ encyclopedia
☐ atlas   ☐ novel
☐ cookery book   ☐ book of poems
☐ dictionary   ☐ travel guide
☐ do-it-yourself guide ☐ wine guide

3a What do you think?

Work in groups of four. Which of these books have you got at home? Which would you like to win as a prize?

☐ atlas   ☐ English dictionary
☐ book of crossword   ☐ grammar book
  puzzles   ☐ Guinness Book
☐ cookery book   of Records
☐ do-it-yourself guide   ☐ medical guide
☐ encyclopedia   ☐ travel guide to Europe

What type of book would you give to the following people: a sixteen-year-old boy or girl, someone who's just retired, your teacher?

▶ ▭ Before you go on to Panorama Plus, do the speaking exercises on the cassette.

Starter

Work in groups of three. What makes you buy a book? Decide which of these points are most important to you: the title, the author, the picture on the cover, the price, the number of pages, what someone has told you about the book. Are there any other important points, apart from these?

Where do you think these numbers and words go in the text? Number them 1 to 15.

☐ 5½   ☐ 1949   ☐ 350,000   ☐ members   ☐ typists
☐ 90   ☐ 8,400   ☐ guests   ☐ photographer ☐ visitors
☐ 1492 ☐ 135,000 ☐ journalists ☐ public   ☐ writers

Factfile on the

Frankfurt Book Fair

◆ The Frankfurt Book Fair, which takes place every year in early October, is the biggest and most important event of this kind in the world. More than (**1**) publishers from over (**2**) countries show their books there.

◆ It's enormous – (**3**) square metres in area, which is about the size of sixteen football fields. It's so big that a free bus service is provided to connect the various halls.

◆ There are more than (**4**) books on show, 100,000 of which are new titles.

◆ A book fair was recorded in Frankfurt as early as (**5**), and for the next two hundred years the city was the centre of the European book trade. In the seventeenth century, Leipzig became more important. However, in (**6**) the Book Fair returned to Frankfurt.

◆ The Book Fair lasts for (**7**) days, and attracts over a quarter of a million (**8**). On the first three days, 60,000 (**9**) of the book trade meet, talk, do deals and make new connections. Then, for the last two days, the Fair is open to the (**10**).

◆ You will find every kind of book there, from tomorrow's best seller to the latest specialist and technical titles. But you can't *buy* a book – except for the specially signed copies in the *Lesewelt im Lesezelt* (Books in the Big Top), where (**11**) read from their books.

◆ Besides books, there is a post office, a kindergarten, fire and first aid services, a police station, shops, and restaurants serving meals, snacks and drinks. You can book hotel rooms and trains and air tickets, too, and several banks have a branch there. There's also a translation and a secretarial service with (**12**), a party service, and a Job Centre. You can also hire a (**13**), a video recorder or a hostess, if you need one. And for the 8,000 (**14**), there is a press centre. Finally, you're always close to an information stand, which can deal with any other enquiries you may have.

◆ A special occasion is the party – by invitation only – given on the last night of the Fair for nearly 3,000 foreign and German (**15**).

◆ Perhaps the most important thing to take to the Frankfurt Book Fair is a comfortable pair of shoes!

1 Has anyone in your class been to the Frankfurt Book Fair, or to another international fair? If yes, ask him/her about it.

2 If you went to the Book Fair for one day, what would you want to see?

3 Imagine you are working at one of the information stands. Which six questions do you think you'd hear most often?

4 Choose a writer you know. If you met this writer, what questions would you ask her/him?

Did you know?

◆ The world's largest library is the Library of Congress, which is in Washington DC, in the USA. It contains over 26 million books, and 60 million other items.

◆ The thickest book in the world was printed in Basle, and is 2.75m thick.

◆ Germany is top of the table of European newspapers, with over 300 daily papers. It's also got one of Europe's best-selling daily newspapers, *Bild*, which has sold around six million copies a day.

Library of Congress, Washington

◆ The heaviest newspaper is the *Sunday New York Times*, which weighs almost 6.5 kg.

◆ In America, an advertisement on the back cover of a popular magazine can cost over $500,000. Even inside, it can cost over $400,000.

◆ Walt Disney Productions spent almost $4 million in advertisements in *Time* magazine on 7 November 1988, which was Mickey Mouse's 60th birthday.

Advertising in the UK

▣ You will hear a college lecturer giving some information about advertising in the UK. Listen and put these types of advertising in the order that she mentions them. One isn't mentioned.

☐ outdoor advertising (posters etc.)
☐ press
☐ commercial radio
☐ cinema
☐ commercial TV
☐ direct mail
☐ small ads

Listen again and make notes on each of the types.

Now compare your notes with a partner. Use your notes to write four sentences about advertising in the UK.

Piccadilly Circus, London

1 What kinds of things are bought or sold through small ads? Have you ever used them? How many other kinds of small ads can you think of? (e.g. lost and found, ...)

2 Now choose one of the following things and write your own small ad: something for sale, something wanted, accommodation offered (sharing your house or flat), lonely hearts (looking for a partner), something lost.

Then work with another student. Imagine you're interested in his/her ad. Ring him/her up to find out more.

1 Starter: Things in common

Work with a partner. Find four things that you and your partner have in common. Write these things down. Two of them should begin with *Both of us ...*, and the other two should begin with *Neither of us ....*

> Both of us live on the third floor.

> Neither of us has got a bicycle.

Make a group of four with two other students, and tell them about the things you and your partner have in common. Can you change any of your sentences into statements about all four of you with *All of us ...* or *None of us ...*?

2 Preposition practice

Complete the answers to the three questions below.

Where was the advert?

1 .... television.

2 .... the newspaper.

3 .... my mail.

4 .... the radio.

What do adverts try to do?

5 Give information .... a product.

6 Show a product .... an original way.

7 Work .... people's feelings.

8 Have an influence .... what people buy.

9 Bring some colour .... people's lives!

What are you reading at the moment?

10 A book .... art.

11 A book written .... Agatha Christie.

12 A book .... poems.

13 A book .... my local library.

14 A Chinese novel .... translation.

3 How much do you know?

Work with a partner. Read each starter sentence carefully. Then decide if the statements that follow the sentence are true (T), false (F) or not clear (?).

1 *Most of the students, some of whom were in their forties, couldn't read at all.*

...... Some of the students were in their forties.

...... All of the other students were younger than forty.

...... None of the students could read at all.

...... Most of the students couldn't read at all.

...... Some of the students could read a bit.

2 *Sally said she wouldn't be able to come to the party on Saturday.*

...... Sally doesn't know if she can come or not.

...... Sally might be able to come to the party.

...... Sally would like to come to the party.

...... Sally won't be at the party.

3 *You can ask anyone who is here in this room now about it, and you'll get a good answer.*

...... There's only one person you can ask.

...... All of the people in the room would be able to answer your question.

...... You need to ask all the people in the room.

...... You can choose one of the people in the room to ask, it doesn't matter which person.

...... Nobody can answer your question.

4 *Both Diana and Thomas were out when the fire started. Neither of them knows how it started. The police can interview either of them this evening if necessary.*

...... Diana was out when the fire started.

...... Diana and Thomas were together when the fire started.

...... Thomas knows how the fire started.

...... Thomas is the only person the police can interview this evening.

...... Diana and Thomas can be interviewed this evening.

Now compare your answers with another student. Discuss any differences you've got, and try to decide which answer is correct.

4 Words, words, words: verbs and nouns

Fill in the missing verbs or nouns here – there's no rule to follow!

	VERB	NOUN
1	act (in a theatre)	
2	advertise	
3	be afraid	
4		complaint
5		decision
6	entertain	
7		explanation
8	influence	
9	inform	
10	produce	
11		refusal
12		sale
13		thought
14		threat
15	translate	

Work with a partner. Choose three pairs of words and write a sentence for each pair. Here's an example:
He refused my invitation, but at least his refusal was friendly!

5 With your partner!

Partner A, look at this page. B, please look at page 57 . Partner A. Complete these sentences.

1 My favourite sport is ....

2 I enjoy .... at the weekends.

3 I'm reading a book about ....
at the moment.

4 I can ...., but I can't

....

5 I've never been to ....

6 I saw .... last week.

7 I'll be .... on Saturday afternoon.

Now listen to B's sentences. Make notes on what he/she says. B will also listen to your sentences and make notes.

Find a new partner and report what B told you like this: *Karin said her favourite ... was ...*

6 Write as much as you can!

Imagine that you borrowed one of the above books from a neighbour of yours. You've finished reading it. Write about the book. You could start like this:
Last week I saw one of my neighbours and she gave me a book to read. It was called ...

Write as much as you can in ten minutes.

Now make a group with other students in your class who chose the same book as you. Read what you've written to your group. How different were your ideas about the book?

7 Out and about!

For the next seven days you should look at adverts everywhere you can – in newspapers and magazines, on posters, on television, in the cinema etc. Make a list of the English words that you see in the advertisements, together with the products they helped to advertise. Make your notes like this:

word	product
super	cigarettes, car, holiday

Units 1 & 2 / Revision Plus: Exercise 6 (page 13)

Partner B. You're going to ask A for some advice in the following situations. Before you ask A, write down the advice that you would give someone else in the same situations.

- You always feel tired.
- You haven't got enough money to buy a new car.
- You know that you watch too much television.
- You've lost all your keys.

I think you should ...   My advice is to ...

Why don't you ...?   If I were you, I'd ...

Now tell A your problems and see if his/her advice is the same as the advice that you would give (or is A's advice even better?).

Units 3 & 4 / Revision Plus: Exercise 3 (page 26)

Partner B. You and your partner have got six questions together. First of all, put the words in the correct order to make the second half of questions a-c and the first half of questions d-f. Your partner will read the beginnings of questions a–c. Choose the correct ending and read it so that he/she can complete those sentences. You should complete them, too. Now you do the same with d–f. In the end you should have six complete questions.

a ..... this / read / if / one / morning / you'd / to / wanted

if you'd wanted to read one this morning ?

b ..... dinner / you'd / yesterday / if / to / invited / someone

if

c ..... London / shopping / if / in / you'd / week / gone / last

if

d drunk / you / what / have / would
What would you

e restaurant / you / which / would / chosen / have
Which

f you / gone / have / would / where
Where

When you've got the six questions, tell each other your answers.

With your partner – Partner B

Unit 5 & 6 / Revision Plus: Exercise 2 (page 40)

Partner B. You are going for an interview for a job in a travel agency. Before A interviews you, decide the following things. (Don't be yourself, imagine you are a different person!)

How old are you? (any age but older than 20) ....

Which two of these languages can you speak?

☐ English   ☐ Italian
☐ French   ☐ Spanish

Can you drive a car? ....

Answer these four questions – decide on two positive answers and two negative answers:

Do you enjoy travelling?	☐ yes	☐ no
Are you good at using a computer?	☐ yes	☐ no
Are you willing to work at weekends? ☐	yes	☐ no
Are you good at speaking to large groups of people?	☐ yes	☐ no

Answer these four questions:

Do you smoke?	☐ yes	☐ no
Do you live very near a station?	☐ yes	☐ no
Do you like big dogs?	☐ yes	☐ no

How much office experience have you had?   .... years

Now answer A's questions. Then make a group of four with two other students, and listen to what A says about you. Are you satisfied with the result of your interview?

Unit 7 & 8 / Revision Plus: Exercise 6 (page 55)

Partner B. Complete these sentences.

1 My favourite food is ....

2 I enjoy .... when I'm on holiday.

3 I'm planning to ....

4 I can ...., but I can't
....

5 I've never met ....

6 I ate .... last week.

7 I won't be .... tomorrow.

Now listen to A's sentences. Make notes on what he/she says. A will also listen to your sentences and make notes.

Find a new partner and report what A told you like this: *Mark said his favourite ... was ...*

Information for teachers

Unit 2 / Step 2: Exercise 2b (page 9)

Alan – since 1988
Barbara – for six years
Clare & Tony – for four years
David – since 1990
Eric & Liz – since 1989
Ian & Peter – for three years
Jenny – since 1984
Marina – since 1991
Sandra & Tim – since 1987

Unit 5 / Step 1: Starter (page 30)

postman	taxi driver
shop assistant	police officer
secretary	farm worker
bus driver	teacher

Unit 7 / Step 2: Starter (page 46)

Madonna
Nelson Mandela
Steffi Graf
Liz Taylor
Franz Beckenbauer
Marlon Brando
Brigitte Bardot
The Queen
The Pope

Unit 1 / Step 1

1 Reading: A new life in Australia

The Simpsons and the Clarks are just two of the many British families who have emigrated to Australia, where 80% of the people come from families that were originally British.

Until the end of World War II most immigrants to Australia came from the British Isles. Then the Australians decided to let more Europeans come to Australia. Since the Second World War more than 4 million people have emigrated to Australia, but only about 10 % of the immigrants came from Germany and the Netherlands.

In the 1970s for the first time, the Australian Government also decided to let in large numbers of people from Asia and the Pacific so that today 600,000 Asians live in Australia.

Brisbane, where Tony Simpson moved, is the capital of Queensland, the sunshine state to the north of Sydney. Brisbane is the third largest city in Australia and famous for its relaxed lifestyle and friendly people. In Perth, the capital of Western Australia, the Clarks also enjoy eight hours of sunshine a day all the year round, although in Perth they are far away from the rest of the country. Perth is also a long way from Alice Springs right in the middle of Australia. During the winter months (May to September) thousands of tourists use the town of Alice Springs as a centre when they visit the deserts and rocky areas of Central Australia. It is 450 kilometres away from Ayers Rock, the world's largest monolith.

Doreen Clark says she loves "*the* sunshine, *the* space and *the* freedom", because she is talking about the sunshine, the space and the freedom she has in Perth. When you use abstract nouns there is no definite article; you say *I love sunshine, space and freedom.*

Tony Simpson tells us that he found a job as an engineer. In German there is no indefinite article: *Ich bin Ingenieur.* However, in English with professions you must use the indefinite article.

All this information is to *remind you* that there is a lot to *remember* (remind = jdn. an eine Sache erinnern; remember = *sich erinnern an*). Remember that a pronoun usually follows the word *remind: We've got some lovely photos to remind **us** of the two years we spent in Australia.*

Unit 1 / Step 1

1b Vocabulary

The UK (*The United Kingdom*) is the official name for England, Wales, Scotland and Northern Ireland. However, *Britain* is often used to mean the UK, although Britain or Great Britain only includes England, Wales and Scotland. *The British Isles* is a geographical expression for the UK and the Republic of Ireland with the islands near their coasts. Remember Scotland or Northern Ireland are not the same as England. You should say *Britain* or the *UK* when you are talking in general.

Unit 2 / Step 1

1 Reading: The changing face of Britain

In both the UK and America people often move houses a number of times during their lives. In the USA over 5 million people move between states each year and many millions move to somewhere else inside their own states and cities. When people have come to the end of their working lives, they often decide to move away from the towns to the country or to the coast.

The USA is famous for its mobile homes, large caravans which can be pulled to another place if and when you want a change.

The British often have romantic ideas about country life and many people would like to have a pub or small hotel in a village or spend the last part of their lives in a country cottage. Many Britons do not like living in the centre of towns and usually live in the suburbs. About 60 % of Britons own their own homes and most people live in houses and not flats.

In English when you are talking about people in general you say *most people* and there is no definite article. Compare it to the German: *die meisten Leute.* When Margaret Templer is talking about the British she says: *For most of us, the typical British village has pretty cottages and little shops.* Again here there is no article, but in German you say: *die meisten von uns.*

Margaret Templer reports that the villagers have been feeling angry for a long time. After the verb *feel* you have an adjective: *he feels angry.* This is because you are describing a state (= *Zustand*) not an activity. You have already seen this with the verb *to be: it is sad.* All verbs which are like the verb *to be* take an adjective: *he looks sad, he seems happy, he gets angry, it sounds good, it feels hard,* or *it becomes clear.*

In English the word *river* is used for both *Strom* and *Fluß*, and a *stream* is a small river, ein *Bach.* But when you are talking about a lot of traffic or a lot of people you can also say a *stream of traffic, a stream of visitors.*

Language & Culture

Units 1&2 / Panorama Plus

Factfile on Australia

Australians, or in informal English, *Aussies* live in *Oz*, or as the *Brits* say *Down Under*. These are all friendly expressions for the people or country. The *Kiwis* are of course the New Zealanders. However, when the Australians and New Zealanders call a British person a *Pom* or a *Pommy*, it is not always a very friendly expression. Feelings about the British are rather mixed.

Most Australians, as you found out in Factfile, live in the cities on the coast, where they enjoy both the beautiful beaches and their clean and attractive cities. For many the outback is a flat, hot and lonely (= *einsam*) place, and not the land of hope and adventure that it is for some. The outback is the name of the land on the other side of the Great Dividing Range, a chain of highlands from Cape York in northern Queensland to the southern coast of Tasmania.

For the children who live in the outback, the School of the Air is the only way they can get any education. One of the new subjects which students can study is Japanese. In Queensland alone 25,000 students are studying the language. For Australia, Asia has never been so important. It takes almost half of Australia's exports.

Film and television programmes also earn a lot of money abroad for Australia, and a programme which has become a great favourite in Europe is *The Flying Doctors*. The Flying Doctor Service started in 1928. Today there are over 40 planes which serve two-thirds of the country. They say that if you phone for a doctor, he will be there in not more than two hours.

The nearest school for the children in the outback may be hundreds of miles away. You say the *nearest* school when you mean the one nearest to them. The *next* school is the one after that: *The **nearest** school is 150 miles away and the **next** one is at least 300 miles from here.*

Unit 3 / Step 1

1 Reading: Sport for all – your free guide to getting fitter

You find sports that people play in Britain in most English-speaking countries. People play traditional games like *rugby* and *cricket* and *soccer* (football) in Australia, New Zealand, and South Africa. Cricket and soccer never became popular in the USA, where *baseball* and American football are the most popular national sports. If you are in the USA on the 2nd January, turn on the television, anywhere in the country, at any time, on any station and you will see football from early morning until late at night. The year begins with a sports orgy. The Americans hope to export American football to Europe. There are now some clubs in Europe and you can sometimes see games on TV.

The word *sport* is used to describe the activity in general and is uncountable: *I like sport.* A sport (countable noun) is a special kind of sport: *Which sports do you play?* We use the word *sports* in many combinations like *sports car, sportsman, sportswoman* and *sportswear.*
Sport keeps you fit because you get plenty of *exercise* (= *Bewegung*). In the morning you must do your *exercises* (= *Übungen*). *An exercise* (countable noun) is also what you do for your homework to practise your English. Countable and uncountable nouns are a bit of a problem but don't worry you will get a lot of *practice* (= *Übung*).
In Exercise 2 in this unit you will find the word *equipment*. This is another uncountable noun and you can't just use the indefinite article *an*, you have to say *a piece of equipment.*
Sport should be *fun*. That means that you should enjoy it. But when you fall over, people may think you look *funny*. You will make them laugh.

Unit 3 / Step 2

3 A choice of sports

When you use the pound or dollar sign, it always comes in front of the sum of money: £425 and $500. However, when you speak you say *four hundred and twenty-five pounds* and *five hundred dollars*. Dollars and cents are used in Australia as well as the USA and Canada.

Unit 4 / Step 1

1 Reading: Your A-Z guide to pets

Most small pets such as birds or hamsters are easy to look after but *fish* are perhaps the easiest. *Fish* is both singular and plural in normal spoken English, and *sheep* also has no -*s* in the plural, although both are countable nouns: you say *two fish, three sheep* etc. *Advice* and *information* are uncountable nouns so they have no plural and you must say *pieces of information/advice. Furniture* is another uncountable noun and is used in the same way as *equipment*: *Furniture is often rather expensive.* Look back at the note in Unit 3/Step 1, Exercise 2 on *equipment*.
When you talk about an animal or a pet in general you can say *it*: *Your pet can hurt **itself**.* However, pet owners will say *he* or *she* when they talk about their own animals.

Language & Culture

Unit 4 / Step 1
1c A ten-minute conversation!

In this exercise you have to decide which is the most suitable pet for a *ten-year-old boy*. When a time word like *days, months, years* etc. comes in front of the noun there is no *-s* on the end of the word and the words are joined by hyphens (-). When the time word follows the noun then you have the normal plural with *-s*: *The boy is ten years old*. In Unit 3/Step 2: A choice of sports you heard that *a seven-day stay* in the country costs £390.

Units 3&4 / Panorama Plus
Too old at twenty?

Tennis as we know the game today became popular in the middle of the last century. The first Wimbledon Championship for amateurs took place in 1877 with 200 *spectators*, and the first women's singles in 1884. *Lawn tennis* spread to America, Australia and New Zealand and Canada. In Europe the French were the first to hold national championships in 1891. Over the past hundred years different nationalities have dominated the championships in Wimbledon: the French, the British, the Australians and the Americans, but since the 1970s many Europeans have also won the championships and now it seems to be the turn of the Germans!

Boris Becker was only 17 when he won the men's singles title. When you talk about ages you can use the short form: *He was 17* or the more formal full form: He was seventeen years old. Remember the preposition in English is *at*: at 17 or *at the age of 17* he won the title. Compare it to the German: *mit siebzehn*.

Children *practise* for hours and they need a lot of *practice*. In British English the verb is with an *s* and the noun with a *c*. It is the same with *license/ licence*: Although dogs have to be *licensed*, he hasn't got a *licence*. In American English the usage is not so clear and the verb *practice* is with a *c* and the noun can be written with a *c* or an *s*.

Unit 5 / Step 1
1 Reading: Thinking of changing your career?

Jackie Woods has had eight years *work experience*. She does not mention her *secretarial training*, but she probably did a *commercial course* at a commercial college after she finished school. Many young people in Britain are not always trained for their jobs, but learn *on the job*. Only 40% of young people over 16 get some form of training. Many people in Britain would like to have a situation like the one in Germany, where over 90% of sixteen to twenty-year-olds are apprentices or are trained for their job. There is also less *in-service training* in Britain, which means that employees go on courses regularly to get more experience and qualifications.

In her letter to the *employment agency* Jackie wrote: *I would like an interesting job that gives me more responsibility*. She used the more formal form *I would like* in her letter, but in the interview when she is talking she can use the more informal verb: *I want an interesting job*. Remember when you are asking someone for something, it is politer to say *I'd like* rather than *I want*.

Jackie also used the informal word *job* in her letter. In a more formal letter you often use the formal words *post* or *position*, especially when it is a job with responsibility. *Work* is another informal word and remember there is no article: *I'm looking for work*. The word *profession* is generally only used for people who have academic qualifications such as doctors, teachers or lawyers. A *trade* is a skilled job in which you use your hands: *He's an electrician by trade*. When you use the words *employer* (= *Arbeitgeber*) and *employee* (= *Arbeitnehmer*), make sure you put the stress on the right syllable: em**ploy**er [ɪmˈplɔɪə] and employ**ee** [emplɔˈiː]

Unit 6 / Step 1
1 Reading: After work

People who retire before the official retiring age *take early retirement*. As a thankyou for good work and long service some people may be lucky and get a *golden handshake*, a large sum of money from their employers.

Mary Bishop teaches adults to read and write. She does this without getting any money for it because she wants to help people in need. In America and Britain the government often leaves this kind of work to people who are unpaid and are not always trained. However, without these *voluntary workers* many people who need help would not get it. There are of course also a lot of voluntary organisations that employ paid professional people, but they also have to collect money from the public to help run their organisations.

In this passage there are a number of words with hyphens: *fifty-six, ex-prisoners, part-time*. These are words where hyphens are always used: num-

Language & Culture

bers over twenty (*ninety-two*) and with some prefixes, like *ex-* and *co-* (*ex-wife* or *co-worker*). *Part-time*, would look funny as one word. It is a problem to know when to use a hyphen in English and *English-speaking* people often have to look the words up in a dictionary to make sure. Language is also changing. *Weekend* is now written as one word. It used to be *week-end*. When a word becomes a commonly accepted expression it is usually written as one word. In American English many words are written as one word, but they may still have a hyphen in British English. In the text you saw that *traveling* is spelt with one *l* in American and Canadian English. There is also only one *l* in *traveler* and in *traveled*. In British English there are always two *l*s.

Unit 6 / Step 2
2b A visit from Tim's parents

Tim is American and in his conversation with Ann several words are used which are different in British English: *Mom* for *Mum*, *vacation* for holiday and *apartment* for flat. In British English *vacation* is only used for a *university vacation* and an *apartment* could be one of a large, luxurious group of rooms in a palace (*the Queen's apartments*) or perhaps a group of rooms that make up a suite in a hotel. However, American words are used more and more in Britain as a result of the many American films and series on British television, so you will also hear people who use *apartment* in the meaning *flat*.

Unit 7 / Step 1
1 Reading: Advertising – who needs it?

Advertising is one of Britain's most important products. British adverts are often original and creative and also very funny.
There are more than 300 agencies in London, the centre of the UK advertising industry. The British *public* appreciates good advertising and people are well informed and talk about the latest successful ad. *Wordplay*, the clever use of words, is also appreciated by the British public. Recently, however, advertising has started to use sex and shock tactics and many of these ads have not been allowed on TV or can only be shown at a time when children should be in bed. Organisations like Greenpeace or the RSPCA, the British *Tierschutzverband*, have used nasty, shocking pictures with dead animals to make people think about the problems.

Prepositions are always difficult. In this text there are some expressions with the preposition *on* which often cause problems: *They spend millions **on** advertising. We don't realise the influence they have **on** us. And some of the adverts are good, especially **on** TV.*
Especially and *in particular* are two ways of translating *besonders* into English. You have to use *in particular* after the noun: *Children in particular are at risk.* You can only use *especially* before the noun when you are contrasting with something that has come before: *Many people, especially children, are at risk.* You also often find *especially* after prepositions as in: *especially on TV* or *especially with the opposite sex.*

Unit 8 / Step 1
1 Reading: Course No. 208

It is difficult to understand why there are so many people who cannot read and write in countries where almost everyone goes to school. The reason why there are about 7 million *functional illiterates* (functionally illiterate = *praktisch Analphabet*) in Britain, and 27 million in the USA may have something to do with the school system. In USA and Britain you normally do not have to repeat a year. You usually go up into the next class, even if you have difficulties. Children who do learn to read and write often cannot spell properly and make grammar mistakes.

Both the British and American governments are shocked at the level of English in public examinations such as the *GCE A level* in Britain and *SAT* in the States (equivalent to *Abitur*). Both countries have introduced reform programmes to improve the teaching of English in schools.

There are differences between American English and British English in some constructions as well as in the use of some words. Rod Lewis said, *My daughter wrote me from her new home in Germany.* In British English you say *My daughter wrote **to** me.* British people say *I like reading*, but Americans say *I like to read.*

The word *college* is difficult to use. Here Rod went to City College, which is for adult education. In Britain there are similar colleges called *community colleges*, where as an adult you can do courses and take public examinations. However, in American English *college* is also used for *university*. Where an American might say, *I went to college*, an English person says, *I went to university.*

Schlüssel

Unit 1 / Step 1: Before you go on (page 3)

be, was/were, been;
buy, bought, bought;
call, called, called;
decide, decided, decided;
do, did, done;
drink, drank, drunk;
drive, drove, driven;
eat, ate, eaten;
go, went, gone;

have, had, had;
learn, learnt, learnt;
live, lived, lived;
say, said, said;
stay, stayed, stayed;
think, thought, thought;
try, tried, tried;
visit, visited, visited;
write, wrote, written

Unit 2 / Step 1: Before you go on (page 7)

buying   going   swimming
doing   having   travelling
driving   living   working
feeling   seeing

1 Excuse me. I'm (am) looking for Bond Street. Do you know where it is?
2 We aren't (are not) playing tennis at the moment because it's (is) raining.
3 Hey, you! What are you doing? Those are my bags!
4 Please don't make so much noise. The students next door are having a test.

Unit 3 / Step 1: Before you go on (page 17)

1 Which sport would you do if you wanted to get fit?
2 If I lived in the country, I would run five kilometres every day.
3 What would you do if you couldn't go jogging?
4 I think I would buy a bicycle instead.

Unit 4 / Step 1: Before you go on (page 21)

answer, answered, answered;
break, broke, broken;
catch, caught, caught;
enjoy, enjoyed, enjoyed;
feel, felt, felt;
find, found, found;
get, got, got;
give, gave, given;
keep, kept, kept;
kill, killed, killed;
leave, left, left;
make, made, made;
put, put, put;
stop, stopped, stopped;
test, tested, tested

Unit 5 / Step 1: Before you go on (page 31)

being   losing
eating   riding
flying   running
getting up standing up

1 Most people don't like getting up early to go to work.
2 She hates losing when she plays tennis!
3 He keeps fit by running in the woods and riding his bike.
4 We're looking forward to being in New Zealand at Christmas.

Unit 6 / Step 1: Before you go on (page 35)

1 If you feel so ill, you ~~might~~/should/must see a doctor.
2 Could/Will/~~May~~ you help me with my suitcase, please?
3 In the UK, you have to / must/~~might~~ drive on the left.
4 You ~~mayn~~'t/can't/mustn't park here – it's not allowed.

Unit 7 / Step 1: Before you go on (page 45)

1 Yesterday, when I was driving to work, I suddenly remembered that I hadn't locked the front door.
2 When we arrived in Munich, it was raining and we realized that we had forgotten to bring our umbrellas.

Unit 8 / Step 1: Before you go on (page 49)

1 He couldn't read the instructions which came with the walkman.
2 She's the teacher who taught him how to read.
3 There was a time when I used to read a lot.
4 We went to see the house where Shakespeare was born.

Was gibt es im *Homestudy*-Teil?

Der *Homestudy*-Teil umfaßt ausschließlich Materialien, die Sie zu Hause alleine für sich außerhalb des Unterrichts bearbeiten können. Enthalten sind zusätzliche Übungen zu jedem Step der Units vorne im Buch. Es sind in der Regel schriftliche Übungen, doch sind einige zur gezielten Schulung des Hörverstehens gedacht und durch Cassette bzw. CD gesteuert. Die Aufnahmen dazu finden Sie auf den beiden Lernercassetten bzw. Lerner-CDs, die es zu diesem Lehrwerk gibt (Cassetten: Bestell-Nr. 57 573 und 57 574; CDs [Dreierpaket]: Bestell-Nr. 57 527).

Zu allen Übungen des *Homestudy*-Teils gibt es ab Seite 104 einen Lösungsschlüssel. In Ihrem eigenen Interesse sollten Sie natürlich erst dann die Lösungen einsehen, wenn Sie die Aufgaben bearbeitet haben und mit Ihren eigenen Lösungsvorschlägen zufrieden sind. Auch die Tonbandmanuskripte der Hörverstehensübungen finden Sie im Anhang, ab Seite 109. Sie sind übrigens nur für den Fall abgedruckt, daß Sie wirklich große Verständnisschwierigkeiten haben. Sie müssen nicht jedes Wort verstehen, um die Aufgaben lösen zu können.

Ferner finden Sie im *Homestudy*-Teil nach je zwei Units eine Seite mit *Learners' letters*, die Ihnen Hilfen an die Hand geben, wie Sie Ihr Wissen und Lernen verbessern können. Außerdem gibt es nach jeweils zwei Units die Sektion *Test Yourself*, die es Ihnen ermöglicht, in regelmäßigen Abständen Ihre Fortschritte und Ihren Lernerfolg selbst zu überprüfen. Die *Dictionary skills*-Seiten (nach jedem *Test yourself*) vermitteln Ihnen den effektiven Umgang mit einem zweisprachigen Wörterbuch.

Wie arbeite ich mit dem *Homestudy*-Teil?

Besonders wichtig ist der Grundsatz: Lieber wenig aber oft, als viel aber selten; d.h. mehrere kurze Lern- und Übungsphasen pro Woche, z.B. täglich 10 Minuten, sind effektiver als nur einmal die Woche eine lange.

Wenn Sie zu Hause üben, ist es sinnvoll, zunächst die Teile der Unit, die Sie in der Gruppenstunde bearbeitet haben, noch einmal durchzusehen. Sie können die Lektionstexte lesen und – als Abschluß der *Pronunciation*-Übung im *Homestudy*-Teil – auf der Cassette anhören.

Dann können Sie die Übungen zu dem jeweiligen Step hier im *Homestudy*-Teil machen. Nehmen Sie dazu einen Bleistift und tragen Sie Ihre Lösungsvorschläge ein. Wenn Sie mit ihnen zufrieden sind, vergleichen Sie sie mit dem Schlüssel, unterstreichen Sie die Fehler (falls es welche gibt!) und korrigieren Sie sie. Falls Ihnen nicht klar ist, warum Ihre Lösung nicht stimmt, fragen Sie Ihre Kursleiterin / Ihren Kursleiter in der nächsten Stunde. Alle Lösungen könnten Sie dann noch einmal ausradieren und die Übungen einige Tage später wiederholen, auch wenn sie vorher richtig waren. So sichern Sie Ihren Lernerfolg ab.

Wie arbeite ich mit den Lernercassetten?

Ehe Sie die Übungen im *Homestudy*-Teil machen, sollten Sie zunächst die Teile der Unit, die Sie im Unterricht bearbeitet haben, noch einmal durchsehen. Aus diesem Grund sind die Übungen aus dem *Unit*-Teil, die mit einem weißen Cassettensymbol versehen sind, auch auf den Lernercassetten und Lerner-CDs zu finden. Die Nachbereitung nach jeder Gruppenstunde sieht somit folgendermaßen aus: Sie wiederholen als erstes mit Hilfe der Lernercassetten oder -CDs die Teile, die Sie im Unterricht durchgenommen haben. Danach gehen Sie zu den Übungen im *Homestudy*-Teil über, wobei sich die entsprechende Hörübung (falls vorhanden) aus dieser Sektion unmittelbar an die Übungen des *Unit*-Teils anschließt. Das folgende Beispiel – anhand von Unit 2, Step 1 – kann Ihnen helfen, die Übungen auf den Lernercassetten oder -CDs denen des Buches zuzuordnen.

Lernercassette	Seite im Buch
Unit 2, Step 1	
Before you go on: Speaking practice	S. 7
Homestudy: Exercise 2: Giving reasons and causes	S. 67
Exercise 3: Pronunciation	S. 68

1 Revision of tenses

Write the sentences. ? = make a question, – = make a negative sentence, + = make a positive sentence.

He often writes to her.

1 + **yesterday** *He wrote to her yesterday.*

2 ? *(to/yesterday/did/?/her/write/he)* ....

3 ? **tomorrow** *(going/her/he/tomorrow/is/to/to/?/write)* ....

....

4 – *(her/to/going/tomorrow/he/write/isn't/to)* ....

....

5 – **yet** *(hasn't/her/written/yet/to/he)* ....

....

We're going to eat in the pizzeria next Saturday.

6 + **he often** *(6 words)* ....

....

7 ? **has ever** *(7)* ....

....

8 ? **last week** *(8)* ....

....

9 + **last week** *(7)* ....

....

10 + **when the storm began** *(10)* ....

....

....

11 + **enjoys** *(6)* ....

....

2 Pronunciation

These words were all in the reading text in Step 1. Underline the part of the word where the stress is, like this: _telephone_.

1 history	5 natural	9 experience
2 engineer	6 interesting	10 photographs
3 relatives	7 national	
4 distance	8 university	

Check your answers in the key.
🖭 Now listen to the text.

3 🖭 Giving advice

You'll hear some people who are giving advice. Where are the people? Number these places 1 to 4.

☐ in a travel agent's   ☐ in a restaurant
☐ at a railway station   ☐ at an airport

Listen again. In which situations did you hear the expressions? There was more than one in each of the situations.

It would be a good idea to ....

I think you should ....

If I were you, ...

You ought to ....

Why don't you ..*1*..........

My advice is ....

4 Complete the sentences.

Choose the correct verb for each sentence, and write the other missing word in the box.

The verbs are: *are learning, drove, found, is, move, read, reminded, settle, spent, went.*

1 Would you like to ..*move*..... *to* Australia?

2 Before you go there, you should ....
   a book .... the country.

3 He .... a job .... a teacher
   when he arrived there.

4 They .... two or
   three National Parks on their holiday.

5 He .... a lot of money ....
   hotels.

6 A new way of life .... often
   difficult .... first.

7 Are they sorry they ....
   Australia?

8 The children .... a lot ....
   school now.

9 She tried to .... there,
   but it was very difficult for her.

10 Their photos .... me ....
    my holiday there.

5 Remember the words!

Write the words for the things you can see here in the puzzle. In the two boxes you can see the name of a country a lot of British people emigrate to. What is the missing fourth letter? Write it in.

Crossword:
1. SUNSHINE
2. WEST
3. CROWDED
4. EAST
5. PHOTOGRAPH
6. CLOTHES
7. UNHAPPY
8. ENGINEER
9. DOCTOR

Step 2

1 Complete the table.

Complete this table with a form of the verbs on the left. Make sure that the questions go with the answers correctly.

	?	+	−
1 *eat*	Where *did you eat* yesterday?	I *ate* in a restaurant.	I *didn't eat* at home.
2 *live*	Where *does you live*?	He *lifes* in a small village.	He *has never left* near here.
3 *write*	What *was he writing* when her boss came in?	She *was writing* a letter.	She *wasn't writing* his report.
4 *make*	How much more money *is he making* now?	He *is making* a lot more.	He *making* twice his old salary.
5 *speak*	*Has she spoken* to her new neighbours yet?	She *has spoken* to the children.	She *hasn't spoken* to their parents yet.
6 *drink*	How much *had he drunk* by the time she arrived?	He *had drunk* one or two glasses of wine.	He *didn't drink* any whisky or gin.
7 *be*	Where *will you be* at this time tomorrow?	I *will be* at home.	I *want be* at the office.
8 *be*	Where *were you* yesterday morning?	I *was* at the doctor's.	I *wasn't* at work.

65

2 Margaret Templer's CV

Below these lines you can see some information about Margaret Templer, a television journalist who works for Channel Seven in England. Put these words in the correct order to make questions about her. There is one word missing in each question – write that word in, too.

1 live / ..... / Margaret / where ....

2 Margaret / when / ..... / born ....

3 children / got / many / ..... / how / Margaret ....

4 school / where / go / Margaret / ..... / to ....

5 long / she / journalist / for / Radio South / ..... / a / how ....

....

6 journalist / she / how / been / Channel Seven / long / ..... / a / for ....

....

Name: Margaret
                 Templer

Address: 38A Oxford
                 Street
                 Cambridge
                 CM3 7EF

Date of birth: 10. 8. 1954

Nationality: British

Status: Married

Children: Two

Education: Palmers Comprehensive School
                 (Grays, Essex)

                 University of Nottingham
                 (1972-1975)

Foreign
languages: French

Work
experience: 1975-1984: journalist for
                 Radio South (a local radio
                 station)
                 1990-now: journalist for
                 Channel Seven Television

3 ⌨ What has Tom done?

Tom and his wife are going away for a short holiday. Tom is speaking on his secretary's telephone answering machine. What has Tom done? Tick (✔) the boxes.

write the reports: ☐ yes ☐ no ✔ some of them
read the letters: ☐ yes ☐ no ☐ some of them
sign the letters: ☐ yes ☐ no ☐ some of them

see the plans for next year: ☐ yes ☐ no
speak to the boss about the plans: ☐ yes ☐ no
give the computer books to Anna: ☐ yes ☐ no

Now write sentences about what Tom has or hasn't done.

1 *He has written some of the reports.*

2 ....

3 ....

4 ....

....

5 ....

....

6 ....

....

4 Remember the words!

Put these words into seven groups, with four words in each group.

article	Canada	Germany	Italy	New Zealand	shop
Australia	emigrate	go abroad	Japan	newspaper	Spain
beautiful	exciting	great	leave	office	wonderful
book	factory	guy	magazine	relative	
boy	gentleman	Ireland	move	school	

1 The past progressive and the present progressive

What were the people doing when you arrived at the party yesterday?
Find these people in the pictures on the right.
What are they doing now?

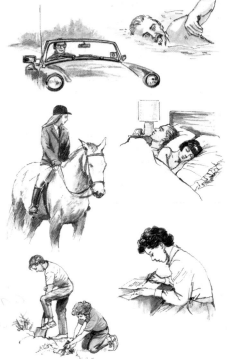

cut, dance, drink, sit, talk, smoke

1 *He was* ~~smoke~~ .... *a cigarette.*
2 *They* ....
3 *He* ....
4 *They* ....
5 *She* ....
6 *She* ....

drive, ride, sleep, swim, work, write

1 *He is* ....
2 ....
3 ....
4 ....
5 ....
6 ....

2 Giving reasons and causes

Choose the correct ending for each sentence.

a We didn't go away because of ...   ☐ it was raining.   ☐ the weather was bad.   ☑ the weather.

b It rained all weekend – that's why ... ☐ the weather was bad.   ☑ we stayed at home.   ☐ no weekend.

c We stayed at home due to ...   ☐ it was raining.   ☐ it rained.   ☑ the rain.

urgündes

🔊 **Listening.** Now listen to the three short texts and complete the sentences.

1 She decided not to take the job because of ....

2 The local authorities decided to build a motorway through the village – that's why ....

   ....

3 The small number of people who voted in the election was probably due to ....

   ....

3 Pronunciation

These words were all in the reading text in Step 1. The letter 'a' isn't the same sound in all the words. Write them in the correct boxes: *village, cottage, farm, grassy, narrow, image, programme, antiques, sad, angry.*

a = [ɪ] as in *sit* [sɪt] (3 words)	a = [aː] as in *aunt* [aːnt] (2 words)	a = [æ] as in *cat* [kæt] (5 words)
village, cottage narrow	*farm, grassy*	*angry, sad, antiques programme, image*

Check your answers in the key. 🔊 Now listen to the text.

4 Remember the words!

Which words can go before these words? Find them in the puzzle.

a *railway* line

a *farm* worker

a *pretty* village

friendly people

correct people

ordinary countryside

beautiful cottages

a *sad* story

a *unspoilt* image

a *quiet* bridge

grass fields

an *antique* shop

a *locked* door

a *run* _ stream

g	m	o	s	r	v	s	l	a	w	s	v	f
d	s	c	o	b	e	a	u	t	i	f	u	l
e	a	j	r	d	b	d	n	l	d	f	r	n
f	v	h	d	p	i	r	f	w	e	v	a	y
a	n	t	i	q	u	e	r	n	o	q	i	a
r	s	u	n	s	p	o	i	l	t	t	l	w
m	g	r	a	s	s	y	e	t	y	j	w	k
b	n	a	r	r	o	w	n	c	p	e	a	g
i	r	f	y	q	n	o	d	k	i	v	y	z
l	g	d	i	k	j	r	l	o	c	k	e	d
u	a	p	r	e	t	t	y	h	a	p	s	u
p	l	e	n	o	x	c	n	r	l	y	t	h

Step 2

1 What have they been doing?

What have these people been doing? Write a sentence for each picture. Use the verbs under the pictures.

clean, paint, play, run, smoke, swim, type, wash

1 She's been *playing tennis*

2 *He's been running*

3 *He's been cleaning the dishes*

4 *She's been washing the car*

5 *He's been painting the floor.*

6 *He's been swimming in the water*

7 *He's been smoking a cigarette*

8 *She's been typing a letter.*

68

2 Write in the verbs.

Write in the correct present perfect form of the verb in brackets. Complete the sentences with *since* or *for*.

1 I (*know*) .... Susan .... last Christmas.

2 They (*live*) .... there .... years.

3 She (*learn*) .... English .... January.

4 They (*be*) .... married .... 1991.

5 He (*drive*) .... that car .... he was 18.

6 She (*wait*) .... for him .... 20 minutes.

7 We (*try*) .... to find a new flat .... a year.

8 I (*have*) .... my computer .... a long time.

since?

for?

3 ☐ Annagret Johnson – a famous author

Listen to this radio interview with Annagret Johnson who is a writer of children's books. Her new book is called *The Kensington Kids*. A London company called MacLong has published the book. Listen carefully and complete these sentences using the present perfect in each sentence. Listen as many times as you like.

1 She .... for more than twenty years.

2 She .... for about ten years.

3 She .... for fifteen years.

4 She .... for twelve years.

5 She .... for eleven years.

6 Her book .... for four weeks.

7 She .... for three weeks.

8 She .... for four years.

4 Remember the words!

All these words were in Unit 1 or Unit 2. Can you remember them? You will need to use all of the letters in the box. Cross the letters off this list when you use them.

1 Men often put their money in one of these. *w* _ _ _ _ _ _

2 A short word for a bicycle. _ _ _ _

3 In the near past. _ _ _ _ _ _ _ _

4 People from other countries who come to live in your country. _ _ _ _ _ _ _ _ _ _ _

5 People in your family. _ _ _ _ _ _ _ _ _

6 A small river. _ _ _ _ _ _

7 People who live in the house next to you. _ _ _ _ _ _ _ _ _ _

8 Not single (people). _ _ _ _ _ _ _

9 The place where you can buy stamps. _ _ _ _   _ _ _ _ _ _

10 The place where you can see a play. _ _ _ _ _ _ _ _

a	a a a a a
b b	c c	d
e e e e e e
e e e e	f f
g g	h h
i i i i i i i
k	l l l l
m m m m
n n n	o o o
p	r r r r r
r r	s s s s s
t t t t t t t t
u	v	✗ y

Dear English Expert,

My English is getting better and better all the time – I'm very happy about that! But sometimes I have a problem. If someone says something to me that I don't understand, I'm just blocked, completely blocked. I don't know what to say or do, and then I get very nervous and panic. Can you help me? Will it always be the end of the world for me if there's something I don't understand?

Yours sincerely,

Markus, Heidelberg

Dear Markus,

Try not to panic. You can usually do something to help yourself if you don't understand. Just ask yourself this question, and follow the advice:

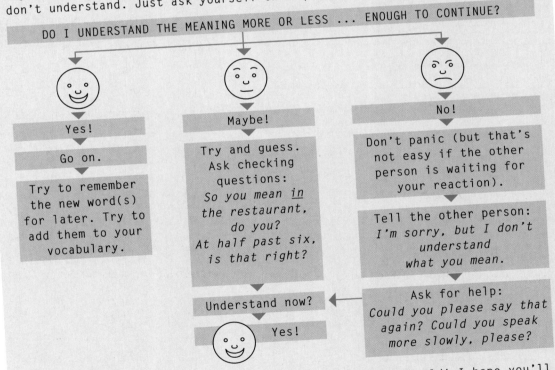

DO I UNDERSTAND THE MEANING MORE OR LESS ... ENOUGH TO CONTINUE?

Yes!

Go on.

Try to remember the new word(s) for later. Try to add them to your vocabulary.

Maybe!

Try and guess. Ask checking questions:
So you mean in the restaurant, do you?
At half past six, is that right?

Understand now?

Yes!

No!

Don't panic (but that's not easy if the other person is waiting for your reaction).

Tell the other person:
I'm sorry, but I don't understand what you mean.

Ask for help:
Could you please say that again? Could you speak more slowly, please?

So: If you don't understand, it isn't the end of the world! I hope you'll feel better about 'not understanding' in the future – it happens to all of us, you know. Don't forget, the other person probably has exactly the same problems in a foreign language, too.

Yours sincerely,
Your English Expert

Test yourself 1

1 Tom's visit to Bristol

leave home (wife) — leave home (Tom) — post letters at station — NOW — 2pm — 8pm — HOTEL PLAZA

Tom bath | to Bristol by train | meeting to make plans for next year | HOTEL PLAZA

Answer these questions. It is now 11.15 am. Use the words in brackets ( ) in your answers.

1 Why is Tom in the train? *(go to Bristol)*
Because he

2 Why is he travelling by train? *(always travel)*
Because he

3 Why didn't he say goodbye to his wife at their flat door when she left? *(have bath)* Because he

4 Why couldn't he say goodbye to his wife when he left home this morning? *(already leave)*
Because she

5 Is Tom tired of sitting in the train? *(only sit in train for 15 minutes)* No, he

6 Has he finished his newspaper yet? *(only start it 10 minutes ago)* No, he

7 Will Tom post his letters in Bristol? *(already post)*
No, he

8 Why has Tom brought last year's reports with him? *(make plans for next year)* Because they

9 Can he go home on the 4 o'clock train? *(still be at the meeting)* No, he

10 Will Tom have to hurry to catch the last train home? *(stay in Bristol until tomorrow)* No, he

Before you go on to Exercise 2, check your answers to this exercise on page 105.

2 Ask about Tom.

Here are the answers to some questions about Tom in Exercise 1. What are the questions? Use the verbs in brackets ( ).

a To Bristol. *(go)*

b By train. *(travel)*

c Having a bath. *(do)*

d For 15 minutes. *(sit)*

e 10 minutes ago. *(start)*

f Yes, he has. *(post)*

g Yes, he will. *(be)*

h Until tomorrow. *(stay)*

3 What's the right order?

Write these words in the correct order to make
sentences or questions. In every one there is a word
you don't need. Cross it out. Example:

*out / need / word / the / cross / ne*X*dn't / don't / you*
Cross out the word you don't need.

1 long / teacher / been / your / how / have / known /
you ? ....
....

2 her / years / for / four / known / since / I've
....
....

3 has / have / how / teaching / long / she / English /
been ? ....
....

4 she's / for / been / think / teaching / I / 1990 /
English / since ....
....
....

5 since / you / English / been / long / learning / how /
have ? ....
....

6 learning / for / am / been / years / three / I've
....
....

4 ☐ Listening

Listen to the conversation and complete these
sentences. You will need to write the word *for* twice
and the word *since* twice.

1 She ....
.... ten years.

2 She ....
.... she was ten.

3 She ....
last Christmas.

4 She...
.... a month.

5 ☐ Dialogue

Listen to the dialogue as many times as you want and
fill in the second part. Two people are talking about
someone who emigrated to Australia a long time ago.

Do you know anybody who decided to emigrate?

....
....
....
....

Why did they decide to leave their home country?

....
....
....
....
....
....

Are they still there?

....
....
....
....
....
....

Where would he like to live?

....
....
....
....
....

Oh, he might be lucky! Who knows?

Dictionary skills 1
Getting to know your dictionary

◆ Everybody who is learning a foreign language needs to have a dictionary. The word list in the back of your course book is very useful, but you probably want to learn and find out about other words, too. You want to be sure about the right word, the right meaning, and how to use and spell it correctly. A dictionary can help you a lot.

There are two types of dictionaries to choose from:

BILINGUAL DICTIONARIES
(English-German, German-English)

dic·tion·ar·y [ˈdɪkʃənrɪ] s Wörterbuch n.

MONOLINGUAL DICTIONARIES
(English-English)

dic·tion·a·ry /ˈdɪkʃənəri ‖ -neri/ n dictionaries a book that gives a list of words in alphabetical order, with their meanings in the same or another language

◆ In *Network Plus 1* there are four pages about using dictionaries. On these pages we are going to look at bilingual dictionaries, because this is what most learners like you choose. We'll introduce you to monolingual dictionaries in *Network Plus 2*.

The most important things to find out about a new dictionary are
  • what is in it,
  • where you can find what you want to find,
  • how you can use it to learn more.

◆ You'll find a lot of different sections in a dictionary. The biggest section is, of course, the alphabetical list of words with their translations. You will also probably find the following sections. Match the German titles for these sections with the English titles on the right. Number them 1-13. If you can't recognize the matching English words – look in a dictionary!

1 Hinweise für den Benutzer	☐ Numbers
2 Erklärung der phonetischen Zeichen	☐ Symbols
3 Wichtige Eigennamen	☐ Abbreviations
4 Abkürzungen	☐ Weights and measures
5 Die Rechtschreibung im amerikanischen Englisch	☐ The English alphabet
6 Die Aussprache des amerikanischen Englisch	☐ Irregular verbs
7 Zahlwörter	☐ American pronunciation
8 Das englische Alphabet	☐ British and American abbreviations
9 Englische Währung	☐ Important proper names
10 Masse und Gewichte	☐ English currency
11 Bildliche Zeichen	☐ Guide to the use of the dictionary
12 Unregelmäßige Verben	☐ American spelling
13 Britische und amerikanische Abkürzungen	☐ Explanation of the phonetic symbols

There's a lot of information in a dictionary, isn't there? The other three 'dictionary' pages will show you some more details.

⟶ page 105

1 What would you ... if you ...?

Put the words of these questions in the right order.
Who could you ask each of these questions to?

1 you / where / if / London / would / worked / in /
live / you ....._Where would you live if_
you worked in London?

I could ask a person who _doesn't work in London._

2 buy / you / what / rich / would / were / you / if ......

....

....

I could ask a person who ....

3 learn / if / night / you / what / go / would / could /
you / to / school ....

....

....

I could ask a person who ....

....

4 travel / how / couldn't / you / drive / would / on/
you / if / holiday ....

....

....

....

I could ask a person who ....

5 film / had / video / you / if / a / rent / which / you /
would ....

....

....

I could ask a person who ....

....

6 live / wanted / if / where / you / emigrate / you /
would / to ....

....

....

....

I could ask a person who ....

....

2 Pronunciation

These words were all in the reading text in Step 1.
Underline the part of the word where the stress is,
like this: re<u>mem</u>ber.

1 regularly	5 especially	9 comfortable
2 popular	6 private	10 quality
3 generally	7 fortunately	11 appreciate
4 disability	8 obviously	12 opportunity

Check your answers in the key.
🖭 Now listen to the text.

3 🖭 Explaining something

You're going to hear what some students wrote about
two different sports. Their teacher has got all the
sentences and is reading them to the class. Complete
the sentences and write a *T* in the box if it's about
tennis, and an *F* if it's about football.
You'll hear these words on the cassette, and you'll
also have to write them:

goal   **kick a ball**   **handle a ball**   **boot**

1 You need a ball ....

.... ☐

2 You have to try to hit the ball ....

....

.... ☐

3 The players are allowed to kick the ball, ...

....

.... ☐

4 You need ....

.... ☐

5 The players wear ....

....

.... ☐

6 The point of the game is to get ....

.... ☐

7 You use a piece of equipment to ....

.... ☐

8 You don't need any other ....

.... ☐

4 Remember the words!

All these words were in Step 1. Combine words from the three boxes to make expressions you could use to talk about sport.

1 wear	6 join	☐ a private	☐ the extra	☐ countryside	☑ shoes
2 start	7 improve	☐ the local	☐ good-quality	☐ fitness	☐ courts
3 remember	8 discover	☑ comfortable	☐ public	☐ cost	☐ sport
4 play on	9 buy	☑ the ideal	☐ the golden	☐ rules	☐ shoes
5 pay		☐ your all-round		☐ club	

Step 2

1 What would you have done?

Write questions like the one in the example. Use the words in brackets.

1 I didn't see the accident. *(what / do)* *What would you have done if you had seen the accident ?*

2 She didn't go to university. *(what / study)* ....

....

3 He didn't phone her. *(what / say)* ....

4 We didn't have a holiday last year. *(where / go)* ....

....

5 He didn't write to them. *(what / ask)* ....

6 I wasn't late for my train. *(when / arrive there)* ....

....

2 ▭ A late start

Listen to Christine's story. Which of these pictures illustrate the story correctly, and which aren't right?

Now listen again and complete these sentences.

1 If she .... so late, she .... breakfast at home.

2 If she .... the bus, she .... her brother.

3 If she .... a taxi, she .... before ten.

4 If she .... for the next bus, she .... the accident.

5 If she .... so late, she .... her job.

6 If she .... in the office that afternoon, she .... the advert.

3 How to do it

Write these words at the beginning of the sentences to show the order in which you have to do these things.

First of all	Secondly	Then	Finally

Here are some words you need to understand:

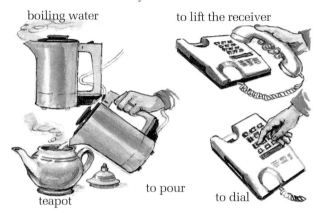

boiling water   to lift the receiver

teapot   to pour   to dial

1   How to make tea

.... you pour out the water and put the tea into the teapot.

.... wait for a few minutes before you drink the tea.

First of all................ you warm the teapot with hot water.

.... you pour the boiling water onto the tea.

2   How to make a photocopy of a letter

.... you press a button on the machine.

.... you put your paper into the photocopier.

.... your copy comes out of the machine.

.... you write your letter on a piece of paper.

3   How to make a phone call from a pay phone

.... you dial the number of the person you'd like to speak to.

.... wait for the other person to answer.

.... put the money into the phone.

.... lift the receiver.

Here are some more sentences about making a phone call from a pay phone. Write these words at the beginning of the sentences. Use each word once.

Fortunately	In fact	Obviously

.... you need some coins to make the call.

.... if the other person isn't at home, you get your money back.

.... if you don't use all the coins that are in the phone, you get them back when you finish your conversation.

4   Remember the words!

Here are pictures to show you what Christine enjoys doing in her free time. Some of these things are sports and some of them aren't. Write words for these things in the correct column. There's a word that ends with *-ing* on every line.

SPORTS Christine enjoys	NON-SPORTS Christine enjoys
....	....
....	....
....	....
....	....
....	....
....	....

1 Past and past participle

Write the verbs here in the correct column and then complete the other two columns.

ate, be, broke, did, drink, drove, forgotten, given, gone, put, seen, send, won, written

eat	*ate*	*eaten*
....	....	....
....	....	....
....	....	....
....	....	....
....	....	....
....	....	....
....	....	....
....	....	....
....	....	....
....	....	....
....	....	....
....	....	....
....	....	....

2 ▦ Having a discussion

When you have a discussion or a conversation with someone, you might want to agree or disagree with the other person. You might also want to express your own opinion and sometimes to change the topic. Listen to the six short conversations. What does the woman do in each of them. Number this list 1 to 6.

☐ She doubts whether what he says is true.
☐ She accepts what he says, but doesn't agree completely.
☐ She completely agrees with him.
☐ She doesn't agree with him at all.
☐ She expresses her own opinion.
☐ She changes the topic.

Which of the above sentences does the picture illustrate?

3 Pronunciation

In all these groups of three words there is one word in which the underlined letters make a different sound. Which word is the different one?

(companion)	*station*	atten*tion*
1 fo**llow**	h**ow**ever	**ow**ner
2 am**ou**nt	f**ou**nd	sh**ou**ld
3 **th**ink	whe**th**er	**th**e
4 **per**fect	whe**th**er	**per**son
5 comp**a**nion	ex**a**mple	ex**a**mined
6 **wh**ole	**wh**ether	**wh**at
7 deci**s**ion	con**s**ider	ad**v**ice
8 **ea**sy	**hea**lthy	(to) l**ea**d

Check your answers in the key.
☐ Now listen to the text.

4 Complete the sentences.

You can fill seven of these gaps with the word *of*. The other seven gaps need seven different words. Do you know what they are? If you can't think of the seven different words, there's a list of ten to choose from at the end of the exercise.

1 They wanted to find a companion .... their mother.

2 The amount .... money she had just wasn't enough.

3 Everybody gave her plenty .... advice.

4 Her house was examined .... an expert.

5 She asked her neighbour to look .... her house while she was away.

6 She spent lots .... time and energy looking for a new house.

7 She gave them a bottle of champagne .... a thank-you present.

8 The man wasn't the owner .... the house.

9 The age .... the house was a disadvantage.

10 .... the other hand, its age also made it very attractive.

11 It was very difficult .... decide.

12 The size .... the garden was perfect.

13 She went to the town hall and asked for more information .... the town.

14 That was probably the best way .... getting information.

Choose from: *about, after, as, by, for, from, on, over, through, to.*

5 Remember the words!

Here are some adjectives that were in Step 1, but the letters of the words they were with are in the wrong order. Write these words correctly.

1	worst	*hitgn*	....	7 right	*ehcioc*	....
2	whole	*yad*	....	8 helpful	*vacdie*	....
3	valuable	*runfitrue*	....	9 good	*adei*	....
4	suitable	*seetsprn*	....	10 dangerous	*tebjosc*	....
5	simple	*dugie*	....	11 daily	*reeisexc*	....
6	sharp	*vinkse*	....	12 common	*seens*	....

Step 2 _____

1 ⌨ A new job

Paul is talking to a friend, Anna, in a pub. Paul's got a new job and Anna works for the same company, but she's in a different department. Listen, fill in the missing words and choose the right ending for each sentence.

1 Paul found it rather .... to ....
☐ people's names.
☐ where his office was.

2 He .... to ....
☐ a list of names and jobs.
☐ a plan of the office building.

3 His new boss .... him to ....
☐ him Robert.
☐ him Rob.

4 Paul .... to ....
☐ Anna's colleagues.
☐ Anna's boss.

5 Anna could perhaps .... him to ....
☐ about the company.
☐ the people's names.

6 Someone offered to show him .... to ....
☐ the fax.
☐ the phone system.

7 Paul's boss has already .... him to ....
☐ a drink with him.
☐ dinner at his home.

8 Paul thinks that this is a .... to ....
☐ for a short time.
☐ for at least two years.

2 Passive forms

Write the correct form of the verb in the gaps. They are all passive.

Every week the reports (*write*) .... by Mr Charlton and (*give*) ....

to our boss. Last week one report (*not finish*) .... on time because Mr Charlton had an

accident and his leg (*break*) .... in two places. The other car (*drive*) ....

by a drunk! He, Mr Charlton – not the drunk, (*take*) .... to hospital by ambulance and

(*examine*) .... by an excellent doctor. He (*bring*) .... home

yesterday, but before he left hospital, he (*tell*) .... to stay at home for three weeks. This

week's reports (*already give*) .... to someone else.

3 It's all different!

You used to live in this place, but you left here 20 years ago. You've come back to have a look but, as you can see, many things have changed.

 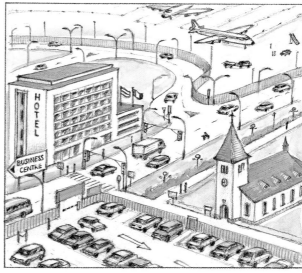

Complete these sentences about the changes. Use each of these verbs, in the passive form, once:
build, close, construct, cut down, demolish, move, open, replace, take away, widen

1 An airport and a hotel *have been* ....

2 The trees ....

3 A motorway ....

4 The lake .... by a car park.

5 The children's play equipment ....

6 The zoo ....

7 A business centre ....

8 The church ....

9 The houses ....

10 The roads ....

4 Learn some new words!

Here are some more words for animals that you can usually see in a zoo. Match the words with the pictures. If you don't know, guess!

	bear		elephant		hippopotamus		monkey		rhinoceros		tiger
	camel		giraffe		lion		parrot		snake		zebra

Check your answers in the key.
☐ If you don't know how to say these words, listen to them on your cassette.

Learners' letters 2
I forget the new words!

Dear English Expert,
J'd like to know more English words, but J forget most of the new words that we meet in the lesson. What can J do? Am J too stupid to learn English? And how can J learn other new words, J mean words that aren't in my course book? Can you give me any advice?
Yours sincerely,
Anna, St. Gallen

Dear Anna,
NO! You aren't too stupid to learn English. Most students find it diffi-cult to remember words, because they don't use their English very often.
There are a lot of different ways of learning vocabulary. For example, there's the vocabulary list in your course book. Here's something you can try: cover[1] the column[2] on the left so that you can't see the English words, then try to write down the missing word in the column on the right. The German translation in the middle will help you.

whether ['weðə]	ob	I don't know ~ to go or not.
amount [ə'maʊnt]	Betrag, Höhe, Menge	He had to pay a large ~ of money.
attention [ə'tenʃn]	Aufmerksamkeit, (Be)Achtung	Can I have your ~, please!

I asked my students for some ideas for you. Here are some of them:

> I write the new words on cards and then I read them every day on the bus.

> I make sentences for myself with the new words in them. These sentences are important or interesting for me, so I remember them better.

> Before every lesson, I choose three new words from the last lesson – and I try to use them. It's usually possible, and then I feel very pleased with myself.

> I travel home with another student after our lesson. We often make a little 'vocabulary test' on the train. Sometimes we do this on the phone in the middle of the week.

Now, what about learning other new words. You could try to:
- collect vocabulary about topics that interest you. Find the words in a dictionary, ask friends, ask your teacher. If you're really interested, you'll probably remember them.
- read more. Don't try to learn (or even understand) all the new words in a story or article, just the most important ones.
- add to the vocabulary that you learn at school. For example, in Unit 4 you had the word *leather* – make a word group of ten things that are usually or sometimes made of leather.
And don't forget, your dictionary can help you a lot!

All the best,
Your English Expert

---

¹ cover = zudecken; ² column = Spalte

80

1 If ...

Complete these questions and answer them with the words from the boxes on the right.

meet the Queen		buy	to the police station
see a ghost		say	at it
lose your passport		go	a flat
win a lot of money		shout	'hello'

1 What would you do if you _met the Queen?_ _____ I'd say 'hello'. _____

2 What would you do if you .... ? ....

3 What would you do if you .... ? ....

4 What would you do if you .... ? ....

Now do the same here, like this:

5 What would you have done if you _'d met the Queen?_ _____ I'd have said 'hello'. _____

6 What would you have done if you .... ? ....

7 What would you have done if you ....
.... ? ....

8 What would you have done if you ....
.... ? ....

2 Which is correct?

Choose the correct part (a, b or c) to complete these questions, and write in the answers. Always use the short form with an apostrophe (') in the answers.

1 Which sport would you take up
  a ☐ if you have time?   b ☐ if you had time?   c ☐ if you'd had time?
  (*table tennis*) ..... _I'd_ ....

2 What will you do
  a ☐ if you lose your job?   b ☐ if you lost your job?   c ☐ if you'd lost your job?
  (*a computer course*) ....

3 What would you have bought
  a ☐ if you have enough money?   b ☐ if you had enough money?   c ☐ if you'd had enough money?
  (*a CD player*) ....

4 a ☐ Who will do the work   b ☐ Who would do the work   c ☐ Who would have done the work
                                                                    if the others aren't there?
  (*I*) ....

5 a ☐ Where will you stay   b ☐ Where would you stay   c ☐ Where would you have stayed
                                                                    if you went to the party?
  (*with friends*) ....

6 a ☐ What will you say   b ☐ What would you say   c ☐ What would you have said
                                                                    if you'd been at the meeting?
  ("*I don't agree!*") ....

3 Short forms

In this text there are twelve short forms, write the twelve words in full.

Caroline was late again for work on Monday. <u>She'd</u> have been at the station before the train left if she'd got up earlier. She knew that. "I know," she thought. "I'll get up very early tomorrow." Well, Caroline's never been very good at getting up. In fact, she's a very sleepy person in the mornings. So, on Monday evening, she phoned a friend and said, "If you've got time, could you please phone me in the morning when you're ready to leave? I don't want to miss the train again!"
The next morning the phone rang at half past five, and her friend said, "I'm sorry to ring so early, but I'd have told you if you'd asked me. I have to be at the airport at six." Caroline didn't go back to sleep.

1 *would*	5	9 ....
2	6	10 ....
3	7	11 ....
4	8	12 ....

4 The new zoo

A class of schoolchildren visited the new zoo in their town, and then they wrote about it. Rewrite their sentences, beginning with the words in italics, and use the passive form.

1 They feed *the animals* once a day.
   The animals ....

2 They've moved *the elephants* from the old zoo.
   ....
   ....

3 They shouldn't allow *dogs* in the zoo.
   ....
   ....

4 They opened *the new zoo* last week.
   ....

5 They bought *some new animals* before the zoo moved.
   ....
   ....

6 The zoo needs *a lot of animal food* every day.
   ....
   ....

5 ⌨ Listening

What happened yesterday? Listen to the radio report on a break-in at a supermarket. Complete these sentences with verbs.

1 Two cars ...... *were stolen.* ....

2 A small window ....

3 All the money ....

4 Four bottles of wine ....

5 One of the cars ....

6 The other car ....

6 ⌨ Dialogue

Listen to the dialogue as many times as you want and fill in the second part. A woman wants to buy a pet for her children. She's talking to a man in the pet shop.

I want to buy a dog for my children, and I'd like some advice.

....
....
....
....

Yes, I mean there are five of us who can take it for walks.

....
....
....

We live in a flat. Perhaps it would be better to have a cat.

....
....
....
....

Yes, a cat would be easier, wouldn't it?

....
....
....
....

Well, I'll discuss this with the family, and come back next week.

Dictionary skills 2
Learning from your dictionary

◆ If you look up a word in the German-English half of your dictionary, this is what you can find out:

the stress[1] of
the German
word

the part of speech[2] of the
German word (here:
f = feminine noun)

These two things are interesting for an
English person who is learning German,
but probably not for you, especially if
German is your first language.

Karri'ere *f* career: ~ **machen** make a
career for o.s., *weitS.* get to the top.

the English translation of the word (here: o.s. = oneself *sich*,
weitS = *in weiterem Sinne* – you can find out what these
letters mean in the section called Abbreviations)

◆ If you want to know more about the English word, look it up in the English-German half of the
dictionary. There you can find out:

where to divide[3]
the word

the part of speech (s =
Substantiv or noun)

the phonetics show you
how to pronounce
the word, and the ' shows
you the stress

ca·reer [kə'rɪə] *s* **1.** Karriere *f*, Laufbahn
f: *enter upon a* ~ e-e Laufbahn ein-
schlagen; *make a* ~ *for o.s.* Karriere
machen; **2.** Beruf *m*: ~ *diplomat* Be-
rufsdiplomat *m*; ~ *girl* (*od.* **woman**)
Karrierefrau *f.* **ca·reer·ist** [kə'rɪərɪst] *s*
Karrieremacher *m.*

what the word
means in German

word combinations

expressions with
the word in them

other words that come
from the word

◆ So, you see – you don't get exactly the same information in these two parts. What can you see
where?

	English-German	German-English
	dic·tion·ar·y ['dɪkʃənrɪ] *s* Wörterbuch *n.*	**Wörter|buch** *n* dictionary. **~verzeich-nis** *n* list of words, vocabulary.
The English word	✔	✔
The German word	....	....
The English pronunciation	....	....
The stress of the English word	....	....
Where you can divide the English word	....	....
The part of speech of the word	....	....

Question 1: If you look up a German word, does the dictionary tell you how to pronounce the
English translation? ☐ yes ☐ no

Question 2: If you can't pronounce the word, and the dictionary doesn't help you in the German-
English list – what are you going to do?

☐ pronounce it wrongly for the rest of my life.
☐ look up the English word in the English-German list.

⊶ page 106

---

[1] the stress = Betonung; [2] the part of speech = Wortart; [3] divide = trennen

1 Infinitive or gerund?

Choose the right verb for each sentence. Use each verb only once. Decide if you need an infinitive (with *to*) or a gerund (with *-ing*). For example, you'll have to choose between *to go* and *going* for sentence 1.

The verbs: *be, buy, change, come, do, drive, go, live, remember, smoke.*

1 I'd like .... to Paris.

2 I want .... a CD player for my son.

3 I enjoy .... through the countryside.

4 My teacher asked me .... this exercise.

5 I hate .... late for appointments.

6 We like .... where we live now.

7 She's looking forward to .... home at Christmas.

8 I've decided .... my job.

9 I don't like smokers who like .... as soon as the day begins!

10 It's sometimes difficult .... the new words.

2 Pronunciation

These words were all in the reading text in Step 1. Look at the parts of the words that are underlined. Match pairs of sounds – one from the list on the left with one from the list on the right.

1 sat<u>is</u>fied	5 d<u>e</u>tails
2 kn<u>ow</u>ledge	6 w<u>or</u>king
3 dr<u>ea</u>ms	7 direct<u>or</u>
4 d<u>i</u>vorced	

- ☐ f<u>ir</u>m
- ☐ bel<u>ow</u>
- ☐ lawy<u>er</u>
- ☐ br<u>igh</u>t
- ☐ c<u>o</u>nversations
- ☐ w<u>a</u>ste
- ☐ thr<u>ee</u>

Check your answers in the key.

😐 Now listen to the text.

3 Developing a conversation

Match the beginnings of sentences and questions on the left with the endings and answers on the right.

1 Sorry to interrupt but

2 Could you explain

3 Talking of interviews,

4 While we're on the subject of PDA,

5 Do you know what I mean?

6 What do you think?

- ☐ No, I'm not sure that I do.
- ☐ your last point again?
- ☐ I didn't understand your last point.
- ☐ have you ever had problems with them?
- ☐ I completely agree with you.
- ☐ I'd like to ask you a bit about their work.

😐 Listen and check your answers.

Now listen again. Was the woman's reaction to these sentences friendly or unfriendly?

	1	2	3	4	5	6
friendly						
unfriendly						

4 Remember the words!

Write the missing words in the puzzle. You can then complete the sentence at the end of the exercise with the word in the box.

She hasn't got a job, she's (**9**). Last month she saw an (**3**) for an interesting job in the newspaper. So she (**1**) for it. She had most of the necessary (**10**) and so she sent them the (**2**) of her work experience. They offered her an (**6**) and when she spoke to them she wasn't nervous at all, she was perfectly (**7**). Unfortunately, she didn't get the job because her (**11**) of French wasn't good enough. She'll have to take a course in French because she (**4**) badly in the last examinations she took, but perhaps she'll (**8**) them next time. The problem was that the last course wasn't very interesting – in fact, it was very (**5**)!

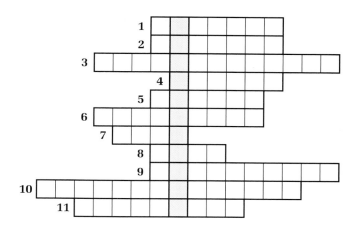

The people at Professional Development Agency say that they can help you to learn how to give a

better .... at interviews.

Step 2

1 The unpopular colleague

Why don't the others in the office like this man? Because …

1 *(arrive late)* *he's always arriving late,* ....

2 *(sit with his feet on the desk)* ....

3 *(read the newspaper)* ....

4 *(phone his girlfriend)* ....

5 *(smoke)* ....

6 *(drink coffee)* ....

7 *(give orders)* ....

2 📖 Gerunds

Caroline went to PDA for advice about interviews. Her problem was that she always said she could do everything. Then when she started the job she found that she wasn't suitable for it at all. Now she knows that it's better to say what is true when the interviewer asks a question like *Can you ...? Do you like ...?* Listen to part of her interview and write eight ticks (✔) in this table.

	like	enjoy	not like	hate	good at	bad at
meet people	✔					
type						
write reports						
use a computer						
phone companies abroad						
speak French						
speak other languages						
work alone						

What do you know about Caroline?

1 *She likes meeting people.* ....

2 ....

3 ....

4 ....

5 ....

....

6 ....

7 ....

....

8 ....

3 Infinitive or gerund?

Choose a different verb from the list for each of these pairs of sentences. Complete one of the sentences with the infinitive *(to change)*, and the other with the gerund *(changing)*.

The verbs: change, *drive, leave, live, ride, save, take, travel.*

1 Have you ever thought about *changing* .... your job?

Would you like *to change* .... your job?

2 I love .... in Wales.

I'd love .... in Wales.

3 She's too nervous .... the examination.

She's very nervous about .... the examination.

4 I used .... in my job.

I enjoy .... in my job.

5 She hates .... her car at night.

She never wants .... her car at night.

6 I'm good at .... electricity.

It's good .... electricity.

7 He knows it was a mistake .... school so young.

He regrets .... school so young.

8 He's bad at .... a bicycle.

He's never learnt how .... a bicycle.

4 Remember the words!

There was an opposite for each of these words in either Step 1 or Step 2. Can you remember them? You will need to use all the letters in the box. Cross the letters off this list when you use them.

1 badly-paid *w* _ _ _ - _ _ _ _

2 same _ _ _ _ _ _ _ _ _

3 employer _ _ _ _ _ _ _ _

4 special _ _ _ _ _ _ _ _

5 nervous _ _ _ _ _

6 borrow _ _ _ _ _

7 male _ _ _ _ _ _

8 strong _ _ _ _

a a a a a c	k l l l l l
d d d e e e	m m m n n n
e e e e e e	o o p p r r r
f f f i i i	t ✗ w y y

1 Some modal verbs

Choose the best word for the sentences. Use each of these words only once: *can't, might, must, mustn't, needn't, should, shouldn't.*

When you are in England:

1 You .... drive on the left.

2 You .... walk everywhere in London, taxis are cheaper than at home.

3 You .... drive on the right.

4 You .... be able to get tickets for *Cats*, although it's difficult.

5 You .... try to speak English as often as possible.

6 You .... forget to give the taxi drivers a tip.

7 You .... watch any German television programmes.

How can you begin these two questions?

Can	Will	Could	May

8 .... / .... I help you?

9 .... /.................. /.................. you help me?

2 What's the missing word?

All the words that are missing from these sentences have got the letter *o* in them, and they're all different. What are they?

1 He retired at the age .... fifty.

2 They moved .... a smaller house.

3 Suddenly they had time .... each other.

4 They've seen many sunsets .... the ocean.

5 She felt guilty at first .... having nothing to occupy her life.

3 ⌨ Meeting people you know

Listen to the six dialogues. In which dialogue do you hear each of these expressions? Number the expressions 1-6.

☐ Give my love to Suzie, won't you?

☐ Many happy returns of the day.

☐ How are things?

☐ Take care.

☐ Cheerio.

☐ Cheers!

Now listen to the dialogues again and write the other person's reaction to the expressions above (1- 6):

1 ....
....

2 ....
....

3 ....
....

4 ....
....

5 ....
....

6 ....

4 Pronunciation

All of these words from the text in Step 1 have got the letter *s* in them, once or more than once.
Do these letters make an *s* sound or a *z* sound?

1 suppose *s z*	7 thousands _ _
2 sights _ _	8 wasting _
3 sunrises _ _ _	9 suddenly _
4 sunsets _ _ _	10 progress _
5 museums _ _	11 useless _ _
6 capitals _	

Check your answers in the key.

⌨ Now listen to the text. Can you hear the difference? (It's sometimes difficult to hear the difference, isn't it?)

5 Remember the words!

These words were used together in the texts in Step 1. Match the words on the left with those on the right.

1 go	7 feel	☐ my time	☐ of having nothing to do
2 see	8 (nothing to) occupy	☐ adults to read	☐ guilty
3 take	9 contact	☑ all over the world	☐ thousands of photographs
4 keep	10 teach	☐ progress	☐ the sights
5 become tired	11 make	☐ a diary	☐ a local group
6 waste	12 prove	☐ that we're not useless	☐ my life

Step 2

1 A lazy day

Tom made a list of things that he wanted to do yesterday, but he decided to have a lazy day. Write sentences about the things he should have done.

1. phone the doctor   X can't find number
2. buy some wine   X not enough money
3. clean the car   X not enough time
4. do the washing   X washing machine broken
5. take books back to library   X library closed
6. write to Aunt Mary   X can't find her letter
7. make list for tomorrow   ✓ same as today!

1 *He should have phoned the doctor, but he didn't because he couldn't find the number.*

2 ....

....

3 ....

....

4 ....

....

5 ....

....

6 ....

....

2 Complete the sentences.

Complete the sentences. You'll need *should have*, *shouldn't have* and *could have* for each situation. These are the verbs you'll need: 1 *catch, go out, take;* 2 *come, find, stay;* 3 *be, break, make;* 4 *choose, phone, try.*

1 You .... without your coat this morning, it was much too cold and wet.

   You .... a very bad cold. You .... your umbrella, too.

2 The party was really good. You .... with us.

   You .... at home. I'm sure you .... a babysitter.

3 They .... their legs up there in the mountains. It was very stupid of them to go.

   They .... the trip without a guide. They .... more realistic about it.

4 He .... to cook something so difficult. He ....

   something that was easy to make. I mean, he .... for a pizza!

3 Too many employees

The International Hotel has got problems. They've got too many employees, and some of them have to go. There are two young people who are both very good at their jobs, so it's difficult to decide who should go.

Part A: Put the words in brackets in the right order to make sentences about these two people.

1 She works *(does/faster/than/he)* ....

2 But he can *(she/French/speak/can/than/better)* ....

3 She can *(car/but/drive/can't/a/he)* ....

4 He has had *(has/than/experience/she/more)* ....

5 She is *(friendly/him/more/than)* ....

6 He's *(than/older/her)* ....

7 But he wants *(more/does/than/money/she/earn/to)* ....

8 She got *(examination/did/results/than/he/better)* ....

9 He learnt *(computer/the/faster/about/did/she/than)* ....

10 She's got *(he/than/voice/better/a/telephone/has)* ....

Check your answers in the key.

☐ **Part B:** Now listen to the manager and his wife. 1 ☐ 2 ☐ 3 ☐ 4 ☐ 5 ☐
They're talking about their two employees.
Are the statements above (1-10) true (T) or false (F)? 6 ☐ 7 ☐ 8 ☐ 9 ☐ 10 ☐

4 Remember the words!

Fill in all the vowels to complete the words on the right. The meanings are on the left.

1 100% sure = d _ f _ n _ t _ l y   4 it happened quickly, not expected = s _ d d _ n l y

2 often = f r _ q _ _ n t l y   5 it was clear = _ b v _ _ _ s l y

3 fortunately = l _ c k _ l y   6 in the end = f _ n _ l l y

With five of these six words you can take the *'ly'* away, and you've still got an English word.

Which one is different? ....

Learners' letters 3

Why is spelling so difficult?

Dear English Expert,
One of my biggest problems in English is the spelling. Why is it so difficult? Are there any rules? If I hear an English word, I often have no idea how to spell it. Is it possible to <u>learn</u> English spelling? Please help me!
Yours sincerely,
Karl, Innsbruck

Hello, I'm a ghoti

A ghoti !?! yes
gh - laugh = f
o - women = i
ti - station = sh

Dear Karl,
Yes, English spelling is a bit difficult, you're right. Look at these words. The five words in each group have exactly the same sound[1], but you write that sound in five different ways!

| tree me dream key piece | wear share pair there their |

It isn't easy to give spelling rules, because there are always exceptions. Here are some tips that will help you to be right more often.

- *ie* or *ei*?
  To make a sound like pl<u>ay</u>, write *e* before *i*: *eight, neighbour*
  To make a sound like tr<u>ee</u>, write *i* before *e*: *field, piece*
  but not after *c*: *receipt*

- If a word ends with *y* and you want to add something, change the *y* to *i*: *baby - babies, study - studies, hurry - hurried, easy - easier, lucky - luckiest, heavy - heavily*
  The *y* doesn't change if you add *-ing*: *study - studying*
  The *y* doesn't change if it follows a vowel[2]: *enjoy - enjoyed*
  (You already know two exceptions: pay - paid, say - said!)

- With short verbs
  → double[3] the consonant[4] at the end if there's one vowel before it: *swim - swimming - swimmer*
  → but don't double the consonant if there's more than one vowel: *dream - dreaming - dreamer*

- With longer verbs
  → double the consonant if the last syllable[5] of the verb is stressed: <u>begin</u> - beginning - beginner
  → but don't double the consonant if the last syllable is not stressed: <u>visit</u> - visiting - visitor
  (You already know an exception: <u>travel</u> - traveller!)

- Drop the *e* at the end of a verb if there's a consonant before it and you want to add something: *write - writing - writer*

This is probably more than enough for now. And remember - you already know some exceptions, and you'll certainly learn some more!
And don't vorget, if yu wright a letter to a frend and their ar sum speling mistakes in it, he or she wil probabley understand anyway!
(There are 10 mistakes in this last sentence! Can you find them?)

Yours sincerely,
Your English Expert

○━ page 107

---

[1] sound = Klang; [2] vowel = Selbstlaut; [3] double = verdoppeln; [4] consonant = Mitlaut; [5] syllable = Silbe

1 A letter from Anke

Here's the first letter a student of English wrote to her English penfriend. Anke finds English verbs a bit difficult, and she's made nine verb mistakes in this letter. Underline the nine mistakes and correct them.

Hello! My name's Anke. My hometown is Hamburg where I'm living with my parents and my two brothers. I go to school every day and enjoy to learn English very much. Our English teacher is from England, but she's working in Germany for more than ten years now. She's very good at to teach English and she never thinks about to go back to England again. In my free time I like playing tennis and reading. To write letters is also one of my favourite pastimes. What about you? I'm sure you could doing that – why don't you try? It's sometimes impossible for me finding the right English words. I'm looking forward to get your letter. Please write soon.

	Anke wrote:	She should have written:
1	*I'm living*	....
2	....	....
3	....	....
4	....	....
5	....	....
6	....	....
7	....	....
8	....	....
9	....	....

2 Too often?

Does *always* really mean 'always' here, or does it mean 'too often'? Choose the best verb for each sentence.

1 The postman
☐ is always coming
☐ always comes
at about 8 o'clock so I can get my post before I go to work.

2 Those children
☐ are always taking
☐ always take
flowers from my garden – and not only once a year, on Mother's Day!

3 My friends in Canada
☐ are always phoning
☐ always phone
me on my birthday.

4 She
☐ is always talking
☐ always talks
to her boyfriend instead of working.

5 My neighbour
☐ is always parking
☐ always parks
in front of my garage.

3 Make the pairs.

These ten sentences belong together in pairs. You can complete the first one of each pair with *shouldn't have*, and the second one with *could have*. One has been done as an example. Find and complete the other four pairs.

The pairs: *1* ..... + *7* .... + ... + ... + ... + ...

1 She .....*shouldn't have*..... taken so much money to the casino.

2 She .... caught a bad cold.

3 She .... lost her way.

4 She .... given her baby daughter that knife.

5 She .... walked home in the dark.

6 She .... hurt it.

7 She .....*could have*..... lost it all.

8 She .... gone out in the rain yesterday.

9 She .... cut herself.

10 She .... hit the dog.

4 Rewrite the sentences.

Rewrite the sentences so that they mean the same – but start with the words that are in *italics*. The last word of each sentence should be a verb.

1 John drives fast, but not as fast as *Sarah*.
   Sarah drives even faster than John does.

2 Peter ate a lot, but not as much as *Paul*.

   ....

3 Bob can dance well, but not as well as *Tom*.

   ....

4 Our children have been noisy, but not as noisy as *their children*.

   ....

   ....

5 Jane is happy, but not as happy as *Anna*.

   ....

6 Martin's got a lot of responsibility at work, but not as much as *Tanya*.

   ....

   ....

7 German shoes are expensive, but not as expensive as *Swiss shoes*.

   ....

   ....

8 Liz works hard, but not as hard as *Anna*.

   ....

5 ▭ Listening

Listen to the eight people, and write a sentence about what each person tells you. Use each of these verbs once, followed by another verb: *be afraid of, be bad at, be good at, enjoy, give up, hate, look forward to, think about*.

1 *He's afraid of losing* ....

2 ....

3 .... ten years ago.

4 .... abroad.

5 ....

6 ....

7 ....

8 ....

6 ▭ Dialogue

Listen to the dialogue as many times as you want and fill in the second part. A woman has gone to PDA because she wants a new job.

I'd like to know how PDA can help me. I want to change jobs.

....

....

Yes, it's boring.

....

....

....

Oh, that would be good.

....

....

....

What will you need to know about me?

....

....

....

....

Is that all?

....

....

....

....

....

I see.

....

Yes, fine. I'll do that, thank you.

Dictionary skills 3
Using your dictionary well

You can't find the answers to all your language problems in a dictionary, but you can find answers to a lot of them – if you know how to use the dictionary. Here are answers to some "dictionary problems":

> I wanted to know the English for *ich dachte* – but *dachte* isn't there!

> Question: Which verb does *dachte* come from?

> Look up *denken* and you'll find *think*.

> Look up *think* in the irregular verb list, and you'll find *thought*. **Ich dachte = I thought.**

GOLDEN RULE: If you can't find a word, ask yourself where it comes from.

> I looked up the word *Schuppe* because I wanted to buy some shampoo in London. I saw two English words: *scale* and *dandruff*. I said "I'd like some shampoo please, I've got scales." And the lady in the shop laughed.

> If you'd looked in the English-German half too, you'd have seen the word *fish* with the word *scale*. You'd also have seen the word *hair* with *dandruff!*

GOLDEN RULE: If you don't know which translation you should use, check the words in the other half of the dictionary.

> I had a little accident, I fell down the stairs. An English friend sent me a card and it said "More haste, less speed." I looked for this expression under the word *more*, but I couldn't find it.

> And then you gave up? *Haste* is the key word here, not *more*. If you look under *haste*, you'll find **more ~, less speed = eile mit Weile**. This is also true when you're looking up words in your dictionary!

GOLDEN RULE: Don't think that you can always find an expression under the first word in that expression. Find a key word.

> I wanted to say that something was "schwer zu sagen". I looked up *schwer* and found *heavy*, so I said "heavy to say". I could see on the other person's face that this was wrong!

> You were right *schwer = heavy*. But if you <u>read</u> through the information on *schwer*, you'll also find: **schwer zu sagen = hard to say; schwer zu verstehen = difficult to understand.** You must always do this when a word has more than one translation.

GOLDEN RULE: Don't take the first translation you see. Read through all the information first.

> I looked up *Ehefrau* and found *wife*, and then I made the plural *wifes*. Why doesn't my dictionary tell me that this isn't correct?

> It does tell you, but in the English-German half. The information on irregular forms and words is always there. So: **one wife – two wives.**

GOLDEN RULE: Look in the English-German half for help with irregular forms and words.

1 Which past?

Write the verbs in the correct past tense: the past simple *(went)*, the past progressive *(was/were going)* or the past perfect *(had gone)*.

When I *(1 arrive)* .... home at 6 o'clock, the children *(2 wait)* .... for me.

They *(3 already do)* .... their homework so we *(4 eat)* .... our dinner.

We *(5 watch)* .... a film on television when the phone *(6 ring)* .... It *(7 be)*

.... my husband. He *(8 stand)* .... in a cold garage in Yorkshire –

this is what he *(9 tell)* .... me. His car *(10 be)* .... in the garage because it *(11 break)*

.... down. It *(12 rain)* .... heavily at the time and he

(13 not want) .... to rent a car to drive home. In fact he *(14 already reserve)*

.... a hotel room before he *(15 phone)* .... me. The children

(16 not be) .... very happy about this news because they *(17 make)* .... a cake at school

for him and they *(18 look)* .... forward to giving it to him as a present. I *(19 be)*

.... happy that he *(20 not have)* .... an accident.

2 Complete the sentences.

Match the beginnings and the endings of these sentences and write the missing words in the boxes.

1 What's the difference *between*   ☐ adverts?

2 What's the purpose   ☐ risk than older people.

3 How much influence do adverts have   ☑ the words "silly" and "stupid"?

4 Cigarette producers spend millions   ☐ cigarettes should be allowed.

5 I first read about that computer company   ☐ adverts for cars because I can't drive.

6 I don't pay any attention   ☐ young people?

7 I don't think adverts   ☐ the local press.

8 Children and teenagers are more   ☐ advertising their products.

3 Expressing satisfaction and dissatisfaction

Number these expressions 1 to 6 from the most positive (1) to the most negative (6).

☐ have enough of   ☐ be quite satisfied with   ☐ be sick and tired of
☐ be not happy with   ☐ be very pleased with   ☐ be not very satisfied with

☐ Now listen to the conversation between a factory manager and one of his employees. The manager is new, and he wants to know what the employees think about the company and their work. Write down six sentences, using the expressions 1 to 6 above.

1 *They're very pleased with* ....

2 ....

3 ....

4 ....

5 ....

6 ....

4 Pronunciation

These words were all new in the reading text in Step 1. Underline the part of the word where the stress is, like this: *nasty*

1 nonsense	5 alcohol	9 purpose	13 influence
2 fluently	6 clients	10 provide	14 particular
3 tobacco	7 difference	11 psychologist	
4 products	8 original	12 subconscious	

Check your answers in the key.
⌨ Now listen to the text.

5 Remember the words!

Which word went with *shavers, peas, agency* and *public service* in the reading text in Step 1? Find the four words in the box and write them in.

1 .... shavers   3 .... agency

2 .... peas   4 .... public service

good	original	nasty	advertising
frozen	electric	important	
silly	successful	interesting	

All the other words can go with *adverts*.
Which are negative and which are positive?

+ ....

− ....

Step 2

1 What did they say?

These people on the street were asked about projects for a new town centre in their town. Report what they said, as in the example.

> I can't comment because I don't live in the town. **2**

> I've seen the plans for the centre.

> I like the new bus system. **5**

> I'll probably go shopping there more often. **3**

> We're looking forward to using the new sports centre. **6**

> I never go to the town centre. **1**

> **4**

1 *He said he never went to the town centre.*

2 ....

3 ....

4 ....

5 ....

6 ....

2 ☐ The new town centre – a report

Listen to the results of a questionnaire about the new town centre. Fill in the statistics.

A Do you want to have a traffic-free centre?   Yes .... %   No .... %

B How often do you go to the town centre?

    More than twice a week .... %   Once or twice a week .... %   Never .... %

C Will you go to the centre more often in the future?   Yes .... %   No .... %

D Have you been to any public meetings about the projects?   Yes .... %   No .... %

E Do you think the town centre projects are too expensive?   Yes .... %   No .... %

F Did you answer our first questionnaire?   Yes .... %   No .... %

Now report on the statistics like this: *76% said they wanted a traffic-free centre.*

1 24% said ....

2 51% said ....

3 8% said ....

4 32% said ....

5 11% said ....

6 89% said ....

7 97% said ....

8 53% said ....

3 What are the reactions?

Write the reactions to these sentences.

1 You should have bought the wine yesterday.
But I did buy it....

2 They should go to work by train.
But they do go by train....

3 He should drive more carefully.

  ....

4 They should have written to her yesterday.

  ....

5 You should have told him yesterday.

  ....

6 You should go to bed earlier.

  ....

7 She should have taken her camera yesterday.

  ....

8 He should have gone to the Book Fair yesterday.

  ....

4 Remember the words!

Which words are missing from these sentences?

1 The girls are afraid to walk home after dark. I can understand their *f*.............................. .

2 Companies can advertise their *p*.............. on TV.

3 An advertising agency makes adverts for its
  c.............................. .

4 It's too expensive for us. We can't *a*................ it.

5 Is that true? Is that really the *t*................?

6 He smokes a .....*p*.......................... after dinner.

7 What's the .....*p*.......................... of his visit? Why is he here?

8 When water is under 0° C, it's *f*...................... .

9 I can't wash my hair, there's no *s*...................... .

10 He's excellent at French. He speaks *f*................ .

11 She likes France, in *p*...................... the south.

12 This doesn't make sense, it's *n*...................... .

We used these words to read and talk about

.... in the press or on TV.

1 *When, where, which* or *who*?

Write *when, where, which* or *who* in the boxes and match the two halves of each sentence.

1 I think he's probably the man   *who*   5 I'm sure this is the house

2 We saw the place in Dallas   6 I saw him on the day

3 Have you read the books   7 I preferred the concert

4 I'm looking forward to the day   8 Those are the children

☐ she rents a room.   ☐ I can go back to work.   ☑ won all that money.   ☐ the President was shot.
☐ they told us to read.   ☐ he left for America.   ☐ used to play with us.   ☐ they played yesterday.

2 Talking about likes, dislikes and preferences

Mrs James answered a questionnaire
in the street about things she likes and
doesn't like.
What do you think she said? Complete A,
B and C in each box with these words:

cats	France	shoes
cinema	French	Spanish
coffee	meat	tea
don't wash	milk chocolate	theatre

She likes ...

A the south of ....

B English ....

C her ....

D ....

   ....

She dislikes ...

A old ....

B red ....

C people who ....

D ....

   ....

She prefers ...

A .... to ....

B .... to ....

C the .... to

   the ....

D ....

🔊 Listen to compare your answers with what Mrs James said. You'll hear one more thing that you can add on
the last line of each box.

Now listen again and number these expressions in the order you hear them. Number each group of expressions 1-4.

likes:
☐ I like
☐ I'm rather keen on
☐ I love
☐ I really love

dislikes:
☐ I can't stand
☐ I'm not very keen on
☐ I hate
☐ I don't like

preferences:
☐ I prefer
☐ I'd prefer to
☐ I'd rather
☐ I like ... more than

3 Pronunciation

These words were all in the reading text in Step 1. In each group of three there is one word in which the
underlined letters make a different sound. Which word is the different one?

(country)   course   fourteen

1	refus<u>ed</u>	attend<u>ed</u>	threaten<u>ed</u>
2	l<u>ea</u>st	r<u>ea</u>ding	thr<u>ea</u>tened
3	p<u>u</u>pils	str<u>u</u>ggle	instr<u>u</u>ctions
4	tr<u>a</u>vel	h<u>a</u>ndle	ash<u>a</u>med
5	ser<u>iou</u>s	pr<u>ou</u>d	obv<u>iou</u>sly

6	coll<u>e</u>ge	sh<u>e</u>lf	<u>e</u>ffort
7	d<u>ai</u>ly	afr<u>ai</u>d	s<u>ai</u>d
8	cl<u>a</u>sses	f<u>a</u>ce	ash<u>a</u>med
9	refu<u>s</u>ed	<u>s</u>tudents	adult<u>s</u>
10	<u>s</u>igns	<u>s</u>kill	<u>s</u>imple

Check your answers in the key.
🔊 Now listen to the text.

4 Learn some new words!

Here you can see some things that you can find in other parts of this book. What are they? Match items 1 - 12 with the words below.

1  Animals and us

2   3

6 The amount of time the owner has is important. Some pets need more attention than others – dogs, for example, often need a lot of care and daily exercise. They shouldn't be left inside the whole day, either. Cats, small birds and fish, on the other hand, are usually easy pets to look after and can be left alone during the day.

7   8   9   10

4 **network** ENGLISH PLUS 1

11 **Langenscheidt-Longman** ENGLISH LANGUAGE TEACHING

5   John Potts and Gaynor Ramsey

12   1993

- ☐ authors
- ☐ book title
- ☐ illustration
- ☐ letter
- ☐ paragraph
- ☐ photograph
- ☐ phrase
- ☐ publisher
- ☐ sentence
- ☐ unit title
- ☐ word
- ☐ year of publication

Step 2

1 The party

Who and what was there at the party? Complete the sentences.

1 There were four women at the party, two *of whom were wearing glasses.*

2 There were three plants on the table, one *of which had flowers.*

3 There were five men at the party, two ....

4 There were four children at the party, three ....

5 There were six bottles on the table, two ....

6 There were two cats in the room, one ....

7 There were three girls at the party, one ....

8 There were three books near the table, one ....

2 Who, whose or which?

Make these sentences longer by using the words in *italics* and two more words – *who, whose* or *which*.

1 Rob has got a daughter. (*is / for / works / Roberta / name / IBM*)

Rob, *who works for IBM,* has got a daughter *whose name is Roberta.*

2 The course will be given by Mrs Dubiel. (*next / French / begins / husband / is / week*)

The course, ..., will be given by Mrs Dubiel, ...

3 This book used to belong to my grandmother. (*collected / valuable / is / of / books / poems / now / very*)

This book, ..., used to belong to my grandmother,

....

4 Mr and Mrs Brown have just bought a new house. (*here / year / to / America / is / went / son / very / last / near*)

Mr and Mrs Brown, ..., have just bought a new house,

....

3 ☐ Arranging to meet

John and Pam are on the phone. John answered her "find a partner" ad in the newspaper. They have never met before, but they're going to meet soon. Listen and write down three more things in each of these boxes:

Both of them ...	**Neither of them ...**	**Only one of them ...**
— *think it's a good idea*	— *has answered an ad like this before*	— *lives in the city centre*

4 Remember the words!

Find the words for things you can read. The letters in the box will help you.

1 Which two are published daily, weekly, monthly etc.

a newspaper   *a* ....

2 Which two are about real places and real people?

a ....   *a* ....

3 Which two can you look up information in?

a ....   *an* ....

4 Which one is all dialogue? *a* ....

5 Which one is a story? *a* ....

6 You can read a book of short ....

or a book of ....

```
a a l s t
a b g h i o p r y
a c d i i n o r t y
a a e g i m n z
a e s n p p r e w
e l n o v
a l p y
e m o p s
e i o r s s t
a e l r t v   b k o o
```

Learners' letters 4

Two different Englishes!

Dear English Expert,
Sometimes we hear some American speakers on the cassettes at school – and I can usually understand them well. But last week my neighbour had some visitors from America and so I decided to try to speak English to them! I was happy that they understood me – but I must say it wasn't always easy to understand them. Can these two 'Englishes' be so different? Which English should I learn and speak? Which is better?

Yours sincerely,
Kirstin, Leipzig

Dear Kirstin,
There are some differences between American and British English, but not very many. It doesn't really matter which English you learn - neither is better than the other. The important thing is that you can understand other people. By the way, you get a gold star for 'trying' to speak English to them - well done! Here are a few differences that might interest you. In the vocabulary section you can match the American and the British words yourself.

VOCABULARY
US English

1 apartment	10 gas
2 bill	11 hi
3 cab	12 movie
4 check	13 pants
5 elevator	14 quarter after
6 fall	15 round trip
7 first floor	16 store
8 freeway	17 subway
9 french fries	18 vacation

GB English

- [ ] autumn
- [ ] bank note
- [ ] bill
- [ ] chips
- [ ] film
- [ ] flat
- [ ] ground floor
- [ ] hello
- [ ] holiday
- [ ] lift
- [ ] motorway
- [ ] petrol
- [ ] quarter past
- [ ] return (ticket)
- [ ] shop
- [ ] taxi
- [ ] trousers
- [ ] underground (train)

GRAMMAR
US: <u>Did you see</u> that film yet?
GB: <u>Have you seen</u> that film yet?

US: <u>Do you have</u> a car?
GB: <u>Have you got</u> a car?

SPELLING

US English	GB English
me<u>ter</u>	me<u>tre</u>
thea<u>ter</u>	thea<u>tre</u>
col<u>or</u>	col<u>our</u>
favo<u>rite</u>	favo<u>urite</u>
trave<u>led</u>	trave<u>lled</u>
cance<u>led</u>	cance<u>lled</u>

And then there's the accent. You know, I've got an English friend in Switzerland - and she went to see an American film. Later she said that she had read the German subtitles[1] for the first twenty minutes, because she couldn't understand the English! Kirstin, you aren't alone.

All the best,
Your English Expert

⊙━ page 108

[1] subtitle = Untertitel

Test yourself 4

1 What did they say?

A few months ago there was an advertisement on television for a rather sexy book. People either liked the advert very much or hated it. A reporter asked some people on the street what they thought about it. What did they say?

> I haven't seen the advert.

> I'll certainly never buy that book! I've got better things to do with my time.

> I work in advertising myself. I think it is a well-made ad.

> I like the way the lady speaks.

1 The little girl said _she liked the way the lady spoke_ ....

2 The young man said ....

   He also said ....

3 The old lady said ....

   She also said ....

4 The policeman said ....

2 But he did do it!

Fill in the missing words.

1 Why ...._didn't he do_........ his homework?   But he did do it!

2 Why doesn't she eat meat?   But she _does eat_ .... meat.

3 Why don't they work in the evenings?   But they .... in the evenings.

4 Why .... by bus?   But she does go by bus.

5 Why didn't they phone the police?   But they .... them.

6 Why .... at home?   But they do eat at home.

3 Write the sentences.

Choose two verbs and another word (or two other words!) to write these sentences. Use all of the words once only.

Here are the verbs you can choose from: *be, come, cost, go, have got, live, o~~pen~~, s~~ell~~ speak, stay, want, work*
Here are the other words: *of which, of whom, where, w~~hich~~, who, whose*

1 The new shop, on Sundays too, very good bread.
   The new shop, which opens on Sundays too, sells very good bread. ....

2 The Albany Hotel, our friends always, a new bar.
   ....

3 Bob, next door, for IBM.
   ....

4 The students, three very well, to take the examination.
   ....

5 Their teacher, English excellent, to England once a year.
   ....

6 These books, some from India, a lot.
   ....

4 Which wine?

Use each of these words once to complete this dialogue: *any, anyone, both, either, neither, some, something.*

A: Would you like .... to drink?

B: Yes, please.

A: Would you like .... wine?

B: Yes, please. What have you got? .... dry wine will do.

A: There's this Swiss red, and this French white. .... are very good.

B: But they aren't sweet, are they?

A: No, ... is sweet.

B: Which would be best with this meal?

A: You could choose .... of them.

B: Do you know these wines?

A: Yes. Ask .... who works here. We all know and like them!

5 ⌨ Listening

Last month Amanda's mother talked to Amanda about her future plans. Here's a letter from Amanda's mother to a good friend. Listen to their conversation and complete the letter. Listen as often as you like.

It all happened about a month ago. I went into the dining room and saw Amanda there. She looked very unhappy. Tom was nowhere to be seen. I asked her where Tom was. She said _____. *Then I asked why. She said* _____ *go. She said* _____ *because* _____ *him. She said* _____ *much but* _____ *him. She said* _____ *happier if they* _____. *I asked her what her plans were. She said* _____ *America. She said* _____ *and* _____ *possible. She said* _____ *jobs. She told me not to worry. She said* _____ *. I hope she does. And I hope this was the right decision for both of them, I really do.*

6 ⌨ Dialogue

Listen to the dialogue as many times as you want and fill in the second part. A woman is interviewing a man who didn't or couldn't learn to read when he was a child.

What was life like for you when you couldn't read?

....
....
....
....
....

How did you feel?

....
....
....
....
....

What were you afraid of?

....
....
....
....

And how do you feel now?

....
....

Yes, I'm sure it was.

Dictionary skills 4

Getting to know more about your dictionary

◆ On the first *Getting to know your dictionary* page you saw a list of sections from a bilingual dictionary. Here's that list again, in English only. If you've forgotten what any of these words mean, look back at page 73 for help.

1 Guide to the use of the dictionary
2 Explanation of the phonetic symbols
3 Important proper names
4 Abbreviations (used in the dictionary)
5 American spelling
6 American pronunciation
7 Numbers

8 The English alphabet
9 English currency
10 Weights and measures
11 Symbols
12 Irregular verbs
13 British and American abbreviations

Here are some short excerpts[1] from *Langenscheidts Taschenwörterbuch Englisch*. Where do you think these excerpts come from? Match them to the sections above.

a

[aɪ] my [maɪ], night [naɪt]
[aʊ] now [naʊ], about [ə'baʊt]
[əʊ] home [həʊm], know [nəʊ]

etwa wie in *Mai, Neid*
etwa wie in *blau, Couch*
von [ə] zu [ʊ] gleiten

j

➳ Luftfahrt, *aviation.*
✉ Postwesen, *postal affairs.*
♪ Musik, *musical term.*
△ Architektur, *architecture.*
⚡ Elektrotechnik, *electrical engineering*; Elektronik, *electronics.*

b

1 inch (in.) = 2,54 cm
1 foot (ft) = 12 inches = 30,48 cm
1 yard (yd) = 3 feet = 91,44 cm

f

1,000,000 a *od.* one million *eine Million*
2,000,000 two million *zwei Millionen*
1,000,000,000 a *od.* one billion *eine Milliarde*

k

pres present, Präsens, Gegenwart.
pres p present participle, Partizip Präsens, Mittelwort der Gegenwart.

c

Pall Mall [ˌpæl'mæl] Straße in London.
Palm Beach [ˌpɑːm'biːtʃ] Seebad in Florida (USA).
Pam·e·la ['pæmələ] Pamela f.

g

2. **...re** wird zu **...er**, z. B. center = centre, theater = theatre, ...cre, z. B. massacre; ausgenommen sind die Wörter auf

h

tell – told – told
think – thought – thought
throw – threw – thrown

1 l

1.2 Der in den Stichwörtern auf Mitte stehende Punkt bzw. der Betonungsakzent zeigt an, wo das englische Wort getrennt werden kann:
cul·ti·vate ..., ˌcul·ti'va·tion

d

b. born geb., geboren.
BA Bachelor of Arts Bakkalaureus *m* der Philosophie; **British Airways** (*britische Luftverkehrsgesellschaft*).
B & B bed and breakfast Übernachtung *f* mit Frühstück.

i

£5 (five pounds)
£10 (ten pounds)

e

1. aː wird zu (gedehntem) æ(ː) in Wörtern wie *ask* [æ(ː)sk = ɑːsk], *castle* ['kæ(ː)sl = 'kɑːsl], *grass* [græ(ː)s = grɑːs], *past* [pæ(ː)st = pɑːst] etc.; ebenso in *branch* [bræ(ː)ntʃ = brɑːntʃ], *can't* [kæ(ː)nt = kɑːnt], *dance* [dæ(ː)ns = dɑːns] etc.

m

a [eɪ], b [biː], c [siː], d [diː], m [em], n [en], o [əʊ], p [piː], x [eks], y [waɪ], z [zed].

◆ Where would you look if you wanted to find these things in the dictionary? Write the number of one of the sections above in the box.

☐ He was born in Hamilton, NZ.

☐ I saw something about Purcell on television yesterday evening.

☐ Write the amount, £1.50, on the cheque in words.

☐ He bought her a 2 lb box of sweets for her birthday.

☐ You want to know the past of the verb to *freeze*.

⚷ page 108

---

[1] excerpt = Auszug

Unit 1 / Step 1

1 2 Did he write to her yesterday? 3 Is he going to write to her tomorrow? 4 He isn't going to write to her tomorrow. 5 He hasn't written to her yet. 6 He often eats in the pizzeria. 7 Has he ever eaten in the pizzeria? 8 Did he eat in the pizzeria last week? 9 He ate in the pizzeria last week. 10 He was eating in the pizzeria when the storm began. 11 He enjoys eating in the pizzeria.

2 1 **his**tory, 2 engin**eer**, 3 **re**latives, 4 **di**stance, 5 **nat**ural, 6 **int**eresting, 7 **nat**ional, 8 uni**vers**ity, 9 ex**per**ience, 10 **pho**tographs

3 1 in a restaurant, 2 at an airport, 3 at a railway station, 4 in a travel agent's

It would be a good idea to: 2	You ought to: 3, 4
I think you should: 1, 3, 4	Why don't you: 1
If I were you: 3, 4	My advice is: 2

4 2 read / about, 3 found / as, 4 drove / through, 5 spent / on, 6 is / at, 7 went / to, 8 are learning / at, 9 settle down, 10 reminded / of

5

1	s	u	n	s	h	i	n	e
2		w	e	s	t			
3	c	r	o	w	d	e	d	

			z				
4		e	a	s	t		
5 p	h	o	t	o	g	r	a	p	h
6		c	l	o	t	h	e	s
7	u	n	h	a	p	p	y
8 e	n	g	i	n	e	e	r
9		d	o	c	t	o	r

Unit 1 / Step 2

1 2 does he live / lives / doesn't live, 3 was she writing / was writing / wasn't writing, 4 is he making / 's/is making / isn't making, 5 Has she spoken / 's/has spoken / hasn't spoken, 6 had he drunk / 'd/had drunk / hadn't drunk, 7 will you be / 'll/will be / won't be, 8 were you / was / wasn't

2 (The missing word is in *italics*.) 1 Where *does* Margaret live? 2 When *was* Margaret born? 3 How many children *has* Margaret got? 4 Where *did* Margaret go to school? 5 How long *was* she a journalist for Radio South? 6 How long *has* she been a journalist for Channel Seven?

3 yes / some of them / yes / no / no.
2 He has read the letters. 3 He has signed some of the letters. 4 He has seen the plans for next year. 5 He hasn't spoken to the boss about the plans. 6 He hasn't given the computer books to Anna.

4 article, book, magazine, newspaper
Australia, Canada, Ireland, New Zealand (English speaking)

Germany, Italy, Japan, Spain
emigrate, go abroad, leave, move
factory, office, school, shop
beautiful, exciting, great, wonderful
boy, gentleman, guy, relative

Unit 2 / Step 1

1 1 He was smoking a cigarette. 1 He's/is swimming. 2 They were sitting on the table. 2 They're/are sleeping. 3 He was talking to a woman. 3 He's/is driving. 4 They were dancing. 4 They're/are working in the garden. 5 She was cutting a cake. 5 She's/is writing a letter. 6 She was drinking champagne/wine. 6 She's/is riding a horse.

2 a the weather, b we stayed at home, c the rain.

1 the long hours. 2 nobody wants to live here now. 3 the beautiful weather and the football match on television.

3 first box: village, cottage, image
second box: farm, grassy
third box: narrow, programme, antiques, sad, angry

4
a **railway** line	a **sad** story
a **farm** worker	a **typical** image
a **pretty** village	a **wide** bridge
ordinary people	**grassy** fields
unfriendly people	an **antique** shop
unspoilt countryside	a **locked** door
beautiful cottages	a **narrow** stream

g	m	o	s	r	v	s	l	a	w	s	v	f
d	s	c	o	b	e	a	u	t	i	f	u	l
e	a	j	r	d	b	d	n	l	d	f	r	n
f	v	h	d	p	i	r	f	w	e	v	a	y
a	n	t	i	q	u	e	r	n	o	q	i	a
r	s	u	n	s	p	o	i	l	t	t	l	w
m	g	r	a	s	s	y	e	t	y	j	w	k
b	n	a	r	r	o	w	n	c	p	e	a	g
i	r	f	y	q	n	o	d	k	i	v	y	z
l	g	d	i	k	j	r	l	o	c	k	e	d
u	a	p	r	e	t	t	y	h	a	p	s	u
p	l	e	n	o	x	c	n	r	l	y	t	h

Unit 2 / Step 2

1 1 She's been playing tennis. 2 He's been running. 3 They've been painting (their bathroom). 4 She's been washing her car. 5 He's been cleaning (the living room). 6 They've been swimming. 7 He's been smoking (a cigarette). 8 They've been typing (letters).

2 1 I've / have known / since, 2 They've / have been living (have lived) / for, 3 She's / has been learning / since, 4 They've / have been married / since, 5 He's / has been driving (has driven) / since, 6 She's / has been waiting / for, 7 We've / have been trying / for, 8 I've / have had / for

3 1 's been a writer/'s been writing books, 2 's been writing children's books, 3 's been working for MacLong, 4 's been married, 5 's been living in London, 6 's been in the (book)shops, 7 's been visiting bookshops/'s been signing books, 8 's been teaching (painting to) children in Kensington. (Die Langform *has* ist statt *'s* überall möglich.)

4 1 wallet, 2 bike, 3 recently, 4 immigrants, 5 relatives, 6 stream, 7 neighbours, 8 married, 9 post office, 10 theatre

Test yourself 1

1 1 Because he's/is going to Bristol. 2 Because he always travels by train. 3 Because he was having a bath. 4 Because she had already left. 5 No, he's/has only been sitting in the train (there) for fifteen minutes. 6 No, he only started it ten minutes ago. 7 No, he's/has already posted them. 8 Because they're going to make plans for next year. 9 No, he'll/will still be at the meeting. 10 No, he's staying / he's going to stay in Bristol until tomorrow.

2 a) Where is Tom going? b) How is he travelling to Bristol? c) What was he doing when his wife left home this morning? d) How long has he been sitting in the train? e) When/How long ago did he start reading his newspaper? f) Has he (already) posted his letters? g) Will he still be at the meeting at four o'clock / in Bristol this evening/...? h) How long is he staying / is he going to stay in Bristol?

3 1 How long have you known your teacher? (been) 2 I've known her for four years. (since) 3 How long has she been teaching English? (have) 4 I think she's been teaching English since 1990. (for) 5 How long have you been learning English? (since) 6 I've been learning for three years. (am)

4 1 She's been working / has worked / has had an interesting job in Perth for ten years. 2 She's been living in Australia since she was ten. 3 She's been married since last Christmas. 4 She's been looking for a new house for a month.

5 See tapescript on page 110.

Dictionary skills 1

Numbers in the column on the right: 7, 11, 4, 10, 8, 12, 6, 13, 3, 9, 1, 5, 2

Unit 3 / Step 1

1 2 What would you buy if you were rich? / who isn't rich. 3 What would you learn if you could go to night school? / who can't go to night school. 4 How would you travel on holiday if you couldn't drive? / who can drive. 5 Which film would you rent if you had a video? / who hasn't got a video. 6 Where would you live if you wanted to emigrate? / who doesn't want to emigrate.

2 1 **reg**ularly, 2 **pop**ular, 3 **gen**erally, 4 disa**bil**ity, 5 es**pec**ially, 6 **pri**vate, 7 **for**tunately, 8 **ob**viously, 9 **com**fortable, 10 **qual**ity, 11 a**pprec**iate, 12 oppor**tun**ity

3 1 You need a ball that is about as big as an orange. 2 You have to try to hit the ball so that the other player

can't hit it back. 3 The players are allowed to kick the ball, but they aren't allowed to handle it. 4 You need two or four players for this sport. 5 The players wear special boots so that they can kick the ball better. 6 The point of the game is to get more goals than the others. 7 You use a piece of equipment to hit the ball. 8 You don't need any other equipment, only a ball.

Tennis: 1, 2, 4, 7. Football: 3, 5, 6, 8.

4 2 start the ideal sport, 3 remember the golden rules, 4 play on public courts, 5 pay the extra cost, 6 join a private club, 7 improve your all-round fitness, 8 discover the local countryside, 9 buy good-quality shoes

Unit 3 / Step 2

1 2 What would she have studied if she had gone to university? 3 What would he/she have said if he had phoned her? 4 Where would you have gone if you had had a holiday last year? 5 What would he have asked if he had written to them? 6 When would you have arrived there if you had been late for your train?

2 Good pictures: 2, 3, 5. Not good: 1, 4. 1 hadn't got up / would have eaten/had 2 hadn't missed / wouldn't have seen/met 3 had taken / would have arrived at the office/reached the office 4 hadn't waited / wouldn't have seen/heard 5 hadn't been/arrived so late / wouldn't have lost 6 had worked/been / wouldn't have read/seen

3 tea: Secondly, Finally, First of all, Then photocopy: Then, Secondly, Finally, First of all phone call: Then, Finally, Secondly, First of all Obviously, Fortunately, In fact

4 **sports:** swimming, climbing, horse riding/riding a horse, skiing, cycling/riding a bike, playing tennis **non-sports:** cooking, dancing, reading, taking photos, watching TV, listening to music

Unit 4 / Step 1

1 be, was/were, been; break, broke, broken; do, did, done; drink, drank, drunk; drive, drove, driven; forget, forgot, forgotten; give, gave, given; go, went, gone; put, put, put; see, saw, seen; send, sent, sent; win, won, won; write, wrote, written

2 5, 3, 2, 1, 6, 4

3 1 however, 2 should, 3 think, 4 whether, 5 example, 6 whole, 7 advice, 8 healthy

4 1 for, 2 of, 3 of, 4 by, 5 after, 6 of, 7 as, 8 of, 9 of, 10 on, 11 to, 12 of, 13 about, 14 of

5 1 thing, 2 day, 3 furniture, 4 presents, 5 guide, 6 knives, 7 choice, 8 advice, 9 idea, 10 objects, 11 exercise, 12 sense

Unit 4 / Step 2

1 1 Paul found it rather difficult to remember people's names. 2 He decided to make a plan of the office building. 3 His new boss told him to call him Rob. 4 Paul wants to meet Anna's colleagues. 5 Anna could

perhaps help him to learn about the company.
6 Someone offered to show him how to use the fax.
7 Paul's boss has already invited him to have a drink
with him. 8 Paul thinks that this is a good place to work
for at least two years.

2   are written, are given, wasn't finished, was broken,
was driven, was taken, was examined, was brought, was
told, have already been given

3   1 have been built/constructed, 2 have been cut
down, 3 has been built/constructed, 4 has been
replaced, 5 has been taken away, 6 has been closed,
7 has been opened, 8 has been moved, 9 have been
demolished, 10 have been widened

4   1 camel, 2 lion, 3 rhinoceros, 4 zebra, 5 bear,
6 giraffe, 7 monkey, 8 tiger, 9 hippopotamus,
10 elephant, 11 parrot, 12 snake

Test yourself 2

1   What would you do if
2 you saw a ghost? I'd shout at it. 3 you lost your
passport? I'd go to the police station. 4 you won a lot of
money? I'd buy a flat.

What would you have done if
6 you'd seen a ghost? I'd have shouted at it. 7 you'd lost
your passport? I'd have gone to the police station.
8 you'd won a lot of money? I'd have bought a flat.

2   1b I'd take up table tennis. 2a I'll do a computer
course. 3c I'd have bought a CD player. 4a I'll do it (the
work). 5b I'd stay with friends. 6c I'd have said "I don't
agree!"

3   2 had, 3 will, 4 has, 5 is, 6 have, 7 are, 8 do not,
9 am, 10 would, 11 had, 12 did not

4   1 are fed once a day. 2 have been moved from the old
zoo. 3 shouldn't be allowed in the zoo. 4 was opened
last week. 5 were bought before the zoo moved.
6 is needed every day.

5   1 were stolen. 2 was broken. 3 was taken. 4 were
drunk. 5 has been found. 6 hasn't been seen.

6   See tapescript on page 112.

Dictionary skills 2

	English-German	German-English
The English word	..✔..	..✔..
The German word	..✔..	..✔..
The English pronunciation	..✔..	......
The stress of the English word	..✔..	......
Where you can divide the English word	..✔..	......
The part of speech of the word	..✔..	..✔..

Question 1: no
Question 2: look up the English ... (we hope)

Unit 5 / Step 1

1   1 to go, 2 to buy, 3 driving, 4 to do, 5 being (US: to
be), 6 living, 7 coming, 8 to change, 9 smoking (US: to
smoke), 10 to remember

2   6, 4, 7, 1, 2, 5, 3

3   5, 2, 1, 3, 6, 4
friendly: 1, 4, 6; unfriendly: 2, 3, 5

4   1 applied, 2 details, 3 advertisement, 4 failed,
5 boring, 6 interview, 7 calm, 8 pass, 9 unemployed,
10 qualifications, 11 knowledge

Missing word: *performance*

Unit 5 / Step 2

1   2 He's always sitting with his feet on the desk. 3 He's
always reading the newspaper. 4 He's always phoning
his girlfriend. 5 He's always smoking. 6 He's always
drinking coffee. 7 He's always giving orders.

2   2 She's good at typing. 3 She likes writing reports.
4 She enjoys using a computer. 5 She doesn't like
phoning companies abroad. 6 She's good at speaking
French. 7 She's bad at speaking other languages.
8 She hates working alone.

3   2 living / to live; 3 to take / taking; 4 to travel /
travelling; 5 driving / to drive; 6 saving / to save;
7 to leave / leaving; 8 riding / to ride

4   1 well-paid, 2 different, 3 employee, 4 ordinary,
5 calm, 6 lend, 7 female, 8 weak

Unit 6 / Step 1

1   1 must, 2 needn't, 3 mustn't, 4 might, 5 should,
6 shouldn't, 7 can't, 8 Can/May I help you?
9 Can/Will/Could you help me?

2   1 of, 2 into, 3 for, 4 over, 5 about

3   4, 1, 5, 6, 2, 3

1 Well, thank you. How did you know it's my birthday
today? 2 Bye. It was nice talking to you. See you again
soon, I hope. 3 Cheers. Here's to our plans for next year.
4 Yes, of course. She'll be sorry, she didn't see you. Bye.
5 Oh, fine thanks. I feel much better about my job now.
6 Yes, you too. Bye.

4   2 s, s; 3 s, z, z; 4 s, s, s; 5 z, z; 6 z; 7 z, z; 8 s; 9 s; 10 s;
11 s, s

5   6, 10, 1, 11, 4, 12, 5, 7, 3, 2, 9, 8

Unit 6 / Step 2

1   2 He should have bought some wine, but he didn't
because he didn't have enough money. 3 He should
have cleaned the car, but he didn't because he didn't
have enough time. 4 He should have done the washing,
but he didn't because the washing machine was broken.
5 He should have taken the books back to the library, but
he didn't because the library was closed. 6 He should
have written to Aunt Mary, but he didn't because he
couldn't find her letter.

2   1 shouldn't have gone out / could have caught /
should have taken; 2 should have come / shouldn't have
stayed / could have found; 3 could have broken /
shouldn't have made / should have been; 4 shouldn't
have tried / should have chosen / could have phoned

3 Part A: 1 faster than he does. 2 speak French better than she can. 3 drive a car but he can't. 4 more experience than she has. 5 more friendly than him. 6 older than her. 7 to earn more money than she does. 8 better examination results than he did. 9 about the computer faster than she did. 10 a better telephone voice than he has.

Part B: 1 T, 2 T, 3 F, 4 F, 5 T, 6 F, 7 T, 8 T, 9 F, 10 T

4 1 definitely, 2 frequently, 3 luckily, 4 suddenly, 5 obviously, 6 finally. Different: luckily / lucky – the *y* changes to *i*, then add *ly*.

The different one: luckily – *y* changes to *i*, then add *-ly*

Learners' letters 3

The last sentence should read: And don't forget, if you write a letter to a friend and there are some spelling mistakes in it, he or she will probably understand anyway!

Test yourself 3

1 1 I'm living / I live; 2 to learn / learning; 3 she's working / she's (she has) been working; 4 to teach / teaching; 5 to go / going; 6 to write / writing; 7 doing / do; 8 finding / to find; 9 get / getting

2 1 always comes, 2 are always taking, 3 always phone, 4 is always talking, 5 is always parking

3 2 could have, 3 could have, 4 shouldn't have, 5 shouldn't have, 6 could have, 8 shouldn't have, 9 could have, 10 shouldn't have

The pairs: 1+7, 8+2, 5+3, 4+9, 10+6

4 2 Paul ate even more than Peter did. 3 Tom can dance even better than Bob can. 4 Their children have been even noisier than our children have. 5 Anna is even happier than Jane is. 6 Tanya's (has) got even more responsibility at work than Martin has. 7 Swiss shoes are even more expensive than German shoes are. 8 Anna works even harder than Liz does.

5 1 He's afraid of losing his job. 2 She's looking forward to seeing *Cats*. 3 He gave up smoking ten years ago. 4 She enjoys/is enjoying travelling abroad. 5 He was good at speaking French. 6 She hates working (US: to work) in the garden. 7 He's thinking about buying a new car. 8 She's bad at using the computer.

6 See tapescript on page 113, 114.

Unit 7 / Step 1

1 1 arrived, 2 were waiting, 3 had already done, 4 ate, 5 were watching, 6 rang, 7 was, 8 was standing, 9 told, 10 was, 11 had broken, 12 was raining, 13 didn't want, 14 had already reserved, 15 phoned, 16 weren't, 17 had made, 18 were looking, 19 was, 20 hadn't had

2 2 of adverts? 3 on young people? 4 on advertising their products. 5 in the local press. 6 to adverts for cars because I can't drive. 7 for cigarettes should be allowed. 8 at risk than older people.

3 5, 2, 6; 4, 1, 3

1 They're very pleased with the working hours. 2 They're quite satisfied with the holidays they get. 3 Some of them aren't very satisfied with the new rules about Sunday work. 4 Some of them aren't happy with the no smoking rule. 5 Most of them have had enough of all the noise outside the factory. 6 They're sick and tired of the coffee.

4 1 **non**sense, 2 **flu**ently, 3 to**bacc**o, 4 **pro**ducts, 5 **al**cohol, 6 **cli**ents, 7 **diff**erence, 8 o**rig**inal, 9 **pur**pose, 10 pro**vide**, 11 psy**chol**ogist, 12 sub**con**scious, 13 **in**fluence, 14 par**tic**ular

5 1 electric, 2 frozen, 3 advertising, 4 important.

Positive: good, original, successful, interesting.
Negative: silly, nasty

Unit 7 / Step 2

1 2 She said she couldn't comment because she didn't live in the town. 3 She said she would probably go shopping there more often. 4 She said she had seen the plans for the centre. 5 He said he liked the new bus system. 6 They said they were looking forward to using the new sports centre.

2 A 76/24, B 41/51/8, C 68/32, D 11/89, E 97/3, F 47/53

1 ... they didn't want a traffic-free centre. 2 ... they went to the town centre once or twice a week. 3 ... they never went to the town centre. 4 ... they wouldn't go to the centre more often in the future. 5 ... they had been to a/some public meeting(s) about the projects. 6 ... they hadn't been to any public meetings about the projects. 7 ... they thought the projects were too expensive. 8 ... they hadn't answered the first questionnaire.

3 3 But he does drive carefully. 4 But they did write to her. 5 But I did tell him. 6 But I do go to bed early. 7 But she did take her camera. 8 But he did go to the Book Fair.

4 1 fears, 2 products, 3 clients, 4 afford, 5 truth, 6 pipe, 7 purpose/point, 8 frozen, 9 shampoo, 10 fluently, 11 particular, 12 nonsense

Missing word: *advertisements*

Unit 8 / Step 1

1 2 where the President was shot. 3 which they told us to read. 4 when I can go back to work. 5 where she rents a room. 6 when he left for America. 7 which they played yesterday. 8 who used to play with us.

2 She likes – A: the south of France, B: English milk chocolate, C: her cats, D: windy days. She dislikes – A: old shoes, B: red meat, C: people who don't wash, D: smoke. She prefers – A: tea to coffee, B: French to Spanish, C: the theatre to the cinema, D: white wine to water

likes: 2, 4, 1, 3; dislikes: 3, 2, 4, 1; preferences: 1, 3, 4, 2

3 1 attended, 2 threatened, 3 pupils, 4 ashamed, 5 proud, 6 college, 7 said, 8 classes, 9 adults, 10 signs

4 1 unit title, 2 illustration, 3 photograph, 4 book title, 5 authors, 6 sentence, 7 paragraph, 8 phrase, 9 letter, 10 word, 11 publisher, 12 year of publication

Unit 8 / Step 2

1 3 two of whom had moustaches. 4 three of whom were girls. 5 two of which were empty. 6 one of which was sleeping/sitting on the piano. 7 one of whom had long hair. 8 one of which was open.

2 2 The course, which begins next week, will be given by Mrs Dubiel, whose husband is French. 3 This book, which is very valuable now, used to belong to my grandmother, who collected books of poems. 4 Mr and Mrs Brown, whose son went to America last year, have just bought a new house, which is very near here.

3 Both of them: are 45, work in a bank, enjoy going to the cinema and the theatre. Neither of them: smokes, has got (any) children, is busy this weekend/at the weekend. Only one of them: has got a car, has been married (before), plays tennis.

4 1 a magazine; 2 a travel book / a biography; 3 a dictionary / an atlas; 4 a play; 5 a novel; 6 stories / poems

Learners' letters 4

Vocabulary: 1 flat, 2 bank note, 3 taxi, 4 bill, 5 lift, 6 autumn, 7 ground floor, 8 motorway, 9 chips, 10 petrol, 11 hello, 12 film, 13 trousers, 14 quarter past, 15 return, 16 shop, 17 underground, 18 holiday

Test yourself 4

1 2 he worked in advertising himself / he thought it was a well-made ad. 3 she would certainly never buy that book / she'd got better things to do with her time. 4 he hadn't seen the advert.

2 3 do work, 4 doesn't she go, 5 did phone, 6 don't they eat

3 2 The Albany Hotel, where our friends always stay, has got a new bar. 3 Bob, who lives next door, works for IBM. 4 The students, three of whom speak very well, want to take the examination. 5 Their teacher, whose English is excellent, goes to England once a year. 6 These books, some of which come from India, cost a lot.

4 something, some, any, both, neither, either, anyone

5 It all happened about a month ago. I went into the dining room and saw Amanda there. She looked very unhappy. Tom was nowhere to be seen. I asked her where Tom was. She said he'd (had) gone. Then I asked why. She said she'd (had) told him to go. She said she couldn't marry him because she didn't love him. She said she'd (had) always liked him very much but she knew she couldn't marry him. She said she thought they would both be happier if they didn't get married. I asked her what her plans were. She said she was looking for a job in America. She said she wanted to move away and she would leave as soon as possible. She said she'd (had) already applied for two jobs. She told me not to

worry. She said she knew what she was doing. I hope she does. And I hope this was the right decision for both of them, I really do.

6 See tapescript on page 115.

Dictionary skills 4

2a, 10b, 3c, 13d, 6e, 7f, 5g, 12h, 9i, 4k, 11j, 1l, 8m

13 (New Zealand), 3 (an English composer), 9 (one pound fifty pence), 10 (lb = pound), 12 (froze)

Unit 1 / Step 1: Exercise 3 (page 64)

1
- I must say this really isn't very good. I hope it's alright, I don't want to be ill this evening.
- Why don't you complain about it? After all, you're paying for it.
- Yes, I know. But perhaps it's just me. Perhaps I just don't like it, or something.
- Well, I think you should call the manager now, and tell him. It's too late to tell him when you've eaten it all!
- Yes, you're right there. Excuse me, please. Could I speak to the manager for a moment.

2
- I know, it's late, I'm sorry, but I can't do anything about it. Don't you think it would be a good idea just to sit down somewhere and wait?
- But I don't want to wait. I want to go. And I want to go now.
- Madam, if a plane's got a technical problem nobody goes anywhere. So my advice to you is to go and buy yourself a newspaper and have a nice drink in the restaurant.
- Umph.

3
- Well, the only one that gets you there in time for lunch is this one. It leaves London very early in the morning. It's an Intercity, of course.
- But I don't live in London. I can't get to London early enough for that one.
- Yes, I see. Well, if I were you, I'd stay in a hotel the night before. There's a small hotel very near here that's not too expensive. You can be right here on the platform in five minutes!
- And can I buy a ticket then?
- You can, but if you want my advice I think you ought to buy it now. You might not have very much time on that morning. I also think you should make a seat reservation. A lot of people travel on that early Intercity.

4
- And what time do I have to be there?
- You ought to be there an hour before, so that means about three o'clock.
- I see. Is there a place to park my car out at the airport?
- Yes, but if I were you, I'd take a taxi. It's cheaper in the end.
- Oh. And the hotel is booked?
- Yes, everything's fine with the hotel. That's no problem. And if you want a car when you arrive there ..., it's too late to book it from here so I think you should go to the car hire desk when you arrive at the airport there. I'll send them a fax, and tell them you're coming.
- Oh, fine. Oh, thanks very much. Goodbye.
- Bye. Have a nice trip.

Unit 1 / Step 2: Exercise 3 (page 66)

Hi, listen, it's almost time for me to go now, so I've just got a couple of messages that are important for you. First of all, I haven't written all of the reports that I wanted to do before leaving. Sorry about that. I've done some of them, they're on your desk. You'll be happy to know that I had time yesterday to read all those letters that you typed for me. Thanks very much, by the way, for getting all those finished so quickly. I've signed them, but there are two that I haven't signed because there are mistakes in them. Sorry, you'll have to correct those please. They're all on your desk. What else is there to tell you? Oh yes, I've seen the plans for next year. I saw them yesterday afternoon but I didn't have time to speak to the boss about them, so I'll have to speak to him as soon as I get back from my holiday. Could you tell him that, please? Thanks. Oh, and the last thing: I couldn't give Anna the computer books yesterday. You remember she asked for them. Well, I couldn't find them anywhere. Do you know where they are? If you know where they are, could you please give them to Anna for me? Thanks again. Right, I think that's all. I'm really looking forward to this short break and I'll see you in a week. Don't work too hard while I'm away! Bye.

Unit 2 / Step 1: Exercise 2 (page 67)

1
- How did the interview go then?
- Well, I think it went very well.
- Tell me a bit more about the job. Is the salary good?
- Yes, great. Much better than my salary at the moment. And the work is very interesting.
- What's the office like, and the boss?
- The office is beautiful. Very modern. And the boss, well she couldn't be nicer. But I'm not taking the job.
- Why not, it's perfect, isn't it?
- Nearly perfect. The problem is the long hours. I don't want to work four ten–hour days a week. I'm sure I wouldn't like long hours like that.
- Oh, what a pity.

2
- It was this time last year that they decided to build a motorway through our beautiful village.
- And has that decision made a very big difference to you?
- Yes, it certainly has.
- How?
- Well, that's not difficult. Nobody wants to live here now. That's the difference it's made.

3
And those were the results of our local elections. The number of people who voted this time was very small. Only 26% of the people in this city voted. Experts say that there were probably two reasons for this. One reason was probably the beautiful weather, and the other was probably the football match on television. Well, we can't choose the weather but next time we hold elections here, we certainly won't have them on the same day as the football final.

Unit 2 / Step 2: Exercise 3 (page 68)

- I'm very pleased to have Annagret Johnson with me here in the studio to talk about her latest book. Hello Annagret.
- Hello.
- Well, first of all, congratulations on your latest book,

called *The Kensington Kids,* which was published last
month.
- Thank you.
- Tell me, when did you start writing books?
- Well, I've been a writer for more than twenty years now.
- Oh, as long as that?
- Yes, but I haven't been a writer of children's books for
all that time. I started writing children's books about
ten years ago.
- So, does that mean you also started working for your
London publisher, MacLong, ten years ago?
- No, I started working for MacLong fifteen years ago.
And for the first five years I wrote very different sorts
of books.
- Oh? What did you use to write?
- Well, I'd prefer not to talk about those books now, if
you don't mind. I'm really only interested in children's
books.
- Oh, I see. Well, tell me, why do you write about
children and cities all the time?
- Cities interest me. I lived in a big city when I was a
child, and then later I lived in the country. I saw then
that a child's life in the city is very, very different from
life in the country. They see and hear so much more,
and very different things.
- Do you still live in the country?
- Oh, no. I got married twelve years ago and then just
one year later my husband and I came to live here in
North London. And I'm still here, as you can see.
- Now about your new book, *The Kensington Kids.* How
long has the book been in the shops now?
- Oh, it must be four weeks now, yes it's four weeks
exactly.
- And are you happy with the results?
- Am I happy? Yes, I am. I've been visiting bookshops
and signing books for the last three weeks. It's been
great.
- Well, that's really good news. Once again,
congratulations. Oh, by the way, why is the book about
children in Kensington? You don't live in Kensington.
- No, I don't. I've been teaching painting to children
there, just one day a week for the last four years. It's
very interesting what you can learn from kids. I know a
lot more about life on the streets of Kensington than
most people who live there.
- Oh, that's interesting, from kids' paintings to a book
about kids. Good luck for this book and all your future
books, too. And thank you for being with us today.
- Thank you.

Test yourself 1: Exercise 4 (page 72)
- Where do you work, Samantha?
- I work in Perth. I moved there ten years ago, and I've
had a very interesting job there since the day I moved.
In fact, that was ten years ago this month that I got the
job there.
- But how long have you been living in Australia then,
you've been here more than ten years, haven't you?
- Yeah, sure have. Now how long have I been living
here? Well, let's say from the year I was ten right up to
now!

- Oh, I see – you don't want to tell me how old you are.
Well, how's life, anyway?
- Fine. Well, I've got some news for you. I got married
last Christmas.
- Oh, congratulations. What's the lucky man's name?
- He's called Ben. He's great. We want to have a family
quite soon, so we're looking for a new house.
- Is that difficult in Perth?
- Oh, I don't really know. I only started looking a month
ago. I guess I'll find something soon.
- Oh, I hope so. I'm sure you will.
- Yes, I've looked at a couple of places but I haven't
really …

Test yourself 1: Exercise 5 (page 72)
- Do you know anybody who decided to emigrate?
- Yes, several years ago, some relatives of mine went
abroad and settled down in southern Australia.
- Why did they decide to leave their home country?
- My uncle had always said that London was too
crowded for him and that he wanted to live in a
country with a lot of sunshine and a lot of space.
- Are they still there?
- Yes, they've been there now for a long time but he's
been feeling homesick recently, and wants to return to
England. But he doesn't want to come back to London.
- Where would he like to live?
- He'd like to find a pretty cottage in an unspoilt village
somewhere. I think he'll find that many of these nice
places have disappeared. Perhaps he ought to stay
where he is!
- Oh, he might be lucky! Who knows?

Unit 3 / Step 1: Exercise 3 (page 74)
Right, now, I'm going to read you eight of the sentences
that people wrote. You write those sentences down,
okay? Right. Number one: You need a ball that is about
as big as an orange. Two: You have to try to hit the ball
so that the other player can't hit it back. Three: The
players are allowed to kick the ball, but they aren't
allowed to handle it. Four: You need two or four players
for this sport. Five: The players wear special boots so
that they can kick the ball better. Six: The point of the
game is to get more goals than the others. Seven: You
use a piece of equipment to hit the ball. And sentence
eight: You don't need any other equipment, only a ball.
And that's all, those were the eight sentences. Now I
wonder if you've written them all …

Unit 3 / Step 2: Exercise 2 (page 75)
Oh, god it was a bad day, at least in the beginning it was.
But it turned out better later on. First of all, I got up late
– I mean really late. You know, I didn't even have time
to have breakfast at home. And I just love having a long,
leisurely breakfast at home – but no – no time, so it was
no breakfast for me! Then I ran out of the apartment as
fast as I could, and you know what – the bus left the
stop just as I got there. So, I missed my bus, too. Well, I
was sort of standing there, when along came my brother
on his bike. Now, I hadn't seen my brother in a while
and so it wasn't bad that I'd missed the bus – I saw my

brother. We talked for a bit and he said I should take a taxi, but I decided that would be too expensive. I know, I know – if I'd taken a taxi, I would have arrived at the office before ten o'clock, and that wouldn't have been so bad. But I didn't. I waited for the next bus. And you know, while I was standing there I suddenly heard this big bang – and there was this accident I saw, in the middle of the road. It wasn't a very bad accident, but it stopped the bus and made me even later. So, in the end I arrived at the office just before eleven o'clock. The boss was so angry, he was just so angry with me that he told me to go, then and there. Pow! Go! I'd lost my job. Well, it wasn't a very interesting job anyway! Well, I suddenly found I had a free afternoon, no office work for me. So I went downtown and went to my favourite coffee shop and read the newspapers there for a while. In one of the papers, I saw an ad for a very interesting job, with a better salary than my ex–job. So, a bit later in the afternoon, I called these people and asked them about the job. They asked me to go and see them first thing the next morning. And I didn't get up late the next morning, I can tell you.

Unit 4 / Step 1: Exercise 2 (page 77)

1
- Well, what did you think of the film then?
- I thought it was very interesting. In fact, I thought it was excellent.
- You didn't, did you? I couldn't agree with you less. I thought it was awful, absolutely awful. It just didn't say anything – nothing at all.
- Oh.

2
- Look, here are the two paintings that I like best. I just wondered what you think? Which one would you buy?
- Let me see – this one.
- Yeah! Exactly the one I chose. Great! It's really nice, isn't it.
- Yes, super.

3
- It's difficult to know what to do in that situation, but I think one possible answer would be to ask the old lady what she really wants to do.
- Yes, I think you're probably right there. That would be a very good way of solving the problem. But do you think she really knows what would be best for her? I'm not sure she can decide, you know.

4
- It was really great to see so much sport on television, wasn't it? We were talking about the football final in the office this morning. We all thought it was absolutely great that the Spanish team won the gold medal – there in Spain! Fantastic.
- Talking of Spain, that would be a good place for our next holiday, wouldn't it?
- Yes, you know, that last goal – sorry – what did you say?

5
- Do you know what I heard this morning?
- No, what?

- Someone told me that they're going to close the supermarket near the station because of the new shopping centre outside the town.
- Oh, I can't imagine they'll do that. I mean, they only opened the supermarket last year, didn't they?

6
- That programme was really good last night, wasn't it? But I'm not really sure that I agree with all the things they said. I mean, it isn't that easy is it? What do you think?
- If you ask me, I think they should forget the idea and make some new plans. I've always thought their plans were very strange.
- Mmm.

Unit 4 / Step 2: Exercise 1 (page 78)
- Well, the job seems quite good. I've been there for a week now.
- That's great, I'm glad you like it.
- It was terribly difficult at first, with so many people.
- What was so difficult?
- Well, I found it rather difficult to remember people's names. There are so many of them. And also, the building is so big. I know where my office is and I know where the canteen is and that's about all.
- Yes, it's really big, isn't it? But I like that!
- Yeah, I'm sure I will, too. I decided to make a plan of the office building so that I can find other people when I need them.
- How do you like your boss? Mr Evans, isn't it?
- Yeah, that's right. Robert Evans. In fact, he told me to call him Rob.
- Oh, that's very friendly. But that's typical of you Americans, isn't it?
- Yeah. I just wish I knew more people.
- Well, I could introduce you to my colleagues, or my boss, if you like.
- Mm, I don't think I want to meet your boss – but your colleagues ...
- Well, do you want to meet them?
- Yeah, I want to meet them. That's a good idea. But you know, there's another problem. There's so much to learn.
- Well, I could help you to learn a bit more about the company in general, if that would help.
- Oh, yeah – that would help a lot, thanks. The others are very helpful, too, you know. Someone offered to show me how to use the fax machine. I've never used one before. And Rob, my boss, is really very friendly. I think it's because we're both Americans. I mean, he's already invited me to have a drink with him – one day next week.
- Oh, that's nice of him. It really is a good place to work, you know.
- Yeah, I think it's a good place to work, too. I think I'll stay there for two years or maybe more!
- Good. Well, I've been there for three years, and I still like it. Come on, let's celebrate your new job. What can I get you to drink?

Test yourself 2: Exercise 5 (page 82)

There was a break-in at the local K supermarket yesterday evening. The robbers stole two cars from the station car park. Then they drove to George Street and broke a small window at the back of the supermarket. While they were in the supermarket, they took all the money and they also drank four bottles of wine. They were probably in no condition to drive after that, but they drove away! The police have found one of the cars near the airport. Nobody has seen the other car since yesterday evening. If you have any information that you think might help the police on this matter, please call your local police station as soon as possible. And now on to our sports news for today. The local football league ...

Test yourself 2: Exercise 6 (page 82)

- I want to buy a dog for my children, and I'd like some advice.
- First you should consider whether or not a dog is really the most suitable choice. Will the dog get enough exercise, for example?
- Yes, I mean there are five of us who can take it for walks.
- And are you prepared to deal with the problems of having a young dog in your home?
- We live in a flat. Perhaps it would be better to have a cat.
- A cat is an ideal pet to be kept in a flat. Dogs can often suffer badly, and then the owner later discovers that the decision was a bad one.
- Yes, a cat would be easier, wouldn't it?
- Yes, obviously cats are less nervous and need less attention. They're also popular because they hardly ever attack young children, or damage the home.
- Well, I'll discuss this with the family, and come back next week.

Unit 5 / Step 1: Exercise 3 (page 84)

1
- If the governments cooperated, the instability of the economic situation could be brought to an end, in fact by any one of the governments we have. The result of this would be positive for all of us, that's quite clear. And that's all ...
- Sorry to interrupt but I didn't understand your last point.
- Oh, I'm sorry – perhaps I said it all a bit too fast. Let me explain again. As you know, things have changed in our money market very recently and ...

2
- If anything goes wrong with this machine, you can bring it back here. There's a lifetime guarantee.
- Could you explain your last point again?
- Madam, a lifetime guarantee is a lifetime guarantee. Sir, can I help you? Let me show you ...

3
- And then of course they immediately wrote and offered me an interview.
- Talking of interviews, have you ever had any problems with them?

- Of course not. Why should I have problems with interviews? Now let me continue. So I phoned and told them ...

4
- So I thought the only thing to do was to contact PDA and ask them for advice.
- While we're on the subject of PDA, I'd like to ask you a bit about their work.
- Oh yeah, I'd be happy to tell you anything you want to know. They're a very good company. They offer all sorts of advice on how to ...

5
- And then you put that in there like that, but be careful not to put it too near this. That could be dangerous. Do you know what I mean?
- No, I'm not sure that I do.
- Oh come on. Why don't you concentrate a bit more? I told you this last week. If only you'd listen.

6
- We could stay in London the night before, and then catch the first train to York. I'd prefer to get there early.
- Oh, I completely agree with you. That's a great idea. Yes, let's do that. Then we could go ...

Unit 5 / Step 2: Exercise 2 (page 86)

- Right. Well, what you've told me up to now, Caroline, sounds fine. Now, I need to ask you some more questions. Now, I know you like meeting people, you've already told me that. And I can see that you do like it. And you're good at typing. Your diploma here shows me that. Now what about writing reports and using a computer. Those are two very important things.
- Oh, I like typing reports. I've always liked doing that. And I enjoy using a computer. I've even got one at home.
- Oh good. And what about speaking on the phone? Have you got a good telephone voice?
- Well, yes, but only in England. I mean, I don't like speaking to companies abroad on the phone. I don't know why. I just don't like it.
- Oh well, perhaps you could learn to like it a bit more!
- Mm, maybe.
- What about foreign languages?
- I'm good at French, very good.
- And other languages?
- Well, I learnt a bit of German, but I must say that my German's not very good, in fact it's bad.
- Well, French would be more important, but perhaps you could improve your German a bit, and possibly start learning Spanish.
- Oh, yes. I think I'd find Spanish easier.
- One last question. How would you feel about working alone?
- Oh, I'd hate that. I want a job so that I can be with other people, and not alone at home. No, I want to work in a team.
- Yes, I can understand that very well. Now, I'd like to show you this job description. It's ...

Unit 6 / Step 1: Exercise 3 (page 87)

1
- Oh, hello. Oh! Yes, I remember. Many happy returns of the day.
- Well, thank you. How did you know it's my birthday today?

2
- Oh dear, it's past five. I really must go, I've got visitors this evening. Cheerio.
- Bye. It was nice talking to you. See you again soon, I hope.

3
- Here are our drinks. Cheers!
- Cheers. Here's to our plans for next year.
- Yes, to our plans.

4
- Well, it's time for me to go. I'm sorry I'm in such a hurry. Give my love to Suzie, won't you?
- Yes, of course. She'll be sorry, she didn't see you. Bye.
- Bye.

5
- Oh, hello. I didn't expect to see you here. How are things?
- Oh, fine thanks. I feel much better about my job now.
- Oh, good. I'm glad to hear that.

6
- Well, I must be on my way now. Bye. Take care.
- Yes, you too. Bye.

Unit 6 / Step 2: Exercise 3 (page 89)

- Well, what do you think about these two, George?
- I don't know. It's very difficult to know what to do, isn't it? I mean she works faster than him, but then on the other hand he can speak French better than she can. Both those two things are important.
- Yes, but she can also drive a car, don't forget that.
- Well, he can, too, now. He passed his test last week.
- Oh, that's good. He didn't tell me that. And he's had more experience than she has.
- No, I'm sorry my dear – that's not right. I looked at their papers last night. They've had exactly the same amount of experience. He was away for a year when he didn't work. I think he was travelling or something.
- Well, who do you think is more friendly – because that's important.
- Yes, it is. Well, I must say, she is more friendly. She's always very friendly to everybody. He isn't always.
- And he's younger than she is. Is that a good thing or a bad thing?
- I don't think that's very important – and he's not very much younger, only a couple of years.
- Yes, he's younger, but he wants to earn more money than her, for the same job! Because he's a man, I suppose.
- Yes, that's not really fair, is it? They should earn the same money for the same job.
- Yes, I quite agree. I'm glad you think like that, too. And don't forget that her examination results at the hotel school were better than his were.
- Yes, that's true, too. And she was much faster at learning to use the computer. That's interesting – you

always expect men to be better at these things, don't you?
- Yes, that just shows you, doesn't it? Yes, she's very good at the computer.
- And she's better on the telephone, too. His voice is really rather bad on the phone.
- Well, it looks as if she's got more good points than he has.
- Yes, it does. Oh dear, I'd better talk to him in the morning. You know, I wish we could keep both ...

Test yourself 3: Exercise 5 (page 92)

1 A lot of people in my company heard yesterday that they're going to lose their jobs soon. I hope that doesn't happen to me. I don't know what I'd do. Oh, dear I think it might, but I hope not ... I don't know what I'd do.

2 I've got a ticket to see *Cats* next week. I can't wait.

3 I used to smoke. I used to smoke a lot. But I stopped ten years ago.

4 My new job's really interesting. I often have to travel abroad. I like that very much.

5 When I was at school we had lots of different lessons. I wasn't very good at school – but my best subject was French. I could speak French really well. It was the only thing I could do really well, I think.

6 Well, there are a lot of things you have to do when you've got a house. Our house is only small, but it's a lot of work. I can do most things, but not work in the garden. I can't stand that. It's awful. Please, never ask me to work in the garden with you – it's the last thing I'd want to do.

7 My car is a bit too old really. I want to buy a new one. But I don't know which one yet. I don't know when I'll buy it. A car costs a lot of money, you know, it needs a bit of thought before you buy one.

8 I can type very well, I can speak French and German well and I can take shorthand. But you know, I just can't use the computer. I try, but I always make mistakes. I'm just not good at it.

Test yourself 3: Exercise 6 (page 92)

- I'd like to know how PDA can help me. I want to change jobs.
- Can you tell me why you aren't satisfied with your present job?
- Yes, it's boring.
- I see. Well, we can help you in many ways. We can give you some help with applying for jobs.
- Oh, that would be good.
- And we can help you to give a better performance at interviews.
- What will you need to know about me?
- We'll need to know about your qualifications, your work experience and, of course, the kind of job you're looking for.
- Is that all?
- No. We'll need to know what you can do. Can you type, take shorthand and use a computer? What knowledge have you got of other languages? Things like that.

- I see.
- Why don't you take this form home and fill in all the details.
- Yes, fine ... I'll do that, thank you ...

Unit 7 / Step 1: Exercise 3 (page 94)
- Now I'd like you to tell me as much as you can about what you know about this factory and about the people who work here. What do the men like? What are the things they don't like? As you know, I'm new to this job, and I want to make this factory the best possible place in town to work.
- Well, as far as I know, all the employees and I mean all of them are very pleased with the working hours. It was a good idea to introduce flexi-time.
- Good.
- They are also all quite satisfied with the holidays they get. You gave everyone three days more per year, that was very good and really helped to increase motivation. But some of them are not very satisfied with the new rules about Sunday work. You know, before they could do more overtime at the weekends than now.
- Yes, yes. I know that. But we just had to change that. There's really nothing I can do about it.
- Yes, well – and then there's the no smoking rule. Some of them aren't happy with that at all.
- Yes, that's clear – but we'll soon have a new smokers' room in the new building – so then that will be okay, won't it?
- Yes, I should think so. Now most of the men say that they've had enough of all the noise outside the factory. But they know that you're putting up two new buildings so they'll just have to wait. When will the new buildings be finished. Do you know?
- Yes, in three months' time. Then that will be the end of the noise. I'll be very happy about that too, I can tell you. Well, it sounds as if they're all happy, in general.
- Yes. Oh, there's one last thing. They asked me to tell you that they're sick and tired of the coffee. I must agree with them. We get the worst coffee in the whole of the world out of those machines.
- Yes, I'm sorry about the coffee. They're right to complain. It is terrible, isn't it? Please tell them from me that there are new coffee machines coming in next month – and the coffee's excellent! Well, thanks for your help. I hope you'll always feel you can come and tell me about the problems the men have, you know, I'd like to think ...

Unit 7 / Step 2: Exercise 2 (page 96)
And now to finish our report on what is happening in the town centre, we'd like to give you the results of a short questionnaire that was carried out on the streets of our town yesterday. The first question asked was: Do you want to have a traffic-free centre? 76% said yes, and 24% said no to that. Then we asked the question: How often do you go to the town centre? The answers: 41% go there more than twice a week, 51% go there once or twice a week and 8% never go there. The third question was this: Will you go to the centre more often in the future? We wanted to know if people think the new centre will be more attractive to them. 68% said yes, and 32% said no. The next question was about public meetings and if people have been to them. 11% said yes to this and 89% said no. Then we asked: Do you think the town centre projects are too expensive? Well, we weren't surprised by this answer, and you probably won't be either. 97%, yes 97 said yes, and only 3% said no. And the last question: Did you answer our first questionnaire? Well, 47% said yes and 53% said no. So, there we are – the town centre projects are going very well, and we're all looking forward to a bright, new, modern centre in the not too distant future. Many thanks to all those people who had the time to stop and answer our questionnaire.
And now it's time to go on to that story that we began yesterday about the family ...

Unit 8 / Step 1: Exercise 2 (page 97)
- We're interested in knowing more about what people like and don't like etc. Do you mind if I ask you just three short questions?
- No, I don't mind at all.
- Well, first of all, can you tell me four things that you really like very much?
- Oh, that's easy! I love the South of France. Then I like English milk chocolate very much. Oh, and I really love my cats. I've got two of them. And I'm rather keen on windy days.
- Oh, windy days! That's unusual!
- Yes, well in some ways I'm an unusual person.
- And what things do you dislike?
- Dislike – I don't like old shoes very much. I'm not very keen on red meat either. And what else? Oh, yes, I can't stand people who don't wash. I think it should be possible for everybody to have a wash, don't you? And last of all, I hate smoke.
- Right. And now for some preferences – you know, you prefer this to that ...
- This to that. Yes, I prefer tea to coffee. I like French more than Spanish – the language, I mean. I'd prefer to go to the theatre than to the cinema. And – one more – yes, I'd rather drink white wine than water.
- Yes, I think I would, too. Well, thank you very much for your interesting answers. And although it isn't windy today, I hope you have a nice afternoon.
- And the same to you. Goodbye.
- Bye.

Unit 8 / Step 2: Exercise 3 (page 99)
- Hello, 327 561.
- Oh, hello, is that John?
- Yes.
- Hello, this is Pam. You answered my ad ...
- Oh, yes. Hello Pam. Oh, that's nice that you've called. I've never done this before and so I wasn't really sure ...
- No, I've never done it before either, but I think it's a good idea.
- Oh, yes. So do I. Now, shall we meet soon?
- Yes, if possible. I live in the city centre, and you?

- No. No, I don't live in the centre but I've got a car so that's no problem.
- Oh, I haven't got one, I don't need one where I live. I think we should know a little bit about each other before we meet. I'm 45, how old are you?
- I'm 45, too. That's a good start. And I don't smoke, do you?
- No, and I can't stand smoky places. Have you got any children?
- No, I haven't. I haven't been married either.
- Oh, I've been married – just once – a long time ago! But I haven't got any children. What else should I ask?
- Well, how about your work? What do you do?
- I work in a bank ...
- Oh, that's funny. Now I work in a bank, too. Oh, dear – we don't want to talk about work now, do we?
- Oh, goodness me, no. What do you do at the weekends? In the summer I play tennis a lot.
- Oh, dear! I don't play tennis. I'm not very sporty at all, I'm afraid. I enjoy going to the cinema and the theatre. Do you?
- Oh, yes, very much. I love both the cinema and the theatre. Listen, perhaps it would be easier to talk if we met. What do you think?
- Yes, I think you're right. How about the weekend? Are you busy this weekend?
- No, no I'm not busy this weekend. Well, what do you think about ...

Test yourself 4: Exercise 5 (page 102)

- Oh, hello Amanda. Where's Tom?
- He's gone.
- Oh? I thought he was staying to dinner. Why has he gone?
- I told him to go. Mummy, I can't marry him, because I don't love him. I've always liked him very much, but I know I can't marry him. I think we'll probably both be happier if we don't get married!
- Well, what are your plans now, Amanda?
- I'm looking for a job in America. I want to move away, and I'll leave as soon as possible. I've already applied for two jobs.
- Oh dear! Are you sure ...?
- Don't, worry mummy. I know what I'm doing.
- Oh, I hope you do, dear.

Test yourself 4: Exercise 6 (page 102)

- What was life like for you when you couldn't read?
- It was hell. Adults can read. At least, that's what people expect. But I couldn't even read simple texts like signs, advertisements or instructions.
- How did you feel?
- Threatened and ashamed. Reading is a skill we need for so many things. I was willing to make the effort to learn, but I didn't know how. I think fear was also a problem.
- What were you afraid of?
- Of telling other people that I couldn't read. Then I found a course at the City College, and it changed my life.
- And how do you feel now?

- I'm a different person. I feel proud that I refused to give up. It was a struggle, you know.
- Yes, I'm sure it was. I hope that if there are other people listening ...

Übersicht der wichtigsten grammatischen Bezeichnungen

Deutsch	Englisch	Lateinisch	Erläuterung
Bedingungssatz	conditional clause / *if*-clause	Konditionalsatz	gibt die Bedingung an, unter der etwas geschieht, z.B. *If he comes in the morning, he won't meet me.*
Befehlsform	imperative	Imperativ	z.B. *Walk straight on.*
Besitzfall	genitive	Genitiv	2. Fall; antwortet auf die Frage Wessen?
Bezugssatz	relative clause	Relativsatz	beschreibt Personen oder Dinge aus dem Hauptsatz näher, z.B. *The policeman who stopped my car is my brother.*
	contact clause		Sonderform des Relativsatzes, in dem das Relativpronomen weggelassen wird, z.B. *Have you bought the things we need for the party?*
Bindewort	conjunction	Konjunktion	verbindet Sätze miteinander, z.B. *if, when*
Eigenschaftswort	adjective	Adjektiv	beschreibt, wie eine Person oder eine Sache ist, z.B. *nice, beautiful, okay*
Einzahl	singular	Singular	z.B. *dog, newspaper*
Frageanhängsel	question tag		z.B. *The weather is fine, isn't it?*
Fragewort	question word	Interrogativpronomen	z.B. *Where? What? How?*
Fürwort	pronoun	Pronomen	steht für andere Wörter in Sätzen
besitzanzeigendes Fürwort	possessive pronoun	Possessivpronomen	zeigt Besitz oder Zugehörigkeit an. Einige besitzanzeigende Fürwörter werden wie Eigenschaftswörter gebraucht, z.B. *my book, their dog;* andere werden wie Hauptwörter verwendet, z.B. *Whose book is this? It's mine.*
bezügliches Fürwort	relative pronoun	Relativpronomen	steht als Verbindungswort zwischen Sätzen für eine Person oder Sache, z.B. *who, which, that. I'd like a car which isn't too expensive.*
hinweisendes Fürwort	demonstrative pronoun	Demonstrativpronomen	weist auf eine Person oder Sache hin, z.B. *this town, these postcards*
persönliches Fürwort	personal pronoun	Personalpronomen	steht für eine Person oder Sache, z.B. *he, him, we, us, it*
rückbezügliches Fürwort	reflexive pronoun	Reflexivpronomen	verweist auf den Satzgegenstand zurück, z.B. *I enjoyed myself at the party.*
Gegenwart	present	Präsens	z.B. *I can whistle. He cooks wonderful omelettes.*
vollendete Gegenwart	present perfect	Perfekt	macht Aussagen über Ereignisse und Tätigkeiten, die einen direkten Bezug zur Gegenwart (,bis jetzt') haben, z.B. *I have always helped him.*
Geschlechtswort (Begleiter des Hauptworts)	article	Artikel	zeigt das grammatische Geschlecht von Hauptwörtern an, z.B. *der Tisch, die Lampe, das Buch*

Deutsch	Englisch	Lateinisch	Erläuterung
bestimmtes Geschlechtswort	definite article	bestimmter Artikel	z.B. *der, die, das, the*
unbestimmtes Geschlechtswort	indefinite article	unbestimmter Artikel	z.B. *ein, eine, a/an*
Grundform	infinitive	Infinitiv	z.B. *do, eat*
Grundzahlen	cardinal numbers	Kardinalzahlen	z.B. *one, two, three*
Hauptwort (Namenwort)	noun	Substantiv	wird benutzt, um Menschen, Tieren, Dingen und abstrakten Begriffen ihren Namen zu geben, z.B. *Peter, dog, love*
Hilfszeitwort	auxiliary verb	Hilfsverb	‚hilft‘ dem Hauptzeitwort; z.B. *He* **can** *cook. She* **will** *come.*
-ing-Form	gerund	Gerundium	Zeitwort, das durch Anhängen von *-ing* zum Hauptwort gemacht wird. Im Satz kann es als Satzgegenstand oder Satzaussage auftreten, z.B. *I enjoy listen**ing** to classical music. Smok**ing** is bad for you.*
Leideform	passive	Passiv	sieht das Geschehen vom Betroffenen aus, z.B. *Sometimes even children **are attacked** by dogs.*
Mehrzahl	plural	Plural	z.B. *dog**s**, newspaper**s***
Mitlaut	consonant	Konsonant	z.B. *b, c, d, f* usw.
Mittelwort der Vergangenheit	past participle	Partizip Perfekt	Formen wie *gespielt, gegessen, gegangen;* engl. z.B. *played, eaten, gone*
Ordnungszahlen	ordinal numbers	Ordinalzahlen	z.B. *first, second, third*
indirekte Rede	reported speech		berichtet über das, was gedacht oder gesagt wurde, z.B. *He says/thinks (that) his wife is ill.*
Satzaussage	predicate		alle Satzteile, die nicht zum Satzgegenstand gehören, z.B. *Peter **reads the newspaper.***
Satzergänzung	object	Objekt	Satzglied, das das Zeitwort ergänzt (3.+ 4. Fall).
	direct object	direktes Objekt/ Akkusativobjekt	4. Fall (Akkusativ); antwortet auf die Frage *Wen?* oder *Was?*, z.B. *Peter reads **the newspaper**.*
	indirect object	indirektes Objekt/ Dativobjekt	3. Fall (Dativ); antwortet auf die Frage *Wem?*, z.B. *Ann gave **me** a book.*
Satzgegenstand	subject	Subjekt	Person oder Sache, über die im Satz eine Aussage gemacht wird (1. Fall), z.B. **Peter** *reads the newspaper.*
Selbstlaut	vowel	Vokal	*a, e, i, o, u*
Steigerung	comparison		
1. Steigerungsstufe	comparative	Komparativ	z.B. *small**er**, **more** modern*
2. Steigerungsstufe	superlative	Superlativ	z.B. *(the) old**est**, (the)* **most** *expensive*

Deutsch	Englisch	Lateinisch	Erläuterung
Stützwort	prop-word		wird benutzt, um Wiederholungen des Hauptworts zu vermeiden, z.B. *My father bought a new car. He's got a Japanese* **one** *now.*
Umstandswort	adverb	Adverb	steht bei Zeit- oder Eigenschaftswörtern und drückt die Art und Weise aus, in der etwas geschieht *(**schnell** laufen)* oder den Grad einer Eigenschaft *(**sehr** alt);* z.B. *quickly, well, never*
Vergangenheit	past	Imperfekt/ Präteritum	Formen wie *kam, lachte;* engl. z.B. *stayed, did, ate*
vollendete Vergangenheit	past perfect	Plusquamperfekt	macht Aussagen über Vorgänge oder Zustände, die vor einem anderen Ereignis oder einer anderen Tätigkeit in der Vergangenheit abgeschlossen waren, z.B. *I went out after I **had done** my homework.*
Verhältniswort	preposition	Präposition	z.B. *in, on, between, at*
Verlaufsform	progressive form/ continuous form		drückt aus, daß eine Tätigkeit oder ein Geschehen gerade abläuft bzw. gerade im Gange war, als eine andere Handlung eintrat, z.B. *John **is watching** TV at the moment. Silvia **was reading** a book when the phone rang.*
Vollverb	full verb		das ,Hauptzeitwort', das die eigentliche Bedeutung besitzt, z.B. *can **help**, will **come***
Zeitwort	verb	Verb	drückt Handlungen, Vorgänge und Zustände aus, z.B. *go, watch, be*
Zukunft	future	Futur	macht Aussagen über Zukünftiges, Geplantes oder unmittelbar Bevorstehendes, z.B. *He **will stay**. I **will go** home.*

Grammar

Inhaltsverzeichnis

Die Ziffern G 1, G 2, etc. beziehen sich auf die Kapitelnummern in diesem Grammatikanhang.

1 Wiederholung der wichtigsten Zeiten / Review of tenses

Die wichtigsten Zeiten in der englischen Sprache sind Ihnen bekannt, auch wenn ihre Anwendung manchmal noch Probleme bereitet. Zur Veranschaulichung und Wiederholung dienen die nachstehenden tabellarischen Übersichten mit Benutzungshinweisen, die grundlegende Einsichten und Regeln vermitteln wollen. Über Feinheiten und Ausnahmen wird noch gesondert zu sprechen sein.

Gegenwart	present simple	I **am** very busy, but I **like** my work.
	present progressive	I **am working** very hard (at the moment).

Durch die beiden Zeitformen der Gegenwart werden gegenwärtige Zustände oder Tätigkeiten beschrieben.

Vergangen-heit	past simple	What **did** you **do** last Monday? I **wasn't** at home, I **went** to Frankfurt.
	past progressive	He **was reading** a newspaper, when the phone rang.
	past perfect	**Had** you **heard** about the play before you saw it? No, I **hadn't heard** about it before.

Die Zeitformen des **past tense** stehen zur Verfügung, wenn über vergangene Zustände oder Tätigkeiten berichtet wird, die in der Vergangenheit abgeschlossen wurden.

Mit dem **past perfect** wird über ‚vorzeitige' in der Vergangenheit abgeschlossene Zustände oder Tätigkeiten gesprochen.

present perfect	(1) I **have lived** in Nevada for 3 years now, but I **have** never **been** to Las Vegas.
	(2) – **Have** you **read** this new book by William Boyd? – Yes, I **have**. I **have read** all his books. Paul **has applied** for a better job. They **have made** a lot of mistakes in these letters. Look.

Eine Sonderstellung nimmt die Zeit des **present perfect** ein, die anders als im Deutschen benutzt wird und nicht eindeutig den Zeitblöcken der **Gegenwart** oder der **Vergangenheit** zugeordnet werden kann. Sie drückt aus, daß eine Tätigkeit oder ein Zustand in der Vergangenheit begann und bis in die Gegenwart andauert (1), bzw. daß die Folgen und Resultate einer zwar schon abgeschlossenen Handlung bis in die Gegenwart spürbar sind (2).

Zukunft	(1) This time next year we **will** all be a year older.
	(2) – What **are** you **doing** after the lesson? – I **am meeting** a friend for a drink.
	(3) We **are going to** spend our holidays in Canada this year.
	(4) – When **does** the performance **start**? – It **starts** at 7.30 p.m.

Für die **Zukunft** stehen Ihnen mehrere sprachliche Möglichkeiten zur Verfügung: **will** zum Ausdruck zukünftiger Ereignisse oder Handlungen, die sich gleichsam ‚zwangsweise' ergeben werden (1), das **present progressive** in zukünftiger Bedeutung, um etwas konkret Geplantes auszusagen (2), **going to** zum Ausdruck einer ‚festen Absicht', einer Entschlossenheit, etwas zu tun (3) und das **present simple** in zukünftiger Bedeutung als ‚timetable future' (4), wenn von (meist offiziell) festgelegten Terminen und Zeiten gesprochen wird.

2 Vergleiche und Gegensätze / Comparisons and contrasts

(1) **Better** late **than** never.
I like this picture **better than** the other one.

She is **as tall as** my sister.
I don't like her **as much as** my sister.

(2) She **is** taller than I **am** / than **me**.
She **is** as tall as you **are** / as **you**.

She **liked** Australia better than he **did** / than **him**.
She **works** as hard as I **do** / as **me**.

They **can** dance better than we **can** / than **us**.
You **can't** read as fast as I **can** / as **me**.

(3) She's keen on foreign food, **but** I'm **not**.
We **aren't** happy about the changes, **but** he **is**.

You **like** pop music, **but** I **don't**.
You **don't** like pop music, **but** I **do**.

They **can** speak Spanish, but we **can't**.
You **shouldn't** feel sorry, but they **should**.

Will man mit Hilfe von Eigenschafts- oder Umstandswörtern Vergleiche in ganzen Sätzen anstellen, benutzt man **than** nach einem Komparativ, um Unterschiede auszudrücken, und **as .... as** für Gemeinsamkeiten (1). In Satzvergleichen wird das Verb **be** wiederholt. Vollverben aber werden durch die entsprechende Form von **do** ersetzt. Hilfsverben werden im Regelfall wiederholt. Das Voll- oder Hilfsverb kann aber auch, wie im Deutschen, ganz wegfallen. Die persönlichen Fürwörter werden in solchen Fällen im 4. Fall verwendet (2). **But** hilft, Gegensätze auszudrücken. Dabei wird das Verb **be** wiederholt. Vollverben werden durch die entsprechende Form von **do** ersetzt. Hilfsverben bleiben erhalten (3).

3 Noch mehr Umstandswörter / More adverbs

Umstandswörter haben Sie im gesamten Kursverlauf häufig angetroffen. Ihre Bildung und Verwendung und ihre Steigerungsstufen sind Ihnen durch stetigen Gebrauch geläufig (*English Network 1, Grammar 18*, S. 123-124; *English Network 2, Grammar 2*, S. 113 und *English Network 3, Grammar 1*, S. 112-113).

(1) **First of all**, put your paper in the machine.
Secondly/Then choose the correct size.
Finally, press the red button to start.

(2) **Naturally**, sport is good for you.
Swimming is **especially** healthy.
Fortunately, the tennis court is near here.
Obviously, golf is more expensive than tennis.

Diese Umstandswörter helfen Ihnen, Ratschläge und Empfehlungen, Ereignisse oder Tätigkeiten in ihrer Reihen- oder Abfolge darzustellen (1). Umstandswörter **kommentieren** auch Aussagen und teilen **die Meinung und Bewertung des Sprechers** mit (2). Stehen sie am Satzanfang, werden sie durch ein Komma abgetrennt und besonders hervorgehoben und betont.

4 *some* und *any*, *both* und *the two*, *either* und *neither* / *some* and *any*, *both* and *the two*, *either* and *neither*

4.1 *some* und *any* / *some* and *any*

Sie erinnern sich sicher an die Grundregel des Gebrauchs von **some** und **any**, nach der **any** in Frage- und verneinten Aussagesätzen und **some** in bejahten Aussagen zu benutzen ist (*English Network 1, Grammar 3*, S. 112):
– *Have you got* **any** *presents for me?*
– *Here are* **some** *presents for you.*
– *I haven't got* **any** *presents for you.*
Grundsätzlich gilt diese Aussage auch bei Zusammensetzungen mit **some** und **any**.

Any und seine Zusammensetzungen können in bejahenden Aussagesätzen in der Bedeutung von *jede(r/s) beliebige(r/s), jede(r/s) ohne Ausnahme* benutzt werden (*English Network 3, Grammar 2.1*, S. 114):
You can ask **any** *neighbour /* **any** *of the neighbours for help.*
Anybody *will be glad to help in a situation like this.*

"Would you like to see some photos of your wife and kids?"

Beware of pickpockets = Vorsicht Taschendiebe; kids = Kinder

(1) Have you got **some** French wine?

(2) Would you like **some** wine? Can I offer you **something** (to drink)? Shall I order **some** coffee for you?

Wird **some** im Fragesatz verwendet, erwartet man eine positive Antwort (1). Es handelt sich bei solchen Sätzen oft nicht eigentlich um Fragen, sondern meist um Angebote, Aufforderungen oder Vorschläge (2).

4.2 *both* und *the two* / *both* and *the two*

Both und **the two** bedeuten auf deutsch *alle beide*.

(1) **Both** friends were hurt. **Both** (of them) were taken to hospital.

(2) **The two** books belong to me.

Both kann alleinstehend oder in Verbindung mit einem Hauptwort verwendet werden und betont die Zusammengehörigkeit von Personen oder Dingen (1).
The two steht grundsätzlich mit einem Hauptwort und wird verwendet, wenn die Zusammengehörigkeit nicht so wichtig ist oder gar keine Rolle spielt (2).

4.3 *either* und *neither* / *either* and *neither*

You can take **either** cassette. **Either** (of them) is interesting.

Either kann allein oder in Verbindung mit einem Hauptwort benutzt werden und bedeutet *jede(r/s) von zweien = entweder der/die/das eine oder der/die/das andere von beiden.*

Neither cassette is the one I really want. **Neither** (of them) is very interesting.

Neither ist die Verneinung von **either** und bedeutet *keine(r/s) von beiden.*

5 Besondere Anwendungen von *do* und *did* / Special uses of *do* and *did*

(1) You (really) **do** work too much, that's why you look so tired.

(2) I don't mind working, but I **do** sometimes complain about my colleagues.

(3) They **did** say that they would help me, but now they seem to have forgotten.

Durch den zusätzlichen Gebrauch von **do** wird der durch das Hauptverb ausgedrückte Vorgang nachdrücklich hervorgehoben und betont (1). Diese Hervorhebung unterstreicht häufig einen Gegensatz (2) und drückt einen Widerspruch (3) aus.

6 Verben, die keine Verlaufsform bilden / Verbs not normally used in the progressive

to be	*sein*	to need	*brauchen,*
to believe	*glauben*		*benötigen*
to belong	*gehören*	to prefer	*vorziehen*
to forget	*vergessen*	to remain	*bleiben*
to hate	*hassen*	to remember	*sich erinnern*
to hear	*hören*	to see	*sehen*
to know	*kennen,*	to seem	*scheinen*
	wissen	to think	*denken*
to like	*mögen*	to understand	*verstehen*
to love	*lieben,*	to want	*wollen,*
	gern haben		*wünschen*
to mean	*bedeuten*		

⚠ Es gibt eine Reihe von Verben, die dauerhafte Zustände beschreiben, und Verben des **Denkens** und **Erkennens**, die in der Regel keine Verlaufsform bilden.

"I think you're right. The goldfish wasn't such a good idea."

I **don't understand** why you didn't come at once.
I **need** your help now.
This coat **belongs** to me.
What **do** you **think** Sheila will do?

7 *always* und die Verlaufsform der Gegenwart und Vergangenheit / *always* and the present/past progressive

The child **is always crying**.
Das Kind schreit (aber auch) immer! (Wie störend!)

He **was always talking** about his job.
Er erzählte andauernd von seiner Arbeit (und ging mir damit auf die Nerven).

Die Verlaufsform wird für die Vergangenheit und Gegenwart in Verbindung mit **always** bei wiederholten Handlungen benutzt, wenn der Sprecher damit sein Mißbehagen und einen Vorwurf oder Tadel zum Ausdruck bringen möchte.

He **is always forgetting** his keys.
You**'re always hearing** strange noises.
You**'re always remembering** things too late.
They **were always seeing** ghosts/things.

Die Verlaufsform kann auch mit bestimmten Verben benutzt werden, die in der Regel dauerhafte Zustände beschreiben und bei denen man diese Form eigentlich **nicht** erwarten würde (vgl. *Grammar 5*). Der Sprecher möchte in solchen Fällen seine Verärgerung, seine Mißbilligung oder zumindest sein Erstaunen nachdrücklich zum Ausdruck bringen.

8 Das Perfekt mit *since* und *for* / The present perfect with *since* and *for*

Die Übersetzung des deutschen Worts *seit* kann durch **since** und **for** vorgenommen werden. Dabei wird die Zeitform der Gegenwart in deutschen *seit*-Sätzen (*Ich lebe seit zehn Jahren in Australien.*) gemäß der Ihnen bekannten Regel in der englischen Sprache zum Perfekt (I **have lived** in Australia **for** ten years.), da ein Bezug zur Gegenwart hergestellt wird (*English Network 3, Grammar 7*, S. 116-117).

(1)	We **have known** Mr Taylor **for** more than a year.
(2)	We **have known** him **since** April 1992.
(2)	Susan **has written** six letters **since** nine o'clock,
(1)	but she **has not written** one in German **for** a week.

Mit **for** wird eine Zeit**dauer** oder **-spanne** angegeben, die bis an die Gegenwart heranreicht (1), und mit **since** ein Zeit**punkt**, von dem aus sich die Handlung bis in die Gegenwart erstreckt (2).

Frage	How long has she known him? How long have you been here?
Aussage	She has known him **since** last Christmas. We have been here **for** four months.
Frage	**How long** have you had this book?
Aussage	I have had it **since** my teacher **gave** it to me.

Gelegentlich findet sich in Verbindung mit **since** auch das **past simple. Since** entspricht in solchen Sätzen *seit(dem)*.

9 Die Verlaufsform des Perfekts / The present perfect progressive

Die Verlaufsform wird aus dem Perfekt des Hilfsverbs **be** und der **ing**-Form des Voll- oder Hauptverbs gebildet.

Aussage	I've (=I **have**) **been reading** since ten.
Frage	What **have** you **been doing**?
Verneinung	We **haven't** (=have not) **been reading**.
Aussage	We**'ve** (=We **have**) been working all morning.

(1)	Why are you so late? **I've been waiting** for half an hour.
(2)	**We've been working** for more than five hours now.
(3)	He can't dance tonight. His legs hurt. He **has been playing** football all afternoon.

"You've been climbing the tree again."

Die Verlaufsform des Perfekts wird verwendet, wenn von Handlungen die Rede ist, die gerade erst abgeschlossen wurden (1), die in der Vergangenheit begonnen haben und in der Gegenwart noch andauern (2) und die zwar in der Vergangenheit abgeschlossen wurden, aber noch Folgen in der Gegenwart haben (3).

10 Bedingungs- oder Konditionalsätze (*if*-Sätze) / *if*-clauses

Verschiedene Typen von Bedingungssätzen haben Sie schon im zweiten und dritten Band von *English Network* kennengelernt (*Band 2: Grammar 12*, S. 121 und *Band 3: Grammar 5*, S. 115), so daß Ihnen das Grundmuster ihrer Bildung schon bekannt ist.

In dem nunmehr auftretenden, letzten Typ dieser Reihe von Bedingungssätzen, der in Grammatiken auch mit dem Begriff **third conditional** belegt ist, wird von einer Situation in der Vergangenheit gesprochen, die nicht eingetreten ist. Man stellt sich vor, was man *getan hätte* oder was *geschehen wäre*, wenn dieses oder jenes *(nicht) eingetreten* oder *(nicht) passiert wäre.*

if-Satz (Nebensatz)	Hauptsatz
If I'd (=I **had**) **asked** him,	he **would have told** us.
If I'd (=I **had**) **known** that,	I **would have been** happy.
If they **hadn't** (=**had not**) **smoked** that much,	they **would have lived** longer.
If you **hadn't** (=**had not**) **been** so lazy,	you **wouldn't** (=**would not**) **have had** such bad exam results.
If she **had eaten** all that food,	she **would have been** sick.

Nebenstehend sehen Sie verschiedene Kombinationsmöglichkeiten in Haupt- und Nebensatz: Grundsätzlich wird im *if*-Satz das **past perfect** (*English Network 3, Grammar 8*, S. 117), und im Hauptsatz **would have + Mittelwort der Vergangenheit** verwendet. Sie werden schon selbst bemerkt haben, daß bei einleitendem *if*-Satz der Hauptsatz durch ein Komma abgetrennt wird. Dieses Komma bedeutet eine kleine Sprechpause.

measles = Masern

11 Weitere Typen von Relativsätzen / More types of relative clauses

11.1 Notwendige und nicht notwendige Relativsätze / Defining and non-defining relative clauses

Bezugs- oder Relativsätzen sind Sie im Kursverlauf immer wieder begegnet (*English Network 2, Grammar 11*, S. 120-121 und *English Network 3, Grammar 18*, S. 123), so daß Ihnen die grundlegenden Satzmuster sicherlich keine Schwierigkeiten mehr bereiten:

*He is the man **who** lives near here.*
*This is the photo **which/that** shows my house.*

*Is this the man (**who/that**) you were talking about?*
*Is this the photo (**which/that**) you wanted to show me?*

(1) The students, **who** by the way are quite young, have learnt a lot.
They came to our last course, **which** was about Canadian literature, every Friday afternoon.

(2) This is the teacher **who** teaches the course.
This is the course (**that**) I was talking about.

Wenn Relativsätze Zusatzinformationen bieten, die für das Verständnis des Hauptsatzes entbehrlich sind, werden sie durch Komma(ta) abgetrennt (1). Notwendige Relativsätze hingegen vermitteln Informationen, die zum Verständnis des Hauptsatzes unverzichtbar sind. Bei ihnen wird auf das Komma verzichtet (2).

11.2 Relativpronomen in notwendigen und nicht notwendigen Relativsätzen / Relative pronouns in defining and non-defining relative clauses

		Personen	Sachen
Notwendige Relativsätze (1, 3, 5)	1./4. Fall 2. Fall	who/that whose	which/that
Nicht notwendige Relativsätze (2, 4, 6)	1./4. Fall 2. Fall	who whose	which

(1) There's the Frenchman **who/that** works at IBM.
(2) Janet Williams, **who** you know, also works there.
(3) There's the restaurant **which/that** sells the best pizzas in town.
(4) But my favourite restaurant, **which** I visit regularly, is Chinese.
(5) I spoke to one of the reporters **whose** articles I had read.
(6) But Angela Roppin, **whose** articles I always read, wasn't there.

Die Ihnen bekannten Relativpronomen **who** und **which** werden in notwendigen und nicht notwendigen Relativsätzen gleichermaßen verwendet (1-4). **That** kann in nicht notwendigen Relativsätzen nicht gebraucht werden (2, 4). **Whose** (= *dessen/deren*) ist, wie alle Relativpronomen, unveränderlich und findet sich in beiden Typen von Relativsätzen (5, 6).

Aus *English Network 3 (Grammar 18,* S.123) wissen Sie, daß das Relativpronomen wegfallen kann, wenn es Ergänzung (Objekt) ist. Dies gilt aber nicht für nicht notwendige Relativsätze. In den Beispielsätzen (2) und (4) kann **who** bzw. **which** (hier Ergänzung/Objekt) nicht entfallen.

11.3 Relativpronomen mit Präpositionen / Relative pronouns with prepositions

There were 50 people at the party, ten **of whom** I knew.
They had lots of food, most **of which** was very good.

The people (**who/that**) I talked **to** were all very interesting.
The music (**which/that**) we listened **to** was great.

Nach einer **Präposition** kann nur **whom** (Personen) oder **which** (Sachen), nicht aber *who* oder *that* stehen. Wird die **Präposition** aber am **Satzende** nachgestellt, verwendet man **who, which** oder **that.**

12 Die indirekte Rede / Reported speech

Der Begriff **indirekte Rede** wird verwendet, wenn über das berichtet wird, was gedacht oder gesagt wurde. Wörtliche Aussagen der direkten Rede werden in Nebensätzen vermittelt, die durch Verben des Sagens, Denkens und Meinens eingeleitet werden: *„Er sagt, daß seine Frau krank ist/sei." „Er denkt/ meint, seine Frau sei krank." = "He says/thinks (that) his wife is ill."*

12.1 Die indirekte Rede mit einleitenden Verben in der Gegenwart / Reported speech with reporting verbs in the present

When I ask her how hard she works,
Sue always answers, "I **work** very hard."
She **answers** (that) she **works** very hard.

Tom says, "I **worked** very hard in my last job."
Tom **says** (that) he **worked** very hard in his last job.

Last year they went to France for their holidays.
They think, "We **will do** the same this year."
They **think** (that) they **will do** the same this year.

Nach einleitendem Verb in der Gegenwart können im nachfolgenden Nebensatz viele Zeitformen auftreten. Die Zeit der direkten Rede ändert sich bei der Umwandlung in die indirekte Rede nicht.

12.2 Die indirekte Rede mit einleitenden Verben in der Vergangenheit / Reported speech with reporting verbs in the past

(1) Paul said, "Life **is** very hard in America."
Paul **said** (that) life **was** very hard in America.

(2) His wife replied, "I **liked** the American way of life."
His wife **replied** (that) she **had liked** the American way of life.

(3) They both thought, "Our children **will not want** to stay there."
They both **thought** (that) their children **would not want** to stay there.

(4) They both agreed, "We **have** always **enjoyed** being with American friends."
They both **agreed** (that) they **had** always **enjoyed** being with American friends.

Steht der Hauptsatz aber in der Vergangenheit (**past, past perfect**), so muß auch im Nebensatz der indirekten Rede eine Zeit der Vergangenheit stehen.
Beachten Sie, wie die Zeiten der direkten Rede ,verschoben' werden. Die zugrunde liegende Regel wird **Zeitenfolge** oder auch **sequence of tenses** genannt. Auch die Personalpronomen ändern sich, aber das ist in der deutschen Sprache ebenso der Fall.

(1) present ⟶ past
(2) past ⟶ past perfect
(3) will-future ⟶ would
(4) present perfect ⟶ past perfect

"He said he wouldn't eat it without tomato sauce."

Mit diesem Grundwissen wird es Ihnen nicht schwer fallen, für weitere Zeitformen der direkten Rede die Entsprechungen in der indirekten Rede zu finden:

"I **am looking** for a new job." ⟶ He told us (that) he **was looking** for a new job.
"I **had** no luck in my old job." ⟶ He told us (that) he **had had** no luck in his old job.
"I **can work** very hard." ⟶ He said (that) he **could work** very hard.

13 Das Passiv / The passive

Bei dieser Form – mitunter auch ,Leideform des Verbs' genannt – wird das Geschehen vom Betroffenen her gesehen. Der Täter ist weniger wichtig als die Tat selbst oder ihre Ergebnisse. *„Einladungen wurden verschickt."* Es ist unerheblich, wer sie geschrieben und zur Post gebracht hat, wichtig ist, daß sie verschickt wurden.

13.1 Die Bildung der Passivform / The formation of the passive

Im Englischen wird das Passiv mit einer Form des Hilfsverbs **be** und dem **Mittelwort der Vergangenheit**, dem **Partizip Perfekt**, gebildet. Vergleichbar verfahren wir in der deutschen Sprache, wenn wir das Partizip Perfekt und *werden* miteinander verbinden, um das Passiv zu konstruieren:

be attack**ed**	=	**angegriffen werden**
be seen	=	**gesehen werden**

13.2 Verwendung der Passivform / Use of the passive

> (1) A lot of space **is needed by** large animals.
> Valuable objects **can be damaged by** pets.
> Sometimes even children **are attacked by** dogs.
> A prize **was offered** for the best song.
> Two new computers **have been bought** for our office.

> (2) This problem **will be solved** next year,
> because the road **will be repaired**.
> The decision to do that **has** just **been taken**.
> And the houses **are going to be painted** next year, too.

Der Vorgang, der Ablauf des Geschehens oder der erreichte Zustand, das Resultat wird besonders hervorgehoben und betont. Die Täter oder Verursacher **können** am Satzende durch **by** angeschlossen werden. Häufig läßt man sie aber ganz weg, wenn es uninteressant ist, durch wen etwas getan oder veranlaßt wurde (1).
Das Passiv kann **von allen Zeiten** gebildet werden, obwohl erfahrungsgemäß die Passivformen der Gegenwart und Vergangenheit überwiegen (2).

14 Der Infinitiv mit *to* / The infinitive with *to*

Diese Form des Englischen haben Sie im Kursverlauf schon mehrfach angetroffen und geübt (*English Network 3, Grammar 17.1-17.3, S. 122-123*), so daß an dieser Stelle keine wesentlich neuen Informationen auf Sie warten, sondern eher eine Erinnerung an eine schon bekannte und – hoffentlich – beherrschte Struktur mit ihren Anwendungsmöglichkeiten.

> (1) He has always **planned to come**.
> We **hope to see** him again soon.
>
> (2) It's **difficult to keep** one's promises.
> That's not really **hard to believe**.
>
> (3) Sheila is **the best person to be** our director.
>
> (4) She has always been **the first to come** and **the last to go**.

Der Infinitiv mit **to** steht – wie Sie wissen – nach bestimmten Verben (1),

Adjektiven (2),

Superlativen (3),

bestimmten Zahlwörtern (4).

> Yesterday I didn't know **what to do**, **whether to translate** the letters first or **to do** something else. I asked my friend **when to translate** them.
>
> She wanted to help me and told me **which** job **to do** first and **where to begin**.
>
> I have never learnt **how to repair** an engine.
> Do you know **how to start** the car?

Weiterhin steht der Infinitiv nach Fragewörtern wie **what, when, where, whether, which** und **how**, die häufig Verben wie **to ask, to know, to learn, to show, to teach, to tell** und **to understand** folgen.

Aufzählungen und rhetorische Fragen finden sich häufig in Zeitungstexten, wie die nachstehende Anzeige in der Tageszeitung *Daily Express* beweist, in der für ein kostenloses Buch zur Verbesserung der Englischkenntnisse mit den folgenden vollmundigen Worten geworben wurde, die wahre Wunderdinge versprechen:

What this free book will show you:
How to stop making embarrassing mistakes in English!
How to become a fluent conversationalist and effective
* public speaker!*
How to increase your word power!
How to read faster and better!
How to put punch into your writing!
How to pass English examinations!
How to develop self-confidence!
How to increase your thinking power!

15 *ing*-Form (gerund)

Dieser Form sind Sie schon in den Abschnitten 15 des 2. Bandes (S. 122) und 16.1-16.3 des 3. Bandes (S. 121-122) von *English Network* begegnet.

(1) I **like learning** English, and I really **enjoy travelling** to England.

(2) I have never **thought about learning** French.

(3) I'm **fond of using** my knowledge, I'm **keen on speaking** the foreign language and I think I'm now quite **good at writing** it, too.

(4) I also take great **interest in studying** the development of the English language.

(5) **Learning** is a healthy exercise for anybody.

Die ***ing*-Form** findet sich nach bestimmten Verben (1), nach Verben mit fester Präposition (2), nach Eigenschaftswörtern mit fester Präposition (3), Hauptwörtern mit fester Präposition (4), und dient nicht zuletzt als Subjekt eines Satzes / als Satzgegenstand (5). Diese Funktion kann im übrigen auch die **Infinitiv-Konstruktion** übernehmen: ***To travel*** *round the world is something a lot of people would like to do once in their life.*

"My husband's not very keen on flying."

16 *could have done* und *should have done / could have done* and *should have done*

(1) She **could/should have helped** me. Why didn't she? You **could/should have sent** a letter, but I never received one.

(2) She **could have helped** you if she had known. I **could have sent** a letter if I had known your address.

(3) They left at two, now it's five o'clock so they **should have reached** Dublin by now.

Die Verbindung von **could/should + have + Mittelwort der Vergangenheit** drückt eine Möglichkeit aus, die zwar in der Vergangenheit bestand, aber nicht genutzt wurde (1). Die Wortfolge ist für deutschsprachige Lerner oft gewöhnungsbedürftig. Sie findet sich häufig im Hauptsatzteil von Bedingungssätzen (2). **Should + have + Mittelwort der Vergangenheit** drückt mitunter auch eine Annahme aus (3).

rattle = klappern; screw = Schraube; loose = locker

17 Stammformen unregelmäßiger Verben / Principal parts of irregular verbs

Grundform	Vergangenheit	Perfekt	
be	was/were	have (has) been	sein
beat	beat	have beaten	schlagen
become	became	have become	werden
begin	began	have begun	beginnen
break	broke	have broken	brechen
bring	brought	have brought	bringen
build	built	have built	bauen
burn	burnt	have burnt	(ver)brennen
buy	bought	have bought	kaufen
catch	caught	have caught	fangen, erreichen
choose	chose	have chosen	(aus-)wählen
come	came	have come	kommen
cost	cost	have cost	kosten
cut	cut	have cut	schneiden
dig	dug	have dug	graben
do	did	have done	tun, machen
draw	drew	have drawn	zeichnen
dream	dreamt	have dreamt	träumen
drink	drank	have drunk	trinken
drive	drove	have driven	(Auto) fahren
eat	ate	have eaten	essen
fall	fell	have fallen	fallen
feel	felt	have felt	(sich) fühlen
feed	fed	have fed	füttern
fight	fought	have fought	(be)kämpfen
find	found	have found	finden
fly	flew	have flown	fliegen
forget	forgot	have forgotten	vergessen
get	got	have got	bekommen
give	gave	have given	geben
go	went	have gone	gehen, fahren
grow	grew	have grown	wachsen
hang	hung	have hung	hängen
have	had	have had	haben
hear	heard	have heard	hören
hit	hit	have hit	treffen, schlagen
hold	held	have held	halten
hurt	hurt	have hurt	verletzen, (sich) weh tun
keep	kept	have kept	(be)halten, bleiben
know	knew	have known	wissen, kennen
learn	learnt	have learnt	lernen
leave	left	have left	verlassen, abfahren
lend	lent	have lent	leihen
let	let	have let	(zu)lassen
lie	lay	have lain	liegen, sich legen
lose	lost	have lost	verlieren
make	made	have made	machen
mean	meant	have meant	meinen, bedeuten
meet	met	have met	treffen, begegnen
pay	paid	have paid	(be-)zahlen
put	put	have put	stellen, legen
read	read	have read [red]	lesen
ride	rode	have ridden	reiten, fahren

Grundform	Vergangenheit	Perfekt	
ring	rang	have rung	anrufen, klingeln
run	ran	have run	laufen, rennen
say	said	have said	sagen
see	saw	have seen	sehen
sell	sold	have sold	verkaufen
send	sent	have sent	schicken
shine	shone	have shone	scheinen
shoot	shot	have shot	(er)schießen
show	showed	have shown	zeigen
shut	shut	have shut	schließen, zumachen
sing	sang	have sung	singen
sit	sat	have sat	sitzen
sleep	slept	have slept	schlafen
speak	spoke	have spoken	sprechen
spell	spelt	have spelt	buchstabieren
spend	spent	have spent	verbringen, ausgeben
spoil	spoilt	have spoilt	verderben, vernichten; verwöhnen
spread	spread	have spread	(sich) ausbreiten, verbreiten
stand	stood	have stood	stehen
steal	stole	have stolen	stehlen
strike	struck	have struck	schlagen
swim	swam	have swum	schwimmen
take	took	have taken	nehmen
teach	taught	have taught	unterrichten, lehren
tell	told	have told	sagen, erzählen
think	thought	have thought	denken
understand	understood	have understood	verstehen
wear	wore	have worn	tragen
win	won	have won	gewinnen
write	wrote	have written	schreiben

In den nachfolgenden Wortschatzanhängen *Vocabulary* und *Dictionary* wird die Aussprache in eckigen Klammern nach jedem Eintrag angegeben. Dazu wird eine spezielle Lautschrift verwendet, deren wichtigste Symbole hier erläutert werden.

Symbol	Beispielwort	Aussprache
ə	number	wie *e* in deutsch *singe*
ɪ	in	wie *i* in deutsch *in*
ɪə	here	wie *ie* in deutsch *hier*
iː	meet	wie *ie* in deutsch *Knie*
e	yes	etwa wie *e* in deutsch *fett*
eɪ	day	nicht wie deutsch *ei*, sondern [e] + [ɪ]
eə	where	wie *air* in deutsch *fair*
æ	thanks	zwischen deutschem *a* und *ä*
aɪ	nice	wie *ei* in deutsch *Eile*
aʊ	how	wie *au* in deutsch *flau*
ɑː	father	wie *ah* in deutsch *Kahn*
ɒ	coffee	wie *o* in deutsch *Motte*
ɔɪ	boy	wie *eu* in *deutsch*
ɔː	four	wie *o* in deutsch *Borke*
ʌ	come	wie *a* in deutsch *Klatsch*
ʊ	look	wie *u* in deutsch *Butter*
ʊə	tourist	[ʊ] + [ə]
əʊ	no	[ə] + [ʊ]
uː	too	etwa wie *u* in deutsch *Tuch*
ɜː	early	etwa wie *ö* in deutsch *Segeltörn*
v	have	wie *v* in deutsch *Virus*
θ	thanks	wie ein gelispeltes *ß* in deutsch *Biß*
ð	this	wie ein gelispeltes *s* in deutsch *Sand*
s	seat	wie *ß* in deutsch *Muße*
z	please	wie *s* in deutsch *Museum*
ʃ	she	wie *sch* in deutsch *fesch*
ʒ	television	wie *g* in deutsch *Regie*
tʃ	cheers	wie *tsch* in deutsch *Klatsch*
dʒ	German	[d] + [ʒ]
ŋ	song	wie *ng* in deutsch *singen*
r	repeat	nicht wie ein deutsches r, sondern vorn im Munde gesprochen
w	we	nicht wie ein deutsches w, sondern durch die Lippen wie [uː]

Der hochgestellte Strich ' steht in Wörtern mit mehr als einer Silbe vor dem Teil des Wortes, der am stärksten betont wird. Der tiefgestellte Strich ‚ bedeutet, daß die folgende Silbe auch etwas betont wird.
Bei Sätzen werden im *Vocabulary* nur die Hauptbetonungen angegeben, nicht aber alle Betonungen im Einzelwort angeführt.

Hier finden Sie eine Auflistung aller englischen Wörter und Wendungen, die Sie in diesem Buch kennenlernen. Sie erscheinen in derselben Reihenfolge, wie sie vorne im Buch vorkommen.

In der linken Spalte steht jeweils das englische Wort oder die Wendung und dahinter in eckigen Klammern die Aussprache. Einen Leitfaden zur Aussprache finden Sie auf der Vorseite. In der mittleren Spalte erscheint die deutsche Übersetzung und in der rechten Spalte ein Satzbeispiel, in dem das englische Wort stehen könnte. Wenn Sie die Vokabeln einmal gelernt haben, können Sie diese rechte Spalte benutzen, um sich selbst abzufragen. Sie decken dabei die linke Spalte zu und versuchen, die durch das Zeichen ~ markierte Lücke mit dem richtigen Wort zu füllen.

Die **fettgedruckten** Wörter und Wendungen sind besonders nützlich. Sie werden sie öfter brauchen und sollten sie deshalb vorrangig lernen. Die Wörter in normalem Druck sind in diesem Buch noch nicht so wichtig.

Alle Wörter und Wendungen sind in dieser Wortliste nur dort aufgeführt, wo sie zum ersten Mal vorkommen. Wenn Sie ein Wort zu einem späteren Zeitpunkt nochmals nachschlagen möchten, finden Sie die Aussprache und Übersetzung in der alphabetischen Wortschatzliste ab Seite 149.

UNITS 1 & 2

I **move** [muːv]	Umzug, (Fort)Bewegung; (*hier:* new moves = Neubeginn)	

UNIT 1 *Step 1*

S common ['kɒmən]	gemeinsam, allgemein, üblich, gewöhnlich	
in common [ɪn 'kɒmən]	gemeinsam	
dislike [dɪs'laɪk]	nicht mögen; Abneigung	
1 like about [ˌlaɪk ə'baʊt]	schätzen an, gern haben an	
crowd; crowded [kraʊd; 'kraʊdɪd]	(Menschen)Menge; überfüllt	The train station was very ~.
history ['hɪstərɪ]	Geschichte	Jane is studying ~ at university.
expect; expectation [ɪk'spekt; ˌekspek'teɪʃn]	erwarten; Erwartung	We ~ed 40 people but only 20 came.
settle ['setl]	sich niederlassen; *auch:* zahlen, abrechnen	In 1980 we ~d in Australia.
settle down [ˌsetl 'daʊn]	sich ansiedeln, einleben	It took us a long time to ~ at the new school.
miss [mɪs]	vermissen	You'll ~ me when I've gone.
relative ['relətɪv]	Verwandte(-r)	All our ~s came to the birthday.
distance ['dɪstəns]	Entfernung	Columbus travelled a great ~ in 1492.
long-distance [ˌlɒŋ 'dɪstəns]	Fern-	~ phone calls are expensive.
feel homesick [ˌfiːl 'həʊmsɪk]	Heimweh haben	After three weeks on holiday I began to ~.
however [haʊ'evə]	jedoch, dennoch	John has blue eyes. His brother, ~, has brown ones.
success; successful [sək'ses; sək'sesfʊl]	Erfolg; erfolgreich	The show was a great ~.
western ['westən]	westlich, West-	Many Japanese people visit ~ Europe.
natural ['nætʃrəl]	natürlich, normal	I prefer holidays to work, but that's ~.
sunshine ['sʌnʃaɪn]	Sonnenschein	Most people prefer ~ to rain.
space [speɪs]	Weite, Raum, freier Platz, Lücke; *auch:* Weltraum	There's lots of ~ in countries like Australia.
freedom ['friːdəm]	Freiheit	We can do what we like, when we like. We have lots of ~.
photograph; photographer ['fəʊtəgrɑːf, fə'tɒgrəfə]	Foto; Fotograf(-in)	He always carries a ~ of his wife.
remind of [rɪ'maɪnd əv]	erinnern an	Christmas ~s me ~ my childhood.

1b definition [ˌdefɪˈnɪʃn] — Erklärung, Umschreibung
   make sb. do sth. — *hier:* jdn. zu etwas veranlassen, zwingen — The boy ~ the little girl cry.

   e.g. (= for example) [iːˈdʒiː] — z.B. (= zum Beispiel) — I like warm countries, ~ France or Italy.

   missing [ˈmɪsɪŋ] — fehlend — My bag is ~. I can't find it.
   northern [ˈnɔːðn] — nördlich, Nord- — ~ England is colder than the south.
   southern [ˈsʌðən] — südlich, Süd- — Texas is in the ~ United States.
   eastern [ˈiːstən] — östlich, Ost- — ~ Europe has changed a lot since 1990.

   United Kingdom (UK) [juːˌnaɪtɪd ˈkɪŋdəm] — Vereinigtes Königreich *(Großbritannien und Nordirland)* — The ~ includes Britain and Northern Ireland.
   Ireland [ˈaɪələnd] — Irland — Northern ~ is a part of the UK.
   Wales [weɪlz] — Wales *(Teil Großbritanniens)* — Only a few people in ~ speak Welsh.

   Irish [ˈaɪrɪʃ] — irisch(-e, -er, -es); Ire, Irin — He's from Ireland. He's ~.
2 **mention** [ˈmenʃn] — erwähnen — He didn't ~ her name.
   expert (on) [ˈekspɜːt] — Experte, Expertin, Fachmann (für) — She's an ~ on American history.
   emigrate [ˈemɪɡreɪt] — auswandern
   advise [ədˈvaɪz] — raten
   expression [ɪkˈspreʃn] — Ausdruck, Äußerung — What's the English ~ for that?
   realistic [ˌrɪəˈlɪstɪk] — realistisch, wirklichkeitsnah, sachlich — The film gave a ~ picture of life during the war.

   cost [kɒst] — (Un)Kosten, Preis, Aufwand — The ~ of the holiday was more than I expected.

   ought to [ɔːt tə] — sollte(-st, -t, -n) — You ~ tell him you can't come.
   practical [ˈpræktɪkl] — praktisch, geschickt — Cars are often more ~ than public transport.

UNIT 1 *Step 2*

S **abroad** [əˈbrɔːd] — nach/in Übersee, ins/im Ausland — He spent his last holiday ~.
1 review (of) [rɪˈvjuː] — Rückblick (auf)
1d memory (of) [ˈmemərɪ] — Gedächtnis, Erinnerung (an)
   go round [ˌɡəʊ ˈraʊnd] — vorbeigehen, besuchen
   hold (held, held) [həʊld, held] — halten (hielt, gehalten) — He likes to ~ her hand.
1e **library** [ˈlaɪbrərɪ] — Bücherei, Bibliothek — The ~ had many old books.
   excite; exciting [ɪkˈsaɪt; ɪkˈsaɪtɪŋ] — erregen, aufregen; aufregend — The film was very ~.
   guy [ɡaɪ] — Bursche, Typ — He's not that kind of ~.
   firm [fɜːm] — Firma — He works for a large ~.

UNIT 2 *Step 1*

S ping-pong [ˈpɪŋpɒŋ] — Tischtennis; *hier:* Wechselspiel
   belong to [bɪˈlɒŋ tə] — gehören — This coat ~s ~ me. It's mine.
   contrasting [kənˈtrɑːstɪŋ] — gegensätzlich
1 **take place** [ˌteɪk ˈpleɪs] — stattfinden, sich ereignen — The wedding will ~ next May.
   railway [ˈreɪlweɪ] — Eisenbahn — John is proud of his model ~.
   review [rɪˈvjuː] — Rundschau
   pretty [ˈprɪtɪ] — hübsch — She looks ~ when she smiles.
   cottage [ˈkɒtɪdʒ] — Häuschen — They have a small ~ in the country.
   all around [ˌɔːl əˈraʊnd] — ringsumher, überall — People were standing ~.
   grass; grassy [ɡrɑːs; ˈɡrɑːsɪ] — Gras; grasbedeckt, Gras- — The ~ area is perfect for picnics.
   field [fiːld] — Feld — The ~ was full of corn.
   stream [striːm] — Bach — The mountain ~ had cool, clear water.

   run (ran, run) [rʌn, ræn, rʌn] — *hier:* fließen (floß, geflossen) — The Thames ~s through London.
   image [ˈɪmɪdʒ] — Bild; Image — Many people have a false ~ of America.

   what is it like? [ˌwɒt ɪz ɪt ˈlaɪk] — wie ist es?, wie sieht es aus? — ~ to ride a motorbike?

all over [ˌɔːl 'əʊvə]	überall, in ganz …	People drink Coke ~ the world.
unspoilt [ˌʌn'spɔɪlt]	unverdorben, unbeschädigt	Some parts of France are still ~.
disappear [ˌdɪsə'pɪə]	verschwinden	The sun ~ed behind a large building.
antique [æn'tiːk]	Antiquität, Antiquitäten-	~s are often expensive.
lock [lɒk]	abschließen, zusperren	~ the door when you leave.
sad [sæd]	traurig	He was ~ when his dog died.
ordinary ['ɔːdnrɪ]	gewöhnlich, einfach	It has been an ~ sort of day.
line [laɪn]	Linie; Zeile; (Telefon)Leitung	The London to Brighton ~ is very busy.
service ['sɜːvɪs]	Dienst(leistung)	The bus ~ here is terrible.
1a correct; correction [kə'rekt; kə'rekʃn]	berichtigen; richtig; Korrektur, Verbesserung	The teacher ~ed the tests.
1b spoil (spoilt, spoilt) [spɔɪl, spɔɪlt]	verderben (verdarb, verdorben), vernichten, ruinieren; *auch:* verwöhnen	The noise outside ~t the concert.
good-looking [ˌgʊd'lʊkɪŋ]	gutaussehend, attraktiv	He's a handsome, ~ man.
combination [ˌkɒmbɪ'neɪʃn]	Kombination, Verbindung	
smile [smaɪl]	Lächeln; lächeln	She gave me a big ~.
2 cause [kɔːz]	Ursache, Grund; veranlassen, verursachen, bewirken	Sweet foods are a ~ of toothache.
run (ran, run) [rʌn, ræn, rʌn]	*hier:* betreiben, führen *(Geschäft)*	His aunt ~s a small shop.
villager ['vɪlɪdʒə]	Dorfbewohner(-in)	
develop; development [dɪ'veləp; dɪ'veləpmənt]	(sich) entwickeln; Entwicklung	The political situation could ~ into a crisis.
result [rɪ'zʌlt]	Ergebnis	The ~s of the test were very useful.
due to ['djuː tə]	wegen, infolge von	The plan was changed ~ bad weather.
B write out [ˌraɪt 'aʊt]	ausschreiben, vervollständigen	
hey [heɪ]	hallo, he	"~! Mind the wet paint!"

UNIT 2 *Step 2*

1 for [fɔː, fə]	seit	He has lived in Germany ~ six years.
period ['pɪərɪəd]	Periode, Zeitraum	
1b present ['preznt]	gegenwärtig, momentan	She doesn't like her ~ job.
bike [baɪk]	Fahrrad	He decided to go into town by ~.
2 present perfect progressive [ˌpreznt 'pɜːfɪkt prə'gresɪv]	Verlaufsform der vollendeten Gegenwart	
recent; recently ['riːsnt; 'riːsntlɪ]	neu, jüngst; vor kurzem, unlängst	I ~ bought a new washing machine.
2a reply [rɪ'plaɪ]	Antwort; antworten	Did you get a ~ to your letter?
goodness ['gʊdnɪs]	du meine Güte!, mein Gott!	"Oh my ~! What a terrible storm!"
wallet ['wɒlɪt]	Brieftasche	He lost his ~ on the train.
2b TV station [tiː'viː ˌsteɪʃn]	Fernsehsender	The local ~ shows great programmes.
immigrant ['ɪmɪgrənt]	Einwanderer	There are many ~s in New York.
extra ['ekstrə]	zusätzlich, Zusatz-	
3 compare [kəm'peə]	vergleichen	The professor ~d his students' exam results.
3a advantage; disadvantage [əd'vɑːntɪdʒ; ˌdɪsəd'vɑːntɪdʒ]	Vorteil; Nachteil	Living in a large city has many ~s.

UNITS 1 & 2 *Panorama Plus*

S kangaroo [ˌkæŋgə'ruː]	Känguruh	Australia is the home of the ~.
sheep *(Ez/Mz)* [ʃiːp]	Schaf(-e)	Wool comes from ~.
hundred ['hʌndrəd]	hundert	Birmingham is a ~ miles from London.

Factfile on Australia

(fact)file ['fækt,faɪl]	Bericht, Dossier	All the details are in the ~.
plant [plɑ:nt]	Pflanze	All ~s need water to live.
young *(Ez/Mz)* [jʌŋ]	(Tier)Junge(-n)	The animal fed its babies, i.e. its ~.
pouch [paʊtʃ]	Beutel	A baby kangaroo lives in its mother's ~.
grow (grew, grown) [grəʊ, gru:, grəʊn]	wachsen (wuchs, gewachsen)	Flowers ~ in the garden.
outback ['aʊtbæk]	Hinterland *(in Australien)*	There are many sheep farms in the ~.
station ['steɪʃn]	*hier:* (Zucht)Farm	Farms in Australia are sometimes called ~s.
huge [hju:dʒ]	riesig	She ate a ~ ice cream. It was enough for three!
hectare ['hekteə]	Hektar *(Flächenmaß)*	He has fifty ~s of land.
raise [reɪz]	(hoch)heben, errichten; *hier:* züchten	They ~d sheep on the farm.
system ['sɪstəm]	System	The tube ~ in London is difficult to understand for some people.
allow [ə'laʊ]	erlauben, ermöglichen	Joe wouldn't ~ Tom to read his book. He said 'no' when Tom asked him.
each other [ˌi:tʃ 'ʌðə]	einander, sich (gegenseitig)	Neighbours should help ~.
(even) though [('i:vn) ðəʊ]	obwohl	He was tired, ~ he hadn't done much.
apart [ə'pɑ:t]	(ab)gesondert, abseits; *hier:* voneinander entfernt	The two men stood ten metres ~.
provide [prə'vaɪd]	geben, liefern, versorgen	The sun ~s us with light.
patient ['peɪʃnt]	Patient(-in)	The doctor has many ~s.
emergency [ɪ'mɜ:dʒənsɪ]	Notfall	Quick! This is an ~.
truck [trʌk]	Lastwagen	This ~ can carry 40 pianos.
several ['sevrəl]	mehrere	~ letters arrived this morning.
trailer ['treɪlə]	Anhänger	They need a tractor and a ~ to transport all the wood.
coast [kəʊst]	Küste	The land by the sea is the ~.
plain [pleɪn]	Ebene	A ~ is a wide open space.
extremely [ɪk'stri:mlɪ]	äußerst	It was ~ hot last summer.
flat [flæt]	flach	Holland is a very ~ country.
edge [edʒ]	Rand, Kante, Grenze	He stood at the ~ of the lake.
desert ['dezət]	Wüste	The air in the ~ is hot and dry.
maximum ['mæksɪməm]	Maximum, Höchst-	Some cars have a ~ speed of about 200 km per hour.
Celsius *(Abk:* **C**) ['selsɪəs]	Celsius *(Temperaturmaß)*	It was 50° ~ in the desert.
stretch [stretʃ]	Fläche, Strecke	This ~ of road is very flat.
track [træk]	Gleis	Trains travel along ~s.
press [pres]	drücken	He ~ed the money into my hand.
button ['bʌtn]	Knopf	The on/off ~ is on the right.
second ['sekənd]	Sekunde	Please wait for a ~.
imagine [ɪ'mædʒɪn]	sich vorstellen	
break down [ˌbreɪk 'daʊn]	*hier:* eine Panne haben, stehenbleiben *(Auto)*	

Did you know?

population [ˌpɒpjʊ'leɪʃn]	Bevölkerung	The ~ of China is extremely high.
spread out (spread, spread) [spred, spred]	(sich) ausbreiten (breitete aus, hat ausgebreitet)	They ~ the food for the picnic.
direction [dɪ'rekʃn]	Richtung; *auch:* Anweisung, Vorschrift	He looked in my ~.

Australia and the USA

suburban [sə'bɜ:bən]	Vorstadt-, kleinstädtisch	I prefer ~ life to village life.

UNITS 1 & 2 *Revision Plus*

2	**discuss; discussion** [dɪ'skʌs; dɪ'skʌʃn]	diskutieren; Diskussion	The students had to ~ a difficult problem.
3	**own; owner** [əʊn; 'əʊnə]	besitzen; Besitzer(-in)	They pay rent to the ~ of the house.
	suddenly ['sʌdnlɪ]	plötzlich	It ~ started to rain.
	so [səʊ]	deshalb, darum, also	It got cold, ~ she put her coat on.
	nostalgic [nɒ'stældʒɪk]	nostalgisch	
4	noun [naʊn]	Substantiv, Hauptwort	
	add [æd]	hinzufügen	Can you ~ my name to the list?
	wave [weɪv]	Welle	He stood on the beach and watched the ~s.
	form [fɔːm]	bilden	
	cloud [klaʊd]	Wolke	The sun disappeared behind a big ~.
	creamy ['kriːmɪ]	kremig	The chicken came with a ~ sauce.
	dust; dusty [dʌst; 'dʌstɪ]	Staub; staubig	She cleaned the ~ off the table.
	rainy ['reɪnɪ]	regnerisch, verregnet	An umbrella is useful on ~ days.
	salty ['sɔːltɪ]	salzig	The food he cooks is always ~.
	sand; sandy [sænd; 'sændɪ]	Sand; sandig, Sand-	The children built castles in the ~.
	sleep; sleepy [sliːp; 'sliːpɪ]	Schlaf; schläfrig, müde	She sometimes talks in her ~.
	smell; smelly [smel; 'smelɪ]	Geruch, Duft; übelriechend, muffig	The ~ of the flowers filled the room.
	smoky ['sməʊkɪ]	qualmend, verräuchert	I don't like ~ pubs.
	look up [ˌlʊk 'ʌp]	nachsehen, nachschlagen	
5	**exchange** [ɪks'tʃeɪndʒ]	(aus)tauschen; Tausch	You can always ~ the book for another one.
6	**creative** [kriː'eɪtɪv]	kreativ, einfallsreich	The pictures she draws are very ~.
7	paper ['peɪpə]	Zeitung *(umgangssprachlich)*	
	forecast ['fɔːkɑːst]	Vorhersage	

STORY 1 _____

accent ['æksent]	Akzent	reporter [rɪ'pɔːtə]	Reporter(-in)
Englishman ['ɪŋglɪʃmən]	Engländer	some [sʌm]	irgendein(-e, -er, -es)

UNITS 3 & 4 _____

UNIT 3 *Step 1* _____

1	**free** [friː]	kostenlos	The best things in life are ~.
	especially [ɪ'speʃəlɪ]	besonders	Some card games are ~ good for children.
	adult ['ædʌlt]	Erwachsene(-r)	The film was for ~s only.
	class [klɑːs]	Kurs, Unterricht	He has a French ~ every Monday night.
	gold; golden [gəʊld; 'gəʊldən]	Gold; golden, aus Gold	Her ~ hair shone in the sun.
	rule [ruːl]	Regel, Vorschrift	The ~s of the game are easy to understand.
	first of all ['fɜːst əv ˌɔːl]	zuallererst, vor allen Dingen	~, you have to do your homework.
	finally ['faɪnəlɪ]	schließlich, letztendlich	~, he thanked us for coming.
	(un)popular [(ˌʌn)'pɒpjʊlə]	(un)beliebt, (un)populär	Football is very ~ in most countries.
	general ['dʒenərəl]	allgemein	Men are ~ly taller than women.
	keep (kept, kept) [kiːp, kept]	sich halten, bleiben (blieb, geblieben)	He ~s fit by jogging.
	make sure [ˌmeɪk 'ʃɔː]	sich vergewissern, feststellen	Please ~ you lock the door.

join [dʒɔɪn]	beitreten, sich anschließen; verbinden	I ~ed the tennis club last year.
ideal [aɪˈdɪəl]	ideal, geeignet	The weather was ~ for a picnic.
be overweight [biː ˌəʊvəˈweɪt]	Übergewicht haben	It isn't healthy to ~.
suffer (from) [ˈsʌfə]	leiden (an)	She regularly ~s from bad headaches.
disability [ˌdɪsəˈbɪlətɪ]	Behinderung	Because of his ~, he couldn't walk.
support [səˈpɔːt]	(unter)stützen; *hier:* tragen; Unterstützung	Do you ~ any political groups?
improve [ɪmˈpruːv]	verbessern	Visiting London really ~d my English.
all-round [ˌɔːlˈraʊnd]	allgemein, Gesamt-	Although he has a cold, his ~ health is very good.
private [ˈpraɪvɪt]	privat	This land is ~ property.
(un)fortunately [(ˌʌn)ˈfɔːtʃnətlɪ]	(un)glücklicherweise	~, noone was hurt in the accident.
court [kɔːt]	(Gerichts)Hof; *hier:* Tennisplatz	They booked a tennis ~.
obviously [ˈɒbvɪəslɪ]	offensichtlich, natürlich	He has ~ never played tennis before.
at times [ˌət ˈtaɪmz]	zeitweise	The airport is very busy ~.
stress [stres]	Streß, Druck	There's a lot of ~ in this job.
increase [ɪnˈkriːs]	steigern, vergrößern, erhöhen	The supermarket ~d its prices last week.
discover [dɪˈskʌvə]	entdecken	Columbus ~ed America in 1492.
countryside [ˈkʌntrɪsaɪd]	Landschaft	The ~ in this area is beautiful.
quality [ˈkwɒlətɪ]	Qualität	His clothes are of the highest ~.
appreciate [əˈpriːʃɪeɪt]	schätzen, würdigen	I really ~ your help.
opportunity [ˌɒpəˈtjuːnətɪ]	Gelegenheit, Möglichkeit	He never had an ~ to go to America.
1a contain [kənˈteɪn]	beinhalten, enthalten	
disabled [dɪsˈeɪbld]	behindert	Stairs can be a problem for ~ people.
1b all over the world [ɔːl ˌəʊvə ðə ˈwɜːld]	auf der ganzen Welt	English is spoken ~.
by myself [ˌbaɪ maɪˈself]	allein	I did all the work ~.
ice hockey [ˈaɪs ˌhɒkɪ]	Eishockey	
cycle [ˈsaɪkl]	radfahren	Why don't you ~ to school?
sail [seɪl]	segeln	It's better to ~ your boat on the sea than on a lake.
basketball [ˈbɑːskɪtbɔːl]	Basketball	
volleyball [ˈvɒlɪbɔːl]	Volleyball	
handball [ˈhændbɔːl]	Handball	
squash [skwɒʃ]	Squash	
race [reɪs]	rennen, rasen; Rennen	The shortest distance for a ~ is 100 metres.
2 badminton [ˈbædmɪntən]	Badminton, Federball	
skate [skeɪt]	Schlittschuh laufen	
windsurf [ˈwɪndsɜːf]	surfen	
equipment [ɪˈkwɪpmənt]	Ausrüstung	Skiing ~ is rather expensive.
hit (hit, hit) [hɪt, hɪt]	treffen (traf, getroffen), schlagen, (zusammen)stoßen	In tennis you have to ~ the ball very hard.
point [pɔɪnt]	(Kern)Punkt, Stelle; Ziel, Zweck	What is the ~ of the game?

UNIT 3 *Step 2* ————————

1 third conditional [ˈθɜːd kənˈdɪʃənl]	Bedingungssatz (Typ 3): die unwirkliche Bedingung in der Vergangenheit	
clause [klɔːz]	Satz *(grammatisch)*	
notice [ˈnəʊtɪs]	bemerken, beachten; Notiz, Beachtung	He didn't ~ that he had made a mistake.

1a **shout (at)** [ʃaʊt] — (laut) rufen, (an)schreien; Ruf, Schrei — A good teacher never ~s at his students.

risk [rɪsk] — Risiko, Gefahr; riskieren — He ~ed his life to help the girl.

take many risks [ˌteɪk ˌmenɪ ˈrɪsks] — viele Risiken eingehen — People who climb mountains often ~.

practise [ˈpræktɪs] — üben — I must ~ my English more often.

cheat [tʃiːt] — mogeln, schummeln — He always ~s when he plays cards.

cup [kʌp] — Pokal, Siegerpreis — Germany won the world ~ in 1990.

beat (beat, beaten) [biːt, biːt, ˈbiːtn] — schlagen (schlug, geschlagen) — Tom usually ~s me at tennis.

hero (heroes) [ˈhɪərəʊ, ˈhɪərəʊz] — Held (Helden) — He was a good soldier, but no ~.

1b **lazy** [ˈleɪzɪ] — faul — He doesn't work much; he's ~.

careless [ˈkeəlɪs] — unvorsichtig, unaufmerksam, nachlässig — John is a very ~ driver.

captain [ˈkæptɪn] — Kapitän — Who is the ~ of this ship?

weigh; weight [weɪ; weɪt] — wiegen; Gewicht — How much do you ~? – My present ~ is 84 kg.

put on weight [ˌpʊt ɒn ˈweɪt] — zunehmen *(Gewicht)* — Have you ~ since we last met?

drug [drʌg] — Droge — Taking ~s is against the law.

prison; prisoner [ˈprɪzn; ˈprɪznə] — Gefängnis; Gefangene(-r) — He was sent to ~ for murder.

1c **age** [eɪdʒ] — Alter(sstufe) — Nobody knows her true ~.

at the age of [ət ˌði: ˈeɪdʒ əv] — im Alter von …, mit … Jahren — He left school ~ 16.

2a scramble [ˈskræmbl] — *hier:* durcheinanderbringen, verdrehen

suitable [ˈsuːtəbl] — passend, geeignet — Those clothes are not really ~ for an interview.

figure [ˈfɪgə] — Figur, Aussehen — She went on a diet to improve her ~.

2b combine [kəmˈbaɪn] — verbinden, kombinieren

in fact [ɪn ˈfækt] — tatsächlich, eigentlich — Skiing is ~ harder than it looks.

welcome (to) [ˈwelkəm] — begrüßen (bei) — He ~d the visitors to the factory.

3 choice [tʃɔɪs] — (Aus)Wahl

talk [tɔːk] — Gespräch

canoe [kəˈnuː] — Kanu fahren, paddeln — He ~d all the way down the river.

UNIT 4 *Step 1*

us [ʌs, əs] — *hier:* wir — "Open the door – it's only ~!"

S **(black)board** [(ˈblæk)bɔːd] — Tafel

collect [kəˈlekt] — (ein)sammeln — His hobby is ~ing stamps.

whole [həʊl] — gesamt, ganz — The ~ family was here at Christmas.

1 **hamster** [ˈhæmstə] — Hamster — Many children have ~s as pets.

rabbit [ˈræbɪt] — Kaninchen — You shouldn't keep ~s in small boxes.

guinea pig [ˈgɪnɪ pɪg] — Meerschweinchen — ~s are popular pets in England.

chapter [ˈtʃæptə] — Kapitel — I only read one ~ of the book.

companion [kəmˈpænjən] — Begleiter(-in), Gefährte(-in), Freund(-in) — His greatest ~ was his dog.

choice [tʃɔɪs] — (Aus)Wahl — You have no ~ in the matter.

common [ˈkɒmən] — gemeinsam, allgemein, üblich, gewöhnlich — Cats are quite ~ pets.

sense [sens] — Sinn, Sinnesorgan — His story didn't make ~.

common sense [ˌkɒmən ˈsens] — gesunder Menschenverstand, Vernunft — Use your ~.

simple [ˈsɪmpl] — einfach — The rules of the game are ~.

avoid [əˈvɔɪd] — (ver)meiden — She always tries to ~ me.

decision [dɪˈsɪʒn] — Entscheidung — It was a difficult ~ to make.

consider [kənˈsɪdə] — überlegen, erwägen; *auch:* halten für — Have you ever ~ed buying a car?

careful [ˈkeəfʊl] — genau, gründlich — She's a very ~ worker.

whether ['weðə]	ob	I don't know ~ to go or not.
amount [ə'maʊnt]	Betrag, Höhe, Menge	He had to pay a large ~ of money.
attention [ə'tenʃn]	Aufmerksamkeit, (Be)Achtung	Can I have your ~, please!
care [keə]	(Für)Sorge	Old people often need a lot of ~.
daily ['deɪlɪ]	täglich, Tages-	He likes to take a ~ shower.
exercise ['eksəsaɪz]	*hier:* Auslauf, Bewegung	Jogging is a good form of ~.
vet [vet]	Tierarzt, Tierärztin	Her dog was sick so she took it to the ~.
helpful ['helpfʊl]	hilfreich, nützlich	The man at the tourist office was ~.
examine [ɪg'zæmɪn]	prüfen, untersuchen	The doctor ~d her broken leg.
proper ['prɒpə]	richtig, passend, geeignet	It wasn't the ~ thing to say.
lead (led, led) [liːd, led]	führen (führte, geführt)	Follow me – I'll ~ the way.
1a **sharp** [ʃɑːp]	scharf	The knife was very ~.
reach [riːtʃ]	erreichen, reichen (an etw.)	The ship took a week to ~ America.
deal (with) [diːl]	umgehen, sich befassen (mit)	A doctor ~s with sick people.
energy ['enədʒɪ]	Energie	Young people usually have more ~ than old people.
tidy ['taɪdɪ]	sauber, ordentlich	His desk was very ~.
tidy up [,taɪdɪ 'ʌp]	aufräumen, säubern	The children had to ~ their rooms.
around [ə'raʊnd]	um ... herum; ungefähr; *hier:* in	He likes to work ~ the garden.
tool [tuːl]	Werkzeug	I need some ~s to repair my bike.
nervous ['nɜːvəs]	nervös	He was ~ before the examination.
attack [ə'tæk]	angreifen	The girl was ~ed last night.
valuable ['væljʊəbl]	wertvoll	We have many ~ antiques.
furniture ['fɜːnɪtʃə]	Möbel	I bought some new ~ for the office.
damage ['dæmɪdʒ]	beschädigen; Schaden	Little Jimmie ~d my furniture with a hammer.
prepare [prɪ'peə]	vorbereiten, zubereiten	I've thought about everything. I'm ~d now.
1b connect [kə'nekt]	verbinden, in Zusammenhang stehen	
pig [pɪg]	Schwein	~s eat almost anything.
cow [kaʊ]	Kuh	~s produce milk.
beef [biːf]	Rind(fleisch)	He eats cold ~ sandwiches every day.
lamb [læm]	Lamm(fleisch)	People often eat ~ at Easter.
pork [pɔːk]	Schweinefleisch	~ is eaten with apple sauce.
product; production ['prɒdʌkt; prə'dʌkʃn]	Produkt, Erzeugnis; Produktion	Cheese and butter are milk ~s.
bacon ['beɪkən]	Speck	The English sometimes eat ~ and eggs for breakfast.
leather ['leðə]	Leder	She is wearing a ~ jacket.
sausage ['sɒsɪdʒ]	Wurst	He burnt the ~s.
2 note (down) [nəʊt]	notieren, aufschreiben	Joe got lots of ~s for his birthday.
toy [tɔɪ]	Spielzeug	He kept two birds in a ~.
cage [keɪdʒ]	Käfig	Cold is the ~ of hot.
opposite ['ɒpəzɪt]	Gegenteil	I ~ that he will come.
doubt [daʊt]	(be)zweifeln	She ~ed the present with thanks.
accept [ək'sept]	annehmen, akzeptieren, anerkennen	The visitor was a ~ stranger.
complete [kəm'pliːt]	völlig, vollständig; vervollständigen, (aus)füllen	
2a **aloud** [ə'laʊd]	laut	Read the text ~, please!

UNIT 4 *Step 2* _____

S chianti [kɪ'æntɪ]	Chianti *(ital. Rotwein)*	He ordered a bottle of ~.
1 passive ['pæsɪv]	Passiv, Leideform	
monkey ['mʌŋkɪ]	Affe	The ~ sat in the tree.

1a shoot (shot, shot) [ʃuːt, ʃɒt] — (er)schießen (schoß, geschossen) — The robber ~ the policeman.
solve [sɒlv] — lösen, klären — They cannot ~ the problem.
murder [ˈmɜːdə] — Mord — The ~ happened on Sunday evening.

ballpoint pen [ˈbɔːlpɔɪnt ˌpen] — Kugelschreiber — I prefer ~s to pencils.
1b cancel [ˈkænsl] — streichen, absagen — I must ~ the newspaper next week.
1c water [ˈwɔːtə] — (be)wässern, gießen — Don't forget to ~ my flowers.
gate [geɪt] — Tor, Pforte; *auch:* Flugsteig, Gate — She painted the garden ~ blue.
hang (hung, hung) [hæŋ, hʌŋ] — hängen (hing, gehangen) — He ~ his coat on the back of the chair.

2a various [ˈveərɪəs] — verschieden, mehrere — There are ~ reasons why I can't come.

couple [ˈkʌpl] — Paar — Jack and Jill are a lovely ~.
a couple of [ə ˈkʌpl əv] — einige, ein paar — I'll be there in ~ hours.
3 staff [stɑːf] — Personal — It's difficult to find good ~.
contact [ˈkɒntækt] — Kontakt, Beziehung; sich mit jdm. in Verbindung setzen — A baby needs ~ with its mother.

3a lonely [ˈləʊnlɪ] — einsam — A big city can be a ~ place.

UNITS 3 & 4 *Panorama Plus*

S sportsman/sportswoman [ˈspɔːtsmən, ˈspɔːtswʊmən] — Sportler/-in — Most ~ train very hard.

Too old at twenty?
title [ˈtaɪtl] — Titel, Überschrift — He won the European ~ three years ago.

gymnastics [dʒɪmˈnæstɪks] — Turnen, Gymnastik — ~ is quite a difficult sport.
dive [daɪv] — tauchen — He ~d under the water.
champion [ˈtʃæmpjən] — Meister(-in), Sieger(-in) — He is a tennis ~.
teenage [ˈtiːnˌeɪdʒ] — jugendlich, Jugend- — Italian ~ fashion is very popular in America.

force [fɔːs] — zwingen — His mother ~d him to drink milk.
control [kənˈtrəʊl] — Kontrolle; kontrollieren — The car went out of ~.
starlet [ˈstɑːlət] — Sternchen; Star — Few ~s are successful as adults.
stop [stɒp] — abhalten — She ~ped the baby from falling.
ruin [ˈrʊɪn] — ruinieren, zerstören; Ruine; Ruin, Untergang — The picnic was ~ed by the rain.

take part in [ˌteɪk ˈpɑːt ɪn] — teilnehmen an — Ten people will ~ the race.
practice [ˈpræktɪs] — Übung, Üben — You need a lot of ~ to become a champion.

hardly [ˈhɑːdlɪ] — kaum — There are ~ any flowers in the park.

kid [kɪd] — Kind — Most ~s like watching TV.
make it to the top [ˌmeɪk ɪt tə ðə ˈtɒp] — es bis zur Spitze schaffen, ganz nach oben kommen — You can ~ if you try.
aspect [ˈæspekt] — Aspekt, Gesichtspunkt

Did you know?
human [ˈhjuːmən] — Mensch; menschlich — Some ~s live to be over 100.
cheetah [ˈtʃiːtə] — Gepard — The ~ is the fastest animal.
speed [spiːd] — Geschwindigkeit — What is the maximum ~ of the car?
swift [swɪft] — Mauersegler — They have some ~s in their garden.
falcon [ˈfɔːlkən] — Falke — His hobby is training ~s.
jump [dʒʌmp] — springen — She ~ed out of the boat.
balloon [bəˈluːn] — Ballon — I always wanted to go up in a ~.

A working relationship
relationship (with) [rɪˈleɪʃnʃɪp] — Beziehung, Verhältnis (zu) — Do you have a good ~ with your father?

show jumper [ˈʃəʊ ˌdʒʌmpə] — Springreiter(-in); Springpferd — She wants to be a ~.
dolphin [ˈdɒlfɪn] — Delphin — ~s are very clever animals.
sniffer dog [ˈsnɪfə dɒg] — Spürhund — The ~ found drugs in his suitcase.
acceptable [əkˈseptəbl] — akzeptabel, annehmbar
bull [bʊl] — Stier — He has five ~s on his farm.
fox [fɒks] — Fuchs — ~es like eating chickens.
hunt [hʌnt] — jagen — The police are ~ing the robber.

UNITS 3 & 4 *Revision Plus*

4 **own** [əʊn] — eigen, einzig — I'd like to drive my ~ car.
5 **powerful** [ˈpaʊəfʊl] — mächtig, stark, (zug)kräftig — The wind was very ~.
helpless [ˈhelplɪs] — hilflos — She is quite ~ due to her disability.
useless [ˈjuːslɪs] — nutzlos, unbrauchbar — This broken bottle is ~.
6 **hurricane** [ˈhʌrɪkən] — Hurrikan, Wirbelsturm — Many people were killed by the ~.

STORY 2 _____

envelope [ˈenvələʊp] — Briefumschlag
fan [fæn] — Fan, Anhänger
go to see sb. [ˌgəʊ tə ˈsiː] — jdn. besuchen
personality [ˌpɜːsəˈnælətɪ] — Persönlichkeit

receiver [rɪˈsiːvə] — Empfänger(-in); *hier:* Telefonhörer
says, it ~ [ˌɪt ˈsez] — es heißt, steht (geschrieben)

UNITS 5 & 6 _____

UNIT 5 *Step 1* _____

1 **career** [kəˈrɪə] — Karriere, Beruf — Being a doctor is a good ~.
depend on [dɪˈpend ɒn] — abhängen von — I can't decide by myself. It ~s ~ you.
responsibility [rɪˌspɒnsəˈbɪlətɪ] — Verantwortung — The job carries a lot of ~.
duty [ˈdjuːtɪ] — Pflicht, Aufgabe; Dienst — It is your ~ to do your best.
profession; professional [prəˈfeʃn; prəˈfeʃənl] — Beruf; professionnel, Berufs-, Fach- — It was a ~ theatre group.
agency [ˈeɪdʒənsɪ] — Agentur, Büro — I found a job in an advertising ~.
satisfy [ˈsætɪsfaɪ] — zufriedenstellen — Are you ~ed with your new car?
apply [əˈplaɪ] — sich bewerben — He is going to ~ for the job.
fail [feɪl] — versagen, verfehlen, durchfallen — He ~ed the examination.
below [bɪˈləʊ] — unten — See ~ for our telephone number.
detail [ˈdiːteɪl] — Detail, Einzelheit — All the ~s are in the report.
qualification [ˌkwɒlɪfɪˈkeɪʃn] — Qualifikation — She had the right ~s for the job.
dream [driːm] — Traum — I had a strange ~ last night.
dream (dreamt, dreamt) [driːm, dremt] — träumen (träumte, geträumt) — He ~ of becoming a famous actor.
waste [weɪst] — Verschwendung; verschwenden; öde, leer, nutzlos — That film was a ~ of money.
divorced [dɪˈvɔːst] — geschieden — She is ~ with two children.
lawyer [ˈlɔːjə] — Rechtsanwalt — Most ~s earn a lot of money.
director [dɪˈrektə] — Direktor — A company ~ works long hours.
take shorthand [ˌteɪk ˈʃɔːthænd] — stenografieren — A secretary must be able to ~.
knowledge [ˈnɒlɪdʒ] — Kenntnis, Wissen — My ~ of history is very good.
dull [dʌl] — träge, langweilig, eintönig, trübe — The day was ~ and grey.
boring [ˈbɔːrɪŋ] — langweilig — The play was rather ~.
positive [ˈpɒzətɪv] — positiv, bejahend — He is hoping for a ~ answer.
humour [ˈhjuːmə] — Humor — He has no sense of ~.
interest [ˈɪntrəst] — Interesse; interessieren — London is a city of special ~.
bright [braɪt] — fröhlich, heiter, hell; *hier:* klug — He was a very ~ child.

embarrass [ɪmˈbærəs]	in Verlegenheit bringen, verwirren	He likes to ~ his little sister.
embarrassed [ɪmˈbærəst]	verlegen	I was ~ when I fell over in the road.
express [ɪkˈspres]	ausdrücken; ausdrücklich, *auch:* Eil-	Words cannot ~ how sad I am.
calm [kɑːm]	ruhig	You must stay ~ in an emergency.
performance [pəˈfɔːməns]	Ausführung, Vorstellung, Darstellung	His ~ in the play was super.
1a weak [wiːk]	schwach	He felt ~ after the illness.
aim [eɪm]	Ziel	His ~s in life are not realistic.
1b male [meɪl]	männlich	Many hospitals have ~ nurses.
argue [ˈɑːgjuː]	argumentieren, streiten	He ~s with his brother all the time.
clever [ˈklevə]	klug	She was a really ~ child.
female [ˈfiːmeɪl]	weiblich	Men often don't like having a ~ boss.
pass [pɑːs]	vorbeigehen, -fahren; (herüber)reichen; *hier:* bestehen *(Prüfung)*	Tom ~ed all his examinations.
salesman/saleswoman [ˈseɪlzmən, ˈseɪlzˌwʊmən]	Verkäufer(-in)	The ~ said the dress looked very nice.
unemployed [ˌʌnɪmˈplɔɪd]	arbeitslos	He has been ~ for a year now.
2 organize [ˈɔːgənaɪz]	organisieren	It is important to ~ your time well.
interrupt; interruption [ˌɪntəˈrʌpt; ˌɪntəˈrʌpʃn]	unterbrechen; Unterbrechung	The phone call was ~ed.
subject [ˈsʌbdʒɪkt]	Thema	I think we should change the ~.
be on the subject of ... [ˌbiː ɒn ðə ˈsʌbdʒɪkt əv]	sich mit dem Thema ... befassen	The lesson will ~ French history.
tourism [ˈtʊərɪzm]	Tourismus	~ is big business in London.

UNIT 5 *Step 2*

1a cough [kɒf]	Husten	He had a bad ~ from smoking.
lend (lent, lent) [lend, lent]	leihen (lieh, geliehen)	Can you ~ me your car for an hour?
use [juːz]	Gebrauch, Nutzen, Sinn	The ~ of the progressive tenses is a difficult thing to learn.
regret [rɪˈgret]	bedauern	I ~ not learning French as a child.
imagine [ɪˈmædʒɪn]	sich vorstellen	I can't ~ being 100 years old.
1b spare time [ˌspeə ˈtaɪm]	Freizeit	
favourite [ˈfeɪvrɪt]	Lieblings-	Apples are my ~ fruit.
pastime [ˈpɑːstaɪm]	Zeitvertreib, Hobby	Football is one of his ~s.
2a mad [mæd]	verrückt	
drive s.o. mad [ˌdraɪv ˈmæd]	jdn. verrückt machen	
bark [bɑːk]	bellen	The dog ~ed all night.
dig (dug, dug) [dɪg, dʌg]	graben (grub, gegraben)	He ~ a hole in the garden.
pick (up) [pɪk]	(auf)heben, aufnehmen; abholen; *hier:* pflücken *(Blumen)*	They ~ed all the flowers.
2b past [pɑːst]	vergangen, früher	
extra [ˈekstrə]	zusätzlich, Zusatz-	He works in a pub to earn ~ money.
3a stressful [ˈstresfʊl]	anstrengend, streßig	
typist [ˈtaɪpɪst]	Schreibkraft	The ~ finished all the letters.
officer [ˈɒfɪsə]	Offizier, (Polizei)Beamter/Beamtin	The police ~ took a lot of risks.

UNIT 6 *Step 1*

third [θɜːd]	dritte(-r, -s)	Wednesday is the ~ day of the week.
1 retirement [rɪˈtaɪəmənt]	Ruhestand	
former [ˈfɔːmə]	früher(-e, -er, -es), ehemalig	He is a ~ colleague of mine.

garden ['gɑ:dn]	Gartenarbeit betreiben	Father likes ~ing very much.
above [ə'bʌv]	oben	They live in a flat ~ a shop.
above all [ə,bʌv 'ɔ:l]	vor allem	He is a good man and ~ a good father.
sight [saɪt]	Sicht(weite), Anblick; Sehenswürdigkeit	We're going to look at the ~s tomorrow.
sunrise ['sʌnraɪz]	Sonnenaufgang	The ~ was very beautiful.
sunset ['sʌnset]	Sonnenuntergang	The clouds are often red at ~.
ocean ['əʊʃn]	Ozean	They crossed the Atlantic ~ to reach America.
capital ['kæpɪtl]	Hauptstadt	Paris is the ~ of France.
diary ['daɪərɪ]	Tagebuch	She wrote in her ~ every day.
record ['rekɔ:d]	Aufzeichnung, Wiedergabe; Rekord	He keeps a ~ of all the money he spends.
feeling ['fi:lɪŋ]	Gefühl	I get the ~ I'm being watched.
suppose [sə'pəʊz]	annehmen, vermuten	I ~ I'll get married one day.
guilty ['gɪltɪ]	schuldig	The court found the prisoner ~.
occupy ['ɒkjʊpaɪ]	in Besitz nehmen, besetzen, innehaben; *hier*: ausfüllen	He can ~ his time well.
activity [æk'tɪvətɪ]	Aktivität, Tätigkeit, Unternehmung	Tennis is a healthy sports ~.
weekly ['wi:klɪ]	wöchentlich, pro Woche, Wochen-	The magazine comes out ~.
progress *(Ez/Mz)* ['prəʊgres]	Fortschritt(-e)	His ~ at school was rather slow.
prove [pru:v]	beweisen	You cannot ~ that I am wrong.
1a **mainly** ['meɪnlɪ]	hauptsächlich	I ~ go shopping at the supermarket.
1b **go to see sb.** [,gəʊ tə 'si:]	jdn. besuchen	I must ~ Tom today.
continent ['kɒntɪnənt]	Kontinent	There are five ~s in the world.
2 **many happy returns of the day!** [mænɪ hæpɪ rɪ'tɜ:nz əv ðə 'deɪ]	herzlichen Glückwunsch zum Geburtstag!	
how are things? [,haʊ ɑ: 'θɪŋz]	wie geht es (dir/Ihnen/euch)?	
how are you keeping? [haʊ ɑ: jʊ 'ki:pɪŋ]	wie geht es dir/Ihnen/euch?	
here's to you! [,hɪəz tə 'ju:]	auf dein/Ihr/euer Wohl!	
look after yourself! [,lʊk ɑ:ftə jɔ:'self]	mach's gut!, paß auf dich auf!	
cheerio! [,tʃɪərɪ'əʊ]	mach's gut!, tschüs!	
give my love to ... [,gɪv maɪ 'lʌv tə]	grüße / grüßen Sie / grüßt ... ganz lieb von mir	
2a **touch** [tʌtʃ]	Berührung, Verbindung, Kontakt; berühren	They stayed in ~ for many years.
B **in italics** [ɪn ɪ'tælɪks]	in Kursivschrift	

UNIT 6 *Step 2*

S **paper** ['peɪpə]	Zeitung *(umgangssprachlich)*	I read the ~ every morning.
1 **luckily** ['lʌkɪlɪ]	glücklicherweise	~ the driver saw the child.
1a **risky** ['rɪskɪ]	riskant, gefährlich	
1b **climber** ['klaɪmə]	Bergsteiger(-in)	A ~ must have good equipment.
save [seɪv]	retten; *auch*: aufheben, aufbewahren	Thank you! You ~d my life.
trouble ['trʌbl]	Mühe, Schwierigkeiten, Probleme, Ärger; (pol.) Unruhen	There was ~ in the pub last night.
make every mistake in the book [meɪk 'evrɪ mɪ,steɪk ɪn ðə 'bʊk]	jeden erdenklichen Fehler machen	
route [ru:t]	Route, Strecke	This ~ is very busy.
poor [pɔ:]	*hier*: schlecht, ungeeignet	The food in this restaurant is ~.
alive [ə'laɪv]	lebend, am Leben	My grandmother is still ~.
2 **comparison** [kəm'pærɪsn]	Vergleich	
contrast ['kɒntrɑ:st]	Gegensatz	
repeat [rɪ'pi:t]	wiederholen	Could you ~ that, please?

2 comparison [kəm'pærɪsn] — Vergleich
contrast ['kɒntrɑːst] — Gegensatz
repeat [rɪ'piːt] — wiederholen — Could you ~ that, please?
2a frequent ['friːkwənt] — häufig — He is a ~ visitor to the zoo.
2b plan [plæn] — planen — They ~ned a holiday in France.
Mom [mɒm] — Mutti *(amerik.)* — Ask your ~ if you can go.
please [pliːz] — zufriedenstellen, erfreuen; (jdm.) gefallen — He'll do anything to ~ her.

3 definitely ['defɪnɪtlɪ] — bestimmt, zweifellos — She's ~ not coming.
retirement [rɪ'taɪəmənt] — Ruhestand — My dad is enjoying his ~.

UNITS 5 & 6 *Panorama Plus*

Sun City, Arizona

science ['saɪəns] — Naturwissenschaft — He wants to study ~.
science-fiction [ˌsaɪəns 'fɪkʃn] — Science-fiction-, utopisch — I like ~ stories.
curve [kɜːv] — Kurve — He drove round the ~ too fast.
circle ['sɜːkl] — Kreis — The children all stood in a ~.
silent ['saɪlənt] — ruhig, still — The house was completely ~.
surface ['sɜːfɪs] — Oberfläche — The table had a plastic ~.
recognize ['rekəgnaɪz] — (wieder)erkennen — She didn't ~ me.
exception [ɪk'sepʃn] — Ausnahme — Every rule has an ~.
citizen ['sɪtɪzn] — Bürger(-in) — He is a British ~.
safe; safety [seɪf; 'seɪftɪ] — sicher; Sicherheit — I don't think this bridge is ~.
youth [juːθ] — Jugend — The ~ of today have a lot of money.

oriented ['ɔːrɪentɪd] — orientiert — America is a very money-~ country.

society [sə'saɪətɪ] — Gesellschaft — Modern ~ is full of problems.
remain [rɪ'meɪn] — bleiben — She ~ed in the house all day.
environment [ɪn'vaɪərnmənt] — Umgebung — The house is nice but the ~ is awful.

persuade [pə'sweɪd] — überreden, überzeugen
argument ['ɑːgjʊmənt] — Argument; Streit — I wasn't persuaded by his ~s.
difficulty ['dɪfɪkəltɪ] — Schwierigkeit

Did you know?

great-grandmother [ˌgreɪt'grænˌmʌðə] — Urgroßmutter — How old is your ~?
unemployment [ˌʌnɪm'plɔɪmənt] — Arbeitslosigkeit, Arbeitslosen- — ~ is increasing quickly.
figure ['fɪgə] — Zahl — Have you seen the most recent sales ~s?
out of work [aʊt əv 'wɜːk] — arbeitslos — He has been ~ for a year.
United States (US) [juˌnaɪtɪd 'steɪts] — Vereinigte Staaten von Amerika — The President of the ~ is a powerful man.

Losing your job – it might be a good move!

steward/stewardess ['stjʊəd, ˌstjʊə'des] — Steward/Stewardeß — The ~ offered him a drink.
specialist ['speʃəlɪst] — Spezialist(-in) — He is a ~ in American history.

UNITS 5 & 6 *Revision Plus*

S imagination [ɪˌmædʒɪ'neɪʃn] — Vorstellungskraft, Phantasie — He doesn't have very much ~.
maybe ['meɪbiː] — vielleicht
2 willing ['wɪlɪŋ] — gewillt, bereit — He wasn't ~ to pay for the meal.
non- [nɒn] — nicht-, un- — He booked a ~stop flight.
smoker ['sməʊkə] — Raucher(-in) — Are you still a ~?

any ['enɪ] — irgendein(-e, -er); jede(-r, -s) (beliebige)

3 speaker ['spiːkə] — Sprecher(-in) — The professor is the last ~ this evening.

5 inform [ɪn'fɔːm] — informieren, mitteilen — Will we be ~ed of the result?
qualify ['kwɒlɪfaɪ] — sich qualifizieren, eignen — When will you ~ as a doctor?
application [ˌæplɪ'keɪʃn] — Gesuch, Antrag, Bewerbung — He posted his ~ last week.
drop [drɒp] — fallenlassen; *hier:* weglassen; Tropfen — Don't ~ it, it'll break.

completion [kəm'pliːʃn] — Fertigstellung, Abschluß — When is ~ of the building expected?

satisfaction; dissatisfaction [ˌsætɪs'fækʃn; 'dɪsˌsætɪs'fækʃn] — Zufriedenheit, Befriedigung; Unzufriedenheit — She got no ~ from her work.
writer ['raɪtə] — Schreiber(-in), Autor(-in) — Charles Dickens was a great ~.

STORY 3

blue [bluː] — *hier:* traurig, depressiv — bureau ['bjʊərəʊ] — Büro
boyfriend ['bɔɪfrend] — Freund *(eines Mädchens)* — mirror ['mɪrə] — Spiegel

UNITS 7 & 8

UNIT 7 *Step 1*

1 point of view [ˌpɔɪnt əv 'vjuː] — Standpunkt, Ansicht — I don't agree with your ~.
silly ['sɪlɪ] — dumm — She says a lot of ~ things.
nasty ['nɑːstɪ] — böse, schlimm, gefährlich, fies — The ~ boy hit my little sister.
sex; sexy [seks; 'seksɪ] — Geschlecht; Sex; sexy, aufreizend — There were many ~ scenes in that film.

nonsense ['nɒnsəns] — Unsinn, Blödsinn — Don't talk such ~!
fluently ['fluːəntlɪ] — fließend — He speaks German ~.
pay attention to [ˌpeɪ ə'tenʃn tə] — beachten, Aufmerksamkeit schenken — He doesn't ~ his teachers.

tobacco [tə'bækəʊ] — Tabak — Cigarettes are made from ~.
alcohol ['ælkəhɒl] — Alkohol — Too much ~ is bad for your health.
client ['klaɪənt] — Kunde, Kundin — I'm taking an important ~ to lunch.
press [pres] — Presse *(Zeitung)* — She reads the adverts in the ~.
difference ['dɪfrəns] — Unterschied — It doesn't make any ~.
frozen ['frəʊzn] — (ein)gefroren, Tiefkühl- — ~ food is very expensive.
shaver ['ʃeɪvə] — Rasierapparat — He got a new ~ for Christmas.
original [ə'rɪdʒənl] — original, ursprünglich; *hier:* originell, einfallsreich, neu — That's an ~ tie you're wearing!

purpose ['pɜːpəs] — Zweck, Absicht — What is the ~ of your visit?
anyway ['enɪweɪ] — jedenfalls — ~, she's not coming, so it doesn't matter.

psychologist [saɪ'kɒlədʒɪst] — Psychologe, Psychologin — He wants to be a ~ when he leaves university.

afford [ə'fɔːd] — sich leisten — I can't ~ a new TV.
subconscious [ˌsʌb'kɒnʃəs] — unterbewußt — She thought about it ~ly.
influence ['ɪnfluəns] — Einfluß; beeinflussen — He's a bad ~ on me.
particular [pə'tɪkjʊlə] — besondere(-r, -s), speziell — This ~ colour suits you well.
in particular [ˌɪn pə'tɪkjʊlə] — besonders, vor allem — Children ~ are often ill.
be at risk [biː ət 'rɪsk] — gefährdet sein — Her life ~.
fair [feə] — fair, anständig — The teacher was always ~.
1b cigar [sɪ'gɑː] — Zigarre — I don't like the smell of ~ smoke.
pipe [paɪp] — Pfeife; *auch:* (Rohr)Leitung — My brother smokes a ~.
tin; tinned [tɪn; tɪnd] — (Konserven)Dose; eingemacht, konserviert — ~ pears are nice with cream.

2   **be sick and tired of sth.** [bi: ˌsɪk
       ənd ˈtaɪəd əv ˈsʌmθɪŋ]   etw. satt haben

B   **front** [frʌnt]   Vorderseite, Front, Vorder-   The ~ garden is quite small.

UNIT 7 *Step 2*

S   **blond(e)** [blɒnd]   blond   She has lovely ~ hair.
1   **speech** [spiːtʃ]   Rede   The Prime Minister made an
                                                                                       inportant ~.

        reported speech [rɪˌpɔːtɪd ˈspiːtʃ]   indirekte Rede
        fear [fɪə]   Angst   ~ of flying is quite common.
1a **right** [raɪt]   direkt, gerade   The station is ~ around the corner.
1c **vocabulary** [vəʊˈkæbjʊləri]   Wortschatz   His ~ isn't very large.
2a **switch on/off** [ˌswɪtʃ ˈɒn, ˈɒf]   ein-, ausschalten   Please ~ the radio.
        wash up [ˌwɒʃ ˈʌp]   abwaschen, abspülen   He didn't want to ~.
3   **truth** [truːθ]   Wahrheit   Sometimes the ~ hurts.
        shampoo [ʃæmˈpuː]   Shampoo   Which ~ do you use?
3a mail [meɪl]   Post(sendung)

UNIT 8 *Step 1*

S   **print** [prɪnt]   Gedrucktes, (Ab)Druck; drucken   You must read the small ~ before
                                                                                       you sign anything.

1   **skill** [skɪl]   Fertigkeit, (Fach)Kenntnis   A good secretary needs
                                                                                       shorthand ~s.

        text [tekst]   Text   Have you read the ~ yet?
        pupil [ˈpjuːpl]   Schüler(-in)   The school had 1,000 ~s.
        handle [ˈhændl]   handhaben, umgehen mit,   She ~s children very well.
                                                    fertigwerden

        afterwards [ˈɑːftəwədz]   nachher, hinterher, später   Are you going home ~?
        difficulty [ˈdɪfɪkəltɪ]   Schwierigkeit   He has ~ getting up early.
        effort [ˈefət]   Anstrengung, Mühe   He makes no ~ at all at school.
        college [ˈkɒlɪdʒ]   weiterführende Schule, Hochschule   He went to ~ last year.
        attend [əˈtend]   teilnehmen an, besuchen   I always ~ all my classes.
        basic [ˈbeɪsɪk]   grundlegend, Grund(lagen)-   The ~ problem is that he is lazy.
        be ashamed (of) [bi: əˈʃeɪmd]   sich schämen (für, wegen)   He ~ of his old clothes.
        it says [ˌɪt ˈsez]   es heißt, steht (geschrieben)   ~ 12 o'clock on the card.
        instruction [ɪnˈstrʌkʃn]   Anweisung   Follow the ~s carefully!
        not even [nɒt ˈiːvn]   (noch) nicht einmal   He could ~ remember her name.
        look up [ˌlʊk ˈʌp]   nachsehen, nachschlagen   Can you ~ the word in the
                                                                                       dictionary?

        hell [hel]   Hölle   She made his life ~.
        threat; threaten [θret; ˈθretn]   (Be)Drohung; (be)drohen   He ~ed me with a knife.
        notebook [ˈnəʊtbʊk]   Notizbuch   The policeman wrote the details in
                                                                                       his ~.

        shelf (shelves) [ʃelf, ʃelvz]   Regal(-e)   The ~ was full of books.
        anyone [ˈenɪwʌn]   jeder (beliebige)   Can ~ come to the party?
        real [ˈriːəl]   wirklich, wahr, echt   The holiday was a ~ adventure.
        struggle [ˈstrʌgl]   Kampf, Ringen, Anstrengung   Bringing up six children was a ~.
        refuse; refusal [rɪˈfjuːz; rɪˈfjuːzl] sich weigern, ablehnen;   He ~d to go on holiday with me.
                                                    Ablehnung, Verweigerung

        (some of) whom [huːm]   (von) denen (einige)   There were four people, two of ~ I
                                                                                       knew.

1a **everyday** [ˈevrɪdeɪ]   alltäglich, Alltags-   He wore his ~ clothes to the party.
2   like [laɪk]   Vorliebe
        preference [ˈprefərəns]   Vorliebe, Vorzug
        reader [ˈriːdə]   *hier*: Lesestoff, Lektüre   The class had a Shakespeare play
                                                                                       as a ~.

        biography [baɪˈɒgrəfɪ]   Biographie   Have you read the new ~ of
                                                                                       Marilyn Monroe?

novel ['nɒvl] — Roman, Novelle — I read two ~s while I was on holiday.

detective [dɪ'tektɪv] — Detektiv, Kriminal- — I love reading ~ stories.

non-fiction book [ˌnɒn'fɪkʃn ˌbʊk] — Sachbuch — He only writes ~s.

romance [rəʊ'mæns] — Liebesroman — I read a wonderful ~ about a prince who married a poor girl.

dislike [dɪs'laɪk] — nicht mögen — Most people ~ going to the dentist.

UNIT 8 Step 2

S **kiosk** ['kiːɒsk] — Kiosk — He bought a paper at the ~.

copy ['kɒpɪ] — kopieren, abschreiben, abmalen — Can you ~ the first chapter for me?

1 relative clause [ˌrelətɪv 'klɔːz] — Relativsatz

1a **politics** ['pɒlətɪks] — Politik — She thinks ~ is very boring.

Canadian [kə'neɪdjən] — kanadisch(-e, -er, -es); Kanadier(-in) — Do you have any ~ friends?

fiction ['fɪkʃn] — Erfindung, Dichtung, Romanliteratur — Sir Arthur Conan Doyle is a famous ~ writer.

slang [slæŋ] — Slang, Jargon, Umgangssprache — You shouldn't use ~ in a formal letter.

atlas ['ætləs] — Atlas — We can find it in the ~.

set [set] — Satz, Garnitur, Sammlung etc. — What does the word "~" mean in this sentence?

meaning ['miːnɪŋ] — Bedeutung — He doesn't know the ~ of this word.

available [ə'veɪləbl] — erhältlich, verfügbar — The new product will be ~ next year.

actress ['æktrɪs] — Schauspielerin — Marilyn Monroe was a great ~.

poem ['pəʊɪm] — Gedicht — He wrote ~s when he was younger.

second-hand [ˌsekənd'hænd] — gebraucht, aus zweiter Hand — He bought a ~ car.

2 **any** ['enɪ] — irgendein(-e, -er); jede(-r, -s) (beliebige) — You can take ~ bus into town.

either ['aɪðə] — jede(-r, -s) (von zweien), beide — We can watch ~ film.

neither ['naɪðə] — keine(-r, -s) (von zweien) — She wore ~ of her two new dresses.

2a **get (got, got)** [get, gɒt] — holen (holte, geholt) — I'll ~ you a glass of water.

aspirin ['æsprɪn] — Aspirin(tablette) — If you have a headache, take an ~.

bored [bɔːd] — gelangweilt — I was ~ at home, so I went out.

2b **tiger** ['taɪgə] — Tiger — The ~ belongs to the cat family.

gorilla [gə'rɪlə] — Gorilla — ~s eat bananas.

zoo [zuː] — Zoo — She took the children to the ~.

2c **downtown** ['daʊntaʊn] — in der/die Innenstadt (amerik.) — All the big stores are ~.

3 **cookery book** ['kʊkərɪ bʊk] — Kochbuch — He can't cook without a ~.

encyclopedia [ɪnˌsaɪklə'piːdjə] — Nachschlagewerk, Lexikon — The ~ was full of mistakes.

3a **crossword (puzzle)** ['krɒswɜːd (ˌpʌzl)] — Kreuzworträtsel — I can't finish the ~, it's too hard.

UNITS 7 & 8 Panorama Plus

S **author** ['ɔːθə] — Autor(-in) — Agatha Christie was a successful ~.

cover ['kʌvə] — (Buch)Umschlag, Einband — There was a photo on the ~ of the book.

apart from [ə'pɑːt frəm] — abgesehen von — He has no other friends ~ me.

member ['membə] — Mitglied — The club had over 200 ~s.

public ['pʌblɪk] — Öffentlichkeit — The building was closed to the ~.

Factfile on the Frankfurt Book Fair

publisher ['pʌblɪʃə] — Verleger(-in), Herausgeber(-in) — Bookshops buy their books from ~s.

enormous [ɪ'nɔːməs]	enorm, riesig, gewaltig	The new airport is quite ~.
square metre [ˌskweə 'miːtə]	Quadratmeter	My new flat is 50 ~s in size.
connect; connection [kə'nekt; kə'nekʃn]	verbinden, in Zusammenhang stehen; Verbindung, Beziehung	They built a bridge to ~ the two islands.
show [ʃəʊ]	Schau, Ausstellung	Many people visited the flower ~.
trade [treɪd]	Handel, Handels-	~ was very bad last year.
century ['sentʃərɪ]	Jahrhundert	There are a hundred years in a ~.
attract [ə'trækt]	anziehen, anlocken	The new shop ~ed many customers.
deal [diːl]	Geschäft, Handel	They do a lot of business ~s abroad.
make connections [meɪk kə'nekʃnz]	Verbindungen, Kontakte knüpfen	
technical ['teknɪkl]	technisch	I don't understand the ~ details.
besides [bɪ'saɪdz]	außer, neben; außerdem, noch dazu	A supermarket sells many things ~ food.
kindergarten ['kɪndəˌgɑːtn]	Kindergarten	Her son started ~ at the age of four.
aid [eɪd]	Hilfe	The young man rushed to her ~.
serve [sɜːv]	(be)dienen; *hier:* anbieten	Does this restaurant ~ children's meals?
snack [snæk]	Imbiß	She always has a ~ at 11 o'clock.
air [eə]	Flugzeug, Flug-, Luft-	~ travel is very safe.
branch [brɑːnʃ]	Zweig(stelle), Filiale	This bank has two ~es in town.
translation [træns'leɪʃn]	Übersetzung	The ~ of the book was not good.
secretarial [ˌsekrə'teərɪəl]	Schreib-, Büro-	This company needs more ~ staff.
close to ['kləʊs tə]	nahe, dicht an/bei	The shop is ~ the station.
stand [stænd]	(Verkaufs-, Messe)Stand	There were many ~s at the trade fair.
enquiry, enquiries [ɪn'kwaɪərɪ]	(An-, Nach)Frage(n), Erkundigung(en); Auskunft *(Mz)*	The secretary deals with all ~s.
invitation [ˌɪnvɪ'teɪʃn]	Einladung	She sent me an ~ to the party.

Did you know?

contain [kən'teɪn]	beinhalten, enthalten	This box ~s all my old letters.
item ['aɪtəm]	Gegenstand, Stück, Artikel	I need some electrical ~s for the kitchen.
be top of the table [biː ˌtɒp əv ðə 'teɪbl]	an der Spitze stehen	His team ~ at the moment.

Advertising in the UK

lecturer ['lektʃərə]	Vortragende(-r), Dozent(-in)	
outdoor ['aʊtˌdɔː]	draußen, im Freien, Außen-	He enjoys all ~ sports.
poster ['pəʊstə]	Plakat	Have you seen the ~s for the new play?
commercial [kə'mɜːʃl]	kommerziell, geschäftlich; *hier:* Werbe-	There were two ~ breaks during the film.
mail [meɪl]	Post(sendung)	I didn't get any ~ today.
accommodation [əˌkɒmə'deɪʃn]	Unterkunft, Quartier	The hotel ~ was not very good.

UNITS 7 & 8 *Revision Plus*

3	**be in one's forties** [biː ɪn wʌnz 'fɔːtɪz]	zwischen 40 und 50 Jahre alt sein	
4	**action** ['ækʃn]	Handlung, Tat, Aktion	~s are better than words.
	entertain [ˌentə'teɪn]	unterhalten	The clown had to ~ the audience.
	thought [θɔːt]	Gedanke	The ~ of all that food makes me feel ill.

Dictionary

Hier finden Sie sämtliche Wörter und Wendungen des Buches in alphabetischer Reihenfolge. Darüber hinaus enthält das *Dictionary* die wichtigen Wörter aus *English Network 1, 2 + 3*. Neben dem englischen Stichwort, der Aussprache und der deutschen Übersetzung sehen Sie auch, wo das betreffende englische Wort im *Vocabulary* zu finden ist. Viele der Wörter (mit Fundstelle in *Schrägdruck*) brauchen Sie nur zu verstehen. Die übrigen Wörter (Fundstelle in normalem Druck) sollten Sie lernen. Möchten Sie mehr über ein Wort wissen, können Sie es mit Hilfe der Fundortangabe im *Vocabulary* nachschlagen.

Die erste Ziffer der Fundortangabe weist auf den Band hin, in dem das Wort vorkommt, die zweite auf die Unit, die dritte (nach dem Punkt) auf den Step. II/3.2 heißt also *Network 2*, Unit 3, Step 2; PI/1&2P heißt *Network Plus 1*, Units 1 & 2, Panorama Plus. Die anderen Abkürzungen bedeuten:

G = Gazette
I = Introduction (= Wortschatz, der auf der Auftaktseite zu einer Unit erscheint)
P = Panorama (people) bzw. Panorama Plus
R = Revision activities bzw. Revision Plus
S = Story

A

a, an [ə, æn, ən] ein(-e) I/1.1: **three days a week** dreimal pro Woche I/2.3
able ['eɪbl]: **be able to** können II/4.1
about [ə'baʊt] über I/2.1; ungefähr I/3.1: **ask about** fragen nach, sich erkundigen nach III/2.2; **what about …?** wie ist es mit …? I/2.1
above [ə'bʌv] oben *II/1.2*, PI/6.1: **above all** vor allem PI/6.1
abroad [ə'brɔːd] nach/in Übersee, ins/im Ausland PI/1.2
accent ['æksent] Akzent *PI/S1*
accept [ək'sept] annehmen, akzeptieren, anerkennen PI/4.1
acceptable [ək'septəbl] akzeptabel, annehmbar *PI/3&4P*
accident ['æksɪdənt] Unfall II/3.3
accommodation [ə,kɒmə'deɪʃn] Unterkunft, Quartier PI/7&8P
account [ə'kaʊnt] Konto I/5.2
across [ə'krɒs] quer durch, über III/3.1
act [ækt] *hier: (Theater)* spielen, auftreten, darstellen III/6.R
action ['ækʃn] Handlung, Tat, Aktion PI/7&8R
active ['æktɪv] aktiv III/2.2
activity [æk'tɪvəti] Aktivität, Tätigkeit, Unternehmung *II/1.1*, PI/6.1
actor ['æktə] Schauspieler III/4.2
actress ['æktrɪs] Schauspielerin PI/8.2
actually ['æktʃʊəli] eigentlich, wirklich I/1.1
add [æd] hinzufügen PI/1&2R
address [ə'dres] Adresse I/1.3
adjective ['ædʒɪktɪv] Adjektiv, Eigenschaftswort *II/5.3*
adult ['ædʌlt] Erwachsene(-r) PI/3.1
advantage [əd'vɑːntɪdʒ] Vorteil PI/2.2
adventure [əd'ventʃə] Abenteuer III/2.2

advert, ad (= advertisement) [əd'vɜːt, æd] *(Abkürzung)* Anzeige, Reklame II/2.1
advertise ['ædvətaɪz] ankündigen, annoncieren III/1.1
advertisement [əd'vɜːtɪsmənt] Anzeige, Inserat; Reklame, Werbung II/2.1
advice [əd'vaɪs] Rat(schlag) II/3.1
advise [əd'vaɪz] raten *PI/1.1*
afford [ə'fɔːd] sich leisten PI/7.1
afraid [ə'freɪd]: **I'm afraid** ich bedaure, leider I/1.1; **I'm afraid I can't** nein, leider nicht I/1.1; **be afraid (of)** Angst haben (vor) III/2.2
after ['ɑːftə] nach I/2.2; hinter I/3.1; nachdem III/6.2: **after that** danach I/6.1
afternoon [,ɑːftə'nuːn] Nachmittag I/2.2
afterwards ['ɑːftəwədz] nachher, hinterher, später PI/8.1
again [ə'gen] noch einmal, wieder I/2.1
against [ə'genst] gegen III/3.3
age [eɪdʒ] Alter(sstufe) *II/2.3P*, PI/3.2: **at the age of** im Alter von …, mit … Jahren PI/3.2
aged [eɪdʒd] … Jahre alt, im Alter von … II/6.2
agency ['eɪdʒənsi] Agentur, Büro PI/5.1
… ago [ə'gəʊ] vor (+ *Zeitraum*) I/5.2: **a long time ago** vor längerer Zeit I/5.2
agree [ə'griː] zustimmen, übereinstimmen, einverstanden sein II/4.1
aid [eɪd] Hilfe PI/7&8P
aim [eɪm] Ziel PI/5.1
air [eə] Luft II/2.2; Flugzeug, Flug-, Luft- PI/7&8P: **air hostess** Stewardeß III/5.R
airport ['eəpɔːt] Flughafen II/1.1
alcohol ['ælkəhɒl] Alkohol PI/7.1
alive [ə'laɪv] lebend, am Leben PI/6.2

all [ɔːl] alle(-s) I/2.R: **above all** vor allem PI/6.1; **at all** überhaupt II/1.1; **first of all** zuallererst, vor allen Dingen PI/3.1; **not at all** bitte, nichts zu danken I/3.1; **all around** ringsumher, überall PI/2.1; **all day** den ganzen Tag I/5.R; **all his work** seine ganze Arbeit I/5.2; **all over** überall, in ganz … PI/2.1; **all over the world** auf der ganzen Welt PI/3.1; **all right** in Ordnung I/3.1; **all-round** allgemein, Gesamt- PI/3.1; **all the best** alles Gute I/3.3
allow [ə'laʊ] erlauben, ermöglichen PI/1&2P: **be allowed to** dürfen III/6.1
almost ['ɔːlməʊst] beinahe, fast III/6.R
alone [ə'ləʊn] allein I/2.1
along [ə'lɒŋ] entlang I/3.2
aloud [ə'laʊd] laut PI/4.1
alphabet ['ælfəbet] Alphabet *II/1.R*
already [ɔːl'redi] schon, bereits III/4.1
also ['ɔːlsəʊ] auch II/5.1
although [ɔːl'ðəʊ] obwohl III/2.3
altogether [,ɔːltə'geðə] zusammen, insgesamt I/5.1
always ['ɔːlweɪz] immer I/1.3
American [ə'merɪkən] amerikanisch(-e, -er, -es); Amerikaner(-in) I/1.1
amount [ə'maʊnt] Betrag, Höhe, Menge PI/4.1
and [ænd, ənd] und I/1.1
angry ['æŋgri] ärgerlich, verärgert, böse III/3.2
animal ['ænɪml] Tier III/2.R
anniversary [,ænɪ'vɜːsəri] Jahrestag, Jahresfeier III/6.1
another [ə'nʌðə] ein(-e) andere(-r, -s) I/5.3
answer ['ɑːnsə] Antwort I/2.1
answer ['ɑːnsə] antworten I/2.1
antique [æn'tiːk] Antiquität, Antiquitäten- PI/2.1

any ['enɪ] welche, irgendwelche I/2.1; irgendein(-e, -er); jede(-r, -s) *(beliebige) PI/5&6R*, PI/8.2

anybody ['enɪˌbɒdɪ] (irgend) jemand *(bei Fragen und Verneinung)* III/1.1

anyone ['enɪwʌn] (irgend) jemand III/1.2; jeder (beliebige) PI/8.1

anything ['enɪθɪŋ] (irgend) etwas *(in Fragen und bei Verneinung)* III/1.2; alles *(jede beliebige Sache)* III/4.1: **anything else?** noch etwas? *(in Fragen)* I/5.1

anyway ['enɪweɪ] jedenfalls PI/7.1

anywhere ['enɪweə] irgendwo(hin) *(in Fragen und bei Verneinung)* III/1.2

apart [ə'pɑːt] (ab)gesondert, abseits; *hier:* voneinander entfernt PI/1&2P: **apart from** abgesehen von PI/7&8P

apartment [ə'pɑːtmənt] Wohnung, Apartment *(amerik.)* II/5.1

apple ['æpl] Apfel I/6.1

application [ˌæplɪ'keɪʃn] Gesuch, Antrag, Bewerbung PI/5&6R

apply [ə'plaɪ] sich bewerben PI/5.1

appointment [ə'pɔɪntmənt] Verabredung, Termin II/3.1: **make an appointment** eine Verabredung treffen, einen Termin ausmachen II/3.1

appreciate [ə'priːʃɪeɪt] schätzen, würdigen PI/3.1

apprentice [ə'prentɪs] Lehrling, Auszubildende(-r) II/2.I

April ['eɪprəl] April I/2.2

area ['eərɪə] Gebiet I/3.1

argue ['ɑːgjuː] argumentieren, streiten PI/5.1

argument ['ɑːgjʊmənt] Argument; Streit PI/5&6P

arm [ɑːm] Arm II/3.1

around [ə'raʊnd] um ... herum; ungefähr; *hier:* in PI/4.1: **all around** ringsumher, überall PI/2.1

arrange [ə'reɪndʒ] arrangieren, ausmachen II/2.1

arrival [ə'raɪvl] Ankunft, Ankunfts- III/3.1

arrive [ə'raɪv] ankommen I/5.3

art [ɑːt] Kunst I/2.3

article ['ɑːtɪkl] (Zeitungs)Artikel III/1.1

as [æz, əz] wie I/6.3; als I/4.3: **as ... as** so ... wie *(Vergleich)* II/1.2; **as far as** soweit, soviel III/1.3

ashamed [ə'ʃeɪmd]: **be ashamed (of)** sich schämen (für, wegen) PI/8.1

ask [ɑːsk] fragen, (eine Frage) stellen I/2.1: **ask about** fragen nach, sich erkundigen nach III/2.2; **ask for** bitten um I/6.1

aspect ['æspekt] Aspekt, Gesichtspunkt *PI/3&4P*

aspirin ['æsprɪn] Aspirin(tablette) PI/8.2

assistant [ə'sɪstənt] Assistent(-in), Gehilfe, Gehilfin, Mitarbeiter(-in) II/2.1

at [æt, ət] auf I/1.1; an I/3.1: **at 7 o'clock** um 7 Uhr I/2.2; **at all** überhaupt II/1.1; **at home** zuhause I/1.2; **at least** wenigstens, zum mindesten; mindestens III/4.1; **at once** sofort III/6.1; **at the age of** im Alter von ..., mit ... Jahren PI/3.2; **at times** zeitweise PI/3.1; **at work** bei der Arbeit I/1.2

atlas ['ætləs] Atlas PI/8.2

attack [ə'tæk] angreifen PI/4.1

attend [ə'tend] teilnehmen an, besuchen PI/8.1

attention [ə'tenʃn] Aufmerksam-keit, (Be)Achtung PI/4.1: **pay attention to** beachten, Aufmerk-samkeit schenken PI/7.1

attic ['ætɪk] Dachstube, Mansarde II/4.1

attract [ə'trækt] anziehen, anlocken PI/7&8P

attractive [ə'træktɪv] attraktiv, gutaussehend III/2.1

audience ['ɔːdjəns] Publikum, Zuschauer, Zuhörer III/1.3

August ['ɔːgəst] August I/2.2

aunt [ɑːnt] Tante I/2.1

Australia [ɒ'streɪljə] Australien I/5.3

Australian [ɒ'streɪljən] australisch(-e, -er, -es); Australier(-in) II/6.1

Austrian ['ɒstrɪən] österreichisch(-e, -er, -es); Österreicher(-in) I/1.1

author ['ɔːθə] Autor(-in) PI/7&8P

automatic [ˌɔːtə'mætɪk] automatisch, selbsttätig III/4.3

autumn ['ɔːtəm] Herbst I/2.2

available [ə'veɪləbl] erhältlich, verfügbar PI/8.2

average ['ævrɪdʒ] Durchschnitt, Durchschnitts- III/1.3: **an average of** im Durchschnitt, durchschnittlich III/1.3

avoid [ə'vɔɪd] (ver)meiden PI/4.1

away [ə'weɪ] weg, fort III/6.2

awful ['ɔːfʊl] furchtbar, schrecklich, scheußlich III/6.1

B

baby ['beɪbɪ] Baby, Säugling III/2.2

back [bæk] Rücken, Rückseite II/3.1

back [bæk] zurück I/6.1

backache ['bækeɪk] Rückenschmerz(en) II/3.1

background ['bækgraʊnd] Hintergrund III/4.1

bacon ['beɪkən] Speck PI/4.1

bad [bæd] schlecht, schlimm I/4.3

badminton ['bædmɪntən] Badminton, Federball PI/3.1

bag [bæg] Tasche I/4.1

baggage ['bægɪdʒ] (Reise)Gepäck *(amerik.)* III/3.1

baker's ['beɪkəz] Bäcker(laden) II/5.2

balcony ['bælkənɪ] Balkon I/4.1

ball [bɔːl] Ball II/6.2: **ballpoint pen** Kugelschreiber PI/4.2

balloon [bə'luːn] Ballon PI/3&4P

bank [bæŋk] Bank I/2.3: **bank clerk** Bankangestellte(-r) II/2.1; **bank note** Banknote I/5.I

bankrupt ['bæŋkrʌpt] bankrott II/4.2: **go bankrupt** bankrott machen II/4.2

bar [bɑː] Bar, Kneipe, Schnellimbiß usw. I/6.2: **coffee bar** Café I/6.2; **snack bar** Schnellimbiß I/6.2

bar [bɑː] Stange, Riegel; *hier:* Stück III/6.2

barbecue ['bɑːbəkjuː] Barbecue *(Grillfest)* III/6.3

bark [bɑːk] bellen PI/5.2

basement ['beɪsmənt] Kellergeschoß II/4.1

basic ['beɪsɪk] grundlegend, Grund(lagen)- PI/8.1

basketball ['bɑːskɪtbɔːl] Basketball PI/3.1

bath [bɑːθ] Bad(ewanne) I/4.1

bathroom ['bɑːθrʊm] Bad, Badezimmer II/4.1

battery ['bætərɪ] Batterie III/4.3

be (was/were, been) [biː, wɒz/wɜː, biːn] sein (war/waren, gewesen) I/4.1, I/5.1, II/1.1: **be in one's forties** zwischen 40 und 50 Jahre alt sein PI/7&8R

beach [biːtʃ] Strand II/1.1: **beach shoe** Strandschuh, Badeschuh II/1.1

beard [bɪəd] Bart III/2.3

beat (beat, beaten) [biːt, biːt, 'biːtn] schlagen (schlug, geschlagen) PI/3.2

beautiful ['bjuːtəfʊl] schön I/3.3

because [bɪ'kɒz] weil I/3.3: **because of** wegen III/3.3

become (became, become) [bɪ'kʌm, bɪ'keɪm, bɪ'kʌm] werden (wurde, geworden) II/6.1

bed [bed] Bett I/4.2: **in bed** im Bett I/4.2; **bed and breakfast** Zimmer mit Frühstück *(in Privatunterkunft)* I/6.R

bedroom ['bedrʊm] Schlafzimmer II/4.1

beef [biːf] Rind(fleisch) PI/4.1

beer [bɪə] Bier I/5.3

before [bɪˈfɔː] vor *(zeitlich)* I/6.2;
ehe, bevor II/1.3; vorher, zuvor
II/1.3
begin (began, begun) [bɪˈgɪn,
bɪˈgæn, bɪˈgʌn] beginnen (begann,
begonnen), anfangen I/2.2, II/4.3P
beginning [bɪˈgɪnɪŋ] Anfang, Beginn
III/4.1
behind [bɪˈhaɪnd] hinter I/5.1
believe [bɪˈliːv] glauben II/3.3
belong to [bɪˈlɒŋ tə] gehören PI/2.1
below [bɪˈləʊ] unten *II/3.3*, PI/5.1
besides [bɪˈsaɪdz] außer, neben;
außerdem, noch dazu PI/7&8P
best [best] beste(-r, -s) II/1.2: **all the
best** alles Gute I/3.3; **best** am
besten I/5.3; **with best wishes** mit
den besten Wünschen *(am
Briefschluß)* III/1.1
better [ˈbetə] besser II/1.2
between [bɪˈtwiːn] zwischen I/5.1
bicycle [ˈbaɪsɪkl] Fahrrad I/2.2
big [bɪg] groß I/3.1
bike [baɪk] Fahrrad PI/2.2
bill [bɪl] Rechnung I/6.1; Banknote,
Geldschein *(amerik.)* II/5.1
biography [baɪˈɒgrəfɪ] Biographie
PI/8.1
bird [bɜːd] Vogel III/6.2
birth [bɜːθ] Geburt III/1.1
birthday [ˈbɜːθdeɪ] Geburtstag I/3.2:
happy birthday! alles Gute zum
Geburtstag! III/6.1; **to your
birthday!** auf deinen/Ihren/euren
Geburtstag! III/6.1
bit [bɪt]: **a bit** ein bißchen, ein
wenig I/1.1
black [blæk] schwarz I/5.1: **in black
and white** schwarz auf weiß II/5.R
blackboard [ˈblækbɔːd] Tafel PI/4.1
blanket [ˈblæŋkɪt] (Woll)Decke
III/1.2
bless you! [ˈbles juː] Gesundheit!
(beim Niesen) III/6.1
block [blɒk] Block III/2.2: **block of
flats** Wohnblock,
Mehrfamilienhaus *(brit.)* III/2.2
blond(e) [blɒnd] blond PI/7.2
blood [blʌd] Blut III/5.R
blouse [blaʊz] Bluse II/5.1
blue [bluː] blau I/5.1; *hier:* traurig,
depressiv *PI/S3*
board [bɔːd] Tafel PI/4.1
boat [bəʊt] Boot, Schiff III/3.R
body [ˈbɒdɪ] Körper II/3.3
book [bʊk] Buch I/2.R: **non-fiction
book** Sachbuch PI/8.1
book [bʊk] buchen, reservieren I/4.1
bookshop [ˈbʊkʃɒp] Buchladen I/2.R
border [ˈbɔːdə] Grenze I/3.1
bored [bɔːd] gelangweilt PI/8.2
boring [ˈbɔːrɪŋ] langweilig PI/5.1
born [bɔːn]: **was/were born**
wurde(-n) geboren III/1.1

borrow [ˈbɒrəʊ] (aus)borgen,
(aus)leihen II/4.1
boss [bɒs] Chef(-in) I/2.1
both [bəʊθ] beide(-s) I/4.R: **both ...
and** sowohl ... als auch II/1.1
bottle [ˈbɒtl] Flasche I/6.1
boutique [buːˈtiːk] Boutique I/3.3
box [bɒks] Kasten, Kiste, Koffer
III/3.1
Boxing day [ˈbɒksɪŋ deɪ] Zweiter
Weihnachtsfeiertag III/6.3
boy [bɔɪ] Junge III/4.1
boyfriend [ˈbɔɪfrend] Freund *(eines
Mädchens)* PI/S3
bracket [ˈbrækɪt] Klammer *III/5.3*
branch [brɑːnʃ] Zweig(stelle),
Filiale PI/7&8P
bread [bred] Brot I/6.1
break [breɪk] Pause I/2.2: **have a
break** Pause machen I/2.2
break (broke, broken) [breɪk,
brəʊk, ˈbrəʊkən] (zer)brechen
(brach, gebrochen) III/5.2: **break
down** *hier:* eine Panne haben,
stehenbleiben *(Auto)* PI/1&2P
breakfast [ˈbrekfəst] Frühstück
I/4.1: **a full breakfast** ein
englisches Frühstück I/4.1; **bed
and breakfast** Zimmer mit
Frühstück *(in Privatunterkunft)*
I/6.R
bridge [brɪdʒ] Brücke I/3.2
bright [braɪt] fröhlich, heiter, hell;
hier: klug PI/5.1
bring (brought, brought) [brɪŋ,
brɔːt] bringen (brachte, gebracht)
I/5.3, I/6.1, III/4.2: **bring up**
erziehen II/6.1
Britain [ˈbrɪtn] Großbritannien I/3.1
British [ˈbrɪtɪʃ] britisch(-e, -er, -es);
Brite, Britin I/1.1
broadcast [ˈbrɔːdkɑːst] Übertragung,
Sendung III/6.R
brochure [ˈbrəʊʃə] Broschüre II/1.1
brother [ˈbrʌðə] Bruder I/2.1:
brother-in-law Schwager II/6.1
brown [braʊn] braun I/5.1
build (built, built) [bɪld, bɪlt]
bauen (baute, gebaut) III/4.1
building [ˈbɪldɪŋ] Gebäude I/3.2
bull [bʊl] Stier PI/3&4P
bureau [ˈbjʊərəʊ] Büro *PI/S3*
burn (burnt, burnt) [bɜːn, bɜːnt]
(ver)brennen (brannte, gebrannt)
(brit.) III/4.2
bus [bʌs] Bus I/4.2: **bus stop**
Bushaltestelle I/5.2
business [ˈbɪznɪs] Geschäft,
Geschäfts-, Beruf, Handel III/1.1
busy [ˈbɪzɪ] beschäftigt II/2.1; belebt
III/3.1
but [bʌt, bət] aber I/1.2
butcher's [ˈbʊtʃəz] Metzger,
Fleischer(laden) II/5.2

butter [ˈbʌtə] Butter I/6.1
button [ˈbʌtn] Knopf PI/1&2P
buy (bought, bought) [baɪ, bɔːt]
kaufen (kaufte, gekauft) I/5.1,
I/5.2, III/4.1
by [baɪ] mit I/4.I; *(geschrieben)* von
I/5.2; um, bis (spätestens) III/2.1;
durch, indem *III/5.2*: **by myself**
allein PI/3.1; **by plane/train** mit
dem Flugzeug/Zug I/4.I; **by the
sea** am Meer I/3.3; **by the way**
übrigens II/5.1
bye [baɪ] tschüs I/2.1: **bye-bye**
tschüs I/2.1

C

cab [kæb] Taxi *(amerik.)* II/5.1
café [ˈkæfeɪ] Café III/2.2
cage [keɪdʒ] Käfig PI/4.1
cake [keɪk] Kuchen III/2.3
calculator [ˈkælkjʊleɪtə]
Taschenrechner II/2.2
Californian [ˌkælɪˈfɔːnɪən]
kalifornisch(-e, -er, -es);
Kalifornier(-in) I/1.3
call [kɔːl] Anruf I/4.1
call [kɔːl] anrufen I/6.1; rufen III/2.1:
call (back) (zurück)rufen,
(wieder) anrufen III/2.1
called [kɔːld] genannt I/1.1
calm [kɑːm] ruhig PI/5.1
camera [ˈkæmrə] Kamera II/1.1
camping [ˈkæmpɪŋ] Camping,
Zelten III/1.2
campsite [ˈkæmpsaɪt] Zeltplatz I/6.R
can [kæn, kən] können, kann(-st),
könnt I/1.1: **can't stand** nicht
ausstehen können I/6.1
Canadian [kəˈneɪdjən] kanadisch(-e,
-er, -es); Kanadier(-in) PI/8.2
cancel [ˈkænsl] streichen, absagen
PI/4.2
canoe [kəˈnuː] Kanu fahren, paddeln
PI/3.2
capital [ˈkæpɪtl] Hauptstadt PI/6.1
captain [ˈkæptɪn] Kapitän PI/3.2
car [kɑː] Auto I/2.2: **car park**
Parkplatz I/3.2
card [kɑːd] Karte I/5.1: **credit card**
Kreditkarte I/5.2
care [keə] (Für)Sorge PI/4.1: **take
care!** mach's gut!, paß auf dich
auf! III/6.3
care for [ˈkeə fɔː] sich kümmern
um, sorgen für III/4.3
career [kəˈrɪə] Karriere, Beruf PI/5.1
careful [ˈkeəfʊl] vorsichtig II/2.2;
genau, gründlich *II/3.2*, PI/4.1
careless [ˈkeəlɪs] unvorsichtig,
unaufmerksam, nachlässig PI/3.2

carrot ['kærət] Möhre, Mohrrübe I/6.1

carry ['kærɪ] tragen III/3.1

cash [kæʃ] bar, Bargeld I/5.2

cassette [kə'set] Tonbandkassette I/2.2

castle ['kɑːsl] Burg I/4.1

casual ['kæʒʊəl] *hier:* salopp, sportlich *(gekleidet)* III/6.1

cat [kæt] Katze II/6.3

catch (caught, caught) [kætʃ, kɔːt] fangen (fing, gefangen); erreichen *(Verkehrsmittel)* III/3.1; sich holen, zuziehen *(+ Krankheit)* III/6.2

cause [kɔːz] Ursache, Grund PI/2.1

cause [kɔːz] veranlassen, verursachen, bewirken PI/2.1

celebrate ['selɪbreɪt] feiern III/6.I

celebration [ˌselɪ'breɪʃn] Feier, Fest III/6.3

Celsius *(Abk:* **C)** ['selsɪəs] Celsius *(Temperaturmaß)* PI/1&2P

cent [sent] Cent *(amerik. Währung)* III/6.3

centimetre ['sentɪˌmiːtə] Zentimeter III/2.R

central ['sentrəl] zentral, Zentral- II/4.1

centre ['sentə] Mitte, Zentrum I/3.1: **city centre** Stadtmitte, City I/3.1

century ['sentʃərɪ] Jahrhundert PI/7&8P

certain ['sɜːtn] sicher, bestimmt, gewiß II/6.1

certainly ['sɜːtnlɪ] gewiß, natürlich I/6.1

chain [tʃeɪn] Kette II/5.3: **chain stores** *(Läden, die zu einer Kette gehören)* II/5.3

chair [tʃeə] Stuhl II/2.2

champagne [ˌʃæm'peɪn] Champagner, Sekt III/6.1

champion ['tʃæmpjən] Meister(-in), Sieger(-in) PI/3&4P

chance [tʃɑːns] Chance, Möglichkeit III/5.1

change [tʃeɪndʒ] Wechselgeld I/5.1; Veränderung, Wechsel II/3.2

change [tʃeɪndʒ] wechseln I/5.1; sich verändern, ändern III/2.2; umsteigen III/3.1

channel ['tʃænl] Kanal; *hier:* Fernsehprogramm III/1.3

chapter ['tʃæptə] Kapitel PI/4.1

cheap [tʃiːp] billig, preiswert II/1.1

cheat [tʃiːt] mogeln, schummeln PI/3.2

check [tʃek] Rechnung *(amerik.)* II/5.1

check [tʃek] überprüfen III/4.2

check-in ['tʃekɪn] Abfertigungs-, Eincheck- III/3.1: **check-in desk** Abfertigungsschalter III/3.1

cheerio! [ˌtʃɪərɪ'əʊ] mach's gut!, tschüs! PI/6.1

cheers! [tʃɪəz] zum Wohl! III/6.1

cheese [tʃiːz] Käse I/6.1

cheetah ['tʃiːtə] Gepard PI/3&4P

chemist's ['kemɪsts] Apotheke, Drogerie II/5.2

cheque [tʃek] Scheck I/5.2: **traveller's cheque** Reisescheck I/5.2

chianti [kɪ'æntɪ] Chianti *(ital. Rotwein)* PI/4.2

chicken ['tʃɪkɪn] Hähnchen I/6.1

child (children) [tʃaɪld, 'tʃɪldrən] Kind (Kinder) I/1.3

childhood ['tʃaɪldhʊd] Kindheit III/4.1

Chinese [ˌtʃaɪ'niːz] chinesisch(-e, -er, -es); Chinese, Chinesin I/3.3

chips [tʃɪps] Pommes frites I/6.1

chocolate ['tʃɒkələt] Schokolade III/1.2

choice [tʃɔɪs] (Aus)Wahl *PI/3.2*, PI/4.1

choose (chose, chosen) [tʃuːz, tʃəʊz, 'tʃəʊzn] (aus)wählen (wählte, gewählt) III/1.3

Christmas ['krɪsməs] Weihnachten I/6.2: **Christmas Day** Erster Weihnachtstag I/6.2; **Christmas Eve** Heiligabend III/6.R; **merry Christmas!** frohe Weihnachten! III/6.3

church [tʃɜːtʃ] Kirche; Gottesdienst III/5.1

cigar [sɪ'gɑː] Zigarre PI/7.1

cigarette [ˌsɪgə'ret] Zigarette II/3.3

cinema ['sɪnəmə] Kino I/3.2

circle ['sɜːkl] Kreis PI/5&6P

citizen ['sɪtɪzn] Bürger(-in) PI/5&6P

city ['sɪtɪ] Großstadt, Weltstadt I/3.1: **city centre** Stadtmitte, City I/3.1

class [klɑːs] Klasse I/3.2; Kurs, Unterricht PI/3.1: **first class** erste(-r) Klasse II/4.2

classical ['klæsɪkl] klassisch III/5.1

classroom ['klɑːsrʊm] Klassenzimmer I/3.2

clause [klɔːz] Satz *(grammatisch)* PI/3.2: **relative clause** Relativsatz *PI/8.2*

clean [kliːn] säubern, putzen III/2.2

clean [kliːn] sauber III/2.2

clear [klɪə] klar, hell, rein III/3.2

clerk [klɑːk] Sekretär(-in), Büroangestellte(-r) II/2.1

clever ['klevə] klug PI/5.1

client ['klaɪənt] Kunde, Kundin PI/7.1

climb [klaɪm] klettern, besteigen II/4.2

climber ['klaɪmə] Bergsteiger(-in) PI/6.2

clock [klɒk]: **o'clock** Uhr *(bei Zeitangabe)* I/2.2; **at 7 o'clock** um 7 Uhr I/2.2

close [kləʊz] schließen I/4.R

close to ['kləʊs tə] nahe, dicht an/bei PI/7&8P

clothes [kləʊðz] Kleider, Kleidung II/5.I

cloud [klaʊd] Wolke PI/1&2R

cloudy ['klaʊdɪ] bewölkt II/1.2

club [klʌb] Club I/2.3

coach [kəʊtʃ] (Reise)Bus III/3.1

coast [kəʊst] Küste PI/1&2P

coat [kəʊt] Mantel, Jacke II/5.1

cod [kɒd] Kabeljau I/6.1

coffee ['kɒfɪ] Kaffee I/2.2: **coffee bar** Café I/6.2

coin [kɔɪn] Münze I/5.1

cold [kəʊld] Erkältung II/3.2

cold [kəʊld] kalt II/1.2

colleague ['kɒliːg] Kollege, Kollegin III/1.1

collect [kə'lekt] (ein)sammeln PI/4.1

college ['kɒlɪdʒ] weiterführende Schule, Hochschule PI/8.1

colour ['kʌlə] Farbe I/5.2

comb [kəʊm] Kamm II/1.1

combination [ˌkɒmbɪ'neɪʃn] Kombination, Verbindung *PI/2.1*

combine [kəm'baɪn] verbinden, kombinieren *PI/3.2*

come (came, come) [kʌm, keɪm, kʌm] kommen (kam, gekommen) I/1.3, III/2.3: **come out** herauskommen, erscheinen III/1.R; **come true** wahr werden, sich verwirklichen II/6.3

comfortable ['kʌmfətəbl] bequem I/4.3

comment ['kɒment] Kommentar, Be-, Anmerkung *II/6.2*

comment on ['kɒment ˌɒn] kommentieren, sich äußern zu/über III/6.1

commercial [kə'mɜːʃl] kommerziell, geschäftlich; *hier:* Werbe- PI/7&8P

common ['kɒmən] gemeinsam, allgemein, üblich, gewöhnlich *PI/1.1*, PI/4.1: **in common** gemeinsam *PI/1.1*; **common sense** gesunder Menschenverstand, Vernunft PI/4.1

commute (on) [kə'mjuːt] pendeln, hin- und herfahren (mit) III/3.3

companion [kəm'pænjən] Begleiter(-in), Gefährte(-in), Freund(-in) PI/4.1

company ['kʌmpənɪ] Unternehmen I/1.3

compare [kəm'peə] vergleichen PI/2.2

comparison [kəm'pærɪsn] Vergleich *PI/6.2*

competition [ˌkɒmpɪ'tɪʃn] Wettbewerb II/1.3

complain [kəm'pleɪn] sich beschweren II/5.1

complaint [kəm'pleɪnt] Beschwerde II/5.1

complete [kəm'pli:t] vervollständigen, (aus)füllen *II/1.R*, PI/4.1

complete [kəm'pli:t] völlig, vollständig *II/1.R*, PI/4.1

completion [kəm'pli:ʃn] Fertigstellung, Abschluß PI/5&6R

comprehension [ˌkɒmprɪ'henʃn] Verständnis(übung) *II/1.1*

computer [kəm'pju:tə] Computer I/3.2

concern [kən'sɜ:n] Anteilnahme, Sorge III/2.1

concert ['kɒnsət] Konzert III/3.2

condition [kən'dɪʃn] Kondition, Bedingung; Zustand, Beschaffenheit III/6.1

conditional [kən'dɪʃənl]: **third conditional** Bedingungssatz (Typ 3): die unwirkliche Bedingung in der Vergangenheit *PI/3.2*

congratulations [kənˌgrætʃʊ'leɪʃnz] Glückwunsch II/1.3

connect [kə'nekt] verbinden, in Zusammenhang stehen *PI/4.1*, PI/7&8P

connection [kə'nekʃn] Verbindung, Beziehung PI/7&8P: **make connections** Verbindungen, Kontakte knüpfen PI/7&8P

consider [kən'sɪdə] überlegen, erwägen; *auch:* halten für PI/4.1

contact ['kɒntækt] Kontakt, Beziehung PI/4.2

contact ['kɒntækt] sich mit jdm. in Verbindung setzen PI/4.2

contain [kən'teɪn] beinhalten, enthalten *PI/3.1*, PI/7&8P

continent ['kɒntɪnənt] Kontinent PI/6.1

continue [kən'tɪnju:] fortfahren, weitergehen, -machen III/1.1

contradict [ˌkɒntrə'dɪkt] widersprechen *III/2.3*

contrast ['kɒntrɑ:st] Gegensatz *PI/6.2*

contrasting [kən'trɑ:stɪŋ] gegensätzlich *PI/2.1*

control [kən'trəʊl] Kontrolle PI/3&4P

control [kən'trəʊl] kontrollieren PI/3&4P

conversation [ˌkɒnvə'seɪʃn] Unterhaltung, Gespräch III/1.3

cook [kʊk] Koch, Köchin II/1.1

cook [kʊk] kochen, zubereiten I/1.2

cooker ['kʊkə] Herd II/4.2

cookery book ['kʊkərɪ bʊk] Kochbuch PI/8.2

cooking ['kʊkɪŋ] Kochen II/6.R

cool [ku:l] kühl III/6.1

copy ['kɒpɪ] Kopie; Exemplar, Stück *(von Büchern, Zeitungen, Platten etc.)* III/4.2

copy ['kɒpɪ] kopieren, abschreiben, abmalen PI/8.2

corn [kɔ:n] Getreide, Korn; Mais III/6.3

corner ['kɔ:nə] Ecke I/3.2

correct [kə'rekt] berichtigen PI/2.1

correct [kə'rekt] richtig PI/2.1

correction [kə'rekʃn] Korrektur, Verbesserung PI/2.1

cost [kɒst] (Un)Kosten, Preis, Aufwand PI/1.1: **extra cost** Aufpreis II/1.1

cost (cost, cost) [kɒst, kɒst] kosten (kostete, gekostet) III/1.R

costume ['kɒstju:m] Kostüm III/6.R

cottage ['kɒtɪdʒ] Häuschen PI/2.1

cotton ['kɒtn] Baumwolle, aus Baumwolle III/2.3

cough [kɒf] Husten PI/5.2

could [kʊd] könnte(-st, -t, -n) I/4.1; konnte(-t, -st, -n) III/1.2

country ['kʌntrɪ] Land I/3.1: **in the country** auf dem Land I/3.1

countryside ['kʌntrɪsaɪd] Land(schaft) *II/2.3P*, PI/3.1

couple ['kʌpl] Paar PI/4.2: **a couple of** einige, ein paar PI/4.2

course [kɔ:s] Kurs I/2.2; Gang *(einer Mahlzeit)* I/6.1: **main course** Hauptgericht I/6.1

course [kɔ:s]: **of course** selbstverständlich I/5.1

court [kɔ:t] (Gerichts)Hof; *hier:* Tennisplatz PI/3.1

cousin ['kʌzn] Cousin(-e) I/2.1

cover ['kʌvə] (Buch)Umschlag, Einband PI/7&8P

cow [kaʊ] Kuh PI/4.1

crazy ['kreɪzɪ] verrückt II/6.1

cream [kri:m] Creme II/1.1; Sahne III/2.3: **suntan cream** Bräunungscreme II/1.1

creamy ['kri:mɪ] kremig PI/1&2R

creative [kri:'eɪtɪv] kreativ, einfallsreich PI/1&2R

credit card ['kredɪt kɑ:d] Kreditkarte I/5.2

crisis ['kraɪsɪs] Krise II/6.1

cross [krɒs] überqueren III/3.1: **cross out/off** durchstreichen *III/3.2*

crossroads ['krɒsrəʊdz] Kreuzung I/3.1

crossword (puzzle) ['krɒswɜ:d (ˌpʌzl)] Kreuzworträtsel PI/8.2

crowd [kraʊd] (Menschen)Menge PI/1.1

crowded ['kraʊdɪd] überfüllt PI/1.1

cry (cried) [kraɪ, kraɪd] weinen (weinte, geweint), schreien *III/3.R*

cup [kʌp] Tasse I/6.2; Pokal, Siegerpreis PI/3.2

cupboard ['kʌbəd] (Küchen)Schrank II/4.2

curly ['kɜ:lɪ] lockig, gelockt III/2.3

currency ['kʌrənsɪ] Währung I/5.3

curve [kɜ:v] Kurve PI/5&6P

custom ['kʌstəm] Brauch, Gewohnheit, Sitte III/6.I

customer ['kʌstəmə] Kunde(-in) I/6.1

cut (cut, cut) [kʌt, kʌt] schneiden (schnitt, geschnitten) III/4.1: **cut down** *hier:* fällen III/4.1

cycle ['saɪkl] radfahren PI/3.1

D

dad [dæd] Vati I/2.3

daily ['deɪlɪ] täglich, Tages- PI/4.1

damage ['dæmɪdʒ] Schaden PI/4.1

damage ['dæmɪdʒ] beschädigen PI/4.1

dance [dɑ:ns] Tanz, Tanzveranstaltung III/1.2

dance [dɑ:ns] tanzen III/1.2

dancer ['dɑ:nsə] Tänzer(-in) III/1.2

danger ['deɪndʒə] Gefahr III/3.2

dangerous ['deɪndʒərəs] gefährlich III/3.2

dark [dɑ:k] dunkel III/2.1

date [deɪt] Datum; Zeitpunkt III/1.1

daughter ['dɔ:tə] Tochter I/2.1: **daughter-in-law** Schwiegertochter II/6.1

day [deɪ] Tag I/2.2: **all day** den ganzen Tag I/5.R; **the day after tomorrow** übermorgen II/6.2; **the day before yesterday** vorgestern II/6.2; **in the old days** früher III/5.1

dead [ded] tot I/2.1

deal [di:l] Geschäft, Handel PI/7&8P

deal (with) [di:l] umgehen, sich befassen (mit) PI/4.1

dear [dɪə] Liebe(r) ... *(in Briefen)* I/2.3: **oh dear** oje!, meine Güte II/1.1

death [deθ] Tod III/6.2

December [dɪ'sembə] Dezember I/2.2

decide [dɪ'saɪd] beschließen II/2.1: **decide on** sich entscheiden für *III/5.3*

decision [dɪ'sɪʒn] Entscheidung PI/4.1

definitely ['defɪnɪtlɪ] bestimmt, zweifellos PI/6.2

definition [ˌdefɪ'nɪʃn] Erklärung, Umschreibung *PI/1.1*

demolish [dɪ'mɒlɪʃ] ab-, niederreißen III/4.1

dentist ['dentɪst] Zahnarzt II/3.2

department [dɪ'pɑːtmənt] Abteilung II/5.3: **department store** Kaufhaus, Warenhaus II/5.2

departure [dɪ'pɑːtʃə] Abreise, Abfahrt, Abflug III/3.1

depend on [dɪ'pend ɒn] abhängen von PI/5.1

describe [dɪ'skraɪb] beschreiben III/2.1

desert ['dezət] Wüste PI/1&2P

desk [desk] Schreibtisch II/2.2: **information desk** Informations-schalter III/3.1; **check-in desk** Abfertigungsschalter III/3.1

dessert [dɪ'zɜːt] Dessert, Nachspeise I/6.1

detail ['diːteɪl] Detail, Einzelheit *II/6.3*, PI/5.1

detective [dɪ'tektɪv] Detektiv, Kriminal- PI/8.1

develop [dɪ'veləp] (sich) entwickeln PI/2.1

development [dɪ'veləpmənt] Entwicklung PI/2.1

dial ['daɪəl] wählen *(Telefon) II/6.3P*

dialogue ['daɪəlɒg] Dialog *II/1.1*

diary ['daɪərɪ] Tagebuch PI/6.1

dictate [dɪk'teɪt] diktieren III/4.3

dictionary ['dɪkʃənrɪ] Wörterbuch I/2.2

die [daɪ] sterben III/4.1

diet ['daɪət] Ernährung; Diät II/3.3

difference ['dɪfrəns] Unterschied *II/G1*, PI/7.1

different ['dɪfrənt] andere(-r, -s); verschieden I/3.2

difficult ['dɪfɪkəlt] schwierig III/1.3

difficulty ['dɪfɪkəltɪ] Schwierigkeit *PI/5&6P*, PI/8.1

dig (dug, dug) [dɪg, dʌg] graben (grub, gegraben) PI/5.2

dining room ['daɪnɪŋrʊm] Eßzimmer II/4.1

dinner ['dɪnə] warmes Abendessen, warmes Mittagessen I/1.3

direct [dɪ'rekt, daɪ'rekt] direkt III/3.1

direction [dɪ'rekʃn] Richtung; *auch:* Anweisung, Vorschrift PI/1&2P

director [dɪ'rektə] Direktor PI/5.1

dirt [dɜːt] Schmutz III/3.3

dirty ['dɜːtɪ] schmutzig III/2.2

disability [ˌdɪsə'bɪlətɪ] Behinderung PI/3.1

disabled [dɪs'eɪbld] behindert PI/3.1

disadvantage [ˌdɪsəd'vɑːntɪdʒ] Nachteil PI/2.2

disagree [ˌdɪsə'griː] nicht überein-stimmen, nicht zustimmen *II/6.1*

disappear [ˌdɪsə'pɪə] verschwinden PI/2.1

disappoint [ˌdɪsə'pɔɪnt] enttäuschen III/4.1

disco ['dɪskəʊ] Disco, Diskothek III/5.3

discover [dɪ'skʌvə] entdecken PI/3.1

discuss [dɪ'skʌs] diskutieren PI/1&2R

discussion [dɪ'skʌʃn] Diskussion PI/1&2R

disgusting [dɪs'gʌstɪŋ] ekelhaft, widerlich III/4.1

dislike [dɪs'laɪk] Abneigung *PI/1.1*

dislike [dɪs'laɪk] nicht mögen *PI/1.1*, PI/8.1

dissatisfaction ['dɪsˌsætɪs'fækʃn] Unzufriedenheit PI/5&6R

distance ['dɪstəns] Entfernung PI/1.1: **long-distance** Fern- PI/1.1

dive [daɪv] tauchen PI/3&4P

divorced [dɪ'vɔːst] geschieden PI/5.1

do (did, done) [duː, dɪd, dʌn] tun (tat, getan), machen I/1.3, I/4.1, II/2.1: **does** *(Hilfsverb do)* I/2.3; **don't** (= do not), *(Hilfsverb do, Verneinung)* I/2.1

doctor ['dɒktə] Arzt I/5.R: **family doctor** Hausarzt, Hausärztin II/3.1

dog [dɒg] Hund I/2.2

dollar ['dɒlə] Dollar I/5.2

dolphin ['dɒlfɪn] Delphin PI/3&4P

door [dɔː] Tür II/4.1

double ['dʌbl] Doppel- I/1.2

doubt [daʊt] Zweifel III/3.3: **there's no doubt about it** es besteht kein Zweifel III/3.3

doubt [daʊt] (be)zweifeln PI/4.1

down [daʊn] hinunter, herunter III/3.1

downstairs [ˌdaʊn'steəz] unten, (die Treppe) hinunter/herunter II/4.1

downtown ['daʊntaʊn] in der/die Innenstadt *(amerik.)* PI/8.2

dozen ['dʌzn] Dutzend I/3.3

Dr ['dɒktə] *(Abkürzung für Doktor)* II/3.1

draw (drew, drawn) [drɔː, druː, drɔːn] zeichnen (zeichnete, gezeichnet) III/2.R

drawing ['drɔːɪŋ] Zeichnung *I/5.1*

dream [driːm] Traum PI/5.1

dream (dreamt, dreamt) [driːm, dremt] träumen (träumte, geträumt) PI/5.1

dress [dres] Kleid II/5.1: **get dressed** sich anziehen, sich ankleiden II/5.1

drink [drɪŋk] Getränk, Drink; *hier:* Trinken I/6.1

drink (drank, drunk) [drɪŋk, dræŋk, drʌŋk] trinken (trank, getrunken) I/2.2, I/5.2, II/1.2

drive (drove, driven) [draɪv, drəʊv, 'drɪvn] fahren (fuhr, gefahren) I/2.3, II/1.2, II/5.2: **drive s.o. mad** jdn. verrückt machen *PI/5.2*

driver ['draɪvə] Fahrer(-in) II/2.1

drop [drɒp] Tropfen PI/5&6R

drop [drɒp] fallenlassen; *hier:* weglassen PI/5&6R

drug [drʌg] Droge PI/3.2

dry [draɪ] (ab)trocknen, fönen III/3.3

dry [draɪ] trocken III/3.3

due to ['djuː tə] wegen, infolge von PI/2.1

dull [dʌl] träge, langweilig, eintönig, trübe PI/5.1

during ['djʊərɪŋ] während III/1.1

dust [dʌst] Staub PI/1&2R

dusty ['dʌstɪ] staubig PI/1&2R

duty ['djuːtɪ] Pflicht, Aufgabe; Dienst PI/5.1

E

e.g. (= for example) [iː'dʒiː] z.B. (= zum Beispiel) PI/1.1

each [iːtʃ] jede(-r, -s) I/5.1: **30 pence each** je 30 Pence I/5.1; **each other** einander, sich (gegenseitig) PI/1&2P

ear [ɪə] Ohr II/3.1

early ['ɜːlɪ] früh II/2.1

earn [ɜːn] *(Geld)* verdienen I/5.2

east [iːst] Ost-, Osten I/3.1

Easter ['iːstə] Ostern, Oster- III/4.1

eastern ['iːstən] östlich, Ost- PI/1.1

easy ['iːzɪ] leicht III/2.1

eat (ate, eaten) [iːt, eɪt, 'iːtn] essen (aß, gegessen) I/4.2, I/5.2, II/1.2

edge [edʒ] Rand, Kante, Grenze PI/1&2P

editor ['edɪtə] Herausgeber(-in), Redakteur(-in) III/6.R

education [ˌedʒʊ'keɪʃn] Bildung, Erziehung, Ausbildung III/1.1

educational [ˌedʒʊ'keɪʃənl] lehrreich, bildend III/1.3

effort ['efət] Anstrengung, Mühe PI/8.1

egg [eg] Ei III/4.1

either ['aɪðə] jede(-r, -s) *(von zweien)*, beide PI/8.2: **not ... either** auch nicht III/6.1; **either ... or** entweder ... oder III/6.3

election [ɪ'lekʃn] Wahl, Abstimmung III/2.1

electrical [ɪ'lektrɪkl] Elektro-, elektrisch III/3.3

electronic [ˌɪlek'trɒnɪk] elektronisch III/4.1

elephant ['elɪfənt] Elefant II/5.3

elevator ['elɪveɪtə] Lift, Fahrstuhl *(amerik.)* II/5.1

else [els] (sonst) noch; *hier:* andere(-r,-s) III/1.1: **anything else?** noch etwas? *(in Fragen)* I/5.1

embarrass [ɪmˈbærəs] in Verlegenheit bringen, verwirren PI/5.1

embarrassed [ɪmˈbærəst] verlegen PI/5.1

emergency [ɪˈmɜːdʒənsɪ] Notfall PI/1&2P

emigrate [ˈemɪɡreɪt] auswandern *PI/1.1*

employee [emˈplɔɪiː, ˌemplɔɪˈiː] Angestellte(-r) III/3.1

employer [ɪmˈplɔɪə] Arbeitgeber II/2.3

empty [ˈemptɪ] leer II/5.3

encyclopedia [ɪnˌsaɪkləˈpiːdjə] Nachschlagewerk, Lexikon PI/8.2

end [end] Ende III/1.1

end [end] (be)enden III/1.1

ending [ˈendɪŋ] Schluß *III/2.R*

energy [ˈenədʒɪ] Energie PI/4.1

engine [ˈendʒɪn] Maschine, Motor III/5.2

engineer [ˌendʒɪˈnɪə] Ingenieur(-in), Techniker(-in) II/2.1

England [ˈɪŋɡlənd] England *(Teil Großbritanniens)* III/2.3

English [ˈɪŋɡlɪʃ] englisch(-e, -er, -es); Engländer(-in) I/1.1

Englishman [ˈɪŋɡlɪʃmən] Engländer *PI/S1*

enjoy [ɪnˈdʒɔɪ] genießen, Gefallen finden; gern tun II/1.1: **enjoy oneself** sich gut unterhalten, Gefallen finden III/4.1

enormous [ɪˈnɔːməs] enorm, riesig, gewaltig PI/7&8P

enough [ɪˈnʌf] genug I/5.3

enquiry, enquiries [ɪnˈkwaɪərɪ] (An-, Nach)Frage(n), Erkundigung(en); Auskunft *(Mz)* PI/7&8P

entertain [ˌentəˈteɪn] unterhalten PI/7&8R

entertainer [ˌentəˈteɪnə] Entertainer(-in), Unterhaltungskünstler(-in) III/5.1

entertainment [ˌentəˈteɪnmənt] Unterhaltung, Vergnügung III/5.I

entrance [ˈentrəns] Eingang II/4.1: **entrance hall** Eingangshalle, Hausflur II/4.1

envelope [ˈenvələʊp] Briefumschlag *PI/S2*

environment [ɪnˈvaɪərnmənt] Umgebung PI/5&6P

equipment [ɪˈkwɪpmənt] Ausrüstung PI/3.1

especially [ɪˈspeʃəlɪ] besonders PI/3.1

etc. (= et cetera) [ɪt ˈsetərə] und so weiter *II/G1*

Europe [ˈjʊərəp] Europa I/5.1

European [ˌjʊərəˈpiːən] europäisch(-e, -er, -es); Europäer(-in) III/1.3

even [ˈiːvn] selbst, sogar II/5.3: **not even** (noch) nicht einmal II/8.1; **even though** obwohl PI/1&2P

evening [ˈiːvnɪŋ] Abend I/1.3

event [ɪˈvent] Ereignis; Veranstaltung *(Sport)* III/6.3

ever [ˈevə] jemals, schon einmal II/1.1

every [ˈevrɪ] jede(-r, -s) I/2.2

everybody [ˈevrɪˌbɒdɪ] jeder III/1.2

everyday [ˈevrɪdeɪ] alltäglich, Alltags- *II/6.3P*, PI/8.1

everyone [ˈevrɪwʌn] jeder III/1.2

everything [ˈevrɪθɪŋ] alles *(jede einzelne Sache)* III/1.1

everywhere [ˈevrɪweə] überall(hin) III/1.2

exactly [ɪɡˈzæktlɪ] genau III/1.1

examination [ɪɡˌzæmɪˈneɪʃn] Examen, Prüfung II/6.1: **take an examination** eine Prüfung machen, sich einer Prüfung unterziehen II/6.1

examine [ɪɡˈzæmɪn] prüfen, untersuchen PI/4.1

example [ɪɡˈzaːmpl] Beispiel II/1.1: **for example** zum Beispiel II/1.1

excellent [ˈeksələnt] ausgezeichnet I/4.3

except [ɪkˈsept] außer, mit Ausnahme von III/2.1

exception [ɪkˈsepʃn] Ausnahme PI/5&6P

exchange [ɪksˈtʃeɪndʒ] Tausch PI/1&2R

exchange [ɪksˈtʃeɪndʒ] (aus)tauschen PI/1&2R

excite [ɪkˈsaɪt] erregen, aufregen PI/1.2

exciting [ɪkˈsaɪtɪŋ] aufregend PI/1.2

exclusive [ɪkˈskluːsɪv] exklusiv II/5.3

excuse me [ɪkˈskjuːz miː] entschuldigen Sie, entschuldige, entschuldigt bitte I/3.1

exercise [ˈeksəsaɪz] Übung I/2.2; *hier:* Auslauf, Bewegung PI/4.1: **get exercise** Sport treiben, Übungen machen II/3.I

exist [ɪɡˈzɪst] existieren, vorhanden sein III/4.I

exit [ˈeksɪt] Ausgang III/3.1

expect [ɪkˈspekt] erwarten PI/1.1

expectation [ˌekspekˈteɪʃn] Erwartung PI/1.1

expensive [ɪkˈspensɪv] teuer I/4.1

experience [ɪkˈspɪərɪəns] Erlebnis I/6.3; Erfahrung II/6.1

expert (on) [ˈekspɜːt] Experte, Expertin, Fachmann (für) PI/1.1

explain [ɪkˈspleɪn] erklären III/4.1

explanation [ˌekspləˈneɪʃn] Erklärung II/3.1

express [ɪkˈspres] ausdrücken PI/5.1

express [ɪkˈspres] ausdrücklich; *auch:* Eil- PI/5.1

expression [ɪkˈspreʃn] Ausdruck, Äußerung PI/1.1

extra [ˈekstrə] *hier:* Statist III/5.3

extra [ˈekstrə] zusätzlich, Zusatz- *PI/2.2*, PI/5.2: **extra cost** Aufpreis II/1.1

extremely [ɪkˈstriːmlɪ] äußerst PI/1&2P

eye [aɪ] Auge II/2.3

F

face [feɪs] Gesicht III/2.1

face [feɪs] schauen, blicken, liegen II/4.1

fact [fækt] Faktum, Tatsache III/1.3: **in fact** tatsächlich, eigentlich PI/3.2

factfile [ˈfæktˌfaɪl] Bericht, Dossier PI/1&2P

factory [ˈfæktrɪ] Fabrik III/5.1

fail [feɪl] versagen, verfehlen, durchfallen PI/5.1

fair [feə] Messe, Ausstellung I/1.1

fair [feə] blond, hell III/2.3; fair, anständig PI/7.1

faithfully [ˈfeɪθfʊlɪ]: **yours faithfully** mit freundlichen Grüßen *(am Briefschluß)* III/1.1

falcon [ˈfɔːlkən] Falke PI/3&4P

fall [fɔːl] Herbst *(amerik.)* II/5.1

fall (fell, fallen) [fɔːl, fel, ˈfɔːlən] fallen (fiel, gefallen) III/5.1

false [fɔːls] falsch I/3.1

family [ˈfæməlɪ] Familie I/2.1: **family doctor** Hausarzt, Hausärztin III/3.1

famous [ˈfeɪməs] berühmt I/4.3

fan [fæn] Fan, Anhänger *PI/S2*

far [faː] fern, weit I/2.I: **as far as** soweit, soviel III/1.3; **far from** weit von I/3.1

farm [faːm] Bauernhof, Farm II/2.1: **farm worker** Landarbeiter(-in) II/2.1

fashion [ˈfæʃn] Mode III/2.1: **fashion model** Mannequin III/2.1

fast [faːst] schnell I/6.2: **fast-food** Fast Food I/6.2

fat [fæt] dick, fett III/2.3

father [ˈfaːðə] Vater I/2.1: **father-in-law** Schwiegervater II/6.1

fault [fɔːlt] Defekt, Fehler, Schuld, Mangel III/3.3

favourite [ˈfeɪvrɪt] Lieblings- PI/5.2

fax [fæks] (Tele)Fax III/4.2

fear [fɪə] Angst PI/7.2

February [ˈfebrʊərɪ] Februar I/2.2

feed (fed, fed) [fi:d, fed] füttern (fütterte, gefüttert) III/4.3
feeder ['fi:də] *hier:* Fütterungs-apparat, -vorrichtung III/4.3
feel (felt, felt) [fi:l, felt] (sich) fühlen (fühlte, gefühlt) II/3.I: **feel homesick** Heimweh haben PI/1.1; **feel sick** übel, schlecht sein II/3.2; **feel upset** bestürzt, durcheinander sein III/6.2
feeling ['fi:lɪŋ] Gefühl *III/3.3P*, PI/6.1
female ['fi:meɪl] weiblich PI/5.1
few [fju:] wenige, paar III/5.1: **a few** einige, ein paar III/2.1
fiction ['fɪkʃn] Erfindung, Dichtung, Romanliteratur PI/8.2: **non-fiction book** Sachbuch PI/8.1; **science-fiction** Science-fiction-, utopisch PI/5&6P
field [fi:ld] Feld PI/2.1
fight [faɪt] Kampf III/5.1
fight (fought, fought) [faɪt, fɔ:t] kämpfen (kämpfte, gekämpft), erkämpfen, bekämpfen III/5.1: **fight one's way** sich durch-schlagen, -kämpfen III/5.1
figure ['fɪgə] Figur, Aussehen PI/3.2; Zahl PI/5&6P
file [faɪl] Bericht, Dossier PI/1&2P
fill (in) ['fɪl (ɪn)] (aus)füllen I/4.1
film [fɪlm] Film I/1.3: **go to see a film** ins Kino gehen I/1.3; **film star** Filmstar II/1.2
finally ['faɪnəlɪ] schließlich, letztendlich PI/3.1
find (found, found) [faɪnd, faʊnd] finden (fand, gefunden) I/2.3, II/5.3P
fine [faɪn] gut I/2.1: **I'm fine, thanks** danke, mir geht's gut I/2.1
finger ['fɪŋgə] Finger II/3.1
finish ['fɪnɪʃ] (be)enden I/4.R
fire ['faɪə] Feuer III/4.2
fireworks ['faɪəwɜ:ks] Feuerwerk III/6.3
firm [fɜ:m] Firma PI/1.2
first [fɜ:st] erste(-r, -s) I/1.3; zuerst I/6.1: **first class** erste(-r) Klasse II/4.2; **first floor** Erdgeschoß *(amerik.)* II/5.1; **first name** Vor-name I/1.3; **first of all** zuallererst, vor allen Dingen PI/3.1
fish [fɪʃ] Fisch I/6.1
fit [fɪt] fit, in Form II/3.1
fitness ['fɪtnəs] Fitneß II/3.I
flag [flæg] Fahne I/5.2
flat [flæt] Wohnung II/3.1: **two-roomed flat** 2-Zimmer-Wohnung II/4.1
flat [flæt] flach PI/1&2P
flexi-time (= flexible time) ['fleksɪ taɪm] Gleitzeit II/2.1
flight [flaɪt] Flug II/1.1

floor [flɔ:] Fußboden; Etage I/4.1: **on the … floor** in der … Etage I/4.1; **ground floor** Erdgeschoß I/4.1; **first floor** Erdgeschoß *(amerik.)* II/5.1
florist's ['flɒrɪsts] Blumenladen, Blumengeschäft II/5.2
flower ['flaʊə] Blume III/6.2
flu [flu:] Grippe III/6.2
fluently ['flu:əntlɪ] fließend PI/7.1
fly (flew, flown) [flaɪ, flu:, fləʊn] fliegen (flog, geflogen) III/1.1
fog [fɒg] Nebel II/1.2
foggy ['fɒgɪ] neblig II/1.2
follow ['fɒləʊ] (nach/ver)folgen, nachlaufen III/6.1
food [fu:d] Essen I/1.3: **fast-food** Fast Food I/6.2
foot (feet) [fʊt, fi:t] Fuß I/4.2; *(Maßeinheit = 30,48 cm)* III/2.1: **on foot** zu Fuß I/4.2
football ['fʊtbɔ:l] Fußball I/5.2
for [fɔ:, fə] für I/1.2; seit PI/2.2; … lang *(zeitlich)* II/1.1: **for example** zum Beispiel II/1.1
force [fɔ:s] zwingen PI/3&4P
forecast ['fɔ:kɑ:st] Vorhersage *PI/1&2R*
foreign ['fɒrən] fremd, ausländisch III/1.1
forget (forgot, forgotten) [fə'get, fə'gɒt, fə'gɒtn] vergessen (vergaß, vergessen) II/5.R
fork [fɔ:k] Gabel III/1.2
form [fɔ:m] Formular I/4.1; Form, Art III/3.I
form [fɔ:m] bilden *PI/1&2R*
formal ['fɔ:ml] förmlich, offiziell, feierlich; *hier:* vorschriftsmäßig, korrekt *(gekleidet)* III/6.1
former ['fɔ:mə] früher(-e, -er, -es), ehemalig PI/6.1
fortunately ['fɔ:tʃnətlɪ] glücklicherweise PI/3.1
fox [fɒks] Fuchs PI/3&4P
free [fri:] frei I/6.2; kostenlos PI/3.1: **free time** Freizeit II/1.I; **are you free?** hast du / haben Sie / habt ihr Zeit? III/3.R
freedom ['fri:dəm] Freiheit PI/1.1
French [frentʃ] französisch(-e, -er, -es); Franzose, Französin I/1.1: **French fries** Pommes frites *(amerik.)* II/5.1
frequent ['fri:kwənt] häufig PI/6.2
fresh [freʃ] frisch III/2.2
Friday ['fraɪdɪ] Freitag I/2.1
fridge (= refrigerator) [frɪdʒ, rɪ'frɪdʒəreɪtə] Kühlschrank II/4.2
friend [frend] Freund(-in), Bekannte(-r) I/1.3: **make friends** Freundschaft(en) schließen II/3.1
friendly ['frendlɪ] freundlich III/2.2

from [frɒm, frəm] aus I/1.I; von I/2.3: **from … to** von … bis I/2.R
front [frʌnt] Vorderseite, Front, Vorder- *I/5.3P*, PI/7.1: **in front of** vor I/3.1
frozen ['frəʊzn] (ein)gefroren, Tiefkühl- PI/7.1
fruit [fru:t] Frucht, Obst I/6.1
full [fʊl] voll I/4.1: **full-time** ganztägig II/2.3
fun [fʌn] Spaß, Vergnügen III/6.1
funny ['fʌnɪ] lustig, komisch III/5.R
furnished ['fɜ:nɪʃt] möbliert III/4.1
furniture ['fɜ:nɪtʃə] Möbel PI/4.1
further ['fɜ:ðə] weiter, ferner III/6.1
future ['fju:tʃə] Zukunft; Futur II/6.I
future ['fju:tʃə] Zukunfts-, zukünftig III/2.2

G

gallery ['gælərɪ] Galerie I/4.3
gallon ['gælən] Gallone *(Maßeinheit = 4,546 l)* III/3.3
game [geɪm] Spiel III/1.3
gap [gæp] Lücke *III/1.1*
garage ['gærɑ:dʒ] Garage; Tankstelle, (Auto)Werkstatt II/4.1
garden ['gɑ:dn] Garten II/3.2
garden ['gɑ:dn] Gartenarbeit betreiben PI/6.1
gardener ['gɑ:dnə] Gärtner(-in) II/3.3
gas [gæs] Gas, Gas- III/6.1
gate [geɪt] Tor, Pforte; *auch:* Flugsteig, Gate PI/4.2
general ['dʒenərəl] allgemein PI/3.1
gentleman (gentlemen) ['dʒentlmən, 'dʒentlmən] mein(-e) Herr (Herren) *(höfliche Anrede) (amerik.)* III/1.1
German ['dʒɜ:mən] deutsch(-e, -er, -es); Deutsche(-r) I/1.I
gerund ['dʒerənd] Gerundium *III/5.2*
get (got, got) [get, gɒt] bekommen (bekam, bekommen) I/4.R, I/5.2; werden III/2.2; gelangen, kommen III/3.1; holen PI/8.2: **get around** herumkommen, reisen III/3.I; **get dressed** sich anziehen, sich an-kleiden II/5.1; **get exercise** Sport treiben, Übungen machen II/3.I; **get home** zuhause ankommen I/4.R; **get married** heiraten, sich verheiraten II/6.1; **get on well with** gut auskommen mit II/6.1; **get to** ankommen in/bei I/4.R; **get up** aufstehen I/5.2
ghost [gəʊst] Geist, Gespenst III/6.3
girl [gɜ:l] Mädchen III/2.3
give (gave, given) [gɪv, geɪv, 'gɪvn] geben (gab, gegeben) I/3.R, II/3.R, II/5.2: **give up** aufgeben I/6.2

glad [glæd] froh III/6.1
glass [glɑːs] Glas I/6.1
glasses [ˈglɑːsɪz] Brille III/2.1
go (went, gone) [gəʊ, went, gɒn] gehen (ging, gegangen) I/1.3, I/5.2; *hier:* hingehören, passen *III/1.3*: **go for a walk** spazierengehen I/5.R; **go jogging** joggen I/1.3; **go out** ausgehen I/2.R; **go round** vorbeigehen, besuchen *PI/1.2*; **go shopping** einkaufen gehen I/1.3; **go to** gehen in, fahren nach I/1.3; **go to see sb.** jdn. besuchen *PI/S2*, PI/6.1
goddaughter [ˈgɒdˌdɔːtə] Patenkind *(weiblich)* III/6.2
going to [ˈgəʊɪŋ tə] werden *(Form der Zukunft)* II/6.1
gold [gəʊld] Gold PI/3.1
golden [ˈgəʊldən] golden, aus Gold PI/3.1
goldfish [ˈgəʊldfɪʃ] Goldfisch II/1.R
golf [gɒlf] Golf I/2.3
good [gʊd] der (die, das) Gute, Gutes II/5.R
good (at) [gʊd] gut (in) I/2.3: **good-looking** gutaussehend, attraktiv PI/2.1
goodbye [ˌgʊdˈbaɪ] auf Wiedersehen I/2.1
goodness [ˈgʊdnɪs] du meine Güte!, mein Gott! PI/2.2
gorilla [gəˈrɪlə] Gorilla PI/8.2
government [ˈgʌvnmənt] Regierung III/2.1
gram [græm] Gramm I/6.3
grammar [ˈgræmə] Grammatik *II/1.2*
gran (= grandmother) [græn, ˈgrænˌmʌðə] Großmutter, Oma II/6.2
grandmother [ˈgrænˌmʌðə] Großmutter, Oma II/6.1
grass [grɑːs] Gras PI/2.1
grassy [ˈgrɑːsɪ] grasbedeckt, Gras- PI/2.1
great [greɪt] großartig I/1.1
great-grandmother [ˌgreɪtˈgrænˌmʌðə] Urgroßmutter PI/5&6P
Greek [griːk] griechisch(-e, -er, -es); Grieche, Griechin II/1.1
green [griːn] grün I/5.1
greet [griːt] (be)grüßen III/3.R
greeting [ˈgriːtɪŋ] Gruß III/1.R
grey [greɪ] grau I/2.3
grilled [grɪld] gegrillt I/6.2
ground [graʊnd] Boden II/4.1: **ground floor** Erdgeschoß I/4.1
group [gruːp] Gruppe I/4.2
grow (grew, grown) [grəʊ, gruː, grəʊn] wachsen (wuchs, gewachsen) PI/1&2P
guess [ges] (er)raten III/1.2
guest [gest] Gast III/5.1

guide (to) [gaɪd] *hier:* Führer, Handbuch (durch/über) III/6.2: **guide book** Reiseführer III/1.2
guilty [ˈgɪltɪ] schuldig PI/6.1
guinea pig [ˈgɪnɪ pɪg] Meerschweinchen PI/4.1
gun [gʌn] Gewehr, Pistole II/5.2
guy [gaɪ] Bursche, Typ PI/1.2
gymnastics [dʒɪmˈnæstɪks] Turnen, Gymnastik PI/3&4P

H

habit [ˈhæbɪt] (An)Gewohnheit III/1.3
hair [heə] Haar(e) II/6.3: **do one's hair** sich frisieren III/5.1
hairdresser [ˈheəˌdresə] Friseur, Friseuse III/5.R
half [hɑːf] halb, Hälfte I/4.1: **half past six** halb sieben I/4.1
hall [hɔːl] Halle; Flur II/4.1: **entrance hall** Eingangshalle, Hausflur II/4.1
ham [hæm] Schinken I/6.1
hamburger [ˈhæmbɜːgə] Hamburger I/6.2
hamster [ˈhæmstə] Hamster PI/4.1
hand [hænd] Hand II/3.1: **on the other hand** auf der anderen Seite, andererseits III/3.3; **second-hand** gebraucht, aus zweiter Hand PI/8.2
handball [ˈhændbɔːl] Handball PI/3.1
handle [ˈhændl] handhaben, umgehen mit, fertigwerden PI/8.1
handsome [ˈhænsəm] schön *(bei Männern)* II/6.3
hang (hung, hung) [hæŋ, hʌŋ] hängen (hing, gehangen) PI/4.2
happen [ˈhæpən] passieren, geschehen, sich ereignen II/5.1
happy [ˈhæpɪ] glücklich I/6.2: **happy birthday!** alles Gute zum Geburtstag! III/6.1; **many happy returns of the day!** herzlichen Glückwunsch zum Geburtstag! PI/6.1
hard [hɑːd] hart, schwer, fleißig II/2.2
hardly [ˈhɑːdlɪ] kaum PI/3&4P
hate [heɪt] hassen I/6.2
have (had, had) [hæv, hæd] haben (hatte, gehabt) I/2.2; *hier:* essen, zu sich nehmen I/4.R; *hier:* bekommen *(Kinder)* III/2.2: **I'll have (= I will have)** ich nehme I/6.1; **have a nice day** einen schönen Tag noch I/5.1; **have something done** etwas machen lassen III/5.2

have got [hæv ˈgɒt] haben, besitzen I/2.1
have to [ˈhæv tə] müssen II/4.1: **don't have to** nicht müssen II/3.2
he [hiː] er I/1.1
head [hed] Kopf II/3.1
headache [ˈhedeɪk] Kopfschmerzen II/3.2
health [helθ] Gesundheit I/4.3
healthy [ˈhelθɪ] gesund II/3.3
hear (heard, heard) [hɪə, hɜːd] hören (hörte, gehört) II/1.3
heart [hɑːt] Herz III/5.1
heating [ˈhiːtɪŋ] Heizung II/4.1
heavy [ˈhevɪ] schwer III/2.3
hectare [ˈhekteə] Hektar *(Flächenmaß)* PI/1&2P
hell [hel] Hölle PI/8.1
hello [həˈləʊ] Hallo. Guten Tag. Grüß' Gott. Grüezi. I/1.I
help [help] Hilfe I/4.1
help [help] helfen I/4.1
helpful [ˈhelpfʊl] hilfreich, nützlich PI/4.1
helpless [ˈhelplɪs] hilflos PI/3&4R
her [hɜː] ihr(-e) I/2.1; sie, ihr *(Einzahl)* I/2.1
here [hɪə] hier I/2.1: **here you are** hier, bitte *(wenn man etwas überreicht)* I/5.1; **here's to you!** auf dein/Ihr/euer Wohl! PI/6.1
hero (heroes) [ˈhɪərəʊ, ˈhɪərəʊz] Held (Helden) PI/3.2
hers [hɜːz] ihre(-r, -s), der (die, das) ihre II/5.1
hey [heɪ] hallo, he PI/2.2
hi [haɪ] hallo! I/1.1
high [haɪ] hoch II/4.1
hill [hɪl] Hügel, Berg III/5.1
him [hɪm] ihn, ihm I/2.1
hire [haɪə] mieten III/3.1
his [hɪz] seine(-r, -s), der (die, das) sein(ig)e II/5.2
history [ˈhɪstərɪ] Geschichte PI/1.1
hit (hit, hit) [hɪt, hɪt] treffen (traf, getroffen), schlagen, (zusammen)stoßen PI/3.1
hobby [ˈhɒbɪ] Hobby II/1.1
hold (held, held) [həʊld, held] halten (hielt, gehalten) PI/1.2: **hold on** *hier:* dranbleiben, am Apparat bleiben, warten II/2.1
holiday [ˈhɒlədeɪ] Urlaub, Ferien I/1.3: **(public) holiday** Feiertag III/6.3; **on holiday** im Urlaub, in den Ferien III/2.2
home [həʊm] Heim, Zuhause I/1.2; Heimat- III/4.1: **at home** zuhause I/1.2; **get home** zuhause ankommen I/4.R; **take home** nach Hause (mit)nehmen III/1.2
homesick [ˈhəʊmsɪk]: **feel homesick** Heimweh haben PI/1.1

homework ['həʊmwɜ:k]
Hausaufgaben I/2.2
hope [həʊp] Hoffnung I/5.3
hope [həʊp] hoffen I/5.3
horse [hɔ:s] Pferd II/6.3
hospital ['hɒspɪtl] Krankenhaus I/2.3
hot [hɒt] heiß II/1.2: **hot dog** Hot
dog *(heißes Würstchen in einem
Brötchen)* III/6.3
hotel [ˌhəʊ'tel] Hotel I/1.3
hour ['aʊə] Stunde I/4.1: **rush hour**
Hauptverkehrszeit III/3.3
house [haʊs] Haus I/4.2
household ['haʊshəʊld] Haushalt
III/1.3
housewife ['haʊswaɪf] Hausfrau
III/4.3
how [haʊ] wie I/2.1: **how about …?**
wie wäre es mit …? wie wäre es,
wenn …? II/3.1; **how are things?**
wie geht es (dir/Ihnen/euch)?
PI/6.1; **how are you?** wie geht es
dir/Ihnen/euch? I/2.1; **how are
you keeping?** wie geht es
dir/Ihnen/euch? PI/6.1; **how do
you do?** wie geht es Ihnen?,
angenehm! *(höfliche Begrüßungs-
formel)* I/2.1; **how long** wie lange
I/5.1; **how many** wie viele I/2.1;
how much wieviel I/4.1; **how
much is …?** was kostet …? I/4.1
however [haʊ'evə] jedoch, dennoch
PI/1.1
huge [hju:dʒ] riesig PI/1&2P
human ['hju:mən] Mensch PI/3&4P
human ['hju:mən] menschlich
PI/3&4P
humour ['hju:mə] Humor PI/5.1
hundred ['hʌndrəd] hundert
PI/1&2P
hungry ['hʌŋgrɪ] hungrig III/2.3
hunt [hʌnt] jagen PI/3&4P
hurricane ['hʌrɪkən] Hurrikan,
Wirbelsturm PI/3&4R
hurry ['hʌrɪ]: **be in a hurry** es eilig
haben III/3.1
hurry ['hʌrɪ] eilen, hasten III/3.1:
hurry up sich beeilen III/3.1
hurt (hurt, hurt) [hɜ:t, hɜ:t]
verletzen (verletzte, verletzt),
(sich) weh tun III/4.2
husband ['hʌzbənd] Ehemann I/2.1

I

I [aɪ] ich I/1.1: **I see** ach so *(Ausruf)*
I/3.1
ice [aɪs] Eis I/6.1: **ice cream**
Eiskrem I/6.1; **ice hockey**
Eishockey PI/3.1
idea [aɪ'dɪə] Idee I/5.1

ideal [aɪ'dɪəl] ideal, geeignet PI/3.1
if [ɪf] wenn, falls II/3.1; ob III/2.1
ill [ɪl] krank II/3.1
image ['ɪmɪdʒ] Bild; Image PI/2.1
imagination [ɪˌmædʒɪ'neɪʃn]
Vorstellungskraft, Phantasie
PI/5&6R
imagine [ɪ'mædʒɪn] sich vorstellen
PI/1&2P, PI/5.2
immediately [ɪ'mi:dɪətlɪ] sofort I/6.1
immigrant ['ɪmɪgrənt] Einwanderer
PI/2.2
important [ɪm'pɔ:tnt] wichtig I/6.3
impossible [ɪm'pɒsəbl] unmöglich
II/6.1
improve [ɪm'pru:v] verbessern PI/3.1
in [ɪn] in I/1.I: **in black and white**
schwarz auf weiß II/5.R; **in
common** gemeinsam *PI/1.1*; **in
fact** tatsächlich, eigentlich PI/3.2;
in front of vor I/3.1; **in German**
auf deutsch I/1.I; **in order to** um
zu III/5.1; **in particular**
besonders, vor allem PI/7.1
inch (inches) [ɪntʃ, 'ɪntʃɪz] Inch,
Zoll *(Maßeinheit = 2,54 cm)*
III/2.1
include [ɪn'klu:d] einschließen,
beinhalten I/4.1
including [ɪn'klu:dɪŋ] einschließlich
I/4.1
increase [ɪn'kri:s] steigern,
vergrößern, erhöhen PI/3.1
independent [ˌɪndɪ'pendənt]
unabhängig III/6.3
Indian ['ɪndjən] indisch(-e, -er, -es);
Inder(-in) I/3.3
industrial [ɪn'dʌstrɪəl] Industrie-,
industriell I/3.1
industry ['ɪndəstrɪ] Industrie III/5.1
infinitive [ɪn'fɪnətɪv] Infinitiv,
Grundform *III/5.2*
influence ['ɪnflʊəns] Einfluß PI/7.1
influence ['ɪnflʊəns] beeinflussen
PI/7.1
inform [ɪn'fɔ:m] informieren,
mitteilen PI/5&6R
information [ˌɪnfə'meɪʃn]
Information, Auskunft I/3.1:
information desk
Informationsschalter III/3.1
inside [ˌɪn'saɪd] innerhalb, drinnen
II/2.3
instead [ɪn'sted] statt dessen II/3.2:
instead of an Stelle von, statt
III/1.2
instruction [ɪn'strʌkʃn] Anweisung
PI/8.1
instrument ['ɪnstrəmənt] Instrument
III/5.1
insurance [ɪn'ʃʊərəns]
Versicherung, Versicherungs-
III/3.1
interest ['ɪntrəst] Interesse PI/5.1

interest ['ɪntrəst] interessieren PI/5.1
interested (in) ['ɪntrəstɪd]
interessiert (an) II/1.3
interesting ['ɪntrəstɪŋ] interessant
I/3.3
international [ˌɪntə'næʃnl]
international I/1.1
interrupt [ˌɪntə'rʌpt] unterbrechen
PI/5.1
interruption [ˌɪntə'rʌpʃn]
Unterbrechung PI/5.1
interview ['ɪntəvju:] Interview,
Vorstellungsgespräch II/2.1
interview ['ɪntəvju:] befragen,
interviewen III/3.1
into ['ɪntʊ] in, in … hinein III/6.1
introduce … to [ˌɪntrə'dju:s tʊ] …
vorstellen I/1.1
invent [ɪn'vent] erfinden III/6.R
invitation [ˌɪnvɪ'teɪʃn] Einladung
PI/7&8P
invite [ɪn'vaɪt] einladen I/5.3
Ireland ['aɪələnd] Irland PI/1.1
Irish ['aɪrɪʃ] irisch(-e, -er, -es); Ire,
Irin PI/1.1
irregular [ɪ'regjʊlə] unregelmäßig
II/1.I
island ['aɪlənd] Insel II/1.1
it [ɪt] es I/1.1
Italian [ɪ'tæljən] italienisch(-e, -er,
-es); Italiener(-in) I/1.I
italics [ɪ'tælɪks]: **in italics** in
Kursivschrift *PI/6.1*
item ['aɪtəm] Gegenstand, Stück,
Artikel PI/7&8P
itinerary [aɪ'tɪnərərɪ] Reiseroute,
-plan III/3.1
its [ɪts] seine(-r, -s), der (die, das)
sein(ige) *(sächlich)* III/5.3

J

jacket ['dʒækɪt] Jacke, Jakett II/5.1
jam [dʒæm] Marmelade, Konfitüre
III/5.R
January ['dʒænjʊərɪ] Januar I/2.2
Japanese [ˌdʒæpə'ni:z] japanisch(-e,
-er, -es); Japaner(-in) I/2.3
jeans [dʒi:nz] Jeans II/2.2
job [dʒɒb] Arbeit, Stelle I/5.2
jogging ['dʒɒgɪŋ] Jogging II/3.I: **go
jogging** joggen I/1.3
join [dʒɔɪn] beitreten, sich
anschließen; verbinden PI/3.1
joke [dʒəʊk] Scherz, Witz III/1.2
journalism ['dʒɜ:nəlɪzm]
Journalismus III/1.1
journalist ['dʒɜ:nəlɪst] Journalist(-in)
III/1.1
journey ['dʒɜ:nɪ] Fahrt, Reise I/4.1
juice [dʒu:s] Saft I/6.1
July [dʒʊ'laɪ] Juli I/2.2

jump [dʒʌmp] springen PI/3&4P: **show jumper** Springreiter(-in); Springpferd PI/3&4P
June [dʒuːn] Juni I/2.2
just [dʒʌst] nur I/1.1; gerade, soeben; *hier:* einfach III/2.1

K

kangaroo [ˌkæŋɡəˈruː] Känguruh PI/1&2P
keen [kiːn]: **(be) not too keen on** nicht allzu gern mögen I/6.1
keep (kept, kept) [kiːp, kept] halten (hielt, gehalten), behalten III/4.3; sich halten, bleiben PI/3.1: **how are you keeping?** wie geht es dir/Ihnen/euch? PI/6.1
key [kiː] Schlüssel I/4.1
kid [kɪd] Kind PI/3&4P
kill [kɪl] töten III/1.3
kilo [ˈkiːləʊ] Kilo I/6.3
kilometre [ˈkɪləˌmiːtə] Kilometer I/3.1
kind [kaɪnd] Sorte, Art III/1.3
kind [kaɪnd] nett, freundlich I/4.1
kindergarten [ˈkɪndəˌɡɑːtn] Kindergarten PI/7&8P
king [kɪŋ] König III/2.1
kiosk [ˈkiːɒsk] Kiosk PI/8.2
kitchen [ˈkɪtʃɪn] Küche II/4.1
knee [niː] Knie II/3.1
knife (knives) [naɪf, naɪvz] Messer III/1.2
know (knew, known) [nəʊ, njuː, nəʊn] kennen (kannte, gekannt) I/3.1; wissen I/3.3, II/3.3P: **well-known** berühmt, wohlbekannt II/5.3
knowledge [ˈnɒlɪdʒ] Kenntnis, Wissen PI/5.1

L

label [ˈleɪbl] beschriften *II/4.1*
lady [ˈleɪdɪ] Lady, Dame II/5.1
lake [leɪk] See III/6.2
lamb [læm] Lamm(fleisch) PI/4.1
lamp [læmp] Lampe II/4.2
land [lænd] Land, Boden III/6.3
land [lænd] landen I/5.2
lane [leɪn] Gasse I/3.3
language [ˈlæŋɡwɪdʒ] Sprache, Sprach- I/6.R
lantern [ˈlæntən] Laterne III/6.3
large [lɑːdʒ] groß I/6.3
last [lɑːst] dauern, reichen, halten *(+ Zeitraum)* III/5.3
last [lɑːst] letzte(-r, -s) I/4.2; das letzte Mal I/5.2

late [leɪt] spät, verspätet I/4.1
laugh [lɑːf] lachen III/2.1
law [lɔː] Gesetz III/6.2: **brother-in-law** Schwager II/6.1; **daughter-in-law** Schwiegertochter II/6.1; **father-in-law** Schwiegervater II/6.1; **mother-in-law** Schwiegermutter II/6.1; **sister-in-law** Schwägerin II/6.1; **son-in-law** Schwiegersohn II/6.1
lawyer [ˈlɔːjə] Rechtsanwalt PI/5.1
lazy [ˈleɪzɪ] faul PI/3.2
lead (led, led) [liːd, led] führen (führte, geführt) PI/4.1
learn (learnt, learnt) [lɜːn, lɜːnt] lernen (lernte, gelernt) I/3.1, III/1.2
learner [ˈlɜːnə] Lerner(-in) II/2.2
least [liːst] kleinst(-e, -er, -es), wenigst(-e, -er, -es) III/3.3: **at least** wenigstens, zum mindesten; mindestens III/4.1
leather [ˈleðə] Leder PI/4.1
leave (left, left) [liːv, left] verlassen (verließ, verlassen), zurücklassen; (weg)gehen, (weg)fahren II/2.1: **leave for** (weg)gehen, (weg)fahren, (weg)fliegen nach III/3.1
lecturer [ˈlektʃərə] Vortragende(-r), Dozent(-in) *PI/7&8P*
left [left] linke(-r, -s); (nach) links I/3.1: **on the left** links, auf der linken Seite I/3.1; **on your left** links von Ihnen/dir/euch, zu Ihrer/deiner/eurer Linken I/3.2
leg [leg] Bein II/3.1
lemon [ˈlemən] Zitrone I/6.1
lend (lent, lent) [lend, lent] leihen (lieh, geliehen) PI/5.2
less [les] weniger III/2.1
lesson [ˈlesn] Unterrichtsstunde I/2.2
let (let, let) [let, let] (zu)lassen (ließ, gelassen) III/6.2; *hier:* vermieten II/4.3: **let's (= let us)** laß' uns *(+ Vorschlag)* II/1.1
letter [ˈletə] Brief I/2.3; Buchstabe *II/1.R*
library [ˈlaɪbrərɪ] Bücherei, Bibliothek PI/1.2
licence [ˈlaɪsəns] Erlaubnis, Lizenz III/2.2: **driving licence** Führerschein III/2.2
lie (lay, lain) [laɪ, leɪ, leɪn] liegen (lag, gelegen), sich legen III/6.2: **lie down** sich (hin)legen III/6.2
life (lives) [laɪf, laɪvz] Leben II/3.2
lift [lɪft] Lift, Aufzug II/4.1
light [laɪt] Licht I/3.1: **traffic lights** Ampel I/3.1
like [laɪk] Vorliebe *PI/8.1*
like [laɪk] gern haben I/1.1: **I'd like (= I would like)** ich möchte I/4.1; **like about** schätzen an, gern

haben an *PI/1.1*; **like doing** gern tun II/1.1
like [laɪk] wie III/4.1: **like this** wie dies(-e, -es, -er) *II/1.1*; **what is it like?** wie ist es?, wie sieht es aus? PI/2.1
line [laɪn] Linie, Zeile II/4.2, PI/2.1; (Telefon)Leitung PI/2.1
list [lɪst] Liste III/1.3
listen [ˈlɪsn]: **listen for** horchen, lauschen auf III/4.3; **listen to** (zu)hören I/2.2
listener [ˈlɪsnə] (Zu)Hörer(-in) III/6.R
little [ˈlɪtl] klein III/4.1: **a little** ein bißchen, ein wenig III/2.1
live [lɪv] wohnen, leben I/1.3: **live to be a hundred** hundert Jahre alt werden III/2.R
living [ˈlɪvɪŋ] Lebensunterhalt III/5.1: **living room** Wohnzimmer II/4.1
local [ˈləʊkl] lokal, örtlich III/3.1
lock [lɒk] abschließen, zusperren PI/2.1
lonely [ˈləʊnlɪ] einsam PI/4.2
long [lɒŋ] lang I/5.2: **long-distance** Fern- PI/1.1; **how long** wie lange I/5.1
look [lʊk] Blick II/5.1: **have a look** (sich) etw. ansehen II/5.1
look [lʊk] aussehen III/5.2: **look (at)** (an)sehen I/2.1; **look after** sich kümmern um, sorgen für II/6.2; **look after yourself!** mach's gut!, paß auf dich auf! PI/6.1; **look for** suchen nach, sich umsehen nach III/1.1; **look forward to** sich freuen auf III/1.1; **look up** nachsehen, nachschlagen *PI/1&2R*, PI/8.1; **good-looking** gutaussehend, attraktiv PI/2.1
lose (lost, lost) [luːz, lɒst] verlieren (verlor, verloren) II/4.2, III/2.2
lot [lɒt]: **a lot** viel III/1.2; **a lot of** viele I/2.1; **lots of** viele I/3.3
lottery [ˈlɒtərɪ] Lotterie III/2.2
love [lʌv] Liebe III/1.1: **love from** liebe Grüße von *(am Briefschluß)* III/1.1; **give my love to …** grüße / grüßen Sie / grüßt … ganz lieb von mir PI/6.1
love [lʌv] lieben I/6.1
lovely [ˈlʌvlɪ] wunderschön, entzückend II/4.1
low [ləʊ] niedrig, tief, gering III/5.1
luck [lʌk] Glück III/5.1: **good luck!** viel Glück! III/5.1
luckily [ˈlʌkɪlɪ] glücklicherweise PI/6.2
lucky [ˈlʌkɪ] glücklich, Glücks- III/6.3
lunch [lʌntʃ] Mittagessen I/4.R
lunchtime [ˈlʌntʃˌtaɪm] Mittagszeit, -pause II/2.R

M

machine [mə'ʃi:n] Maschine III/1.1
mad [mæd] verrückt PI/5.2: **drive s.o. mad** jdn. verrückt machen PI/5.2
madam ['mædəm] *(höfliche Anrede für eine Kundin)* I/6.1; *(höfliche Anrede für eine Frau im Brief)* III/1.1
magazine [ˌmægə'zi:n] Zeitschrift I/5.1
magnet ['mægnɪt] Magnet III/4.3
mail [meɪl] Post(sendung) PI/7.2, PI/7&8P
main [meɪn] Haupt- I/3.2: **main course** Hauptgericht I/6.1
mainly ['meɪnlɪ] hauptsächlich PI/6.1
make (made, made) [meɪk, meɪd] machen (machte, gemacht), bilden I/2.2, II/6.3P: **make an appointment** eine Verabredung treffen, einen Termin ausmachen II/3.1; **make connections** Verbindungen, Kontakte knüpfen PI/7&8P; **make every mistake in the book** jeden erdenklichen Fehler machen PI/6.2; **make friends** Freundschaft(en) schließen II/3.1; **make it to the top** es bis zur Spitze schaffen, ganz nach oben kommen PI/3&4P; **make sb. do sth.** *hier:* jdn. zu etwas veranlassen, zwingen PI/1.1; **make sure** sich vergewissern, feststellen PI/3.1
make-up ['meɪkʌp] Make-up, Schminke III/6.R
male [meɪl] männlich PI/5.1
man (men) [mæn, men] Mann (Männer) I/3.1
manage ['mænɪdʒ] (es) schaffen, klarkommen I/4.1
manager ['mænɪdʒə] Manager, Geschäftsführer, Direktor III/1.2
many ['menɪ] viele I/2.1: **how many** wie viele I/2.1
map [mæp] (Land)karte, Stadtplan I/5.1
March [mɑːtʃ] März I/2.2
market ['mɑːkɪt] Markt II/5.2
marriage ['mærɪdʒ] Heirat, Hochzeit, Ehe III/4.3P
married ['mærɪd] verheiratet I/2.1: **get married** heiraten, sich verheiraten II/6.1
marry ['mærɪ] heiraten II/2.2
match [mætʃ] Spiel *(Sport)* II/6.R
match [mætʃ] zuordnen II/1.1
material [mə'tɪərɪəl] Material III/4.1
matter ['mætə] Sache, Angelegenheit II/5.1: **it doesn't matter** es macht nichts II/5.1; **is anything the matter?** ist irgend

etwas nicht in Ordnung? III/1.R; **what's the matter?** worum geht es? was ist los? II/5.1
maximum ['mæksɪməm] Maximum, Höchst- PI/1&2P
May [meɪ] Mai I/2.2
may [meɪ] dürfen II/4.1: **may do sth.** vielleicht etwas tun II/2.1
maybe ['meɪbi:] vielleicht PI/5&6R
me [mi:] mich, mir; *auch:* ich I/1.2
meal [mi:l] Essen, Mahlzeit III/3.2
mean (meant, meant) [mi:n, ment] meinen (meinte, gemeint) III/2.1; bedeuten III/4.3
meaning ['mi:nɪŋ] Bedeutung II/3.1, PI/8.2
meat [mi:t] Fleisch I/6.1
media ['mi:dʒə] Medien III/1.I
medical ['medɪkl] medizinisch, ärztlich, Kranken- III/4.2
medicine ['medsɪn] Medizin, Arznei III/1.2
medium-sized ['mi:dɪəm'saɪzd] mittelgroß I/3.1
meet (met, met) [mi:t, met] kennenlernen, treffen (traf, getroffen) I/1.I, I/5.2, II/1.2: **pleased to meet you** angenehm; nett, Sie/dich/euch kennenzulernen I/1.1
meeting ['mi:tɪŋ] Treffen, Versammlung III/1.1
melon ['melən] Melone I/6.1
member ['membə] Mitglied PI/7&8P
memo ['meməʊ] Memo, Notiz, Nachricht III/4.2
memory (of) ['memərɪ] Gedächtnis, Erinnerung (an) PI/1.2
mention ['menʃn] erwähnen PI/1.1
menu ['menju:] Speisekarte I/6.1
merry ['merɪ]: **merry Christmas!** frohe Weihnachten! III/6.3
message ['mesɪdʒ] Mitteilung, Botschaft I/6.3
metal ['metl] Metall, Metall-, metallen III/4.1
metre ['mi:tə] Meter III/2.1
microwave ['maɪkrəˌweɪv] Mikrowelle III/4.3
middle ['mɪdl]: **in the middle** in der Mitte, mitten in III/2.2
midnight ['mɪdnaɪt] Mitternacht II/5.2
might [maɪt]: **might do sth.** vielleicht etwas tun II/2.1
migraine ['mi:greɪn] Migräne II/3.2
mile [maɪl] Meile *(Längenmaß = 1,609 km)* III/3.3
milk [mɪlk] Milch I/6.1
million ['mɪljən] Million I/6.3
millionaire [ˌmɪljə'neə] Millionär(-in) I/5.2
mime [maɪm] mimen, mit Hilfe der Mimik darstellen III/5.2

mind [maɪnd] etwas gegen etwas haben I/5.1; (be)achten, achtgeben auf III/3.1
mine [maɪn] mein(-e, -er, -es), der (die, das) mein(ig)e II/5.1
minus ['maɪnəs] minus I/1.2
minute ['mɪnɪt] Minute I/3.1
mirror ['mɪrə] Spiegel PI/S3
miss [mɪs] Fräulein III/6.1
miss [mɪs] verpassen I/3.1; vermissen PI/1.1
missing ['mɪsɪŋ] fehlend PI/1.1
mistake [mɪ'steɪk] Fehler II/5.1: **make every mistake in the book** jeden erdenklichen Fehler machen PI/6.2
model ['mɒdl] Modell III/2.1: **fashion model** Mannequin III/2.1
modern ['mɒdən] modern I/4.3
Mom [mɒm] Mutti *(amerik.)* PI/6.2
moment ['məʊmənt] Augenblick I/6.1
Monday ['mʌndɪ] Montag I/2.1
money ['mʌnɪ] Geld I/5.I
monkey ['mʌŋkɪ] Affe PI/4.2
month [mʌnθ] Monat I/2.3
moon [mu:n] Mond II/4.2
more [mɔ:] mehr I/6.2: **more again** noch(mals) mehr II/2.3
morning ['mɔ:nɪŋ] Morgen, Vormittag I/2.2: **this morning** heute morgen I/4.R; **in the mornings** vormittags I/2.2
most [məʊst] meiste(-r, -s) II/1.2; am meisten; *hier:* am liebsten III/1.3
mother ['mʌðə] Mutter I/2.1: **mother-in-law** Schwiegermutter II/6.1
motor ['məʊtə] Motor- III/5.R
motorbike ['məʊtəbaɪk] Motorrad III/5.R
motorway ['məʊtəweɪ] Autobahn III/3.3
mountain ['maʊntɪn] Berg I/3.1: **mountain bike** Mountain-Bike, Geländefahrrad III/4.3
moustache [mə'stɑːʃ] Schnurrbart III/2.3
mouth [maʊθ] Mund II/3.1
move [mu:v] Umzug, (Fort)Bewegung PI/1&2I
move [mu:v] (sich) bewegen, umräumen; *auch:* umziehen *(Wohnung)* III/3.3
movie ['mu:vɪ] Film *(amerik.)* II/5.1: **movie theater** Kino *(amerik.)* II/5.1
Mr ['mɪstə] Herr *(Anrede)* II/5.1
Mrs [mɪsɪz] Frau *(Anrede für eine verheiratete Frau)* I/2.1
Ms [mɪz] Frau *(Anrede)* III/1.1

much [mʌtʃ] viel I/2.3: **how much** wieviel I/4.1; **how much is …?** was kostet …? I/4.1
Mum [mʌm] Mutti I/2.3
murder ['mɜːdə] Mord PI/4.2
museum [mjuːˈzɪəm] Museum I/3.2
mushroom ['mʌʃrʊm] Pilz I/6.1
music ['mjuːzɪk] Musik I/3.R
musical ['mjuːzɪkl] Musical III/5.3
musical ['mjuːzɪkl] musikalisch, musisch, Musik- III/5.1
musician [mjuːˈzɪʃn] Musiker(-in), Musikant(-in) II/5.3
must [mʌst] müssen II/2.3: **mustn't** (= **must not**) nicht dürfen II/3.2
my [maɪ] mein(-e) I/1.1
myself [maɪˈself] ich/mir/mich (selbst) III/4.1: **by myself** allein PI/3.1

N

name [neɪm] Name I/1.1: **first name** Vorname I/1.3; **my name's** ich heiße I/1.1; **what's your name?** wie heißen Sie?, wie heißt du/ihr? I/1.1
narrow ['nærəʊ] eng, schmal III/6.1
nasty ['nɑːstɪ] böse, schlimm, gefährlich, fies PI/7.1
national ['næʃənl] national, National-, Landes- III/1.1
nationality, -ies [ˌnæʃəˈnælətɪ] Nationalität, -en I/1.1
natural ['nætʃrəl] natürlich, normal PI/1.1
near [nɪə] nahe (gelegen, -liegend) III/3.3
near [nɪə] in der Nähe von I/1.1
nearly ['nɪəlɪ] fast, beinahe III/3.3
necessary ['nesəsərɪ] nötig, notwendig II/3.2
need [niːd] benötigen I/5.1; brauchen, müssen III/1.1
negative ['negətɪv] negativ, verneinend II/1.2
neighbour ['neɪbə] Nachbar(-in) II/4.3
neither ['naɪðə] keine(-r, -s) *(von zweien)* PI/8.2: **neither … nor** weder … noch III/5.1; **neither/nor do I** ich auch nicht *(Antwort auf eine Frage)* III/6.1
nervous ['nɜːvəs] nervös PI/4.1
never ['nevə] nie II/2.2
new [njuː] neu I/2.3
news [njuːz] Nachrichten I/5.2
newsagent's ['njuːzˌeɪdʒənts] Zeitungsladen, Zeitungsgeschäft II/5.2
newspaper ['njuːsˌpeɪpə] Zeitung I/1.3

next [nekst] nächste(-r, -s) I/2.2; als nächstes III/1.1: **next to** neben I/5.1
nice [naɪs] nett, schön I/1.1: **nice to meet you** angenehm; nett, Sie/dich/euch kennenzulernen I/1.1
night [naɪt] Nacht I/4.1: **at night** in der Nacht, nachts III/1.2
no [nəʊ] nein I/1.1
nobody ['nəʊbədɪ] niemand III/1.2
noise [nɔɪz] Lärm III/3.3
noisy ['nɔɪzɪ] laut III/2.2
non- [nɒn] nicht-, un- PI/5&6R: **non-fiction book** Sachbuch PI/8.1
none [nʌn] kein(-e, -er, -es), niemand III/1.2
nonsense ['nɒnsəns] Unsinn, Blödsinn PI/7.1
no one ['nəʊwʌn] niemand III/1.2
nor [nɔː]: **nor do I** ich auch nicht *(Antwort auf eine Frage)* III/6.1
normal ['nɔːml] normal II/2.3
north [nɔːθ] Norden, Nord- I/2.R
northern ['nɔːðn] nördlich, Nord- PI/1.1
nose [nəʊz] Nase II/3.1
nostalgic [nɒˈstældʒɪk] nostalgisch *PI/1&2R*
not [nɒt] nicht I/1.1: **not at all** bitte, nichts zu danken I/3.1; **not even** (noch) nicht einmal PI/8.1
note [nəʊt] Note, Notiz I/5.I: **bank note** Banknote I/5.I; **take notes on** sich Notizen machen über III/1.3
note (down) [nəʊt] notieren, aufschreiben *PI/4.1*
notebook ['nəʊtbʊk] Notizbuch PI/8.1
nothing ['nʌθɪŋ] nichts II/3.1
notice ['nəʊtɪs] Notiz, Beachtung PI/3.2
notice ['nəʊtɪs] bemerken, beachten PI/3.2
noun [naʊn] Substantiv, Hauptwort *PI/1&2R*
novel ['nɒvl] Roman, Novelle PI/8.1
November [nəʊˈvembə] November I/2.2
now [naʊ] jetzt I/1.3: **now that** seitdem, jetzt wo III/1.3
nowhere ['nəʊweə] nirgendwo(hin) III/1.2
number ['nʌmbə] Zahl, Nummer I/1.2
number ['nʌmbə] (durch)numerieren, zählen *II/2.1*
nurse [nɜːs] Krankenschwester II/6.1

O

object ['ɒbdʒɪkt] Gegenstand III/4.1
obviously ['ɒbvɪəslɪ] offensichtlich, natürlich PI/3.1

occasion [əˈkeɪʒn] Gelegenheit, Anlaß III/6.I
occupy ['ɒkjʊpaɪ] in Besitz nehmen, besetzen, innehaben; *hier:* ausfüllen PI/6.1
ocean ['əʊʃn] Ozean PI/6.1
October [ɒkˈtəʊbə] Oktober I/2.2
of [ɒv, əv] von I/1.3: **of course** selbstverständlich I/5.1
offer ['ɒfə] Angebot I/4.1
offer ['ɒfə] anbieten III/1.1
office ['ɒfɪs] Büro I/4.2: **office assistant** Bürogehilfe, Bürogehilfin II/2.1
officer ['ɒfɪsə] Offizier, (Polizei)Beamter/Beamtin PI/5.2
often ['ɒfn] oft I/1.3
oh [əʊ] Null *(in Telefonnummern)* I/1.2
oil [ɔɪl] Öl III/3.3
okay (= OK) [ˌəʊˈkeɪ] in Ordnung; *hier:* mir geht's gut I/2.1
old [əʊld] alt I/3.1
omelette ['ɒmlət] Omelett I/1.2
on [ɒn] auf I/1.3; an III/1; *hier:* über III/5.1: **on a train** im Zug, in der Bahn I/4.2; **on foot** zu Fuß I/4.2; **on Saturdays** samstags I/1.3; **on television** im Fernsehen I/5.1; **on the … floor** in der … Etage I/4.1; **on your left** links von Ihnen, zu Ihrer Linken I/3.2; **on your right** rechts, auf der rechten Seite I/3.2
once [wʌns] einmal, einst II/3.2: **at once** sofort III/6.1
one [wʌn]: **a Japanese one** *(Stützwort)* ein(-e) japanische(-r, -s) I/2.3; **one-way ticket** einfache Fahrkarte *(amerik.)* III/3.1
onion ['ʌnjən] Zwiebel I/6.3
only ['əʊnlɪ] einzig II/5.1: **only child** Einzelkind II/2.1
only ['əʊnlɪ] nur III/1.2; erst III/2.2
open ['əʊpən] öffnen I/4.R
open ['əʊpən] offen I/3.3
opera ['ɒprə] Oper, Opern- III/5.3
opinion [əˈpɪnjən] Meinung III/1.3
opportunity [ˌɒpəˈtjuːnətɪ] Gelegenheit, Möglichkeit PI/3.1
opposite ['ɒpəzɪt] Gegenteil *III/2.R*, PI/4.1
opposite ['ɒpəzɪt] gegenüberliegend, entgegengesetzt III/1.3
opposite ['ɒpəzɪt] gegenüber I/5.1
or [ɔː] oder I/1.3
orange ['ɒrɪndʒ] Apfelsine I/6.1
orange ['ɒrɪndʒ] orange I/5.1
order ['ɔːdə] Reihenfolge, Ordnung *II/1.2*; Befehl, Anordnung II/3.2; Bestellung III/4.1: **in order to** um zu III/5.1
order ['ɔːdə] bestellen I/6.1
ordinary ['ɔːdnrɪ] gewöhnlich, einfach PI/2.1

organization [ˌɔːgənaɪˈzeɪʃn] Organisation III/2.1
organize [ˈɔːgənaɪz] organisieren PI/5.1
oriented [ˈɔːrɪentɪd] orientiert PI/5&6P
original [əˈrɪdʒənl] original, ursprünglich; *hier:* originell, einfallsreich, neu PI/7.1
originally [əˈrɪdʒənəlɪ] ursprünglich I/1.1
other [ˈʌðə] andere(-r, -s) I/2.1: **each other** einander, sich (gegenseitig) PI/1&2P
ought to [ɔːt tə] sollte(-st, -t, -n) PI/1.1
our [ˈaʊə] unser(-e) I/1.3
ours [ˈaʊəz] unsere(-r, -s), der (die, das) unsere II/5.2
out [aʊt]: **out of** aus, heraus I/3.2; **be out** *hier:* ausgegangen sein II/2.1; **out of work** arbeitslos PI/5&6P
outback [ˈaʊtbæk] Hinterland *(in Australien)* PI/1&2P
outdoor [ˈaʊtˌdɔː] draußen, im Freien, Außen- PI/7&8P
outside [ˌaʊtˈsaɪd] außerhalb II/2.I; draußen II/2.3
oval [ˈəʊvl] oval III/2.3
over [ˈəʊvə] über I/3.2; mehr als I/3.3: **all over** überall, in ganz … PI/2.1; **all over the world** auf der ganzen Welt PI/3.1; **over there** da drüben I/5.1
overweight [ˌəʊvəˈweɪt]: **be overweight** Übergewicht haben PI/3.1
own [əʊn] besitzen PI/1&2R
own [əʊn] eigen, einzig PI/3&4R
owner [ˈəʊnə] Besitzer(-in) PI/1&2R
oz (= ounce) [aʊns] Unze *(Maßeinheit = 28,35 g)* III/6.2

P

pâté [ˈpæteɪ] Pastete *(franz.)* III/6.2
pack [pæk] (ein)packen III/4.2
packet [ˈpækɪt] Paket, Päckchen I/6.3
page [peɪdʒ] Seite II/1.1
paint [peɪnt] (Mal)Farbe III/4.1
paint [peɪnt] (an)malen, anstreichen III/4.1
pair [peə] Paar II/5.1
pants [pænts] (lange) Hose(n) *(amerik.)* II/5.1
paper [ˈpeɪpə] Papier, Blatt III/2.R; Zeitung *(umgangssprachlich)* PI/1&2R, PI/6.2
parade [pəˈreɪd] Parade III/6.3
paragraph [ˈpærəgrɑːf] Absatz, Abschnitt, Paragraph II/2.3

parcel [ˈpɑːsl] Paket, Päckchen III/4.2
pardon? [ˈpɑːdn] wie bitte? I/3.1
parents [ˈpeərənts] Eltern I/2.1
park [pɑːk] Park I/3.2
park [pɑːk] parken II/2.2
part [pɑːt] Teil I/3.1: **take part in** teilnehmen an PI/3&4P; **part-time** Teilzeit- II/1.1
particular [pəˈtɪkjʊlə] besondere(-r, -s), speziell PI/7.1: **in particular** besonders, vor allem PI/7.1
partner [ˈpɑːtnə] Partner(-in) I/2.1
party [ˈpɑːtɪ] Party II/4.3
pass [pɑːs] vorbeigehen, -fahren; (herüber)reichen; bestehen *(Prüfung)* PI/5.1
passenger [ˈpæsɪndʒə] Passagier, Fahrgast, Reisende(-r) III/3.1
passive [ˈpæsɪv] Passiv, Leideform PI/4.2
passport [ˈpɑːspɔːt] (Reise)Paß II/1.2
past [pɑːst] Vergangenheit III/1.1: **past participle** Partizip Perfekt, Mittelwort der Vergangenheit III/4.2; **past perfect** Plusquamperfekt, Vorvergangenheit III/6.2; **past progressive** Verlaufsform der ersten Vergangenheit II/5.2; **past simple** Imperfekt, erste Vergangenheit I/5.2
past [pɑːst] vergangen, früher PI/5.2
past [pɑːst] an … vorbei I/3.2; nach I/4.1: **half past six** halb sieben I/4.1
pastime [ˈpɑːstaɪm] Zeitvertreib, Hobby PI/5.2
patient [ˈpeɪʃnt] Patient(-in) PI/1&2P
patriotic [ˌpætrɪˈɒtɪk] patriotisch III/6.3
pay [peɪ] Bezahlung, Gehalt II/2.1
pay (paid, paid) [peɪ, peɪd] bezahlen (bezahlte, bezahlt) I/6.1: **pay attention to** beachten, Aufmerksamkeit schenken PI/7.1; **pay for** bezahlen I/5.2
pea [piː] Erbse I/6.1
peace [piːs] Frieden III/6.2
pear [peə] Birne, Birnen- III/6.2
pen [pen] Feder(halter), Füller II/2.2: **ball pen** Kugelschreiber PI/4.2
pence [pens] *(Mehrzahl von* penny) I/5.1: **30 pence each** je 30 Pence I/5.1
pencil [ˈpensl] (Blei)Stift II/2.2
penny [ˈpenɪ] *(brit. Währung);* „Pfennig" III/4.1
people [ˈpiːpl] Leute, Menschen I/1.I
per [pɜː] pro I/4.1: **per cent** (%) Prozent, Prozentsatz III/1.3
perfect [ˈpɜːfɪkt] perfekt, vollkommen, genau richtig II/4.1

performance [pəˈfɔːməns] Ausführung, Vorstellung, Darstellung PI/5.1
perhaps [pəˈhæps] vielleicht I/6.1
period [ˈpɪərɪəd] Periode, Zeitraum PI/2.2
person [ˈpɜːsn] Person I/4.1
personal [ˈpɜːsənəl] persönlich I/1.3
personality [ˌpɜːsəˈnælətɪ] Persönlichkeit PI/S2
persuade [pəˈsweɪd] überreden, überzeugen PI/5&6P
pet [pet] Haustier III/4.3
petrol [ˈpetrəl] Benzin III/3.3
phone [fəʊn] *(Kurzform für)* Telefon I/1.2: **be on the phone to** telefonieren mit III/2.1
phone [fəʊn] anrufen I/5.1
photo [ˈfəʊtəʊ] Foto I/5.2: **take a photo** ein Foto machen I/5.2
photocopier [ˈfəʊtəʊˌkɒpɪə] Fotokopiergerät II/2.2
photocopy [ˈfəʊtəʊˌkɒpɪ] (Foto)Kopie II/2.2
photograph [ˈfəʊtəgrɑːf] Foto PI/1.1
photographer [fəˈtɒgrəfə] Fotograf(-in) PI/1.1
photography [fəˈtɒgrəfɪ] Fotografie II/6.R
phrase [freɪz] Redewendung, Ausdruck III/G1
piano [pɪˈænəʊ] Klavier I/1.2
pick (up) [pɪk] (auf)heben, aufnehmen; abholen; *hier:* pflücken *(Blumen)* PI/5.2
picnic [ˈpɪknɪk] Picknick III/2.2: **have a picnic** picknicken III/2.2
picture [ˈpɪktʃə] Bild III/2.2
pie [paɪ] Pastete; gedeckter Kuchen III/6.3
piece [piːs] Stück III/2.3
pig [pɪg] Schwein PI/4.1
pilot [ˈpaɪlət] Pilot, Flieger II/6.2
ping-pong [ˈpɪŋpɒŋ] Tischtennis; *hier:* Wechselspiel PI/2.1
pint [paɪnt] *(brit. Maßeinheit = 0,568 l);* Halbe (Bier) III/4.1
pipe [paɪp] Pfeife; *auch:* (Rohr)Leitung PI/7.1
pity [ˈpɪtɪ]: **what a pity!** wie schade! III/6.1
pizza [ˈpiːtsə] Pizza III/1.2
place [pleɪs] Ort I/1.1; Platz, Stelle; Haus, Wohnung I/6.R: **take place** stattfinden, sich ereignen PI/2.1
plain [pleɪn] Ebene PI/1&2P
plan [plæn] Plan II/1.1
plan [plæn] planen PI/6.2
plane [pleɪn] Flugzeug I/4.I
plant [plɑːnt] Pflanze PI/1&2P
plant [plɑːnt] pflanzen III/4.2
plastic [ˈplæstɪk] Plastik, aus Plastik III/2.3

platform ['plætfɔ:m] Bahnsteig III/3.3

play [pleɪ] Bühnenstück I/5.2

play [pleɪ] spielen I/1.2

player ['pleɪə]: **record player** (Schall)Plattenspieler III/4.2

pleasant ['pleznt] angenehm, freundlich, erfreulich III/4.2

please [pli:z] zufriedenstellen, erfreuen; (jdm.) gefallen PI/6.2

please [pli:z] bitte I/1.2

pleased [pli:zd] erfreut I/1.1: **pleased to meet you** angenehm; nett, Sie/dich/euch kennenzulernen I/1.1

plenty ['plentɪ]: **plenty of** viel, jede Menge III/4.2

pocket ['pɒkɪt] Tasche *(am Kleidungsstück)* III/6.1

poem ['pəʊɪm] Gedicht PI/8.2

point [pɔɪnt] (Kern)Punkt, Stelle *II/3.3P*, PI/3.1; Ziel, Zweck PI/3.1: **point of view** Standpunkt, Ansicht PI/7.1

police [pə'li:s] Polizei II/2.2: **police station** Polizeiwache I/3.1

policeman [pə'li:smən] Polizist II/2.1

polite [pə'laɪt] höflich III/1.2

political [pə'lɪtɪkl] politisch III/2.1

politics ['pɒlətɪks] Politik PI/8.2

poor [pɔ:] arm III/2.1; *hier:* schlecht, ungeeignet PI/6.2

popular ['pɒpjʊlə] beliebt, populär PI/3.1

population [ˌpɒpjʊ'leɪʃn] Bevölkerung PI/1&2P

pork [pɔ:k] Schweinefleisch PI/4.1

positive ['pɒzətɪv] positiv, bejahend *II/1.2*, PI/5.1

possible ['pɒsəbl] möglich II/3.1

possibly ['pɒsəblɪ] vielleicht, eventuell II/3.1

post [pəʊst] Post I/3.1: **post office** Postamt I/3.1

post [pəʊst] (mit der Post) senden, (Post) aufgeben III/4.2

postcard ['pəʊstkɑ:d] Postkarte I/3.3

poster ['pəʊstə] Plakat PI/7&8P

postman/postwoman ['pəʊstmən, 'pəʊstwʊmən] Postbote/Postbotin III/5.R

potato [pə'teɪtəʊ] Kartoffel I/6.1

pouch [paʊtʃ] Beutel PI/1&2P

pound [paʊnd] Pfund *(englische Währung)* I/5.1

powerful ['paʊəfʊl] mächtig, stark, (zug)kräftig PI/3&4R

practical ['præktɪkl] praktisch, geschickt PI/1.1

practice ['præktɪs] Übung, Üben PI/3&4P

practise ['præktɪs] üben *II/1.1*, PI/3.2

prefer [prɪ'fɜ:] vorziehen I/6.1: **I'd prefer** ich würde vorziehen, ich nehme lieber … I/6.1

preference ['prefərəns] Vorliebe, Vorzug *PI/8.1*

prepare [prɪ'peə] vorbereiten, zubereiten PI/4.1

preposition [ˌprepə'zɪʃn] Präposition, Verhältniswort I/5.1

present ['preznt] Geschenk II/5.I; Gegenwart III/1.1: **present perfect** Perfekt, vollendete Gegenwart, zweite Vergangenheit *II/1.2*; **present perfect progressive** Verlaufsform der vollendeten Gegenwart *PI/2.2*; **present progressive** Verlaufsform der Gegenwart *II/3.2*; **present simple** Präsens, Gegenwart *I/2.2*

present ['preznt] gegenwärtig, momentan PI/2.2

president ['prezɪdənt] Präsident III/2.1

press [pres] Presse *(Zeitung)* PI/7.1

press [pres] drücken PI/1&2P

pretty ['prɪtɪ] hübsch PI/2.1

price [praɪs] Preis I/5.1

prime minister [ˌpraɪm 'mɪnɪstə] Premierminister(-in) III/2.1

prince [prɪns] Prinz II/4.2

princess [prɪn'ses] Prinzessin II/4.2

print [prɪnt] Gedrucktes, (Ab)Druck PI/8.1

print [prɪnt] drucken PI/8.1

prison ['prɪzn] Gefängnis PI/3.2

prisoner ['prɪznə] Gefangene(-r) PI/3.2

private ['praɪvɪt] privat PI/3.1

prize [praɪz] (Sieger)Preis II/1.3

probably ['prɒbəblɪ] wahrscheinlich II/2.1

problem ['prɒbləm] Problem II/2.3

produce [prə'dju:s] produzieren, herstellen, erzeugen III/3.3

product ['prɒdʌkt] Produkt, Erzeugnis PI/4.1

production [prə'dʌkʃn] Produktion PI/4.1

profession [prə'feʃn] Beruf PI/5.1

professional [prə'feʃənl] professionnel, Berufs-, Fach- PI/5.1

professor [prə'fesə] Professor(-in) III/6.2

profile ['prəʊfaɪl] Profil I/1.3

program *(amerik.)* ['prəʊgræm] Programm, Sendung III/1.1

programme *(brit.)* ['prəʊgræm] Programm, Sendung III/1.1

progress *(Ez/Mz)* ['prəʊgres] Fortschritt(-e) PI/6.1

promise ['prɒmɪs] Versprechen I/6.1

pronoun ['prəʊnaʊn] Pronomen, Fürwort *III/4.2*

pronounce [prə'naʊns] aussprechen III/6.2

pronunciation [prəˌnʌnsɪ'eɪʃn] Aussprache *I/2.R*

proper ['prɒpə] richtig, passend, geeignet PI/4.1

property ['prɒpətɪ] Eigentum, Besitz III/3.1: **lost property office** Fundbüro III/3.1

proud (of) [praʊd (əv)] stolz (auf) II/6.2

prove [pru:v] beweisen PI/6.1

provide [prə'vaɪd] geben, liefern, versorgen PI/1&2P

psychologist [saɪ'kɒlədʒɪst] Psychologe, Psychologin PI/7.1

pub [pʌb] Gasthof, Kneipe I/4.2

public ['pʌblɪk] Öffentlichkeit PI/7&8P

public ['pʌblɪk] öffentlich III/3.1

publish ['pʌblɪʃ] veröffentlichen II/2.1

publisher ['pʌblɪʃə] Verleger(-in), Herausgeber(-in) PI/7&8P

pull [pʊl] ziehen III/6.1

pullover ['pʊlˌəʊvə] Pullover II/5.1

pumpkin ['pʌmpkɪn] Kürbis III/6.3

pupil ['pju:pl] Schüler(-in) PI/8.1

purpose ['pɜ:pəs] Zweck, Absicht PI/7.1

push [pʊʃ] stoßen, schieben, stecken III/6.1

put (put, put) [pʊt, pʊt] legen (legte, gelegt), stellen, setzen II/2.2, III/4.2: **put on** *hier: (Kleidung)* anziehen III/6.1; **put on weight** zunehmen *(Gewicht)* PI/3.2; **put through** *hier:* durchstellen II/2.1

Q

qualification [ˌkwɒlɪfɪ'keɪʃn] Qualifikation PI/5.1

qualify ['kwɒlɪfaɪ] sich qualifizieren, eignen PI/5&6R

quality ['kwɒlətɪ] Qualität PI/3.1

quarter ['kwɔ:tə]: **a quarter** Viertel I/4.1

Queen [kwi:n] Königin (von England) II/6.3

question ['kwestʃən] Frage I/2.1: **question mark** Fragezeichen *II/1.1*

questionnaire [ˌkwestʃə'neə] Fragebogen *I/1.2*

quick [kwɪk] schnell II/2.2

quiet ['kwaɪət] ruhig, still III/2.2

quite [kwaɪt] ganz, völlig, ziemlich II/6.1

quiz [kwɪz] Quiz *I/G2*

R

rabbit ['ræbɪt] Kaninchen PI/4.1
race [reɪs] Rennen PI/3.1
race [reɪs] rennen, rasen PI/3.1
radio ['reɪdɪəʊ]: **(on the) radio** (im) Radio III/1.I
railway ['reɪlweɪ] Eisenbahn PI/2.1
rain [reɪn] Regen II/1.3
rain [reɪn] regnen II/1.2
rainy ['reɪnɪ] regnerisch, verregnet PI/1&2R
raise [reɪz] (hoch)heben, errichten; *hier:* züchten PI/1&2P
rather ['rɑːðə] ziemlich III/5.2; lieber, eher III/5.3
reach [riːtʃ] erreichen, reichen (an etw.) PI/4.1
reaction (to) [rɪ'ækʃn] Reaktion (auf) III/4.1
read (read, read) [riːd, red] lesen (las, gelesen) I/1.3, II/1.2
reader ['riːdə] *hier:* Lesestoff, Lektüre PI/8.1
ready ['redɪ] fertig, bereit III/4.3
real ['rɪəl] wirklich, wahr, echt PI/8.1
realistic [ˌrɪə'lɪstɪk] realistisch, wirklichkeitsnah, sachlich PI/1.1
realize ['rɪəlaɪz] sich klarmachen, begreifen, sich im klaren sein (über) III/6.1
really ['rɪəlɪ] wirklich, eigentlich I/3.1
reason ['riːzn] Grund, Begründung III/2.1
receipt [rɪ'siːt] Quittung I/6.1
receiver [rɪ'siːvə] Empfänger(-in); *hier:* Telefonhörer PI/S2
recent ['riːsnt] neu, jüngst PI/2.2
recently ['riːsntlɪ] vor kurzem, unlängst PI/2.2
reception [rɪ'sepʃn] Rezeption, Empfang I/4.1
receptionist [rɪ'sepʃənɪst] Person am Empfang I/4.1
recognize ['rekəgnaɪz] (wieder)erkennen PI/5&6P
recommend [ˌrekə'mend] empfehlen, raten III/3.1
record ['rekɔːd] Aufzeichnung, Wiedergabe; Rekord PI/6.1; Schallplatte III/4.2: **record player** (Schall)Plattenspieler III/4.2
record [rɪ'kɔːd] aufnehmen, aufzeichnen III/4.3
red [red] rot I/5.1
refusal [rɪ'fjuːzl] Ablehnung, Verweigerung PI/8.1
refuse [rɪ'fjuːz] sich weigern, ablehnen PI/8.1
regards [rɪ'gɑːdz]: **give my regards to ...** grüße / grüßen Sie / grüßt ... von mir III/5.1
regret [rɪ'gret] bedauern PI/5.2

regular ['regjʊlə] regelmäßig II/2.3
relationship (with) [rɪ'leɪʃnʃɪp] Beziehung, Verhältnis (zu) PI/3&4P
relative ['relətɪv] Verwandte(-r) PI/1.1
relative clause [ˌrelətɪv 'klɔːz] Relativsatz *PI/8.2*
remain [rɪ'meɪn] bleiben PI/5&6P
remember [rɪ'membə] sich erinnern an, denken an III/1.R
remind of [rɪ'maɪnd əv] erinnern an PI/1.1
rent [rent] Miete II/4.1
rent [rent] mieten II/4.1
repair [rɪ'peə] reparieren III/1.2
repeat [rɪ'piːt] wiederholen PI/6.2
replace [rɪ'pleɪs] ersetzen *II/6.I*
reply [rɪ'plaɪ] Antwort PI/2.2
reply [rɪ'plaɪ] antworten PI/2.2
report [rɪ'pɔːt] Bericht, Nachricht, Meldung III/4.2
report [rɪ'pɔːt] berichten, melden *II/1.2*: **reported speech** indirekte Rede *PI/7.2*
reporter [rɪ'pɔːtə] Reporter(-in) *PI/S1*
reserve [rɪ'zɜːv] reservieren III/3.R
responsibility [rɪˌspɒnsə'bɪlətɪ] Verantwortung PI/5.1
rest [rest] Rest III/5.1
restaurant ['restərõ, 'restərɒnt] Restaurant I/1.3
result [rɪ'zʌlt] Ergebnis PI/2.1
retire [rɪ'taɪə] in Pension gehen, in den Ruhestand treten II/6.1
retired [rɪ'taɪəd] pensioniert, im Ruhestand II/2.I
retirement [rɪ'taɪəmənt] Ruhestand *PI/6.1*, PI/6.2
return [rɪ'tɜːn] Rückkehr, Rück-, Rückfahrkarte III/3.2: **many happy returns of the day!** herzlichen Glückwunsch zum Geburtstag! PI/6.1
return [rɪ'tɜːn] zurückkehren III/3.1
review (of) [rɪ'vjuː] Rückblick (auf) *PI/1.2*; Rundschau *PI/2.1*
rice [raɪs] Reis I/6.1
rich [rɪtʃ] reich II/3.1
ride (rode, ridden) [raɪd, rəʊd, 'rɪdn] reiten (ritt, geritten); fahren II/1.R
right [raɪt] richtig I/1.1; direkt, gerade PI/7.2: **all right** in Ordnung I/3.1; **be right** recht haben II/6.1; **that's all right** bitte, ist schon in Ordnung I/3.1
right [raɪt] (nach) rechts I/3.1: **on the right** rechts, auf der rechten Seite I/3.2
ring [rɪŋ]: **give sb. a ring** jdn. anrufen III/3.1

ring (rang, rung) [rɪŋ, ræŋ, rʌŋ] klingeln, läuten (läutete, geläutet) I/4.1, II/5.2; anrufen II/2.1
risk [rɪsk] Risiko, Gefahr PI/3.2: **be at risk** gefährdet sein PI/7.1; **take many risks** viele Risiken eingehen PI/3.2
risk [rɪsk] riskieren PI/3.2
risky ['rɪskɪ] riskant, gefährlich *PI/6.2*
river ['rɪvə] Fluß I/3.1
road [rəʊd] Straße, Fahrbahn I/3.1
robber ['rɒbə] Räuber II/5.2
robot ['rəʊbɒt] Roboter II/4.2
romance [rəʊ'mæns] Liebesroman PI/8.1
room [ruːm] Zimmer, Raum I/3.2: **two-roomed flat** 2-Zimmer-Wohnung II/4.1
round [raʊnd] rund III/2.3: **all-round** allgemein, Gesamt- PI/3.1
round [raʊnd] (rund) um, um ... (herum) II/6.1
route [ruːt] Route, Strecke PI/6.2
ruin ['rʊɪn] Ruine; Ruin, Untergang PI/3&4P
ruin ['rʊɪn] ruinieren, zerstören PI/3&4P
rule [ruːl] Regel, Vorschrift PI/3.1
run (ran, run) [rʌn, ræn, rʌn] rennen (rannte, gerannt) III/1.2; *hier:* fließen PI/2.1; *hier:* betreiben, führen *(Geschäft)* PI/2.1
rush [rʌʃ] rasen, hetzen, (sich) beeilen III/6.3: **rush hour** Hauptverkehrszeit III/3.3
Russian ['rʌʃən] russisch(-e, -er, -es); Russe, Russin II/1.R

S

sad [sæd] traurig PI/2.1
safe [seɪf] sicher PI/5&6P
safety ['seɪftɪ] Sicherheit PI/5&6P
sail [seɪl] segeln PI/3.1
salad ['sæləd] Salat I/6.1
salary ['sælərɪ] Lohn, Gehalt II/2.3
sale [seɪl] Verkauf II/4.3: **for sale** verkäuflich, zum Verkauf II/4.3
salesman/saleswoman ['seɪlzmən, 'seɪlzˌwʊmən] Verkäufer(-in) PI/5.1
salt [sɔːlt] Salz III/5.R
salty ['sɔːltɪ] salzig PI/1&2R
same [seɪm] der- (die-, das-)selbe; gleich I/3.2: **and the same to you** gleichfalls I/5.1
sand [sænd] Sand PI/1&2R
sandwich ['sænwɪdʒ] Butterbrot I/5.2
sandy ['sændɪ] sandig, Sand- PI/1&2R

satisfaction [ˌsætɪsˈfækʃn]
Zufriedenheit, Befriedigung
PI/5&6R

satisfy [ˈsætɪsfaɪ] zufriedenstellen
PI/5.1

Saturday [ˈsætədɪ] Samstag I/1.3:
on Saturdays samstags I/1.3

sauce [sɔːs] Soße I/6.3

sausage [ˈsɒsɪdʒ] Wurst PI/4.1

save [seɪv] sparen I/5.2; retten;
auch: aufheben, aufbewahren
PI/6.2

say (said, said) [seɪ, sed] sagen
(sagte, gesagt) I/6.1, II/3.1: **it says**
es heißt, steht (geschrieben) *PI/S2,*
PI/8.1

schnaps [ʃnæps] Schnaps *(deutsch)*
III/6.2

school [skuːl] Schule I/2.3

science [ˈsaɪəns] Naturwissenschaft
PI/5&6P: **science-fiction**
Science-fiction-, utopisch PI/5&6P

Scotland [ˈskɒtlənd] Schottland I/1.1

Scottish [ˈskɒtɪʃ] schottisch(-e, -er,
-es); Schotte, Schottin I/1.1

scramble [ˈskræmbl] *hier:*
durcheinanderbringen, verdrehen
PI/3.2

sea [siː] Meer I/3.1

seaside [ˈsiːsaɪd] (Meeres)Küste
III/3.R: **go to the seaside** ans
Meer fahren III/3.R

season [ˈsiːzn] Jahreszeit I/2.3

seat [siːt] Sitzplatz III/3.3

second [ˈsekənd] Sekunde PI/1&2P

second [ˈsekənd] zweite(-r, -s) I/3.1:
second-hand gebraucht, aus
zweiter Hand PI/8.2

secret [ˈsiːkrɪt] Geheimnis II/3.3

secretarial [ˌsekrəˈteərɪəl] Schreib-,
Büro- PI/7&8P

secretary [ˈsekrətrɪ] Sekretär(-in)
III/1.1

section [ˈsekʃn] Abschnitt *II/1.3P*

see (saw, seen) [siː, sɔː, siːn] sehen
(sah, gesehen) I/1.3, I/5.2, II/1.2: **I
see** ach so *(Ausruf)* I/3.1; **see you
… bis …** III/1.1

seem [siːm] (er)scheinen III/5.1

seldom [ˈseldəm] selten II/3.I

-self, -selves [-self, -selvz] (ich, er,
Sie usw.) selbst, selber III/4.1

self-service [ˌself ˈsɜːvɪs] Selbstbedienung, Selbstbedienungs- I/6.2

sell (sold, sold) [sel, səʊld]
verkaufen (verkaufte, verkauft)
I/5.1, II/1.1

seminar [ˈsemɪnɑː] Seminar, Kurs
III/6.R

send (sent, sent) [send, sent]
schicken (schickte, geschickt),
senden II/3.1, III/4.2

sense [sens] Sinn, Sinnesorgan
PI/4.1: **common sense** gesunder
Menschenverstand, Vernunft PI/4.1

sentence [ˈsentəns] Satz I/2.1

September [sepˈtembə] September
I/2.2

serious [ˈsɪərɪəs] ernst(haft) II/3.1

serve [sɜːv] (be)dienen; *hier:*
anbieten PI/7&8P

service [ˈsɜːvɪs] Bedienung I/4.3;
Dienst(leistung) PI/2.1:
self-service Selbstbedienung,
Selbstbedienungs- I/6.2

set [set] Satz, Garnitur, Sammlung
etc. PI/8.2: **set lunch**
(Mittags-)Menü I/6.1

settle [ˈsetl] sich niederlassen; *auch:*
zahlen, abrechnen PI/1.1: **settle
down** sich ansiedeln, einleben
PI/1.1

several [ˈsevrəl] mehrere *III/6.3P,*
PI/1&2P

sex [seks] Geschlecht; Sex PI/7.1

sexy [ˈseksɪ] sexy, aufreizend PI/7.1

shall [ʃæl]: **shall I …?** kann ich …?
(Vorschlag, Angebot) I/4.1; **shall
we …?** sollen wir II/1.1

shampoo [ʃæmˈpuː] Shampoo PI/7.2

share [ʃeə] teilen II/4.3

sharp [ʃɑːp] scharf PI/4.1

shave [ʃeɪv] (sich) rasieren III/4.2

shaver [ˈʃeɪvə] Rasierapparat PI/7.1

she [ʃiː] sie I/1.1

sheep *(Ez/Mz)* [ʃiːp] Schaf(-e)
PI/1&2P

shelf (shelves) [ʃelf, ʃelvz]
Regal(-e) PI/8.1

shine (shone, shone) [ʃaɪn, ʃɒn]
scheinen (schien, geschienen) II/3.2

ship [ʃɪp] Schiff III/6.2

shirt [ʃɜːt] Hemd II/5.1

shock [ʃɒk] Schock, Schreck,
Erschütterung III/5.3

shocked [ʃɒkt] schockiert I/5.3

shoe [ʃuː] Schuh II/1.1: **beach shoe**
Strandschuh, Badeschuh II/1.1

shoot (shot, shot) [ʃuːt, ʃɒt]
(er)schießen (schoß, geschossen)
PI/4.2

shop [ʃɒp] Geschäft, Laden I/2.R:
shop assistant Verkäufer(-in),
Ladengehilfe, Ladengehilfin II/2.1

shopping [ˈʃɒpɪŋ]: **go shopping**
einkaufen gehen I/1.3

short [ʃɔːt] kurz III/2.3

shortage [ˈʃɔːtɪdʒ] Knappheit,
Mangel III/3.3

shorthand [ˈʃɔːthænd]: **take
shorthand** stenografieren PI/5.1

should [ʃʊd] sollte(-st, -t, -n) II/3.1

shoulder [ˈʃəʊldə] Schulter II/3.1:
shoulder-length schulterlang
III/2.3

shout [ʃaʊt] Ruf, Schrei PI/3.2

shout (at) [ʃaʊt] (laut) rufen,
(an)schreien PI/3.2

show [ʃəʊ] Show, Aufführung,
Vorstellung III/5.3; Schau,
Ausstellung PI/7&8P: **show
jumper** Springreiter(-in);
Springpferd PI/3&4P

show (showed, shown) [ʃəʊ, ʃəʊd,
ʃəʊn] zeigen (zeigte, gezeigt)
III/1.3

shower [ˈʃaʊə] Dusche I/4.1:
have/take a shower (sich)
duschen, eine Dusche nehmen
II/5.1

shut (shut, shut) [ʃʌt, ʃʌt]
schließen (schloß, geschlossen),
zumachen III/5.3

sick [sɪk] krank II/3.2: **feel sick** übel,
schlecht sein II/3.2; **be sick and
tired of sth.** etw. satt haben PI/7.1

side [saɪd] Seite III/3.1

sight [saɪt] Sicht(weite), Anblick;
Sehenswürdigkeit PI/6.1: **sight
seeing** Besichtigung von
Sehenswürdigkeiten II/5.3

sign [saɪn] Zeichen, Schild II/3.2

sign [saɪn] unterschreiben II/6.2

silent [ˈsaɪlənt] ruhig, still PI/5&6P

silly [ˈsɪlɪ] dumm PI/7.1

simple [ˈsɪmpl] einfach PI/4.1

since [sɪns] seit (+ *Zeitpunkt*) III/4.1

sincerely [sɪnˈsɪəlɪ]: **yours sincerely**
mit freundlichen Grüßen *(am
Briefschluß)* III/1.1

sing (sang, sung) [sɪŋ, sæŋ, sʌŋ]
singen (sang, gesungen) II/2.2

singer [ˈsɪŋə] Sänger(-in) II/2.2

single [ˈsɪŋgl] unverheiratet I/2.1;
Einzel- I/4.1: **single ticket**
einfache Fahrkarte *(brit.)* III/3.1

sir [sɜː] (mein) Herr *(höfliche
Anrede)* PI/5.1

sister [ˈsɪstə] Schwester I/2.1:
sister-in-law Schwägerin II/6.1

sit (sat, sat) [sɪt, sæt] sitzen (saß,
gesessen), setzen II/2.2

situation [ˌsɪtjʊˈeɪʃn] Situation II/2.I

size [saɪz] Größe II/5.1

skate [skeɪt] Schlittschuh laufen
PI/3.1

skeleton [ˈskelɪtn] Skelett III/6.3

ski [skiː] Ski fahren III/1.2

skill [skɪl] Fertigkeit, (Fach)Kenntnis
PI/8.1

skirt [skɜːt] Rock II/5.1

slang [slæŋ] Slang, Jargon,
Umgangssprache PI/8.2

sleep [sliːp] Schlaf PI/1&2R

sleep (slept, slept) [sliːp, slept]
schlafen (schlief, geschlafen)
II/3.1, III/G2

sleepy [ˈsliːpɪ] schläfrig, müde
PI/1&2R

slim [slɪm] schlank III/2.3

slow [sləʊ] langsam II/2.2
small [smɔːl] klein I/3.1
smell [smel] Geruch, Duft PI/1&2R
smelly ['smelɪ] übelriechend, muffig PI/1&2R
smile [smaɪl] Lächeln PI/2.1
smile [smaɪl] lächeln PI/2.1
smoke [sməʊk] Rauch II/2.2
smoke [sməʊk] rauchen II/2.2
smoker ['sməʊkə] Raucher(-in) PI/5&6R
smoky ['sməʊkɪ] qualmend, verräuchert PI/1&2R
snack [snæk] Imbiß PI/7&8P: **snack bar** Schnellimbiß I/6.2
sneeze [sniːz] Niesen III/6.1
sniffer dog ['snɪfə dɒg] Spürhund PI/3&4P
snow [snəʊ] Schnee II/1.3
snow [snəʊ] schneien II/1.2
so [səʊ] so I/6.1; deshalb, darum, also PI/1&2R: **and so** also II/2.3; **so do I** ich auch *(Antwort auf eine Frage)* III/6.1
soap [səʊp] Seife III/6.2
social ['səʊʃl] sozial, gesellschaftlich III/5.1
society [sə'saɪətɪ] Gesellschaft PI/5&6P
sock [sɒk] Socke, Strumpf II/5.1
sofa ['səʊfə] Sofa II/4.2
soldier ['səʊldʒə] Soldat III/5.1
solve [sɒlv] lösen, klären PI/4.2
some [sʌm] einige, etwas I/3.1; irgendein(-e, -er, -es) *PI/S1*
somebody ['sʌmbədɪ] (irgend) jemand III/1.1
someone ['sʌmwʌn] jemand(-em, -en) II/3.1
something ['sʌmθɪŋ] etwas II/1.1
sometimes ['sʌmtaɪmz] manchmal I/1.3
somewhere ['sʌmweə] irgendwo(hin) III/1.1
son [sʌn] Sohn II/2.1: **son-in-law** Schwiegersohn II/6.1
song [sɒŋ] Lied II/3.2
soon [suːn] bald II/3.1: **the sooner ... the better** je früher ... desto besser III/2.1
sore [sɔː] weh, wund, entzündet II/3.2: **sore throat** Halsentzündung II/3.2
sorry ['sɒrɪ]: **I'm sorry** es tut mir leid I/3.1
sort [sɔːt] Sorte, Art I/1.3: **what sort of** was für I/1.3
sound [saʊnd] klingen, tönen *III/G3*
soup [suːp] Suppe I/6.1
south [saʊθ] Süd-, Süden I/3.1
southern ['sʌðən] südlich, Süd- PI/1.1

space [speɪs] Weite, Raum, freier Platz, Lücke; *auch:* Weltraum PI/1.1
spaghetti [spə'getɪ] Spaghetti I/3.2
Spanish ['spænɪʃ] spanisch(-e, -er, -es); Spanier(-in) I/1.I
spare time [ˌspeə 'taɪm] Freizeit *PI/5.2*
speak (spoke, spoken) [spiːk, spəʊk, 'spəʊkən] sprechen (sprach, gesprochen) I/1.1, I/5.2: **speaking practice** Sprachpraxis *II/1.1*
speaker ['spiːkə] Sprecher(-in) *I/G1*, PI/5&6R
special ['speʃl] Sonder-, speziell I/4.1
specialist ['speʃəlɪst] Spezialist(-in) PI/5&6P
specialist ['speʃəlɪst] Fach-, Spezial- II/5.3
speech [spiːtʃ] Rede PI/7.2: **reported speech** indirekte Rede *PI/7.2*
speed [spiːd] Geschwindigkeit PI/3&4P
spell (spelt, spelt) [spel, spelt] buchstabieren (buchstabierte, buchstabiert) I/1.2, PI/6.1
spelling ['spelɪŋ] Rechtschreibung, Buchstabierweise, Rechtschreib- III/6.2
spend (spent, spent) (on/in) [spend, spent] ausgeben (für) (gab aus, ausgegeben) I/5.2; verbringen II/6.1, III/4.1
spoil (spoilt, spoilt) [spɔɪl, spɔɪlt] verderben (verdarb, verdorben), vernichten, ruinieren; *auch:* verwöhnen PI/2.1
spoon [spuːn] Löffel III/1.2
sport [spɔːt] Sport I/3.1
sportsman/sportswoman ['spɔːtsmən, 'spɔːtswʊmən] Sportler/-in PI/3&4P
spread out (spread, spread) [spred, spred] (sich) ausbreiten (breitete aus, hat ausgebreitet) PI/1&2P
spring [sprɪŋ] Frühling I/2.2
square [skweə] Platz III/6.2
square [skweə] quadratisch; *hier:* eckig, kantig III/2.3: **square metre** Quadratmeter PI/7&8P
squash [skwɒʃ] Squash PI/3.1
staff [stɑːf] Personal PI/4.2
stairs [steəz] Treppe, Treppenhaus II/4.1
stamp [stæmp] Briefmarke I/5.1
stand [stænd] (Verkaufs-, Messe)Stand PI/7&8P
stand (stood, stood) [stænd, stʊd] stehen (stand, gestanden) III/1.2: **can't stand** nicht ausstehen können I/6.1

standstill ['stændstɪl] Stillstand III/3.3: **be at a standstill** stillstehen, ruhen, verstopft sein III/3.3
star [stɑː] Stern I/4.3: **film star** Filmstar II/1.2
starlet ['stɑːlət] Sternchen; Star PI/3&4P
start [stɑːt] Beginn, Anfang I/5.R
start [stɑːt] beginnen, anfangen I/3.2
starter ['stɑːtə] Vorspeise I/6.1; *hier:* Einstieg *II/1.2*
state [steɪt] Staat III/5.R
statement ['steɪtmənt] Aussage, Behauptung *II/6.R*
station ['steɪʃn] Bahnhof I/3.1; *hier:* (Zucht)Farm PI/1&2P: **police station** Polizeiwache I/3.1; **TV station** Fernsehsender PI/2.2
statistics [stə'tɪstɪks] Statistik III/1.3
status ['steɪtəs] Zustand, Status, Stellung; Familienstand III/1.1
stay [steɪ] bleiben I/1.3; *hier:* übernachten I/5.2
steak [steɪk] Steak I/6.1
steal (stole, stolen) [stiːl, stəʊl, 'stəʊlən] stehlen (stahl, gestohlen) III/3.3
step [step] Schritt *II/1.1*
stereo ['sterɪəʊ] Stereo(anlage) II/4.2
steward/stewardess ['stjʊəd, ˌstjʊə'des] Steward/Stewardeß PI/5&6P
still [stɪl] noch (immer) III/4.2
stomach ['stʌmək] Magen III/4.1
stone [stəʊn] Stein III/4.1
stop [stɒp] Haltestelle I/5.2
stop [stɒp] anhalten, aufhören II/2.2; abhalten PI/3&4P
store [stɔː] Laden, Geschäft *(amerik.)* II/5.1: **department store** Kaufhaus, Warenhaus II/5.2
storm [stɔːm] Sturm, Unwetter III/5.1
story ['stɔːrɪ] Geschichte III/1.1
straight [streɪt] gerade III/2.3: **straight on** geradeaus I/3.1
strange [streɪndʒ] fremd(artig), seltsam, komisch III/3.2
stranger ['streɪndʒə] Fremde(-r) I/3.1
stream [striːm] Bach PI/2.1
street [striːt] Straße *(in der Stadt, mit Häusern)* I/3.2
stress [stres] Streß, Druck PI/3.1
stress [stres] betonen *I/2.R*
stressed [strest] gestreßt, unter Druck II/3.I
stressful ['stresfʊl] anstrengend, streßig *PI/5.2*
stretch [stretʃ] Fläche, Strecke PI/1&2P
strike [straɪk] Streik III/3.3
strong [strɒŋ] stark III/1.2
strudel ['struːdl] Strudel I/6.1
struggle ['strʌgl] Kampf, Ringen, Anstrengung PI/8.1

student ['stju:dnt] Student(-in);
auch: Kursteilnehmer(-in) II/1.2
study ['stʌdɪ] studieren III/1.1
stupid ['stju:pɪd] dumm, töricht II/5.1
subconscious [ˌsʌb'kɒnʃəs]
unterbewußt PI/7.1
subject ['sʌbdʒɪkt] *hier:* Subjekt,
Satzgegenstand *III/6.2*; Thema
PI/5.1: **be on the subject of ...**
sich mit dem Thema ... befassen
PI/5.1
suburb ['sʌbɜ:b] Vorort I/3.1
suburban [sə'bɜ:bən] Vorstadt-,
kleinstädtisch PI/1&2P
success [sək'ses] Erfolg PI/1.1
successful [sək'sesfʊl] erfolgreich
PI/1.1
such [sʌtʃ] solch, so, derart III/4.1
suddenly ['sʌdnlɪ] plötzlich PI/1&2R
suffer (from) ['sʌfə] leiden (an)
PI/3.1
sugar ['ʃʊgə] Zucker II/3.3
suggest [sə'dʒest] vorschlagen III/1.1
suggestion [sə'dʒestʃən] Vorschlag
III/2.2
suit [su:t] Anzug III/1.2
suit [su:t] *hier:* kleiden, stehen,
passen zu III/6.1
suitable ['su:təbl] passend, geeignet
PI/3.2
suitcase ['su:tkeɪs] Koffer II/5.3
summer ['sʌmə] Sommer I/2.2
sun [sʌn] Sonne II/1.3
Sunday ['sʌndɪ] Sonntag I/1.3
sunglasses ['sʌnglɑ:sɪz] Sonnenbrille
II/1.1
sunny ['sʌnɪ] sonnig II/1.2
sunrise ['sʌnraɪz] Sonnenaufgang
PI/6.1
sunset ['sʌnset] Sonnenuntergang
PI/6.1
sunshine ['sʌnʃaɪn] Sonnenschein
PI/1.1
suntan ['sʌntæn] (Sonnen)Bräune
II/1.1: **suntan cream**
Bräunungscreme II/1.1
super ['su:pə] herrlich, prima, super
II/4.1
superlative [su:'pɜ:lətɪv] Superlativ
II/1.2
supermarket ['su:pəˌmɑ:kɪt]
Supermarkt I/3.1
support [sə'pɔ:t] Unterstützung PI/3.1
support [sə'pɔ:t] (unter)stützen; *hier:*
tragen PI/3.1
suppose [sə'pəʊz] annehmen,
vermuten PI/6.1
sure [ʃɔ:] sicher I/5.3: **make sure**
sich vergewissern, feststellen PI/3.1
surface ['sɜ:fɪs] Oberfläche PI/5&6P
surname ['sɜ:neɪm] Familienname
I/1.3
sweet [swi:t] süß III/5.R
swift [swɪft] Mauersegler PI/3&4P

swim (swam, swum) [swɪm,
swæm, swʌm] schwimmen
(schwamm, geschwommen) I/1.2,
III/6.2
swimming costume ['swɪmɪŋ
ˌkɒstju:m] Badeanzug II/1.1
swimming pool ['swɪmɪŋ pu:l]
Schwimmbad I/4.3
Swiss [swɪs] schweizerisch(-e, -er,
-es); Schweizer(-in) I/1.1
switch on/off [ˌswɪtʃ 'ɒn, 'ɒf] ein-,
ausschalten PI/7.2
swop [swɒp] tauschen, austauschen
II/6.1
system ['sɪstəm] System PI/1&2P

T

table ['teɪbl] Tisch I/5.2; Tabelle
III/3.2
take (took, taken) [teɪk, tʊk,
'teɪkən] nehmen (nahm, genom-
men) I/3.1, I/5.2, II/1.2; brauchen,
dauern III/3.1: **take a photo** ein
Foto machen I/5.2; **take care!**
mach's gut! paß auf dich auf!
III/6.3; **take home** nach Hause
(mit)nehmen II/1.2; **take many
risks** viele Risiken eingehen
PI/3.2; **take notes on** sich Notizen
machen über III/1.3; **take off** *hier:*
(Kleidung) ausziehen III/6.1; **take
part in** teilnehmen an PI/3&4P;
take place stattfinden, sich
ereignen PI/2.1; **take shorthand**
stenografieren PI/5.1; **take turns**
sich abwechseln *III/4.2*; **take up**
aufnehmen, beginnen II/1.1; **it
takes me ...** ich brauche dafür ...
(*+ Zeitangabe*) III/3.1
takeaway ['teɪkəˌweɪ] „zum
Mitnehmen" I/6.2
talk [tɔ:k] Gespräch *PI/3.2*
talk [tɔ:k] reden I/6.2: **talk to** reden
mit III/1.1
tall [tɔ:l] groß, hochgewachsen III/2.1
tape [teɪp] Streifen, Band; Tonband,
Cassette III/2.2: **tape recorder**
Tonbandgerät, Cassettenrecorder
III/1.2
tax (taxes) [tæks, 'tæksɪz] Steuer,
Abgabe III/5.R
taxi ['tæksɪ] Taxi I/5.2
tea [ti:] Tee I/2.2
teach (taught, taught) [ti:tʃ, tɔ:t]
unterrichten (unterrichtete,
unterrichtet), lehren III/1.3P
teacher ['ti:tʃə] Lehrer(-in),
Kursleiter(-in) II/1.R
team [ti:m] Team, Mannschaft III/3.R
technical ['teknɪkl] technisch
PI/7&8P

teenage ['ti:nˌeɪdʒ] jugendlich,
Jugend- PI/3&4P
teenager ['ti:neɪdʒə] Jugendliche(-r),
Teenager III/1.2
telegram ['telɪgræm] Telegramm
III/4.2
telephone ['telɪfəʊn] Telefon I/1.2
telephone ['telɪfəʊn] telefonieren
I/5.2
telephonist [tɪ'lefənɪst]
Telefonist(-in) II/2.1
television (= TV) ['telɪˌvɪʒn]
Fernsehen, Fernseher I/1.3: **watch
television** fernsehen I/1.3; **on
television** im Fernsehen I/5.1; **TV
station** Fernsehsender PI/2.2
tell (told, told) [tel, təʊld] erzählen,
sagen (sagte, gesagt) I/2.1, II/3.3
temperature ['temprətʃə]
Temperatur II/3.2: **have a
temperature** Temperatur/Fieber
haben II/3.2
tennis ['tenɪs] Tennis I/1.2
tense [tens] Zeit(stufe) *III/4.R*
terminal ['tɜ:mɪnl] Terminal,
Abfluggebäude III/3.1
terrible ['terəbl] schrecklich II/3.1
test [test] Test, Probe, Prüfung III/5.2
test [test] testen, (über)prüfen III/5.2
text [tekst] Text *II/1.1*, PI/8.1
than [ðæn, ðən] als *(Vergleich)*
II/1.1
thank [θæŋk] danken III/6.3: **thank
you very much** vielen herzlichen
Dank I/3.1
thanks [θæŋks] danke I/1.2: **thanks
a lot** danke vielmals I/3.1
that [ðæt, ðət] das I/1.1; jene(-r, -s)
I/5.1; der, die, das; welche(-r, -s)
(Relativpronomen) II/4.1; daß
III/1.3
the [ðə, ði:] der, die, das I/1.I: **the
sooner ... the better** je früher ...
desto besser III/2.1
theatre ['θɪətə] Theater I/3.1
their [ðeə] ihr(-e) *(Mehrzahl)* I/1.3
theirs [ðeəz] ihre(-r, -s), der (die,
das) ihr(ig)e II/5.2
them [ðem, ðəm] sie, ihnen
(Mehrzahl) I/2.1
then [ðen] dann I/1.3; damals III/4.I
there [ðeə] dort I/2.3: **there is** es
gibt, da ist I/3.1
these [ði:z] diese *(Mehrzahl)* I/5.I
they [ðeɪ] sie *(Mehrzahl)* I/1.2: **they
say** man sagt II/5.3
thick [θɪk] dick III/1.2
thin [θɪn] dünn III/6.2
thing [θɪŋ] Ding, Sache I/3.3: **how
are things?** wie geht es
(dir/Ihnen/euch)? PI/6.1
think (thought, thought) [θɪŋk,
θɔ:t] denken (dachte, gedacht),
glauben, meinen I/3.3, II/5.1:

think of sich vorstellen, denken an III/6.I

third [θɜːd] dritte(-r, -s) PI/6.1

thirsty ['θɜːstɪ] durstig III/5.2

this [ðɪs] dies(-e, -er, -es) I/1.1: **this morning** heute morgen I/4.R; **this time** dieses Mal II/1.1

those [ðəʊz] jene *(Mehrzahl)* I/5.1

though [ðəʊ] obwohl PI/1&2P

thought [θɔːt] Gedanke PI/7&8R

thousand ['θaʊznd] tausend III/5.3

threat [θret] (Be)Drohung PI/8.1

threaten ['θretn] (be)drohen PI/8.1

throat [θrəʊt] Hals, Kehle III/3.2: **sore throat** Halsentzündung II/3.2

through [θruː] durch III/5.1

Thursday ['θɜːzdɪ] Donnerstag I/2.1

tick [tɪk] Haken *III/4.1*

tick [tɪk] abhaken *III/4.1*

ticket ['tɪkɪt] Ticket, (Fahr)Karte II/5.2: **one-way ticket** einfache Fahrkarte *(amerik.)* III/3.1; **single ticket** einfache Fahrkarte *(brit.)* III/3.1

tidy ['taɪdɪ] sauber, ordentlich PI/4.1

tidy up [ˌtaɪdɪ 'ʌp] aufräumen, säubern PI/4.1

tie [taɪ] Krawatte II/5.1

tiger ['taɪgə] Tiger PI/8.2

tights [taɪts] Strumpfhose II/5.1

till [tɪl] bis *(Zeitangabe)* III/1.1

time [taɪm] Zeit I/4.1; *hier:* Mal II/5.R: **a long time ago** vor längerer Zeit I/5.2; **at times** zeitweise PI/3.1; **in two days' time** in zwei Tagen III/3.1; **spare time** Freizeit PI/5.2; **this time** dieses Mal II/1.1; **what's the time?** wieviel Uhr ist es? I/4.1; **what time?** (um) wieviel Uhr? I/4.R

timetable ['taɪmˌteɪbl] Fahrplan; Stundenplan III/3.1

tin [tɪn] (Konserven)Dose PI/7.1

tinned [tɪnd] eingemacht, konserviert PI/7.1

tip [tɪp] Trinkgeld III/4.1

tired ['taɪəd] müde I/2.1

title ['taɪtl] Titel, Überschrift PI/3&4P

to [tʊ, tə] zu I/3.2; vor I/4.1

tobacco [tə'bækəʊ] Tabak PI/7.1

today [tə'deɪ] heute I/4.1

together [tə'geðə] zusammen III/1.3

toilet ['tɔɪlɪt] Toilette, WC II/4.1

tomato [tə'mɑːtəʊ] Tomate I/6.1

tomorrow [tə'mɒrəʊ] morgen I/6.1: **this time tomorrow** morgen um diese Zeit I/6.1; **the day after tomorrow** übermorgen II/6.2

tonight [tə'naɪt] heute abend, heute nacht II/4.2

too [tuː] auch I/1.2; *(vorangestellt)* zu, allzu I/6.1

tool [tuːl] Werkzeug PI/4.1

tooth (teeth) [tuːθ, tiːθ] Zahn (Zähne) II/1.1

toothache ['tuːθeɪk] Zahnschmerzen II/3.2

toothbrush ['tuːθbrʌʃ] Zahnbürste II/1.1

toothpaste ['tuːθpeɪst] Zahnpasta II/1.1

top [tɒp] Ober-, oberste(-r, -s) I/4.1: **be top of the table** an der Spitze stehen PI/7&8P; **make it to the top** es bis zur Spitze schaffen, ganz nach oben kommen PI/3&4P; **on top of** (oben) auf II/3.1; **on top of the world** obenauf, rundum glücklich II/3.1

topic ['tɒpɪk] Thema, Gegenstand III/3.1

touch [tʌtʃ] Berührung, Verbindung, Kontakt PI/6.1

touch [tʌtʃ] berühren PI/6.1

tour [tʊə] Tour, (Rund)Fahrt, Ausflug III/3.1

tourism ['tʊərɪzm] Tourismus PI/5.1

tourist ['tʊərɪst] Tourist I/3.1: **tourist office** Fremdenverkehrsbüro III/3.1

towel ['taʊəl] Handtuch II/1.1

tower ['taʊə] Turm III/5.2

town [taʊn] Stadt I/3.1

toy [tɔɪ] Spielzeug PI/4.1

track [træk] Gleis PI/1&2P

trade [treɪd] Handel, Handels- PI/7&8P: **trade union** Gewerkschaft III/2.1

tradition [trə'dɪʃn] Tradition, Überlieferung, Brauch III/6.I

traditional [trə'dɪʃnl] traditionell, herkömmlich II/5.3

traffic ['træfɪk] Verkehr I/3.1: **traffic lights** Ampel I/3.1

trailer ['treɪlə] Anhänger PI/1&2P

train [treɪn] Zug I/4.I: **on a train** im Zug, in der Bahn I/4.2

train [treɪn] (sich) ausbilden, trainieren, eine Ausbildung machen II/2.1

training ['treɪnɪŋ] Ausbildung, Training II/6.1

tram [træm] Straßenbahn *(brit.)* III/3.1

translate [træns'leɪt] übersetzen III/4.2

translation [træns'leɪʃn] Übersetzung PI/7&8P

transport ['trænspɔːt] Transport, Beförderung, Verkehr III/3.I

travel ['trævl] Reise-, Reisen I/3.2: **travel agent** Reisebürokaufmann II/1.1

travel ['trævl] reisen I/4.I

traveller's cheque [ˌtrævləz 'tʃek] Reisescheck I/5.2

treat [triːt] besondere Freude, Genuß III/6.3

tree [triː] Baum III/2.2

trick [trɪk] Trick, Kniff; *hier:* Streich *(spielen)* III/6.3

trip [trɪp] Reise, Ausflug III/1.1

trouble ['trʌbl] Mühe, Schwierigkeiten, Probleme, Ärger; (pol.) Unruhen PI/6.2

trousers ['traʊzəz] (lange) Hose(n) II/5.1: **a pair of trousers** eine lange Hose II/5.1

trout [traʊt] Forelle I/6.1

truck [trʌk] Lastwagen PI/1&2P

true [truː] wahr I/3.1: **come true** wahr werden, sich verwirklichen II/6.3

truly ['truːlɪ]: **yours truly** mit freundlichen Grüßen, hochachtungsvoll *(am Briefschluß)* III/1.1

truth [truːθ] Wahrheit PI/7.2

try [traɪ] versuchen, probieren II/2.1: **try on** anprobieren II/5.1

tube [tjuːb] Rohr, Schlauch, Tube; *hier:* Name für die Londoner U-Bahn III/3.3

Tuesday ['tjuːzdɪ] Dienstag I/2.1

turkey ['tɜːkɪ] Truthahn III/6.3

turn [tɜːn] Reihe III/6.1: **it's my turn** ich bin an der Reihe II/6.1; **take turns** sich abwechseln *III/4.2*

turn [tɜːn] drehen, wenden, abbiegen; ein-, ausschalten I/3.1

twice [twaɪs] zweimal III/1.3

type [taɪp] Typ, Art, Sorte III/5.I

type [taɪp] tippen, mit der Maschine schreiben II/2.2

typewriter ['taɪpˌraɪtə] Schreibmaschine II/2.2

typical ['tɪpɪkl] typisch III/6.3

typist ['taɪpɪst] Schreibkraft PI/5.2

tyre ['taɪə] (Auto)Reifen *(brit.)* III/5.2

U

umbrella [ʌm'brelə] Regenschirm III/1.2

uncle ['ʌŋkl] Onkel I/2.1

under ['ʌndə] unter II/3.1: **feel under the weather** nicht in Form sein II/3.1

underground ['ʌndəgraʊnd] U-Bahn III/3.1

underline ['ʌndəlaɪn] unterstreichen *II/2.3*

understand (understood, understood) [ʌndə'stænd, ʌndə'stʊd] verstehen (verstand, verstanden) II/2.3, III/G3

unemployed [ˌʌnɪm'plɔɪd] arbeitslos PI/5.1

unemployment [ˌʌnɪmˈplɔɪmənt] Arbeitslosigkeit, Arbeitslosen- PI/5&6P

unfit [ˌʌnˈfɪt] nicht fit, schlecht in Form PI/3.2

unfortunately [ˌʌnˈfɔːtʃnətlɪ] unglücklicherweise PI/3.1

unfriendly [ˌʌnˈfrendlɪ] unfreundlich PI/2.1

unhappy [ʌnˈhæpɪ] unglücklich PI/1.1

uniform [ˈjuːnɪfɔːm] Uniform, Dienstkleidung III/2.1

unit [ˈjuːnɪt] Einheit, Lektion I/1.I

United Kingdom (UK) [juːˌnaɪtɪd ˈkɪŋdəm] Vereinigtes Königreich *(Großbritannien und Nordirland)* PI/1.1

United States (US) [jʊˌnaɪtɪd ˈsteɪts] Vereinigte Staaten von Amerika PI/5&6P

university [juːnɪˈvɜːsətɪ] Universität II/6.1

unknown [ˌʌnˈnəʊn] unbekannt PI/3&4P

unlucky [ʌnˈlʌkɪ] unglücklich, Unglücks- III/6.3

unnecessary [ʌnˈnesəsərɪ] unnötig PI/7.1

unpaid [ˌʌnˈpeɪd] unbezahlt PI/6.1

unpopular [ˌʌnˈpɒpjʊlə] unbeliebt, unpopulär PI/3.1

unspoilt [ˌʌnˈspɔɪlt] unverdorben, unbeschädigt PI/2.1

until [ʌnˈtɪl] bis I/3.2

unusual [ʌnˈjuːʒl] ungewöhnlich II/5.3

up [ʌp] hinauf, herauf III/6.1

upset [ʌpˈset]: **feel upset** bestürzt, durcheinander sein III/6.2

upstairs [ˌʌpˈsteəz] oben, (die Treppe) hinauf/herauf II/4.1

urgent [ˈɜːdʒənt] dringend, eilig III/5.1

us [ʌs, əs] uns I/2.1; *hier:* wir PI/4.1

use [juːz] Gebrauch, Nutzen, Sinn PI/5.2

use [juːz] benutzen II/2.1; verbrauchen III/3.3: **used to** früher (etw. [regelmäßig] getan haben); pflegte(-n, -st, -t) zu II/2.1; **be used to sth.** etwas gewohnt sein III/3.3

useful [ˈjuːsfʊl] nützlich III/4.3

useless [ˈjuːslɪs] nutzlos, unbrauchbar PI/3&4R

usually [ˈjuːʒəlɪ] gewöhnlich I/2.2

V ───────────────

valley [ˈvælɪ] Tal III/4.2

valuable [ˈvæljʊəbl] wertvoll PI/4.1

various [ˈveərɪəs] verschieden, mehrere PI/4.2

VAT (= Value Added Tax) [ˌviː eɪ ˈtiː, ˌvæljuː ˈædɪd tæks] Mehrwertsteuer I/4.1

vegetable [ˈvedʒtəbl] Gemüse(art) I/6.1

vegetarian [ˌvedʒɪˈteərɪən] vegetarisch(-e, -er, -es); Vegetarier(-in) I/6.1

verb [vɜːb] Verb, Zeitwort II/1.2: **modal auxiliary verb** modales Hilfsverb *III/1.2*

very [ˈverɪ] sehr I/2.1

vet [vet] Tierarzt, Tierärztin PI/4.1

veteran [ˈvetrən] Veteran, altgedienter Soldat III/6.3

video [ˈvɪdɪəʊ] Video I/3.2

view [vjuː]: **view of** Aussicht auf I/4.1; **point of view** Standpunkt, Ansicht PI/7.1

village [ˈvɪlɪdʒ] Dorf I/3.1

villager [ˈvɪlɪdʒə] Dorfbewohner(-in) *PI/2.1*

visit (to) [ˈvɪzɪt] Besuch, Aufenthalt (in, bei) III/3.1

visit [ˈvɪzɪt] besuchen I/3.R

visitor [ˈvɪzɪtə] Besucher(-in), Gast III/6.3

vocabulary [vəʊˈkæbjʊlərɪ] Wortschatz *II/1.1*, PI/7.2

voice [vɔɪs] Stimme III/4.3

volleyball [ˈvɒlɪbɔːl] Volleyball PI/3.1

vote [vəʊt] wählen, abstimmen III/2.1

W ───────────────

wait [weɪt] warten III/2.3

waiter [ˈweɪtə] Kellner I/6.1

waitress [ˈweɪtrɪs] Kellnerin II/2.1

Wales [weɪlz] Wales *(Teil Großbritanniens)* PI/1.1

walk [wɔːk] Spaziergang I/5.R: **go for a walk** spazierengehen I/5.R

walk [wɔːk] (zu Fuß) gehen I/3.2

wall [wɔːl] Wand, Mauer III/4.1

wallet [ˈwɒlɪt] Brieftasche PI/2.2

want [wɒnt] wollen I/3.2

war [wɔː] Krieg III/6.2

warm [wɔːm] warm III/2.2

warning [ˈwɔːnɪŋ] Warnung III/3.1

wash [wɒʃ] (sich) waschen III/5.2: **wash up** abwaschen, abspülen PI/7.2

washing machine [ˈwɒʃɪŋ məˌʃiːn] Waschmaschine II/4.2

waste [weɪst] Verschwendung PI/5.1

waste [weɪst] verschwenden PI/5.1

waste [weɪst] öde, leer, nutzlos PI/5.1

watch [wɒtʃ] *(tragbare)* Uhr III/5.2

watch [wɒtʃ] zuschauen I/1.3

water [ˈwɔːtə] Wasser I/6.1

water [ˈwɔːtə] (be)wässern, gießen PI/4.2

wave [weɪv] Welle PI/1&2R

wavy [ˈweɪvɪ] wellig, gewellt III/2.3

way [weɪ] Weg I/3.1; Art, Weise III/1.2: **in this way** auf diese Weise III/3.I; **by the way** übrigens II/5.1

we [wiː] wir I/1.2

weak [wiːk] schwach PI/5.1

wear (wore, worn) [weə, wɔː, wɔːn] tragen (trug, getragen), anhaben *(Kleidung)* III/1.2

weather [ˈweðə] Wetter II/1.1: **feel under the weather** nicht in Form sein II/3.1

wedding [ˈwedɪŋ] Hochzeit III/1.3

Wednesday [ˈwenzdɪ] Mittwoch I/2.1

week [wiːk] Woche I/2.2

weekend [ˌwiːkˈend] Wochenende I/4.1

weekly [ˈwiːklɪ] wöchentlich, pro Woche, Wochen- PI/6.1

weigh [weɪ] wiegen PI/3.2

weight [weɪt] Gewicht PI/3.2: **put on weight** zunehmen *(Gewicht)* PI/3.2

welcome [ˈwelkəm]: **you're welcome** bitte (sehr), gern geschehen I/3.1; **welcome (to)** begrüßen (bei) PI/3.2; **welcome to** willkommen in I/4.1

well [wel] gut I/2.1; *etwa:* nun ja I/3.1: **get on well with** gut auskommen mit II/6.1; **well-known** berühmt, wohlbekannt II/5.3

Welsh [welʃ] walisisch(-e, -er, -es); Waliser(-in) I/3.1

west [west] West-, Westen I/3.1

western [ˈwestən] westlich, West- PI/1.1

wet [wet] naß, feucht III/2.2

what [wɒt] was I/1.I; welche(-r, -s) I/1.1: **what about …?** wie ist es mit …? I/2.1; **what a pity!** wie schade! III/6.1; **what is it like?** wie ist es?, wie sieht es aus? PI/2.1; **what time?** (um) wieviel Uhr? I/4.R; **what's the time?** wieviel Uhr ist es? I/4.1

when [wen] wann I/2.2; wenn I/2.3; als I/5.2

where [weə] wo(-hin, -her) I/1.I

whether [ˈweðə] ob PI/4.1

which [wɪtʃ] welche(-r, -s) I/2.3

while [waɪl] Weile II/6.1: **for a while** eine Zeitlang, einige Zeit II/6.1

while [waɪl] während II/4.1

whisky [ˈwɪskɪ] Whisky II/3.3

whistle [ˈwɪsl] pfeifen I/1.2

white [waɪt] weiß I/5.1: **in black and white** schwarz auf weiß II/5.R

who [huː] wer, wem, wen I/5.2

whole [həʊl] gesamt, ganz PI/4.1

whom [huːm]: **(some of) whom** (von) denen (einige) PI/8.1

whose [huːz] wessen II/5.2

why [waɪ] warum I/5.1

wide [waɪd] weit, breit III/4.2

wife (wives) [waɪf, waɪvz] Ehefrau(-en) I/1.3

will [wɪl] *(Hilfsverb, Zukunft)* I/6.1

willing ['wɪlɪŋ] gewillt, bereit PI/5&6R

win (won, won) [wɪn, wʌn] gewinnen (gewann, gewonnen) II/1.3

wind [wɪnd] Wind III/1.2

window ['wɪndəʊ] Fenster II/4.1

windsurf ['wɪndsɜːf] surfen PI/3.1

windy ['wɪndɪ] windig II/1.2

wine [waɪn] Wein I/1.3

winter ['wɪntə] Winter I/2.2

wish [wɪʃ] (Glück)Wunsch III/1.1: **with best wishes** mit den besten Wünschen *(am Briefschluß)* III/1.1; **give my best wishes to …** grüße/grüßen Sie/grüßt … herzlich von mir III/3.1

wish [wɪʃ] wünschen III/3.1

witch [wɪtʃ] Hexe III/6.3

with [wɪð] mit I/1.1

without [wɪ'ðaʊt] ohne III/4.3

woman (women) ['wʊmən, 'wɪmɪn] Frau (Frauen) I/3.1

wonder ['wʌndə] sich fragen, wundern *II/6.3P*

wonderful ['wʌndəfʊl] wunderbar I/1.2

wood [wʊd] Holz; kleinerer Wald III/4.1

wool [wʊl] Wolle, aus Wolle III/2.3

word [wɜːd] Wort I/2.I

work [wɜːk] Arbeit I/1.2: **at work** bei der Arbeit I/1.2; **out of work** arbeitslos PI/5&6P

work [wɜːk] arbeiten I/1.3: **work for** arbeiten bei I/1.3

worker ['wɜːkə] Arbeiter(-in) II/2.1

working hours ['wɜːkɪŋ 'aʊəz] Arbeitszeit, -stunden II/2.3

world [wɜːld] Welt I/5.1: **all over the world** auf der ganzen Welt PI/3.1

worried about ['wʌrɪd ə'baʊt] besorgt, beunruhigt wegen III/2.1

worry ['wʌrɪ] sich sorgen, sich Sorgen machen II/3.3

worse [wɜːs] schlechter, schlimmer II/1.2

worst [wɜːst] schlechteste(-r, -s), schlimmste(-r, -s) II/1.2

would [wʊd]: **I would like** ich möchte I/4.1; **would you mind …?** würden Sie/würdest du/würdet ihr so freundlich sein …? I/5.1

write (wrote, written) [raɪt, rəʊt, 'rɪtn]: **write (down)** (auf)schreiben I/2.1, III/2.3; **write out** ausschreiben, vervollständigen *PI/2.1*

writer ['raɪtə] Schreiber(-in), Autor(-in) PI/5&6R

wrong [rɒŋ] falsch, verkehrt III/2.2

Y

yard [jɑːd] Yard *(Maßeinheit = 0,914 m)* III/6.1

year [jɪə] Jahr I/2.3

yellow ['jeləʊ] gelb I/5.1

yes [jes] ja I/1.1

yesterday ['jestədɪ] gestern I/4.2: **the day before yesterday** vorgestern II/6.2

yet [jet] schon II/6.1: **not yet** noch nicht II/6.1

you [juː] Sie, dich, euch; Ihnen, dir I/1.1; du, ihr I/1.1

young *(Ez/Mz)* [jʌŋ] (Tier)Junge(-n) PI/1&2P

young [jʌŋ] jung II/2.2

your [jɔː] Ihr(-e), dein(-e), euer(eure) I/1.1

yours [jɔːz] Ihre/eure/deine(-r, -s), der (die, das) Ihr/euer/dein(ig)e II/5.2: **yours faithfully** mit freundlichen Grüßen *(am Briefschluß)* III/1.1; **yours sincerely** mit freundlichen Grüßen *(am Briefschluß)* III/1.1; **yours truly** mit freundlichen Grüßen, hochachtungsvoll *(am Briefschluß)* III/1.1

youth [juːθ] Jugend PI/5&6P

Z

zero ['zɪərəʊ] Null I/1.2

zoo [zuː] Zoo *III/G3*, PI/8.2

Adelaide [ˈædəleɪd] — Hauptstadt des Bundesstaats Südaustralien; gegründet 1836; Einwohnerzahl: 1 Mio.

Alice Springs [ˌælɪs ˈsprɪŋz] — Ort im Nordterritorium (Australien); Einwohnerzahl: 22.759

Arizona [ˌærɪˈzəʊnə] — amerik. Bundesstaat im Südwesten der USA; Fläche: 295.260 km²; Einwohnerzahl: 3,4 Mio.; Hauptstadt: Phoenix

Atlantic, The ~ [ðiː ətˈlæntɪk] — Atlantischer Ozean

Ayers Rock [ˌeəz ˈrɒk] — Fels im Nordterritorium (Australien); größter Monolith der Welt; Fläche: 1400 km²

Becker, Boris [ˌbɒrɪs ˈbekə] — (*12.11.67), deutscher Tennisspieler; erster Deutscher, der Juli 1985 in Wimbledon siegte

Biro, Laszlo [ˌlazləʊ ˈbaɪrəʊ] — Erfinder der Kugelschreibers

Bond Street [ˈbɒnd ˌstriːt] — Straße im vornehmen Londoner Geschäftsviertel

Boslem [ˈbɒzləm] — Ort in England

Boston Marathon [ˌbɒstən ˈmærəθən] — Marathonlauf in Boston; Bundesstaat Massachusetts (USA)

Brisbane [ˈbrɪzbən] — Hauptstadt des Bundesstaats Queensland (Ostaustralien); Fläche: 1220 km²; Einwohnerzahl: 1,2 Mio.

Capriati, Jennifer [ˌdʒenɪfə ˈkæprɪətɪ] — amerik. Tennisspielerin

Christie, Agatha [ˌægəθə ˈkrɪstɪ] — (1890-1976), engl. Kriminalschriftstellerin; sie erfand u.a. die berühmten Kriminalisten *Miss Marple* und *Hercule Poirot*

Co-op [ˈkəʊɒp] — Name einer Supermarktkette

Cockney [ˈkɒknɪ] — Bezeichnung für Sprache und Einwohner des Londoner Ostens

Cohen, Leonard [ˌlenəd ˈkəʊæn] — (*21.09.1934), kanad. Sänger und Dichter; bekannte Lieder sind u.a.: *Suzanne, So long Marianne, Bird on a wire*

Cologne [kəˈləʊn] — Köln; Einwohnerzahl: 1 Mio.

Columbus, Christopher [ˌkrɪstəfə kəˈlʌmbəs] — (1451-1506), Entdecker Amerikas

Commonwealth [ˈkɒmənwelθ] — Nationengemeinschaft der brit. Monarchie; zugehörige Staaten sind viele der früheren brit. Kolonien, z.B.: Australien, Neuseeland und Kanada

Concorde [ˈkɒŋkɔːd] — schnelles Verkehrsflugzeug; von der brit. und franz. Luftfahrtindustrie gebaut. Die erste Passagierflugfahrt fand am 21.01.1976 statt.

Corsica [ˈkɔːsɪkə] — Korsika (franz. Mittelmeerinsel); Fläche: 8681 km²; Einwohnerzahl: 250.000; Hauptstadt: Ajaccio

Death Valley [ˌdeθ ˈvælɪ] — Tal inmitten der Mojave-Wüste (Kalifornien, USA); heißestes und trockenstes Gebiet der USA; Fläche: 760 km²

Devon [ˈdevn] — Gegend in Südwestengland; Fläche: 6711 km²; Einwohnerzahl: 988.000

Dobre, Aurelia [ɔːˈriːlɪə ˈdəʊbrə] — rumän. Turnerin

Dod, Lottie [ˌlɒtɪ ˈdɒd] — Tennisspielerin

Egypt [ˈiːdʒɪpt] — Ägypten; Fläche: 1.001.449 km²; Einwohnerzahl: 57 Mio.; Hauptstadt: Kairo

El Pueblo de Nuestra Señora la Reina de los Angeles de la Porciuncula [el ˈpwebləʊ də nʊˈestrə senˈjɔːrə la ˈreɪnə de lɒs ˈændʒəliːz də la pɔːtʃɪˈʊŋkjʊlə] — ursprünglicher Name von Los Angeles; 1781 von den Spaniern gegründet; Fläche: 1200 km²; Einwohnerzahl: 13,5 Mio.

Finland [ˈfɪnlənd] — Finnland; Fläche: 338.145 km²; Einwohnerzahl: 4,9 Mio.; Hauptstadt: Helsinki

Flying Doctor Service, The ~ [ðə ˌflaɪɪŋ ˈdɒktə ˈsɜːvɪs] — ärztlicher Notdienst per Flugzeug, vor allem im Nordterritorium

Fonda, Jane [ˌdʒeɪn ˈfɒndə] — (*21.12.1937), amerik. Filmschauspielerin; auch bekannt aufgrund ihrer politischen Aktivitäten; bekannte Filmrollen u.a.: *Die letzte Entscheidung, Das China Syndrom, Am goldenen See*

Foster, Jay [ˌdʒeɪ ˈfɒstə] — Tischtennisspieler

Glenmore [glen'mɔ:] — erfundener Name einer Stadt

Gorbachev, Mikhail [mɪˌkaɪl 'gɔ:bətʃɒf] — (*02.03.1931), sowjet. Generalsekretär der kommunistischen Partei von März 1985 bis 1991

grass tree [ˌgrɑ:s 'tri:] — Name eines Baumes, der nur in Australien wächst

Greene, Graham [ˌgreɪəm 'gri:n] — (*02.10.1904), engl. Schriftsteller von Romanen und Dramen; bekannte Werke sind u.a.: *Brighton Rock, The Power and the Glory*

Guinness Book of Records [ˌgɪnɪs bʊk əv 'rekɔ:dz] — das Guinness Buch der Rekorde

Helpline Foundation, The ~ [ðə 'helplaɪn faʊn'deɪʃn] — Name einer Hilfsorganisation

Holmes, Sherlock [ˌʃɜ:lɒk 'həʊmz] — Romanfigur von Sir Arthur Conan Doyle

Izumi, Shigechiyo [ʃɪ'getʃɪəʊ ɪ'zu:mɪ] — Mensch, der am längsten gelebt hat

Kittinger, Joseph [ˌdʒəʊzɪf 'kɪtɪŋə] — Mann, der aus einem Ballon 31,333 Meter in die Tiefe sprang

LA [ˌel'eɪ] — Abkürzung für Los Angeles

Leeds [li:dz] — Industriestadt in Nordengland; Zentrum der Bekleidungsindustrie; Einwohnerzahl: 500.000

Library of Congress [ˌlaɪbrərɪ əv 'kɒŋgres] — Nationalbibliothek in Washington DC (USA); erbaut 1897

Loch Ness [ˌlɒk 'nes] — See in Schottland; Länge: 38,5 km; Tiefe: 230 m

Maddox Street ['mædəks ˌstri:t] — Straßenname

Malaya [mə'leɪə] — Teilstaat von Malaysia (Südostasien)

Maradona, Diego [dɪ'eɪgəʊ mærə'dɒnə] — argent. Fußballspieler

Marvella [mɑ:'veɪjə] — Name eines Urlaubsortes

Matterhorn ['mætəhɔ:n] — Berg an der schweiz.-ital. Grenze (4478 m)

Mediterranean, The ~ [ðə ˌmedɪtə'reɪnjən] — das Mittelmeer

Mexico City [ˌmeksɪkəʊ 'sɪtɪ] — Mexiko(-Stadt); Fläche: 1479 km^2; Einwohnerzahl: 15 Mio.

Mickey Mouse ['mɪkɪ maʊs] — Mickymaus; Zeichentrickfigur von Walt Disney; der erste Mickymaus-Film lief 1928

Mingxia, Fu [ˌfu: 'mɪŋksɪə] — chines. Schwimmerin

Mojave Desert [məʊˌhɑ:vɪ 'dezət] — Wüste in Kalifornien (USA); Fläche: 65.000 km^2

Mr Britling [ˌmɪstə 'brɪtlɪŋ] — Name einer Katze

Murder on the Orient Express [ˌmɜ:də ɒn ði: 'ɔ:rɪent ɪk'spres] — *Mord im Orientexpreß* (Kriminalroman von Agatha Christie)

Nullarbor Plain [ˌnʌləbɔ: 'pleɪn] — Nullarborebene (Südaustralien); Fläche: 48.000 km^2

Olympic Games [əˌlɪmpɪk 'geɪmz] — Olympische Spiele

Olympics, The ~ [ðə ə'lɪmpɪks] — die Olympischen Spiele; die ersten weltweiten Spiele fanden 1896 statt

Oswald, Lee Harvey [ˌli: ˌhɑ:vɪ 'ɒzwəld] — mutmaßlicher Mörder von John F. Kennedy

Pattimore, William [ˌwɪljəm 'pætɪmɔ:] — engl. Sportler

Perth [pɜ:θ] — Hauptstadt des Bundesstaats Westaustralien; gegründet 1829; Fläche: 5369 km^2; Einwohnerzahl: 1,1 Mio.

Peru [pə'ru:] — Peru (Südamerika); Fläche: 1.288.217 km^2; Einwohnerzahl: 22,33 Mio.; Hauptstadt: Lima

Picasso, Pablo [ˌpæbləʊ pɪ'kæsəʊ] — (1881-1973), span. Maler und Bildhauer

Poirot, Hercule [hɜ:ˌkju:l 'pwɑ:rəʊ] — Romanfigur von Agatha Christie

Polo, Marco [ˌmɑ:kəʊ 'pəʊləʊ] — (1254-1323), venezian. Kaufmann und Weltreisender

Queensland ['kwi:nzlənd] — Bundesstaat in Ostaustralien; Fläche: 1.727.200 km^2; Einwohnerzahl: 2,83 Mio; Hauptstadt: Brisbane

Romania [ru:'meɪnjə] — Rumänien; Fläche: 237.500 km^2; Einwohnerzahl: 23 Mio.; Hauptstadt: Bukarest

Sahara [sə'hɑ:rə] — Wüste in Nordafrika; Fläche: 8.600.000 km^2

School of the Air [ˌsku:l əv ði: 'eə] — austral. Schulfunksender, vor allem im Nordterritorium: Farmerkinder bekommen Schulunterricht über Funk erteilt

Singapore [ˌsɪŋə'pɔ:] — Singapur (Stadtstaat in Südostasien); Fläche: 626 km^2; Einwohnerzahl: 2,72 Mio.

Smokey ['sməʊkɪ] — Name einer Katze

Sonoran Desert [sə͵nɔːrən ˈdezət] — Wüste in Arizona (USA); Fläche: 310.000 km^2

South Korea [͵saʊθ kəˈrɪə] — Südkorea; Fläche: 99.143 km^2; Einwohnerzahl: 42,5 Mio.; Hauptstadt: Seoul

Sun City [ˈsʌn ͵sɪtɪ] — Stadt in Arizona (USA), die für Rentner errichtet wurde („Rentnerparadies"); Einwohnerzahl: 40.000

Sunday New York Times [ˈsʌndɪ njuː jɔːk ˈtaɪmz] — Wochenendausgabe der New York Times

Supernova [͵suːpəˈnəʊvə] — Name einer Firma

Telford [ˈtelfəd] — Ort in England

Time [taɪm] — amerik. Zeitschrift

Trans-Australian [͵træns ɒˈstreɪljən] — Name eines austral. Fernreisezuges von Adelaide bis Perth

Vancouver [vænˈkuːvə] — Hafenstadt in Westkanada; Fläche: 114 km^2; Einwohnerzahl: 1,5 Mio.

Vicarage Lane [ˈvɪkərɪdʒ ͵leɪn] — Straßenname

Victorians, The ~ [ðə vɪkˈtɔːrɪənz] — hier: die viktorianische Epoche (1837-1901)

Walt Disney Productions [͵wɒlt ˈdɪznɪ prə͵dʌkʃnz] — Name der von Walt Disney gegründeten Zeichentrickfilm-Firma

Washington DC [ˈwɒʃɪŋtən] — Bundeshauptstadt der USA mit eigenem Distrikt; Fläche: 174 km^2; Einwohnerzahl: 3,6 Mio.

Wisconsin [wɪsˈkɒnsɪn] — amerik. Bundesstaat im Norden der USA; Fläche: 145.436 km^2; Einwohnerzahl: 4,8 Mio.; Hauptstadt: Madison

Yuri Gagarin [͵jʊərɪ ˈgɑːgɑːrɪn] — (1934-1968), sowjet. Astronaut, der als erster Mensch die Erde in einem Raumschiff umkreiste

Zermatt [ˈzɜːmæt] — Ort in der Schweiz am Fuß des Matterhorns

People's names

Women

Annette [əˈnet]
Augusta [ɔːˈgʌstə]
Beth [beθ]
Cathy [ˈkæθɪ]
Chantal [ˌʃɒnˈtæl]
Charlotte [ˈʃɑːlət]
Clare [kleə]
Doreen [dɔːˈriːn]
Emily [ˈemɪlɪ]
Jenny [ˈdʒenɪ]
Kim [kɪm]
Laura [ˈlɔːrə]
Liliane [ˈlɪlɪən]
Liz [lɪz]
Marina [məˈriːnə]
Marion [ˈmærɪən]
Nicola [ˈnɪkələ]
Penny [ˈpenɪ]
Petra [ˈpetrə]
Rose [rəʊz]
Sally [ˈsælɪ]

Men

Alan [ˈælən]
Alex [ˈæleks]
Andy [ˈændɪ]
Dave [deɪv]
David [ˈdeɪvɪd]
Graham [ˈgreɪəm]
Harold [ˈhærəld]
James [dʒeɪmz]
Martin [ˈmɑːtɪn]
Mike [meɪk]
Rod [rɒd]
Stephen [ˈstiːvn]

Families

Adams [ˈædəmz]
Ashton [ˈæʃtən]
Bishop [ˈbɪʃəp]
Bruce [bruːs]
Bunge [bʌndʒ]
Charlton [ˈtʃɑːltən]
Churchill [ˈtʃɜːtʃɪl]
Clark [klɑːk]
Conway [ˈkɒnweɪ]
Deacon [ˈdiːkən]
DeLillo [dəˈlɪləʊ]
Eliot [ˈelɪət]
Givens [ˈgɪvnz]
Goodman [ˈgʊdmən]
Hughes [hjuːz]
Lewis [ˈluːɪs]
Macmillan [məkˈmɪlən]
Parsons [ˈpɑːsnz]
Redford [ˈredfəd]
Sharp [ʃɑːp]
Stewart [ˈstjʊət]
Templer [ˈtemplə]
Weiss [vaɪs]
Woods [wʊdz]

Acknowledgements

We are grateful to the following for permission to reproduce/use copyright material:

Illustrations

Jürgen Bartz, München: pp. 3, 10, 11, 55, 79
Shirley Bellwood (BL Kearley), London: pp. 5 (bottom), 7, 9, 12, 17, 18, 19, 21, 22, 31, 34, 40, 41 (top), 54, 64, 65, 67, 68, 69, 71, 72, 74, 75, 76, 77, 84, 87, 92, 95, 97, 98 (top left), 101
Bulls Pressedienst GmbH, Frankfurt: pp. 124 (C: 1992 KFS/Distr. BULLS), 128 (bottom: C: 1993 CREATORS/Distr. BULLS)
Celia Canning (Linda Rogers Associates), London: p. 5 (top)
Kirsten Hagemann, Münster: pp. 20, 23
Donald Harley (BL Kearley), London: p. 27 (top)
Conny Jude, London: p. 44
Bettina Koenig, München: pp. 27 (bottom), 41 (bottom)
Punch (Werner Lüning), Lübeck: pp. 121, 122, 123, 126, 127, 128 (top)
Chris Ryley, Pulborough, Sussex: p. 16
Martin Salisbury (Linda Rogers Associates), London: pp. 14, 28, 42
Heribert Schulmeyer, Köln: pp. 32, 33, 36, 37, 47, 51, 85, 88, 98 (bottom)
Martin Shovel, Brighton: p. 13

Photographs

Air Lingus, Frankfurt: p. 39 (top left)
Beate Andler-Teufel, München: pp. 30, 45 (top; middle right), 48, 66
Australian Tourist Commission, Frankfurt: p. 10
Erich Bach Superbild Archiv, Grünwald-München: pp. VI (2nd from right), 29 (2nd left from bottom)
Barnaby's Picture Library, London: pp. IV (2nd from right), 1 (2nd from bottom)
Bavaria-Verlag Bildagentur GmbH, München-Gauting: pp. V (2nd from right: TCL; right: Anton Geisser), 11 (middle), 15 (bottom left: TCL; bottom right: Anton Geisser), 24 (left: Krebs), 24/25 (background: TCL), 45 (middle left: Hans Reinhard)
Bilderberg Archiv der Fotografen, Hamburg: pp. VII (right: Ellerbrock & Schafft), 43 (bottom right: Ellerbrock & Schafft)
Deutsche Presse Agentur Farbarchiv, Frankfurt: p. 25 (middle top: Klar; middle bottom: Weissbrod)
Focus Photo- und Presse Agentur, Hamburg: pp. 25 (bottom right: David Levenson), 8 (top: Alan Reininger; middle: Michael S. Yamashita), 38/39 (background: MichaelS. Yamashita)

V.K. Guy Ltd. Photo Library, Troutbeck, Windermere: p. 6 (bottom)
Bildagentur Anne Hamann, München: p. 24 (top right: Peter Schnitzler)
IBM Deutschland GmbH, Stuttgart: p. 39 (top left)
IFA Bilderteam GmbH, München-Taufkirchen: pp. V (left: Kronmüller; 2nd from left: Aigner), 15 (1st left from top: Kronmüller; middle left: Aigner), 24 (bottom right: Selma), 25 (top right: BCI), 39 (middle: F. Prenzel), 45 (bottom: Aberham), 53 (bottom: Siebig), 98 (top right: Aberham)
Interfoto Pressebild Agentur, München: p. 39 (bottom right)
Internationales Bildarchiv, München: pp. VII (2nd from right: Horst von Irmer), 43 (2nd left from bottom: Horst von Irmer)
The Image Bank Bildagentur, München: pp. VII (left), 43 (top), VI (2nd from left), 29 (2nd right from top)
Bildarchiv laenderpress, Düsseldorf: p. 2 (top)
Langenscheidt Verlag KG, München: p. 52 (right; left)
Bettina Lindenberg, München: p. 2 (bottom left)
Sonja Lawless, The Basin, Victoria: p. 2 (bottom right)
Bildagentur Mauritius, Mittenwald: pp. 25 (left: Marliani), 39 (bottom: Rawi)
Bernd-Dieter Meier, Göttingen: pp. IV (left), 1 (1st from top)
Monika Moreis, München: pp. IV (right), 1 (bottom), 11 (top right)
Coralia Pastora, München: p. 11 (1st from left)
Bildagentur Pictor International, München: p. 11 (right bottom)
Ina Pleyer, München: pp. VI (left), 29 (1st from top)
TSW Tony Stone Worldwide Bildagentur, München: pp. VI (right: Belinda Banks), 6 (top right), 29 (bottom: Belinda Banks), 53 (top: Patrick Ward)
John Walmsley, Surrey: p. 38 (bottom)
Zentrale Farbbild Agentur GmbH, Düsseldorf: IV (2nd from left: C. Voigt), 1 (2nd right from top: C. Voigt), V (middle: Pacific Stock), 15 (top right: Pacific Stock), VII (2nd from left: E. Silvester), 43 (2nd right from top: E. Silvester), 39 (top right: K&H Benser)

Cover photograph by TSW Tony Stone Worldwide Bildagentur, München

We would like to thank Gabriele Wißner for her editorial work.

We would be very grateful for any information which might assist us in tracing the copyright owners of sources which we have been unable to acknowledge.